Sylvia Wynter

Sylvia Wynter
ON BEING HUMAN AS PRAXIS

Katherine McKittrick, ed.

Duke University Press   Durham and London   2015

© 2015 Duke University Press
All rights reserved
Printed in the United States of America on acid-free paper ∞
Designed by Heather Hensley
Typeset in Arno Pro by Graphic Composition, Inc.

Library of Congress Cataloging-in-Publication Data
Sylvia Wynter : on being human as praxis / Katherine McKittrick, ed.
pages cm
Includes bibliographical references and index.
ISBN 978-0-8223-5820-6 (hardcover : alk. Paper)
ISBN 978-0-8223-5834-3 (pbk. : alk. paper)
1. Wynter, Sylvia. 2. Social sciences—Philosophy. 3. Civilization,
Modern—Philosophy. 4. Race—Philosophy. 5. Human
ecology—Philosophy. I. McKittrick, Katherine.
HM585.S95 2015
300.1—dc23
2014024286

ISBN 978-0-8223-7585-2 (e-book)

Cover image: Sylvia Wynter, circa 1970s. Manuscripts, Archives
and Rare Books Division, Schomburg Center for Research in Black
Culture, The New York Public Library, Astor, Lenox and Tilden
Foundations.

Duke University Press gratefully acknowledges the Canadian Social
Sciences and Humanities Research Council (SSHRC/Insight Grant)
which provided funds toward the publication of this book.

For Ellison

CONTENTS

ACKNOWLEDGMENTS

The rule is love.

SYLVIA WYNTER, *MASKARADE*

It is difficult to imagine this book as a complete and bounded work. While writing and reading and editing and sharing ideas—processes and conversations that have unfolded since about 2006 yet began well before this time—the text and its ideas have been consistently ajar. It has also witnessed, across the planet and with uneven responses, the Arab Spring and ongoing struggles in Syria, increasing man-made disasters and resource exploitation, wide use of unmanned drones, credit crises, the Occupy movements and student protests, the preventable deaths of Troy Davis, Michael Jackson, Mark Duggan, Whitney Houston, Trayvon Martin, and more, the election of Barack Obama, Idle No More, prisoner strikes in Atlanta, California. . . . Indeed, in Toronto, Ontario, where I write from and dwell, and in Kingston, Ontario, the prison-university town where I teach, and across Canada, prisons are, quietly and not, proliferating fictionally benevolent geographies. The 2012 Marikana (Lonmin) strike—the protest of a variety of appalling work conditions—resulted in miners being threatened and killed, reminiscent of, but not twinning, the Sharpeville massacre in 1960. I hope these kinds of events, and the many more unlisted—and it is worth underscoring the asymmetrical time-place reverberations of the events noted and unspoken and yet-to-come—in some small way *connect to* this work, thus drawing attention to the ways in which the ideas put forth are incomplete and unbounded and grounded and, to use Sylvia Wynter's phraseology, correlational. Our work is unfinished.

Any engagement with Sylvia Wynter demands openness. And without the support, conversations, words, creativity, hospitality, commitment, and energy of Sylvia Wynter—her openness to my ideas and this book, and her willingness to return to many conversations left ajar—this project would not have materialized and with this found spaces to critically examine and imagine the unlisted and the unspoken, the yet-to-come, and our unrealized futures. More than this, Sylvia's generosity, coupled with her prodigious knowledge and commitment to meticulously mapping out big ideas in very particular ways, tore up and tore open my mind and my heart as our conversations provided, at least for me, a new context within which to envision radical collaborative and correlational narratives. More specifically, the dialogue, formalized in the chapter "Unparalleled Catastrophe for Our Species?" but underlying the text as a whole, not only is founded on Wynter's invaluable intellectual mentorship and call-and-response but also signals the difficult task of situating our intellectual questions outside our present system of knowledge in order to historicize and share our futures differently. I learned and continue to learn a lot from Sylvia—about reading, writing, and friendship, about the high styles and the low styles, about the intellectual *life* her generation of Caribbean intellectuals amassed, about the science of the word, and about the difficulties of waiting and the pleasures of anticipation. This editor, then, ajar, extends warm appreciation to Sylvia for her ongoing friendship and conversations.

Wading through the openness of not quite arriving at the yet-to-come, and arriving again and again—stopping, too—in our unfinished histories, as these time-space processes are generated from the perspective of the ex-slave archipelago: many colleagues and friends have interrupted and stopped and dwelled on the ideas put forth. The essayists, I thank, for sharing their ideas and for writing challenging pieces that will enhance how we read the work of Wynter and engage decolonial scholarship.

Rinaldo Walcott has worked on this book with me, inside and out, since I began dreaming it. In addition to contributing his ideas within, he was an early interlocutor with Wynter, in Oakland, California, in 2007. This project would be very different if Rinaldo, a stalwart intellectual and stellar friend, did not imagine it with me. I appreciate Rinaldo's critical engagement, his thoughtful insights, and his willingness to engage the creative-intellectual-physiological contours of black life with me. His ideas inspire, and he made this work believable for me, in a world where blackness is an unbelievable and surprising wonder.

In the United States, the United Kingdom, and Canada, many have provided different kinds of maps and spatial clues and nourishment and conversation and support: Simone Browne, Hazel Carby, Ted Gordon, Matthew Mitchelson, Nick Mitchell, Priscilla McCutcheon, Amy Trauger, Abdi Osman, Nik Heynen, Richard Iton, Paul Gilroy, Vron Ware, Thomas Zacharias, Joao Costa Vargas, Omi Osun Olomo, Ben Carrington, Ned Morgan, Austin Clarke, Linda Peake, Joy James, Jafari Allen, Anne Brierley, Leslie Sanders, Ruthie Gilmore, Craig Gilmore, Jason Weidemann, Mark Campbell, Clyde Woods, Dina Georgis, Michelle Wright, Aaron Kamuguisha, Jenny Burman, Barnor Hesse, Christopher Smith.

Traveling between the Ontario cities of Toronto and Kingston, I have had the pleasure of working and thinking with a number of migratory subjects as well as members of Frontenac and Prince Edward Counties: Beverley Mullings, James Miller, Margaret Little, Anastasia Riehl, Hitay Yükseker, Scott Morgan Straker, Christopher Fanning, Terrie Easter Sheen, Scott Morgensen, Dana Olwan, Barrington Walker, Sammi King, Elaine Power, Eleanor MacDonald, Magda Lewis. I have also had the incredible opportunity to teach and be inspired by many students at Queen's University in Kingston, Ontario, with Carla Moore, Naomi Mukai, Jasmine Abdelhadi, Aruna Boodram, Darcel Bullen, Kathryn Travis, Maya Stistki, Katherine Mazurok, AJ Paynter, Stephanie Simpson, Ei Phyu Han, and Yasmine Djerbal really standing out as challenging and exciting scholars.

In addition to Wynter's writings, the work and ideas of Edouard Glissant, Rinaldo Walcott, Hazel Carby, Prince, Alexander Weheliye, Richard Iton, Toni Morrison, bell hooks, TV on the Radio, Hortense Spillers, Betty Davis, Nas, Achille Mbembe, Homi Bhabha, David Scott, Michael Jackson, Robin D. G. Kelly, Paul Gilroy, Saidiya Hartman, Frantz Fanon, Octavia Butler, Kanye West, M. NourbeSe Philip, Zadie Smith, Ebony Bones, Christina Sharpe, Clyde Woods, Stevie Wonder, Ruth Wilson Gilmore, Roberta Flack, YellowStraps, PJ Harvey, Nina Simone, Kara Walker, Chandra Mohanty, Marvin Gaye, Willie Bester, Aimé Césaire, Lil' Kim, Audre Lorde, Chimamanda Adichie, Simone Browne, Edward Said, Donny Hathaway, Mark Campbell, Millie Jackson, Kara Keeling, Angela Davis, Etta James, Gayatri Gopinath, Fred Moten, W. E. B. DuBois, Lisa Lowe, Dionne Brand, Jimi Hendrix, Drexicya, and Stuart Hall, among many others, have allowed me to think big about the intimacies among social justice, creativity, writing, and racial politics. What newness and strangeness and love and sadness and soul so many creative-intellectual ideas bring forth again and again!

Friends, family, and colleagues, too, who have had an eye on this project since it began and have brought their spirited support to the work within—in essay form and not: Alexander Weheliye, Demetrius Eudell, Lisa Lowe, the McKittricks and Zillis, across nomenclatures, and my mother, Valerie Brodrick, who insists we cherish the conviviality of recipes. Mark Campbell, Jack Dresnick, Johanna Fraley, and Nick Mitchell each contributed to different portions of the long conversation between Wynter and McKittrick—transcribing, editing, listening, responding, translating. I can only describe this work as heavy work—difficult, thick, grave. The long conversation has had many, many versions and several iterations, and all of these scholars generously shared their time and ideas with both Sylvia and me between 2007 and 2014. Katherine Mazurok, Stephanie McColl, and Joanne Farall also assisted with some tediously significant bibliographic details, which I thank them for, immensely. Nick Mitchell and Jack Dresnick especially, have been my constants-in-California, working closely with Sylvia but also lending me their ears and ideas and inspiration. During his research at the Institute of the Black World Archives at the Schomburg Center for Research in Black Culture, Nick also—to his surprise—came across the photograph of Wynter that is used for the cover of this text. Ned Morgan, trusted longtime friend, assisted with early copyedits.

At Duke University Press, Jade Brooks and Ken Wissoker have assisted with many aspects of the manuscript, supporting the initial vision, administering the text at each stage, and allowing it to organically unfold while also ensuring that the practicalities were accounted for. More than this, their ongoing excitement about the collection has allowed me to work patiently with Wynter and her ideas and consider the manuscript, as a whole, a meaningful and worthwhile project. What of Wynter without having time to dwell with Wynter? The comments of the anonymous referees, greatly appreciated, were perceptive, straightforward, and amazingly useful and strengthened the overall manuscript.

The insights and support of the already and yet to be listed—Simone Browne, Walcott, and Ray Zilli—have been especially relevant to my ongoing preoccupation with the writings of Sylvia Wynter, and each has differently lived with the discursive and affective outcomes that continue to emerge as I read, write, and think the futures she offers. Zilli has, too, made me at home with these and other difficult ideas by encouraging me to keep unraveling and working them out—which, after many years and a long-standing mistrust of the real and imagined geographies of home, provides a kind of comfortable but unsettling intellectual clarity that demands unexpectedness. Ellison McKittrick Zilli witnessed the final stages of the book and will, I hope, as dedicatee, keep the text, and the ideas Wynter imparts, ajar.

Katherine McKittrick
....

1   YOURS IN THE INTELLECTUAL STRUGGLE
Sylvia Wynter and the Realization of the Living

Human beings are magical. Bios and Logos. Words made flesh, muscle
and bone animated by hope and desire, belief materialized in deeds,
deeds which crystallize our actualities. . . . And the maps of spring always
have to be redrawn again, in undared forms.

SYLVIA WYNTER, "THE POPE MUST HAVE BEEN DRUNK, THE KING OF CASTILE
A MADMAN"

People ask me, "Why don't you write an autobiography?" But I have
never been able to think that way. My generation I think, would find it
impossible to emphasize the personal at the expense of the political.

SYLVIA WYNTER, "THE RE-ENCHANTMENT OF HUMANISM: AN INTERVIEW
WITH SYLVIA WYNTER"

The epigraphs that begin this introduction draw attention to a challenge:
How to introduce the analytical, creative, and intellectual projects of Sylvia
Wynter, as well as her biographical narrative, *all at once*, while also looking
forward, noncircuitously and without anticipatory repetition, to the essays
and conversations within? The challenge folds over, too, to notice the extensive and detailed corpus Wynter has put forth—more than two hundred
texts and presentations—which comprise dramatic plays, translations, essays, plenaries, symposia, and creative works.[1] Her work speaks to a range of
topics and ideas that interweave fiction, physics, neurobiology, film, music,
economics, history, critical theory, literature, learning practices, coloniality,
ritual narratives, and religion and draw attention to epistemological ruptures such as the secularization of humanism, the Copernican leap, Darwin-

ian modes of biological representation, Fanonian sociogeny, the 1960s. The depth with which she reads texts and her innovative approach to thinking through the ways in which we live and tell our stories have resulted in an intellectual oeuvre that patiently attends to the ways in which our specific conception of the human, Man, curtails alterative models of being, the fullness of our interrelated human realization, and a new science of human discourse. Across her creative texts and her essays, Wynter demonstrates the ways in which a new, revalorized perspective emerges from the ex-slave archipelago and that this worldview, engendered both across and outside a colonial frame, holds in it the possibility of undoing and unsettling—*not replacing or occupying*—Western conceptions of what it means to be human.

While readers unfamiliar with Wynter's work can turn to any number of her essays and enter the conversation from a variety of perspectives, much of her vast and detailed writing life is tracked and explored by both Wynter and David Scott in his incredible interview, "The Re-enchantment of Humanism," in *Small Axe*.[2] In this interview Wynter's experiences as an anticolonial figure emerge not as *inciting* the political vision put forth in her writings but rather as *implicit to* a creative-intellectual project of reimagining what it means to be human and thus rearticulating who/what we are. The process of rearticulation is important to highlight because it underscores relationality and interhuman narratives. Here, the question-problem-place of blackness is crucial, positioned not outside and entering into modernity but rather the empirical-experiential-symbolic site through which modernity and all of its unmet promises are enabled and made plain. *With* this, stands Wynter's subjective-local-specific-diasporic anticolonial unautobiography (see the second epigraph here), articulated *alongside* the physiological—neurochemical-induced—wording of hope and desire within the context of total domination (see the first epigraph). Beside phylogeny and ontogeny stands sociogeny/a new science of the word.[3]

Wynter's anticolonial vision is not, then, teleological—moving from colonial oppression outward and upward toward emancipation—but rather consists of knots of ideas and histories and narratives that can only be legible in relation to one another. Here it is crucial to notice that her oeuvre can be compared to and in conversation with Aimé Césaire, Frantz Fanon, W. E. B. DuBois, Elsa Goveia, Jacques Derrida, Michel Foucault, C. L. R. James, and Edouard Glissant, among others; this is an intellectual project that, therefore, practices co-identification and cocitation and honors the conceptual frame it promises. It is through reading across texts and genres, knitting together and critically engaging a variety of intellectual narratives from the natural sciences, the humanities, the social sciences, and art worlds, as these insights are produced in the shadow of colonialism, that Wynter's anticolonial insights come forth. These knots of histories and ideas and relational narratives, together, emerge in different ways throughout this collection. Painstakingly avoiding an overview of key themes in Wynter's work—Man1, Man2, sociogeny, the science of the word, *propter nos*, autopoiesis, counterdoctrines, adaptive truths, archipelagos of poverty—I draw the reader's attention to the essays within, which touch on, extend, and converse with these concepts and, in very different ways, join Wynter in opening up the possibility of a new science of human discourse: "a sense that in every form that is being inscripted, each of us is also in that form, even though we do not *experience* it. So the human story/history becomes the collective story/history of these multiple forms of self-inscription or self-instituted genres, with each form/genre being adaptive to its situation, ecological, geopolitical."[4]

The Essays

This is a project that speaks to the interrelatedness of our contemporary situation and our embattled histories of conflicting and intimate relationalities. The project is about how our long history of racial violence continues to inform our lives and our anticolonial and decolonial struggles. The work thinks about and interrogates how the figure of Man—in Wynter's formulations—is the measuring stick through which all other forms of being are measured. And, it is a work that seeks to ethically question and undo systems of racial violence and their attendant knowledge systems that produce this racial violence as "commonsense." This is not a project of reviling and thus replacing Man-as-human with an ascendant figure; rather it draws attention to a counterexertion of a new science of being human and the emancipatory breach Wynter's work offers. The writers here work closely with the writings of Sylvia Wynter, bringing into focus the ways in which she asks us to think carefully about the ways in which those currently inhabiting the underside of the category of Man-as-human—under our current epistemological regime, those cast out as impoverished and colonized and undesirable and lacking reason—can, and do, provide a way to think about being human anew. Being human, in this context, signals not a noun but a verb. Being human is a praxis of humanness that does not dwell on the static empiricism of the unfittest and the downtrodden and situate the most marginalized within the incarcerated colonial categorization of oppression; being human as praxis is, to borrow from Maturana and Varela, "the realization of the living."[5]

The collection begins with the dialogic text "Unparalleled Catastrophe for Our Species? Or, to Give Humanness a Different Future: Conversations" (cited in this introduction simply as "Conversations"). Building on a discussion and interview that began in 2007, Katherine McKittrick has since spoken and written with Wynter about various aspects of her research and writing. A call-and-response, this piece might be thought of as an extended prologue to the collection: a narrative that sets the stage for the collection's essays by drawing attention to key themes and concepts in Wynter's work; and, a prefatory conversation that highlights Wynter's voice within the context of the collection as a whole. Indeed, the call-and-response is doubled, with Wynter and McKittrick "calling" and "responding" to one another in "Conversations," while "Conversations" provides a context for the remaining essays that, as a whole, bounce off of, riff toward, and particularize Wynter's larger project. As it contextualizes the collection as a whole, "Conversations" is also a narrative that extends beyond Wynter's earlier writings. Completed in early 2014, it begins the collection but might also be read as a text that closes the collection and opens up Wynter's most recent insights— for it is here that she pushes us to think carefully about the ways in which our capacity to produce narrative as physiological beings allows us to critically re-envision our futures in new and provocative ways.

This is followed by two essays that work through the broader conceptual claims that Sylvia Wynter makes in relation to colonialism, coloniality, history, and the ethics of being human. Denise Ferreira da Silva's "Before *Man*: Sylvia Wynter's Rewriting of the Modern Episteme," is one of the first discussions to think extensively about Wynter's research alongside that of Michel Foucault. In her essay, Silva traces Wynter's reading of the ways in which a racial presence is necessary to the expansion, development, and implementation of imperial order and the production of Man-as-human. Here, as in Wynter's work, Silva puts pressure on Foucault's archaeology of knowledge and tables of difference by drawing attention to the ways in which the violence of conquest and colonization are implicit to modernity. Walter Mignolo's contribution, "Sylvia Wynter: What Does It Mean to Be Human?," explores the cognitive shifts incited by Copernican and Darwinian epochs in order to address the ways in which Sylvia Wynter's project itself is situated outside our present order of knowledge. Wynter's perspective and therefore her reading practices, he suggests, are *decolonial scientia* in that she situates herself beyond the crass body politics of colonial knowledge in order to foster adjoined human needs. Mignolo's essay traces the ways in which Wynter's unveiling of reality—as a naturalized autopoietic social system—allows her to read particular moments, from C. L. R. James's Marxism and Fanon's sociogeny to 1492 and the rise of scientific reason, anew.

Bench Ansfield's "Still Submerged: The Uninhabitability of Urban Redevelopment," draws on Wynter's insights to think through the ways in which urban recovery projects and urban studies approaches to post-Katrina New Orleans are bound up in a teleological promise that reproduces sites of blackness, poverty, and struggle as perpetually and naturally condemned. Extending Wynter's discussion of "1492: A New World View" and the ceaseless geographic workings of colonialism, Ansfield asks that we recognize the ways in which post-Katrina New Orleans is a location of ongoing politicized struggles that demand a home *life*: antidemolition struggles, the right to return, the right to stay, as practices that are deeply entwined with an ethics of recognizing alternative claims to humanness. Katherine McKittrick's essay, "Axis, Bold as Love: On Sylvia Wynter, Jimi Hendrix, and the Promise of Science," explores the ways in which science and scientific knowledge emerge in the writings of Sylvia Wynter. Looking at the scientific contours of creative labor, the essay concludes with a discussion of Jimi Hendrix, music making, blackness, and scientific-mathematic knowledge to illuminate Wynter's call to envision the human as bios-mythoi and being human as praxis. Nandita Sharma's "Strategic Anti-Essentialism: Decolonizing Decolonization" focuses on the ways in which displaced and migratory communities—populations who are identifiable as "immigrants" rather than "indigenous"—are, through the language and theorizing of "settler colonialism," produced as colonizing subjects. By dwelling on Wynter's discussion of *propter nos*, Sharma suggests that the inequalities produced through colonialism not be conceptualized vis-à-vis the Manichaean categories of "native" and "nonnative" but rather through the planetary interhuman consequences of 1492 and the resultant shared experience of, and thus resistance to, terror.

Rinaldo Walcott's contribution, "Genres of Human: Multiculturalism, Cosmo-politics, and the Caribbean Basin," reads the Caribbean basin in relation to European modernity. Working with the writings of Sylvia Wynter, Stuart Hall, Edouard Glissant, Edward Kamau Brathwaite, and Jacques

Derrida, among others, Walcott argues the Caribbean region does not offer an easy unified articulation of sameness through difference but rather a space where the constant negotiation of particularities—extending outward from colonial brutalities—produces an ethics of being "yet to come." Carole Boyce Davies's "From Masquerade to *Maskarade*: Caribbean Cultural Resistance and the Rehumanizing Project" invites a complex and unique reading of Wynter's dramatic play not only because she unearths the intellectual provocations found in practices of creativity—her culling of Wynter's theoretical-scholarly insights that are embedded in *Maskarade* is meaningful—but also because she suggests that such practices of creativity are, for postslave black/Caribbean communities, ways to imagine and bring forth integrated and soldered human *and* environmental alternatives to the crude mechanics of capitalism that arose from plantation slavery. Indeed, we can notice in the essays by Boyce Davies and Walcott, if read alongside Sharma's contribution, how Wynter's work draws attention to the ways in which transatlantic slavery—violent displacement—enforced the necessity of blacks to plant themselves as indigenous to the New World. This kind of insight importantly troubles the politics of claiming land alongside racial particularities and takes what is now being called "settler colonialism studies" in a different direction.

Demetrius Eudell's essay, "Come on Kid, Let's Go Get the *Thing*": The Sociogenic Principle and the *Being* of Being Black/Human," closes the collection and situates Wynter's insights within the context of black intellectual history. Eudell's essay surveys key themes that emerge in Wynter's writings and across black studies, and underscores how particular thinkers have, either in part or to a large extent, challenged the overrepresentation of Man. Eudell's essay traces the ways in which black subjects negotiate biocentric racial scripts in relation to their *own inventions* of blackness. The essay uncovers the ways in which Wynter's insights on sociogeny help clarify the process through which blackness—as we know it—becomes a reality.

Yours in the Intellectual Struggle/The Realization of the Living

Over many, many hours Sylvia Wynter generously shared an analytical story that was insightful, creative, prodigious, urgent. The analytical story put forth both in "Conversations" and in her other works is not simply an intellectual treatise; the ideas uncover a synthesizing mind *at work*. Put differently, throughout and within her essays and ideas, Wynter does not simply convey a set of ideas; rather, she demonstrates the difficult *labor* of thinking the world anew. Wynter's ideas are, in a sense, invariably verbs, encoded with active thought processes grappling with the magma of far-reaching challenges—including the unresolved/unsolved problem of race—which has come to confront us as a global human species collectively living with, through, and against the West's incorporating expansion. To engage her research and ideas is not, then, to take up a purely discursive text; rather, her work reveals intellectual *life* and struggle, with Wynter bringing into focus the dimensions of human life itself through her intensely provocative intellectual concerns and the correlated practice of cognition: a mind at work/everything is praxis.

The title of this introduction, "Yours in the Intellectual Struggle: Sylvia Wynter and the Realization of the Living," is meant to signal how we might read the work of Sylvia Wynter and the essays collected here. Many letters Wynter has posted to me, and others, over the years have closed with the words "yours in the intellectual struggle" and have inspired a world that imagines change.[6] But the struggle to make change is difficult within our present system of knowledge; the struggle can, and has, reproduced practices that profit from marginalization and thus posit that emancipation involves reaching for the *referent-we* of Man. Thus, "yours in the intellectual struggle" bears witness to the practice of sharing words and letters while also drawing attention to the possibilities that storytelling and wording bring.

Sylvia Wynter's insights, essays, letters, and shared ideas signal that hers is a generous project, one that allows the authors in this collection and elsewhere to draw attention to new stories of being human that challenge the profitable brutalities that attend the realization of Man-as-human.[7] I suggest that Wynter's closing signature—"yours in the intellectual struggle"—is best conceptualized alongside Maturana and Varela's "the realization of the living." The latter's research on social systems, the biological sciences, and human activities has long informed Wynter's work and points to her understanding that our present analytic categories—race, class, gender, sexuality, margins and centers, insides and outsides—tell a partial story, wherein humanness continues to be understood in hierarchical terms. The realization of the living, then, is a *relational* act and practice that identifies the contemporary underclass as colonized-nonwhite-black-poor-incarcerated-jobless peoples who are not simply *marked* by social categories but are instead identifiably condemned due to their dysselected *human* status. At the same time, as noted earlier, "the realization of the living" must be imagined as inviting *being human as praxis* into our purview, which envisions the human as verb, as alterable, as relational, and necessarily dislodges the naturalization of dysselection.

Wynter and the essayists here do not use categories of disenfranchisement as a starting points; rather, they focus on the ways in which such categories work themselves out in relation to the human, being human, human being, and codes that govern humanness. Wynter's outlook thus identifies that humanness might be newly conceptualized as a relational category, what she describes in "Conversations" as bios-mythoi, that is differentially inscribed by a knowledge system that mathematizes the dysselected. This is to say that human life is marked by a racial economy of knowledge that conceals—but does not necessarily expunge—relational possibilities and the New World views of those who construct a reality that is produced outside, or pushing against, the laws of captivity. It follows, according to Wynter, that we would do well to reanimate and thus more fully realize the co-relational poetics-aesthetics of our scientific selves.

Notes

1. Including, it should be noted, the nine-hundred-page unpublished manuscript, *Black Metamorphosis: New Natives in a New World*, which is housed at the The Schomburg Center for Research in Black Culture, Harlem, New York.
2. Scott, "The Re-enchantment of Humanism," 119–207.
3. Fanon, *Black Skin, White Masks*, 11; Césaire, "Poetry and Knowledge," 134–146.
4. Scott, "The Re-enchantment of Humanism," 206.
5. Maturana and Varela, *Autopoiesis and Cognition*.
6. Wynter discusses her signature in Thomas, "ProudFlesh Inter/Views Sylvia Wynter."
7. Thomas, "ProudFlesh Inter/Views Sylvia Wynter"; Bogues, *After Man, towards the Human*; Eudell and Allen, "Sylvia Wynter."

2 UNPARALLELED CATASTROPHE FOR OUR SPECIES?
Or, to Give Humanness a Different Future: Conversations

Katherine McKittrick: These conversations began in 2007. Since that time, a series of ideas and exchanges have taken place and unfolded into ongoing discussions about humanism, monohumanism, natural scarcity, genetic codes, race, location, and more. This document archives the key ideas that arose through what was originally, in 2007, an "interview" while also assembling, around and through these ideas, the call-and-response conversations between Wynter and McKittrick that have taken place since.[1] The call-and-response has been textual, telephonic, computerized, and musical—with one document repurposing and mashing up the breaking of the levees and geographies of the Ninth Ward with the 2007 "interview" archives, Kansas Joe McCoy and Memphis Minnie, the Detroit electronica band Drexciya, and others.[2] The narratives here, though, in text form, are conversations that draw specific attention to Sylvia Wynter's ongoing concerns about the ways in which the figure of the human is tied to epistemological histories that presently value a *genre* of the human that reifies Western bourgeois tenets; the human is therefore wrought with physiological and narrative matters that systemically excise the world's most marginalized. Here, her comprehensive knowledge of arts, letters, history, geography, science, and nature comes together—in relation to different times and spaces—and provides a meaningful pathway to dwell on what means to be human and, more important, how we might give humanness a different future.

This conversation should be read with Wynter's earlier work in mind. Her writings on the overrepresentation of Man and her conceptualization of Man1 and Man2, which are explored throughout her writings and in the essays collected here, inform much of what is put forth below.[3] The human, in Wynter's writings, is representatively linked to the figure of Man1 (invented by the Renaissance's *studia humanitatis* as *homo politicus* and therefore differentiated but not wholly separate from the *homo religiousus* conception of human) that was tethered to the theological order of knowledge of pre-Renaissance Latin-Christian medieval Europe; this figure opened up a slot for Man2, a figure based on the Western bourgeoisie's model of being human that has been articulated as, since the latter half of the nineteenth century, liberal monohumanism's *homo oeconomicus*.[4] These figures, both Man1 and Man2, are also inflected by powerful knowledge systems and origin stories that explain who/what we are. These systems and stories produce the lived and racialized categories of the rational and irrational, the selected and the dysselected, the haves and the have-nots as asymmetrical naturalized racial-sexual human groupings that are specific to time, place, and personhood yet signal the processes through which the empirical and experiential lives of *all* humans are increasingly subordinated to a figure that thrives on accumulation.

Added to this, Wynter thinks about the neurological responses that such figures induce: with our biblical and Darwinian origin stories in mind, she locates how the human remains beholden to these pervasive knowledge systems. Thus our postbiblical origin stories might also be described as *macro-origin* stories—as they are tightly knitted to the figures of Man1 and Man2 and consequently function to semantically activate the endogenous opiate reward-and-punishment system of the human brain.[5] The paradoxical way in which *race*—as the naturalized and secular organizing principle of those global relations that are wedded to the Darwinian/Malthusian macro-origin stories that iterate and normalize *homo oeconomicus*—will continue, too, to cast an apocalyptic shadow on any possibility of our thereby *just*, existence as a species. We presently live in a moment where the human is understood as a purely biological mechanism that is subordinated to a teleological economic script that governs our global well-being/ill-being—a script, therefore, whose macro-origin story calcifies the *hero figure* of *homo oeconomicus* who practices, indeed normalizes, accumulation in the name of (economic) freedom. Capital is thus projected as the indispensable, empirical, and metaphysical source of all human life, thus semantically activating the neurochemistry of our brain's opiate reward/punishment system to act accordingly!

Sylvia Wynter offers a different origin narrative possibility. Extending Frantz Fanon's new descriptive statement, which redefines our being human in both meta-Freudian and meta-Darwinian terms, she offers an ecumenically human (origin) story. Specifically, she works through the ways in which Fanon's concept of sociogeny (our codes or masks or *mythoi* or origin narratives) is *linked in semantically activating causal terms*, with the *bios* phenomena of phylogeny/ontogeny.[6] Our *mythoi*, our origin stories, are therefore always formulaically patterned so as to co-function with the endogenous neurochemical behavior regulatory system of our human brain. Humans are, then, a biomutationally evolved, hybrid species—*storytellers who now storytellingly invent themselves as being purely biological*. With this, particular (presently biocentric) macro-origin stories are overrepresented as the singular narrative through which the stakes of human freedom are articulated and marked.[7] Our contemporary moment thus demands a normalized origin narrative of survival-through-ever-increasing-processes-of-consumption-and-accumulation. This is reinforced by the epistemological elaboration of a story line—here we should be mindful of the disciplinary discourses of natural scarcity, the bell curve, and so forth, together with the "planet of slums" reality that is before us—which is nevertheless *made to appear, in commonsense terms*, as being *naturally* determined.[8] This commonsense naturalized story is cast as the only *possible* realization of the way the world must be, and "is."

Working alongside W. E. B. DuBois, C. L. R. James, Frantz Fanon, Aimé Césaire, and Elsa Goveia, among others, Wynter dedicates her own past and still ongoing work to the furthering of the "gaze from below" emancipatory legacy. This legacy had been born out of the overall global range of anticolonial and antiapartheid struggles against the overtly imperial and colonial liberal monohumanist premises. Those struggles were to eventually fail; *politically independent* nation-states came to be epistemologically co-opted and globally reincorporated into the Western world system—a system that is now in its postcolonial, postapartheid but still liberal (or now neoliberal) monohumanist symbolically encoded configuration. Because her ongoing work still strives, as her earlier work had done, to fully realize that emancipatory legacy by putting forward an alternative, *yet no less secular*, version of humannesss imagined outside liberal monohumanism, her overall project can be identified as that of a *counterhumanism*—one now ecumenically "made to the measure of the world."[9]

Some preparatory remarks on the document that follows: The discussion is framed by four guide quotes, which, ideally, the reader will keep in mind throughout. The guide quotes are followed by the larger textual document—the conversations. The conversations are divided into sections that the reader can study in order, out of order, separately, or all together. Each section includes a heading and a very short preamble by McKittrick, which leads into the subsequent insights by Wynter. The entire document reflects the questions from the original 2007 conversation, parts of that conversation that have not been reproduced, verbatim, here, and the call-and-response pattern mentioned above. This is to say that the headings, preambles, and insights are anchored to Wynter's ideas and were generated through what I can only describe as a broader conversational praxis. The endnotes—in the spirit of Wynter and others—draw attention to those areas of the conversations that have been omitted in the text but are relevant to thematic concerns and, perhaps more important, will encourage further explorations of narratives that think through and across humanness, location, and knowledge.[10]

Guide Quotes

> We know that when we talk about the processes of civilization, or evaluate human behavior, human organization, or any biological system, *we are concerned with self-corrective systems*. Basically these systems are always *conservative* of something. As in the engine with a governor, the fuel supply is changed to conserve—to keep constant—the speed of the flywheel, so always in such systems changes occur to conserve the truth of some descriptive statement, some component of the *status quo* ... fundamentally, we deal with three of these enormously complex systems or arrangements of conservative loops. One is the human individual. Its physiology and neurology conserve body temperature, blood chemistry, the length and size and shape of organs during growth and embryology, and all the rest of the body's characteristics. This is a system which conserves descriptive statements about the human being, body or soul. For the same is true of the psychology of the individual, *where learning occurs to conserve the opinions and components of the status quo*. ... Second, we deal with the society in which that individual lives—and that society is again a system of the same general kind. ... And third, we deal with the ecosystem, the natural biological surroundings of these human animals.
> —**Gregory Bateson, "Conscious Purpose versus Nature" (emphasis added)**[11]

> How was *Homo oeconomicus* foisted on us? In spite of his elegant foreign name, he is selfish and unmannered, *brutish as Caliban, naïve as Man Friday*. We all love to speak scathingly of him. Judging from the bad press he receives, we actually

dislike him a lot and cannot believe anyone *could really be so greedy and self-ish. He is logical,* but even that is unattractive. His shadow stretches across our thoughts so effectively that *we even use his language for criticizing him.* . . . Our subject is about his origins: *Where did someone without social attributes come from in the first place,* and why has he expanded from a small, theoretical niche to become an all-embracing mythological figure . . . like a *republican parallel to the imperial microcosm of former civilizations*?

—Mary Douglas and Steven Ney, *Missing Persons* (emphasis added)

What if we did not know where we are and who we are? What if all previous answers to the question of who we are were merely based upon the application of an answer given long ago, an answer that does not correspond to what is perhaps asked in the question *now touched upon of who we are*? For we do not now ask about ourselves "as human," assuming we understand this name in its traditional meaning. According to this meaning, man is a kind of "organism" (animal), that exists among others on the inhabited earth and in the universe. We know this organism, *especially since we ourselves are of this type.* There is a whole contingent of "sciences" that give information about this organism—named man—and we collect them together under the name "anthropology."

—Martin Heidegger, *Basic Concepts* (emphasis added)

What is by common consent called the human sciences have their own drama. . . . All these discoveries, all these inquiries lead only in one direction: to make man admit that he is nothing, absolutely nothing—and that he must put an end to the narcissism on which he relies in order to imagine that he is different from the other "animals." . . . This amounts to nothing more nor less than man's surrender. . . . Having reflected on that, I grasp my narcissism with both hands and I turn my back on the degradation of those who would make man a mere [biological] mechanism. . . . And truly what is to be done is to set man free.

—Frantz Fanon, *Black Skin, White Masks*

Toward the Counterauthority of a New Science in the Global Context of Our Contemporary Crisis-Ridden Times

Katherine McKittrick: In the following, Wynter sets out her project, delineating the ways in which the Copernican leap was to be iconic of the Renaissance transformative mutation. She outlines how the redefinition of the meaning of being human during this epoch, within the overall context of a *studia humanitatis* order of knowledge, was being effected, for the first time, in implicitly desupernaturalizing terms. The premise of this counterpoetics, initially realized by Copernicus's new astronomy, later came to be developed as the physical sciences together with their uniquely new self-correcting mode of cognition. This was followed by a redefined purely secular liberal monohumanist figure that enacts, presently, the hegemonically bourgeois *homo oeconomicus* "descriptive statement" of being human: pari passu with the rise and development from the late nineteenth century onward of the Darwinian/neo-Darwinian biological sciences that now underwrite our contemporary epistemological order.[12]

Sylvia Wynter: What I'm going to propose is that we are now challenged with envisioning a new "science of the Word," which I take from Aimé Césaire.[13] This challenge can be likened to that made by Copernicus when he declared that, while it may *seem* absurd, the Earth indeed also moves! Then Galileo tried to support this view, and he was imprisoned by the Inquisition and had to recant specifically that the Earth indeed does not move. Yet of course, the Earth *does* move. Yet, the premise that the Earth did not move was very central to the form of Christian theology that was hegemonic at the time. Thus, as the famous Cardinal Bellarmine—in the later context of Galileo's heresy trial for his defense of Copernicus's thesis—said: if the Earth moves, it would vitiate our entire plan of salvation.[14] Thus the context of that history demonstrates that, within that theologically absolute system of knowledge, the Earth was supposed to be *fixed* at the center of the universe, as the divinely condemned abode of post-Adamic fallen man. Now, many bourgeois scholars keep saying: Oh, Copernicus took man away from the center, thereby *devalorizing* the human. But they are liberal scholars, right? They see the world *biocentrically*. And they do not understand that, seen *theocentrically*—as would have been the case then—*to be at the center was to be at the dregs of the universe*. The center was then the *most degraded* place to be! So when Copernicus says that the Earth also moves, he is *revalorizing* the Earth. With his challenge, what now has to be recognized is that since the Earth also moves, *and is therefore a star like any other*, it also has to be, over against the traditional astronomy, *of the same homogeneous physical substance as the heavenly bodies*! But he's *also* changing the center to the Sun—and instead of the center being a degraded place, it's now an exalted place.[15] So unless we move out of the liberal monohumanist mindset, it's very difficult to see where we've been, where we're going. Once the Earth had been proved to move, medieval Latin-Christian Europe's then hegemonic theologically absolute worldview had begun to come to an end.

Let us say if you were a Christian subject—now you and I, we don't feel the Earth to move, right? But we take it for granted that the natural scientists are right when they tell us it moves. But for those inhabiting the medieval order of Copernicus's time, when they didn't feel the Earth to move, they would say: ah, I am sinful because Adam and Eve fell and this Earth, divinely condemned to be nonmoving, is justly my abode. If the Earth moved, the theo-Scholastic order of knowledge would have to go. It disappeared.

Copernicus's proposed new astronomy fundamentally breached what was, at that time, the still hegemonic and theologically absolute Scholastic order of knowledge. At the same time, the lay or largely secular scholars—the humanists—projected *studia humanitatis*, which had also come to counterpose itself against that of the theologically absolute order of knowledge together with the overall vertically caste-stratified hierarchical order of medieval Latin-Christian Europe; this was a legitimated order of knowledge wherein a vertically hierarchical order was dominated *spiritually* and *epistemologically* by the church and its celibate clergy. Thus, as an imperative function of the above, *before* the challenge of Copernicus's new astronomy, the hierarchies of the order of late Latin-Christian medieval Europe, the latter in both its spiritual (i.e., sexually celibate) and profane (i.e., sexually noncelibate) clergy/laity forms, had anchored itself on, inter alia, an orthodox Ptolemaic astronomy, for which the cosmos had continued to be defined by a projected fundamental (Heaven/Earth) divide. While this millennially held tradition of knowing the macrocosmos and, co-relatedly, the role allocations of the respective microcosmoi of all societal orders in analogically reinforcing or *mirroring* terms, had logically led, at its Ptolemaic best, to a technically proficient yet at the same time epistemologically resigned astronomy.[16] An astronomy and ordering that, although theologically elaborated in then Latin Christianity's monotheistic Heaven/Earth divide terms, had hitherto remained unchallengeable, reaching all the way back as it did, to Greek astronomy (and there evidencing, if philosophically elaborated, the no less fundamental macrocosmic Form/Matter divide).

Copernicus's epochal breaching of the Heaven/Earth divide was only to be made possible during the Renaissance, first, in generic terms, by the revalorizing/reinvention of Latin-Christian medieval Europe's *homo religiosus Adamic fallen Man* as *homo politicus*, a figure now self-governed by its/his reason, articulated as reasons of state. This was a newly invented Renaissance humanist counterpoetics that was projected over and against the Absolute and conceptually all-powerful, *uncaring* and arbitrary God of the church's then late-medieval orthodox theology. In the terms of the latter's counterpoetics, therefore, the relation was now renarrated as one between the traditional biblical Christian God and a mankind *for whose sake* (*propter nos homines*), rather than merely *for the sake* of his own glory (as the then nominalist orthodox theology held), he had indeed *created the Universe*.[17] And he, as Copernicus was to centrally argue, as "the best and most systematic artisan of all," would *have had to have created* the universe's "world machine" according to rules that made it *law-likely* knowable by the human reason of those creatures *for whose sake* he had done so.[18]

The result was that Copernicus's new (1543) astronomy would, over several centuries and with further development by other scholars, come to be fully realized as a uniquely new and *cognitively open*—because, normally, *imperatively self-correcting*—order of knowledge, just as that of the physical sciences. That premise was therefore to also open up a generalized *natural scientific* conceptual space. This conceptual space provided a context for the biological sciences of the late nineteenth and twentieth centuries to become increasingly institutionalized. This conceptual space, then, was therefore to make possible Darwin's epistemological rupture or leap—that is, its far-reaching challenge to Christianity's biblical macro-origin story's theo-cosmogonically projected divinely created divide between an ostensibly generically Christian mankind, on the one hand, and all other species, on the other. These natural (biological) sciences, however—as they too function, for the main part, in cognitively open and self-correcting terms—must be taken into account with the aporia of their now globally hegemonic Janus-faced *purely biocentric* version of humanness.

The Renaissance humanist mutation and resulting eventual disappearance of the theo-Scholastic order of knowledge reveal that our own now purely secular and purely biocentric order of knowledge can also cease to exist; we see an analogical challenge to that advanced by Copernicus when he challenged the order of knowledge of his time. What I'm putting forward as a challenge here, as a wager, is therefore that the human is, meta-Darwinianly, a hybrid being, both *bios* and *logos* (or, as I have recently come to redefine it, *bios* and *mythoi*). Or, as Fanon says, phylogeny, ontogeny, *and* sociogeny, *together, define what it is to be human*. With this hypothesis, should it prove to be true, our system of knowledge as we have it *now*, goes. Because our present system of knowledge is based on the premise that the human is, like all purely biological species, a natural organism; or, the human is defined biocentrically and therefore exists, as such, in a relationship of pure continuity with all other living beings (rather than in one of both continuity and discontinuity).[19] So, if the biocentrists are right, then everything I'm saying is wrong; but, if I am right, I cannot expect them to accept it easily. For our entire order of secular knowledge/truth, as it has to do with *ourselves,* is devastated if we are hybrid beings! If humans are conceptualized as hybrid beings, you can no longer classify human individuals, as well as human groups, as *naturally selected* (i.e., eugenic) and *naturally dysselected* (i.e., dysgenic) beings. This goes away. It is no longer meaningful. So I have to be realistic and say how can I expect people whose *discipline is their identity* to accept this hybrid model? When what they/we are being faced with is the total removal of their discipline as an autonomous field of inquiry? But then think of the dazzling creativity of the alternative challenge that would be opened up!

So if you are an economist, for example—and I'm anticipating myself here—instead of economics as a behavior-regulatory order of discourse that is, how shall I say, *indispensable to the replication of our present economically homogenized world-systemic order,* you remake it instead into a *science of all genre-specific human modes of material provisioning,* this including our contemporary own. How are these past and present economies understood when seen from a post–*homo oeconomicus* perspective? This is going to be related in a sense to what you call geography. But then geography will not exist as a discipline *by itself* anymore. A part of it will be physical geography—what was the Earth like before we came on the scene, even before any living beings came? And then, as all forms of biological life exploded, how did our later auto-instituting of ourselves as uniquely hybrid living beings bring this new form of specifically humanized geography into being? But geography will no longer be an *in-itself;* geography also becomes part of the study of our planet's overall self-organizing environmental-ecological system.

Now what I'm saying has to do with many of the papers and essays you have read. But what I'm saying also goes beyond those papers in order to attempt to make it all more hearable. Therefore, in what we'll be talking about, I'll be bringing in points that are coming from a book I have been working on. The first part of its title—"In the Great Silence of Scientific Knowledge"—is taken from Aimé Césaire, from "Poetry and Knowledge," a talk he gave at a 1946 conference in Haiti. He proposed that as brilliant as the feats of the natural sciences are, they themselves are half starved—because they cannot deal with our human predicament.[20] He then puts forth the idea of a new science, a hybrid science: a science of the Word. This idea is one in which the study of the Word (the *mythoi*) will condition the study of nature (the *bios*). What my work has led me to think about is that—like Cardinal Bellarmine, who had opposed theologically any suggestion that the Earth also moved—we are, collectively, in a similar situation. Specifically, we are stuck, committed to our now secular, no longer theocentric but no less absolute biocentric premise, that the human is also a purely natural organism, like any other. What I have been attempting to put forward on the basis of Césaire's proposed new science will therefore necessarily call for a rewriting of our present now globally institutionalized order of knowledge.

What I've been struggling with and working on, then, is to come up with a way of getting the above across, without falling into the traps laid down by our present system of knowledge, which means that I am often afraid that I will not be able to get it all across, and that's why I was so delighted by your book. In *Demonic Grounds* you are extending—you've caught what I am struggling to say—and you're making it become your own, argued in your terms.[21] And I know that that's how it's going to be, because the struggle we are confronted with cannot be in any way a one-person task. We must now collectively undertake a rewriting of knowledge as we know it. This is a rewriting in which, inter alia, I want the West to recognize the dimensions of what it has brought into the world—this with respect to, inter alia, our now purely naturalized modes or genres of humanness. You see? Because the West *did* change the world, *totally*. And I want to suggest that it is *that* change that has now made our own proposed far-reaching changes *now* as imperative as they are inevitable. As Einstein said, once physical scientists had split the atom, if we continue with our old way of thinking—the prenuclear way of thinking—we drift as a species toward an unparalleled catastrophe.[22]

White Radiance/Aesthetic Normalcy and the Teleology of Our Ostensibly Ecumenically Human Development: The Genre-Specific/Culture-Specific Objective Truths of Economic Development

KM: The enactment of our present biocentric descriptive statement (and thus its eugenic and dysgenic sociogenic codes of symbolic life and death) is linked to the law-like normalization of the corporeal features of Western Europeans in their now ethno-class bourgeois aesthetic configuration. This normalization is most strikingly evident in the consumer marketing of skin-bleaching creams and cosmetic surgery, as well as by the proposed mainline genetic engineering of designer babies. Such techniques and procedures

prescriptively imply that all humans, globally, be corporeally and aesthetically homogenized according to a single genre-specific (ethno-class) Western European model.[23] This model, of course, must be understood against
and with the range of our incomplete postcolonial, postapartheid, post-
1960s "politics of identity/identity politics" emancipatory struggles and,
therefore, the now incomplete (and paradoxical reversal of the) "beautifica-
tion" in bourgeois-consumer terms of, most markedly, blackness. The failure
and eventual co-optation of these struggles are not, as we know, limited to
the corporeal. They reflect, instead, the emergence of a global free-market-
driven and consumer-oriented mimetic desire that is anchored to a single
genre-specific Western European bourgeois model of being that is, itself,
projected onto, and incorporates, all those who belong to the now globally
economically Westernized middle classes; their working classes; and their
criminalized and jobless underclasses. This then reifies an ostensibly *humanly normative* social category: *homo oeconomicus* (the virtuous breadwinner, the stable job holder, the taxpayer, the savvy investor, the master of natural scarcity).[24] This figure also unveils, Wynter explains, the *symbolic death*
of the denizens of the "planet of slums" just as it uncovers the teleological
underpinnings of the story-lie of ostensibly human development, as well as
the reality of climate change/instability, to which, inter alia, it gives rise.[25]

SW: There are two contemporary issues that make this project urgent for
me. One of them is a small-scale issue, although its implications are not. The
Jamaican health minister—I think it was in February [2007]—announced
that they were putting a ban on the sale of skin-whitening cream by un-
licensed vendors because they were selling cheaper versions, which were
harmful.[26] It turned out that all across the country, men and women are
using these skin-whitening creams. At the same time, in several newspa-
per articles, you see that the same thing is going on in Asia. And you find
that many of these women's faces are now blotched, especially the poorer
women. And Olay, for example, is turning out products like White Radi-
ance. In the United States, a $15 billion-a-year plastic surgery industry flour-
ishes. Its clients include everybody—whites themselves but, of course,
many many blacks and many nonwhites, too: those who don't look suffi-
ciently like the Western bourgeoisie's projected Grecian norm of being and
of beauty. Think of the systemically induced self-aversive plastic-surgical
mutilation tragedy of the brilliantly gifted Michael Jackson! James Watson,
one of the two techno-scientists whose feat was to crack the DNA code, un-

derscores a second, correlated but even more extreme issue, specifically, the dangerous ethical implications of his proposal that techno-scientists mainline-genetically engineer designer babies because he said he doesn't like ugly people and he doesn't like stupid people.[27] Ugly and stupid, that is, from his own genre-specific perspective as a Western bourgeois subject who is, however, at the same time, when in his lab, a natural scientist.[28] Okay. So this is what I mean by the biocentric Scholasticism or the bio-Scholasticism, of our present episteme. This is an episteme that functions, with respect to the knowledge of our contemporary world and its systemic reality, *according to the same cognitively closed descriptive statement and its sociogenically encoded truth of solidarity as that of the theo-Scholastic knowledge system of the medieval order of Latin-Christian Europe.* So this is what gives me the urgency, do you see what I mean? For we cannot allow ourselves to *continue* thinking in this way. This way of thinking is linked to the *same* ethno-class mode of behavior-regulatory and cognitively closed order of knowledge that has led to our now major collectively human predicament: the ongoing process of global warming, climate instability, and ecosystemic catastrophe.

Regarding the above, a 2007 report in *Time* magazine on global warming tells us two things: first, that global warming is a result of *human* activities; and, second, that this problem began in about 1750 but accelerated from about 1950 onward.[29] Now, the date 1750 points to the Industrial Revolution. But the article, which builds on the expertise of a U.N. climate panel, fails to explain *why* global warming accelerated in 1950. What happened by 1950? What began to happen? The majority of the world's peoples who had been colonial subjects of a then overtly imperial West had now become politically independent. At that time, we who, after our respective anticolonial uprisings, were almost all now subjects of postcolonial nations, nevertheless fell into the mimetic trap of what Jean Price-Mars calls, in the earlier nineteenth-century case of Haiti, "collective Bovaryism"[30]—because the West is now going to *reincorporate* us neocolonially, and thereby mimetically, by telling us that the problem with us *wasn't* that we'd been imperially subordinated, *wasn't* that we'd been both socioculturally dominated and economically exploited, but that we were *underdeveloped.*[31] The West said: "Oh, well, no longer be a *native* but come and be Man like us! Become *homo oeconomicus!*" While the only way we could, they further told us, become *un-underdeveloped*, was by following the plans of both their and our economists. The catch was that our economists, like the distinguished Caribbean economist Sir Arthur Lewis, had been educated in British imperial universities, like many of us. This is the same kind of model as in the Roman Empire: all the elites of the imperially subordinated populations were educated in Roman imperial schools! And so these mimetically educated elites, proud to be incorporated as Roman citizens, had helped to keep the Roman Empire going; and then when the Roman Empire was going to break down, among such elites you had a scholar like Augustine, who before his conversion to Christianity had been a professor of rhetoric and of the imperial Roman theory of high and low styles. After his conversion he had then taken all of that knowledge, then shifted the above rhetorical strategies to reinforce the revolutionary *sermo humilis* of the then new "gaze from below," postpagan, postclassical monotheistic religion of Christianity—this latter as one whose projected promise of eternal salvation in the City of God will far outstrip the glories of the cities of Man, including that of Rome itself. This is what I call an Augustinian turn, the taking and revising of an existing system of knowledge, in order to create that which is imperatively emancipatorily new.[32]

There is one profound difference here, however. Rome's empire was *Roman*. Instead, as studies of contemporary neocolonialism as well as of its predecessors colonialism and postcolonialism reveal, the West, over the last five hundred years, has brought the *whole* human species into its *hegemonic*, now purely secular (post-monotheistic, post-civic monohumanist, therefore, itself also transumptively liberal *monohumanist*) model of being *human*. This is the version in whose terms the human has now been redefined, since the nineteenth century, on the *natural scientific model* of a *natural* organism. This is a model that *supposedly* preexists—rather than *coexists* with—all the models of other human societies *and* their religions/cultures. That is, all human societies have their ostensibly natural scientific organic basis, with their religions/cultures being merely superstructural. All the peoples of the world, whatever their religions/cultures, are drawn into the homogenizing global structures that are based on the-model-of-a-natural-organism world-systemic order. This is the enacting of a uniquely secular liberal monohumanist *conception* of the human—Man-as-*homo oeconomicus*—as well as of its rhetorical overrepresenting of that member-class conception of being human (as if it is the *class of classes* of being human itself). Guess what happens? Its empirical results, for both good and ill, have been no less large-scale. Yet at the same time, no less *genre-specifically* caused! So that's the terrifying thing with the *Time* report. It thinks the causes of global warming are *human* activities, but they are not! The Masai who were (and are) being displaced have nothing to do with global warming! It's all of us—the Western and mimetically Westernized middle classes—after we fell into the trap of modeling ourselves on the mimetic model of the Western bourgeoisie's liberal monohumanist Man2. But mind you, at the time—just prior to, during, and after the anticolonial and civil rights struggles—what other model was there?[33] Except, of course, for the hitherto neocolonially neglected yet uniquely ecumenically human model put forward by Frantz Fanon from what had been his activist "gaze from below" antibourgeois, anticolonial, anti-imperial perspective. A uniquely ecumenically Fanonian human model that could (and can) in no way law-likely exist within the *vrai* of our present epistemological order. The *vrai* of, that is, in Richard Rorty's terms, its "truth of solidarity" rather than that of, ostensibly, objectivity.[34]

Yet it is precisely within the law-like epistemic terms of the now globally homogenized descriptive statement model of being human specific to the above order that the climate panel's report and recommendations are generated; these terms are also transmitted, postcolonially, by each ex-colony's branch plant university variant of the West's overall liberal monohumanist academic system. Consequently, the report's recommendations must be put forward in the terms set by the master discipline of economics and its disciplinary "truth of solidarity." This means that the genre-specific preprescribed "truth" of economics must itself analogically elaborate an ethno-class *descriptive statement* mode of *material provisioning* that can, law-likely, be *only that* of *homo oeconomicus's* single absolute model of free-market capitalism. This model's imperative supraordinate telos of increasing capital accumulation thereby predefines it as the *only* means of production indispensable to the enacting of the economic system of free-trade-market capitalism's unceasing processes of techno-industrial economic growth. This model can, at the same time, be enacted only on the homogenized basis of the systemic repression of all other alternative modes of material provisioning. In this mode of material provisioning, therefore, there can ostensibly be no alternative to its attendant planetarily-ecologically extended, increasingly *techno-automated*, thereby job-destroying, postindustrial, yet no less fossil fuel–driven, thereby climate-destabilizing free-market capitalist economic system, in its now extreme neoliberal transnational technocratic configuration. The exceptions, however, are those clusters of still extant nomadic or sedentary indigenous traditionally *stateless* societies—for example, those of the Masai, the San, or the Pygmy in Africa, as well as the range of other such societies in Australia, the Americas, and elsewhere. Many of these groups are now being pushed out of their ostensibly "underdeveloped" "places" totally.[35]

The larger issue is, then, the incorporation of all forms of human being into a single homogenized descriptive statement that is based on the figure of the West's liberal monohumanist *Man*. And this conception of being, because ostensibly natural-scientific, is biocentric. So when Fanon says, "I take my narcissism in both hands and I say that the human is not a mere [biological] mechanism," he overturns this biocentric conception.[36] That doesn't mean that this ethno-class natural organism model of the human doesn't bring you knowledge—as Heidegger points out, it brings you all kinds of knowledge.[37] But it is *not* the knowledge of the human reconceptualized in the direction of a hybridly, both *mythoi* and *bios*, being. We therefore now need to initiate the exploration of the new reconceptualized form of knowledge that would be called for by Fanon's redefinition of being human as that of skins (phylogeny/ontogeny) *and* masks (sociogeny). Therefore *bios* and *mythoi*. And notice! One major implication here: *humanness* is no longer a noun. *Being human is a praxis.*[38]

Now with respect to the *challenges* to the single biocentric model of liberal monohumanist Man, the sixties' movements were really the first opening phase of the dynamic in which the series of "isms" (initiated by the black antiapartheid struggle for civil rights, women's rights/feminism, indigenous and other of-color rights, gay and lesbian rights, and so forth) had erupted to challenge Man's episteme, its truth, and therefore its biocentric descriptive statement. And momentarily, they were making these challenges *all together*. Ah, but when you separate them, you retreat into the bourgeois order of things. And that was the remimeticized Bovaryism trap into which we all fell.[39] The sixties' movements had begun that whole ripping apart of the emperor's clothes—and remember, the sixties movements had been fueled by the earlier anticolonial movements all over the world, which had climaxed in Vietnam, Algeria, and elsewhere. All such humanly emancipatory struggles, all then so fiercely fought for! *You bring them together,* and the world system had begun to question itself! To me Derrida's most radical essay was his revised version of a talk he gave at a philosophy conference in 1968, where he refers to the fact that Martin Luther King had been assassinated, that the Vietnam War was going on, and the student uprisings in Paris were in full force. Now his talk was called "The Ends of Man."[40] At the end he asks,

"But who, 'we'?" The *referent-we* of man and of its ends, he implies, is *not* the *referent-we* of the human species itself. Yet, he says, French philosophers have assumed that, as middle-class philosophers, their *referent-we* (that of Man2) is isomorphic with the *referent-we* in the *horizon of humanity*. I am saying here that the above is *the* single issue with which global warming and climate instability now confronts us and that we have to replace the ends of the *referent-we* of liberal monohumanist Man2 with the ecumenically human ends of the *referent-we in the horizon of humanity*. We have no choice.

If we take the report put forth by the climate panel in *Time* seriously, what we find is this: the authors of the report, as natural scientists and also bourgeois subjects, logically assume that the *referent-we*—whose normal behaviors are destroying the habitability of our planet—is that of *the human population as a whole*. The "we" who are destroying the planet in these findings are not understood as the *referent-we* of *homo oeconomicus* (a "we" that includes themselves/ourselves as bourgeois academics). *Therefore, the proposals that they're going to give for change are going to be devastating!* And most devastating of all for the global poor, who have already begun to pay the greatest price. Devastating, because the proposals made, if nonconsciously so, are made from the perspective of *homo oeconomicus* and its attendant master discipline of economics, whose behavior-regulatory metaphysical telos of mastering Malthusian natural scarcity is precisely *the cause* of the problem itself. So for us to deal with global warming, this will call for a far-reaching transformation of knowledge—this pari passu with a new mutation of the answer (its "descriptive statement") that we give to the question as to *who* as humans *we are*. Again, this kind of transformation of knowledge, which had occurred some five hundred years ago and had put forth—what at the time was to be profoundly revalorizing for the secularizing (reasons-of-state) ruling elites of the then Western European population's *referent-we*—an epochally mutational new answer. Seeing that the Renaissance West, in bringing to an end the then totally hegemonic *theologically Absolute*, because cognitively closed, world of late-medieval Latin-Christian Europe—thereby, inter alia, making the Copernican leap and later the physical sciences possible—had also brought into existence what has become today our now planetarily extended, globally incorporated Western and Westernized hegemonically secular world of contemporary modernity—a worldview that is, in transumptively inherited yet dialectical terms, being articulated and engendered as *biologically Absolute*.

Genre-Specific Narratives of Who "We" Are, Césaire's Science of the Word, Fanon's Sociogenic Masks: The Origin of Their/ Our Uniquely Human Codes and the Third Event

KM: Informed, in part, by Erik Erikson's concept of pseudospeciation and Humberto R. Maturana and Francisco J. Varela's theory of autopoiesis, Sylvia Wynter's hypothesis of auto-speciation suggests that we have been uniquely enabled, by means of our origin myths and cosmogonically charted narratives, to subjectively experience ourselves as semantically-neurochemically opiate-rewarded, thereby fictively eusocializing, inter-altruistic, kin-recognizing member subjects of the same *symbolic life kind* (here "kind" refers to our *genre-specific* or *pseudo-species-specific* human groupings—our class, our tribe, and so forth).[41] Our origin myths and cosmogonies, she explains, are the storytelling "grounds" of the institution of initiation, by means of which we fictively auto-institute or pseudospeciate ourselves as hybridly human.[42] Here Wynter highlights the dynamic interaction between our genetic and nongenetic codes—what she describes, respectively, as our *first set of instructions* and our *second set of instructions*—in order to think through how our subjective sense of self and our subjective sense of *we* (the *referent-we* that determines our sense of place-and-kin to be specific) is intimately connected to the interrelational activities *between* or *across* the physiological and the storytelling-symbolic (*bios and mythoi, skins and* masks).

SW: The paleontologist Juan Luis Arsuaga proposes that the human is not only a languaging being but also a storytelling species.[43] In my own terms, the human is *homo narrans.* This means that as a species, our *hybrid* origins only emerged in the wake of what I have come to define over the last decade as the Third Event. The First and Second Events are the origin of the universe and the explosion of all forms of biological life, respectively. I identify the Third Event in Fanonian-adapted terms as the origin of the human as a hybrid-auto-instituting-languaging-storytelling species: *bios/ mythoi.* The Third Event is defined by the singularity of the *co-evolution* of the human brain *with*—and, unlike those of all the other primates, *with it alone*—the emergent faculties of language, storytelling. This co-evolution must be understood concomitantly with the uniquely *mythmaking* region of the human brain, as the brain scientists Andrew Newberg, Eugene D'Aquili, and Vince Rause document.[44] Further, and together with all of the above, as Ernesto Grassi adds, is the already presupposed—*with* the emergence of language—behavior-regulatory phenomenon of religion, together with its vast range of Holy Kosmoi.[45]

Here the insights of both Maurice Gauchet and Ernesto Grassi are relevant; they demonstrate that all human societies had instituted themselves from our origin by means of the phenomenon of religion.[46] Grassi's point in this respect was that in the same way that genetic signs function to necessitate the behaviors of purely organic species, religion—with its "what is to be said" and "what is to be done" sacred imperatives—would have been able to necessitate the behaviors of languaging human groups. Gauchet was to later show the way in which, multimillennially later, the monotheistic Christian religion's concept of Christ's Incarnation would eventually enable the exit from religion and come to function as secular discourses. Then, R. H. Nelson, an economist, demonstrated the way in which the practitioners of our present master discipline of economics discursively function as a *secular priesthood* of the U.S. nation-state's economic system.[47] As well as, therefore, of the overall globally incorporated world-systemic capitalist economic order in its now neoliberal and neo-imperial, *homo oeconomicus* bourgeois ruling-class configuration at a world-systemic level—of which the United States is still its superpower hegemon.

The master discipline of economics functions now, therefore, according to the *same* behavior-regulatory imperatives, and/or laws, that the master discipline of theology had functioned, in the past, for the overall societal order of Christendom. The transumptive correlation between the two master disciplines (theology and economics) thus points to N. J. Girardot's identification of all religions (together with their secular substitutes) as functioning according to a behavior-regulatory formulaic schema of a "significant ill," on the one hand, and its "cure" or "plan of salvation," on the other.[48] Our present episteme's economic system and its formulaic schema delineate, therefore, mankind's enslavement to natural scarcity—which has replaced what had been its/our enslavement to original sin. The new and present plan of salvation is, therefore, that of the unceasing mastery of natural scarcity by means of ever-increasing economic growth![49]

Our third and hybrid level of existence, as shown in these cases, is therefore a domain specific to Aimé Césaire's proposed new science of the Word. Such a science would be defined by the fact that the study of the Word would now determine the study of nature.[50] The implication is this: the study of nature, in this context, will now be specifically a study of the *imple-*

menting bios agency of the human brain. Here the "first set of instructions" (genetic codes) and the "second set of instructions" (nongenetic codes) emerge; the study of the Word in this light is the study of an *agency* that functions according to the laws of nature and its genetically programmed "first set of instructions" (biological genetic codes) whose role *in this bios/mythoi* hybrid context is to *neurochemically implement* the "second set of instructions" (nongenetically chartered origin stories and myths). This dynamic emerges, for example, in the "imagined communities" of our respective ethno-class nation-states: the genre-specific subjects of each such nation-state are enabled to subjectively experience themselves/ourselves in fictively eusocialized terms—this across all stratified status quo role allocations—as inter-altruistic kin-recognizing member subjects of the same *referent-we* and its imagined community. As such, kin-recognizing member subjects law-likely and performatively enact themselves/ourselves as "good men and women" of their/our *kind* according to a *nongenetically* determined, origin-mythically chartered symbolically encoded and semantically enacted set of *symbolic life/death* instructions. *At the same time*, at the level of *bios/the brain*, the above second set of instructions are genetically (neurochemically) *implemented*. This implementation occurs according to the "laws of nature" first set of instructions, with the second set of instructions, thereby, being alchemically *made flesh*!

I discuss these "instructions" further later, but with this in mind, what I want to uncover, to reveal, here is that which lies behind the ostensible truths of our everyday reality, but which we normally cannot see. It is that of the dynamic of what I now call *the autopoiesis of being hybridly human*. I'm getting this concept, autopoiesis, from Maturana and Varela, who wrote the book *Autopoiesis and Cognition*.[51] They were biologists who, for a long while, had been working on the frog's vision. At that time, the orthodox idea was that the frog's environment impacted on the frog, determining what it was to *see*. Maturana and Varela were trying to think outside that paradigm. But they didn't dare until the sixties, when everything turned upside down, including at the university in Chile. Maturana explains:

> Early in May of 1968 the University of Chile entered a state of revolution. The students took over the University in an attempt to reformulate the philosophy that had inspired its organization. I joined them. All standard academic activities stopped and students and some members of faculty tried to say something new. It was not easy. Language was a trap, but the

whole experience was a wonderful school in which one could discover how mute, deaf, and blind one was. It was easy to be caught in one's own ego, but if one succeeded in attaining at least some degree of freedom from it, one began to listen and one's language began to change; and then, but only then, new things could be said.[52]

So you notice we're now saying that social uprisings have tremendous links to the transformation of knowledge? Okay. So Maturana and Varela said they wanted to find a way to say that the living system that is the frog *specifies* what is to be known of the environment. They were therefore talking about an entirely different kind of perception of the world, right? They wanted to think about the idea of biological organisms as *autonomously functioning, living* (i.e., autopoietic) systems. And this is related to our human social systems—a point they also put forward in their later work.[53] Now if you look at living systems such as the beehive, they are purely biological eusocial systems. Our human eusocial systems are instead *hybrid languaging cum storytelling (if biologically implemented) living systems*; but they function according to laws analogous to those regulatory laws of the supra-autopoietic system, which is the beehive. So I call these the *laws of hybrid human auto-speciation*, thereby of *autopoiesis*. Yet what we also find is that these laws, as the very condition of their ostensibly *extrahumanly* mandated functioning, are nevertheless ones that have hitherto been enacted *outside* of our conscious awareness—even though we ourselves have always rigorously and behaviorally adhered to them as indispensable to our respective genre-specific praxes of being hybridly human! And this is precisely the fact with which we must now come to grips: given that as an already *postnuclear* cum post-cracking-the-code-of-our-genome species, we are now faced with an additional climate crisis situation in which it becomes even more imperative that these laws, for the first time in our species' history, be no longer allowed to function *outside our conscious awareness*.

More specifically, while it is clear that as a species we humans ourselves are, with respect to our eusocial behaviors, no longer subordinated to our genetically coded "first set of instructions"—no longer subordinated as are the also highly eusocial bees in a beehive, right?—what we nevertheless normally overlook is the following: that, from our Third Event origin until today, the hybrid laws that engender the empirical reality of our own always genre-specific fictively eusocializing are storytellingly chartered, symbolically encoded, thereby self-organizing living autopoietic systems; these regulatory laws function at our uniquely third level of hybrid *bios/mythoi* existence and, while we ourselves behaviorally enact them, are nevertheless ones of which we have remained unaware. With this, and taking into account our Third Event origin, the following questions emerge: What had been the cost that had to be paid for the bringing into existence of the above, uniquely human, non-primate-like level of existence? What had been the cost of its law-likely mandated mutational singularity that, as a species, wherein, with respect to *all* our behaviors, we alone no longer had to remain subordinated to the sole set of instructions of our genome's DNA code? The answer to the above is one of which we must now for the first time in our existence imperatively become aware. The cost of that exchange? That of our subordination, instead, to our genre-specific storytelling codes of *symbolic life/death*! Their *Words*—or, in Bateson's terms, their *descriptive statements*. Put differently, we need to think about the way in which, for example, our present transnational world-systemic social order must itself continue to be known in the terms of a rigorously elaborated order of knowledge whose truth of solidarity is itself *prespecified* by our present now globally hegemonic purely secular biocentric descriptive statement of the human: its Code, its Word. Thus, our contemporary now globalized order of knowledge, its truths of solidary, are always already preprescribed by the storytelling-chartered code of *symbolic life/death* of *homo oeconomicus* and its descriptive statement. We must therefore now think about *why* it must be so! We must think about why, for example, our present Darwinian *descriptive statement*—that we are purely biological beings—is a descriptive statement *about which* our present globally extended and hierarchized, Western world-systemic societal order enacts and replicates itself as a self-organizing and autonomously functioning autopoietic eusocial system. This, at the same time as the latter system is itself, circularly encoded/re-encoded, enacted by means of a discursively elaborated order of truth/knowledge, which itself, while partly *natural-scientific* on the one hand (this with respect to its *bios* dimensions), must, on the other hand, paradoxically *deny* the storytelling origins of the "ground" that constitutes it as such an order of truth/knowledge. The hybridity of humanness—that we are *simultaneously* storytelling *and* biological beings—is thereby denied.

To understand all human societal orders, you must therefore look for the sociogenic principle. This can be thought of in the same way as physicists' conception of the anthropic principle: that there must be certain dimensions, physical dimensions and so on, that make human life possible. The analogy of this model therefore enables the following hypothesis: in order to understand the functioning of our present world-systemic societal order *as it is*—rather than as it must law-likely represent itself to be within the "truth of solidarity" terms of our present knowledge orders—one must go to the sociogenic principle. Now when we speak in Western terms about *cultures*, we are also talking about that *principle*! Since it is about that principle's always already cosmogonically chartered sociogenic replicator code of *symbolic life/death* that each *culture* auto-institutes itself as a genre-specific autopoietic field. So when I wrote—in a 1997 essay—about feminist thought and Western thought in general as being *a-cultural*, I meant to underscore that they are *a-sociogenic* or *a-autopoietic*.[54] These areas of thought define the human as a purely biological being; their intellectuals cannot therefore recognize their own culture's autopoietic field as being *the genre-specific field* that it is, assuming instead that its field is simply *reality-in-general*. We see the same problem within, if only for the main part, the field of philosophy—which also tends to be *a-cultural, a-sociogenic, a-autopoietic*. Since it, too, can, for the main part, in no way *relativize* being human (except paradoxically, for example, with the also deeply, in other ways problematic, counterphilosophy of Heidegger as well as that of the no less, in some ways also problematic yet also challenging heretical pragmatist philosophy of Rorty). Orthodox philosophy, however, in philosophizing about the West's biocentric man—and philosophizing within the terms of *its own* version and genre and class of being human—must also necessarily assume that it is reasoning instead from the perspective of the *being of being human*, in *class of classes*, therefore, ecumenically human *homo narrans* terms. Mind you, as I mentioned earlier, this does not mean to say that being human (as biocentrically defined in the direction of Heidegger's *animalitas*, and therefore on the model of a natural organism) does not provide useful knowledge. It does: it provides our *present* order of knowledge—an order of knowledge that is indispensable to the continued reproduction of our present neoliberal/neo-imperial, secularly biocentric, global order of words and of things.[55]

This led me to Césaire's science of the Word and thinking about it as the completion of the West's two natural sciences. This, however, presupposes that our very origin as a species be defined by a "Third Event"—and you notice now that we are going to have to redefine the origin of our being human in meta-Darwinian terms? To do so, I see three events as crucial to the understanding of the origin of the planetary world, its universe, as well as of ourselves. Ilya Prigogine identifies the first two events:

The law-event duality is at the heart of the conflicts, which run through the history of ideas in the Western world, starting with the pre-Socratic speculations and continuing right up to our own time through quantum mechanics and relativity. Laws were associated to a continuous unfolding, to intelligibility, to deterministic predictions and ultimately to the very negation of time. Events imply an element of arbitrariness as they involve discontinuities, probabilities and irreversible evolution. We have to face the fact that we live in a dual universe, whose description involves both laws and events, certitudes and probabilities. Obviously the most decisive events we know are related to the birth of our universe and to the emergence of life.[56]

To revisit the above: the First Event is the origin of the universe; the Second Event is the explosion of all forms of biological life. The Third Event, I identify in Fanonian-adapted terms, as the origin of the human as a hybridly auto-instituting, languaging cum storytelling species—which we can trace to the continent of Africa. Yes! The Third Event! And on the continent of Africa, no less! A continent that, as you know—within the terms of the West's religious and secular chartering cosmogonies—has been seen as either the site of the biblical Ham's *cursed descendants* or the site of the *missing link* between apes and fully evolved Western European humans. Now if Africa is instead, in now meta-Western, meta-Darwinian terms, the site of the Third Event, it is thereby the site of our third level of hybrid *bios/mythoi* existence, and concomitantly of our hitherto also genre-specifically instituted orders of consciousness and modes of mind. I would be prepared, like a Christian in a Roman imperial auditorium, to go to the lions in defense of that hypothesis.[57] But I also say that if my wager is wrong, then, Katherine, don't waste your time!

We shall therefore need, though, if my wager is right, to relativize the West's hitherto secular liberal monohumanist conception of our being human, its overrepresentation as the being of being human itself. We need to speak instead of our *genres of being human*.[58] Once you redefine being human in hybrid *mythoi* and *bios* terms, and therefore in terms that draw attention to the relativity and original multiplicity of our *genres* of being human, all of a sudden what you begin to recognize is the central role that our discursive *formations*, aesthetic fields, and systems of knowledge must play in the performative enactment of all such genres of being hybridly human.[59] You will begin to understand, in the case of the latter, that the role of all such knowledge-making practices with respect to each such genre is *not* to elaborate truth-in-general. Instead, the role of such knowledge-making practices is to elaborate the *genre-specific* (and/or *culture-specific*) orders *of truth* through which we know reality, from the perspective of the no less genre-specific *who* that we already are. These genre-specific orders of truth then serve to motivate, *semantically-neurochemically*, in positive/negative *symbolic life/symbolic death* terms, the ensemble of individual and collective behaviors needed to dynamically enact and stably replicate each such fictively made eusocial human order *as an autopoietic, autonomously functioning, languaging, living system*. This system functions according to the same analogical rules, at the third *bios/mythoi* level of our existence, as a beehive functions at the second level. So that in the same way as the bee can never have knowledge of the higher-level system that is its hive, we too can in no way normally gain cognitive access to the higher level of the genre-specific autopoietic living system of our status quo structured social worlds, ones in whose terms we are always already initiated as fictively eusocialized, thereby kin-recognizing subjects.

To resolve the aporia of this cognitive dilemma, I turn again to Césaire's proposed new and hybrid *bios/mythoi* science of the Word. Here because, as he proposed, and as earlier cited, the study of the *Word/the mythoi* will now determine the study of the *bios/of the brain*, and this will thereby enable us to gain an external (demonic ground) perspective on the always already storytellingly chartered/encoded discursive formations/aesthetic fields, as well as of, co-relatedly, our systems of knowledge. And, with this gain insight into how these systems of knowledge, each together with its genre-specific "truth of solidarity," all institute and stably replicate our genres of being hybridly human with the also communitarian viability of each respective societal order.

Yet with all of the above—including, in macro terms, the instituting of our contemporary secular and "single model" liberal (now neoliberal) monohumanist Western/Westernized transnational world system—what again must be emphasized is that the respective "truths" of their knowledge systems are always already *prespecified* by our storytellingly chartered sociogenic replicator code of symbolic *life/death*, its Word and/or Bateson-type "descriptive statement" as rigorously discursively elaborated by its "status quo system of learning" and its overall epistemological order. This order circularly ensures that each such genre-specific regime/program of truth, will law-likely function to *semantically-neurochemically induce* the performative enactment of our ensemble of always already role-allocated individual and collective behaviors within the reflexly and subjectively experienced terms of a cognitively closed, thereby genre-specific and fictively eusocializing, autonomously functioning, higher-level living autopoietic system.

Cosmogonies of Our Planetary Life and Our Chartered Codes of Symbolic Life and Symbolic Death: Fictively Induced Modes of Inter-Altruistic Kin Recognition and Auto-Instituted Pseudospeciated Mode of Kind

KM: Here Wynter elaborates on storytelling beginnings and cosmogonies. She returns to her extension of Frantz Fanon's conception of our being hybridly human, both *bios* and *mythoi*, in order to address the unsolved phenomenon of human consciousness. She explores how our chartering/encoding genre-specific cosmogonies provide the narrative source of our fictively eusocializing subjectivities, thus enabling us to be reborn-through-initiation as always already sociogenically encoded inter-altruistically kin-recognizing members of each *referent-we*. At the same time, however, the law-like reification of each fictively induced and subjectively experienced order of consciousness of each *referent-we* is, itself, absolutized by what Wynter identifies as the law of cognitive closure.

SW: Fanon put forward the idea of our skin/masks, thereby of the hybridity of our being human, in 1952. Crick and Watson cracked the genetic code in 1953. Now, I argue that Fanon's masks enact a "second set of instructions": that of the sociogenic code of symbolic *life/death*. Further, within the overall enactment of each such "second set of instructions," the *ism* of gender is itself—while only one member class—a *founding* member class. Gender is a founding member because in order to auto-institute ourselves as subjects of a genre-specific *referent-we*, we must, first, co-relatedly and performatively enact each such code's "second set of instructions" at the *familial level*, in terms of our *gender roles*. We know of this brilliant concept of the performative enactment of gender from Judith Butler.[60] I am suggesting that the enactments of such gender roles are always a function of the enacting of a specific *genre* of being hybridly human. Butler's illuminating redefinition of gender as a praxis rather than a noun, therefore, set off bells ringing everywhere! Why not, then, the performative enactment of *all our roles*, of all our *role allocations* as, in our contemporary Western/Westernized case, in terms of, inter alia, gender, race, class/underclass, and, across them all, sexual orientation? All as praxes, therefore, rather than *nouns*. So here you have the idea that with being human *everything is praxis*. For we are not purely biological beings! As far as the eusocial insects like bees are concerned, their roles are genetically *preprescribed* for them. Ours are not, even though the biocentric meritocratic IQ bourgeois ideologues, such as the authors of *The Bell Curve*, try to tell us that they/we are.[61]

So the question is: What are the mechanisms, what are the technologies, what are the strategies by which we prescribe our own roles? What is common to all are cosmogonies and origin narratives. The representations of origin, which we ourselves invent, are then retroactively projected onto an imagined past. Why so? Because each such projection is the shared storytelling origin out of which we are initiatedly *reborn*. In this case we are no longer, as individual biological subjects, primarily *born of the womb*; rather, we are both *initiated* and *reborn* as fictively instituted inter-altruistic kin-recognizing members of each such *symbolically re-encoded* genre-specific *referent-we*. This is to say we are all *initiatedly reborn*—renatus in Saint Thomas Aquinas's Christian term—to subjectively experience ourselves as subjects of the same encoded *symbolic life* kind. Why this imperative? Because for all genre-specific subjects who are reborn from the same eusocializing origin myth and/or cosmogony, their *genetically encoded individual biological life* and its attendant imperative of naked self-preservation must at the same time be, via initiation, *aversively experienced* as *symbolic death*.[62] This is the concomitant condition of inducing in all subjects the *mimetic desire* for the group-collective *symbolic life* of its genre-specific *referent-we*, its fictive mode of pseudospeciated *kind*. The centrality of the ritually initiated and enacted storytelling codes, and thus their *positive/negative, symbolic life/ death* semantically-neurochemically activated "second set of instructions," emerges here: these codes are specific to each *kind*. The positive *verbal meanings* attributed to their respective modes of kind are alchemically transformed into living flesh, as its members all reflexly subjectively experience themselves, in the *mimetically desirable*, because opiate-rewarded, placebo terms of that mode of *symbolic life* prescribed by the storytelling code. This at the same time as they subjectively experience their former "born of the womb" purely biological life as *mimetically aversive*, because they are doing so in now opiate-reward-blocked *symbolic death, nocebo* terms.[63] For the preservation of *which* of these lives, then, do you think wars are fought?

In the wake of the answer to the above, we see our chartering cosmogonies as being isomorphic with what we now define as our "cultures"— in both cases we are talking about our hybrid sociogenic codes and their "second set of instructions." These are codes that are even able to *override* where necessary—this with respect to our auto-instituted, non–genetically restricted fictive modes of eusociality—*the first set of instructions* of our own DNA (unlike as is the case with all other primates). The logical corollary is this: our modes of auto-institution, together with their *initiatory* rituals of rebirth—as iconized by the ritual of Christian baptism—are indispensable to the enacting of the human as the only living species on Earth who is the denizen of its third and hybrid *bios/mythoi* level of existence! Our mode of hybrid living being alone—this together with our also hitherto always genre-specific *bios/mythoi* enacted orders of supraindividual consciousness—is thereby to arrive on the scene *all at once*! With the Big Bang of the biomutational Third Event! So you see now why we still can't solve the problem of consciousness? In spite of the most dedicated efforts of natural scientists, brain scientists, and philosophers? For what becomes clear here is that our human orders of consciousness/modes of mind cannot exist *outside* the terms of a specific cosmogony. Therefore, human orders of consciousness/modes of mind cannot *preexist* the terms of the always already mythically chartered, genre-specific code of symbolic life/death, its "second set of instructions" and thus its governing sociogenic principle— or, as Keith Ward puts it, its nonphysical principle of causality.[64]

To give an example: here we are, we are talking and thinking. We are, in fact, reflexly talking and thinking in terms of Darwin's biocosmogonically chartered definitive version—in *The Descent of Man* (1871)—of the British bourgeoisie's ruling class's earlier reinvention of Man1's civic humanist *homo politicus* as that of liberal monohumanist Man2 as *homo oeconomicus*, together with its now fully *desupernaturalized* sociogenically encoded order of consciousness. These are the very terms, therefore, in which we ourselves, in now historically postcolonial/postapartheid contexts, *are*. If in our case, only mimetically so! This at the same time as we are also struggling to think *outside* the limits of the purely biocentric order of consciousness that is genre-specific to the Western bourgeoisie's *homo oeconomicus*. But it's extremely difficult to do, right? You know why? Because Darwinism's powerful, seductive force as a cosmogony, or origin narrative, is due to the fact that it is the first in our human history to be not only *part myth* but also *part natural science*. In fact, this mutation—the part myth/part natural science workings of Darwinism—draws attention to Darwin's powerful neo-Malthusian conceptual leap.[65] A leap by means of which—over and against Cardinal Bellarmine—Darwin was to definitively replace the biblical Creation account of the origin of all forms of biological life, including the major *bios* aspect of our being hybridly human, with a new evolutionary account. Why, then, say that this Darwinian account is only *part science*? Biologist Glyn Isaac, in his essay "Aspects of Human Evolution" (1983), provides the answer. Isaac makes us aware of the ecumenically human trap into which Darwin had also partly fallen:

> Understanding the literature on human evolution calls for the recognition of special problems that confront scientists who report on this topic. Regardless of how the scientists present them, accounts of human origins are read as replacement materials for genesis. They fulfill needs that are reflected in the fact that all societies have in their culture some form of origin beliefs, that is, some narrative or configurational notion of how the world and humanity began. Usually, these beliefs do more than cope with curiosity, they have allegorical content, and they convey values, ethics and attitudes. The Adam and Eve creation story of the Bible is simply one of a wide variety of such poetic formulations. . . . The scientific movement which culminated in Darwin's compelling formulation of evolution as a mode of origin seemed to sweep away earlier beliefs and relegate them to the realm of myth and legend. Following on from this, it is often supposed that the myths have been replaced by something quite different, which we call "science." However, this is only partly true; scientific theories and information about human origins have been slotted into the same old places in our minds and our cultures that used to be occupied by the myths. . . . *Our new origin beliefs are in fact surrogate myths, that are themselves part science, part myths.*[66]

So the trap, you see, is that of the paradox that lies at the core of our meta-Darwinian hybridity. For what I'm saying is that as humans, *we cannot/do not preexist our cosmogonies*, our representations of our origins—even though it is we ourselves who invent those cosmogonies and then retroactively project them onto a past. We invent them in formulaic storytelling terms, as "donor figures" or "entities," who have *extrahumanly* (supernaturally, but now also *naturally* and/or bioevolutionarily, therefore secularly) *mandated* what the structuring societal order of our genre-specific, eusocial or cultural *present* would have to be.[67]

As the French cultural anthropologist Maurice Godelier also makes clear, with respect to the above: we, too, hitherto have also systematically kept the reality of our own agency—from our origins until today—*opaque* to *ourselves*.[68] Thus all our humanly invented chartering cosmogonies, including our contemporary macro (monohumanistic/monotheistic) cosmogonies, are law-likely configured as being extrahumanly mandated.[69] All such sacred theological discourses (Judaism, Islamism, Christianity, for example) continue to function in the already theo-cosmogonically mandated cognitively closed terms that are indispensable to the enacting of their respective behavior-inducing and behavior-regulatory fictively eusocializing imperative. This is especially apparent, too, in the secular substitute monohumanist religion of Darwin's neo-Malthusian biocosmogony: here, in the biocosmogony of *symbolic life/death*—as that of *selection/dysselection* and *eugenic/dysgenic* codes—the *incarnation of symbolic life*, will law-likely be that of the ruling-class bourgeoisie as *the naturally selected (eugenic) master of Malthusian natural scarcity*. With this emerges, cumulatively, the *virtuous breadwinner*, together with his pre-1960s virtuous housewife, and, co-relatedly, the savvy investor, the capital accumulator, or at least the steady job holder.[70] In effect, wealth, no longer in its traditional, inherited freehold landowning form, but in its now unceasingly capital-accumulating, global form, is itself the sole macro-signifier of ultimate *symbolic life*. *Symbolic death*, therefore, is that of having been naturally dysselected and mastered by Malthusian natural scarcity: as are the globally homogenized dysgenic non-breadwinning jobless poor/the pauper/homeless/the welfare queens. Poverty itself, therefore, is the "significant ill" signifier of *ultimate symbolic death* and, consequently, capital accumulation, and therefore *symbolic life* signifies and narrates a plan of salvation that will cure the dysselected significant ill! The systemic reproduction of the real-life categories of both signifiers are indispensable to the continued enactment of the ruling-class bourgeoisie's governing code of *symbolic life/death* and the defining of liberal (now neoliberal) monohumanist Man2. This now purely secular coding of life/death is itself discursively—indeed rigorously—elaborated bio-epistemologically, *on the model of a natural organism*, by the disciplines of our social sciences and humanities, together with their respective genre-specific and ethno-class truths of solidarity.[71] Consequently, within the laws of hybrid auto-institution and/or pseudospeciation the (humanities and social science) disciplinary truths of solidarity enact their biocosmogonically chartered sociogenic code of symbolic life/death, also imperatively calling to be discursively elaborated *in cognitively* (cum psychoaffectively/aesthetically) *closed terms*.

To sum up: the "representations of origin," whose cosmogonies have chartered all (genre-specific) human societies from our origins until now, as always already fictively eusocializing, inter-altruistic, kin-recognizing (even where totally nongenetically related) good men and women member subjects of the same *symbolic life* kind, thereby of the same *referent-we*, have all hitherto, together with our autopoietic social systems, been projected onto a *formulaically invented* origin-mythic past whose time-out-of-time brings into being an invented range of meta-transcendental "donor figures" all conceptualized as the extrahumanly mandating source of their respective story line's symbolically encoded "second set of instructions." This thereby canonizes, once and for all, what the inviolate (status quo) order of their/our *referent-we*'s fictively instituted autopoietic eusocial systems would *have to be*: the genre-specific societal order, that is, of each such autopoietic system's performatively enacted magma of role allocations, these centrally including our roles with respect to the latter's modes of material provisioning, themselves correlated to different degrees of dominance and subordination. As a result, all such relative degrees of domination and subordination *law-likely* come to be reflexly and subjectively experienced by their respective subjects as being *normally, the only possible expression* of that "once upon a time's" *extrahuman* mandating of what the magma of role allocations structuring of each such genre-specific societal order's always already sociogenically encoded *higher level, self-organizing, autonomously functioning, living autopoietic, now humanly* (i.e., storytellingly chartered) *encoded eusocial system*, would have had to be.

The concomitant reification of both small-scale and immensely large-scale systemic injustices that have been indispensable to the institutionalization of all our formulaically invented origin stories and narratively chartered genre-specific modes of fictively eusocializing auto-speciation (or in Erik Erikson's terms, pseudospeciation) has therefore functioned *in a law-like manner* from our origins until today.[72] The result is that our now immensely large-scale systemic injustices, as extended across the planet, are all themselves as law-likely and *co-relatedly indispensable* to the institutionalization of our now purely secular and therefore Western and Westernized liberal/neoliberal Man's *homo oeconomicus*'s biocosmogonically chartering origin narrative![73] In our present case, *homo oeconomicus*'s bio-origin narrative, together with its *sociogenically encoded* genre-specific mode of auto-speciation being itself, is one that epochally and uniquely overrepresents and reifies its genre-specific (ethno-class) *referent-we* as being isomorphic with that of the now *emergent-referent-we* "in the horizon of humanity."[74] Given this overrepresentation, the logic by which it pervasively informs the present is therefore dangerously illusory, seeing that its genre-specific *referent-we* correlatedly overrepresents its ethno-class conceptions—such as, for example, those *human rights* and *crimes against humanity*, together with their ostensibly universally applicable international laws of justice, as applied within an international court of justice—as if these formations were ecumenically human conceptions.[75]

Our Global Problematique: The Praxis of Mind/Minding as It Relates to Our Biocosmogonically Chartered Codes and the Intellectual Imperatives of Our Academic/Public Intellectual/Middle-Class Worldviews

KM: As a figure who partook in and witnessed civil rights and anticolonial struggles, Wynter illuminates the limitations of Marxism and, in doing so, draws attention to the ways in which all (Western and Westernized) anticapitalist and antieconomic critiques, with their sole focus on one form of (economically driven labor) oppression, cannot comprehensively attend to the interrelatedness of our colonial-global predicaments. The ongoing struggles of the ex-slave archipelago, beginning with the anticolonial native labor/ *damnés de la terre* uprisings, as well as the increasingly embattled global archipelagoes of poverty, are therefore themselves nuanced, complex struggles that are folded into multifarious social processes that are intimately linked to, yet can in no way can be identified simply as, *economic*. Wynter thus calls for a solution that understands our global crises in relation to her correlated models of being human (Man1 and Man2) and, therefore imperatively, for interrelated solutions to interrelated problems, rather than as singular and particular dilemmas that merely require singular and particular disciplinary solutions.[76]

SW: How are we *not* to think, after Adam Smith and the Scottish School of the Enlightenment, that all human societies are *not* teleologically determined with respect to their successive modes of economic production that determine *who* they are? How are we *not* to think in terms of an ostensibly universal human history, that itself has been identified as one in which all human societies, without exception, must law-likely move from hunter-gatherer, to pastoral, to agricultural modes of material provisioning, to one based on a manufacturing economy?[77] Therefore, how are we *not* to think in the *same* correlated terms of the teleologically determined hegemony of the *bios* (i.e., the material) aspect of our being human? And after Marx's proposed humanly emancipatory antibourgeois project—one itself that was, in fact, unaware that it had become discursively entrapped in what had been Adam Smith and his contemporaries' eighteenth-century projected modality of a post–landed gentry, *bourgeois* account of *origin*—how are we not to think that this teleological hunter-gatherer-to-manufacturing-accumulating society framework was not indeed *the* template for all of human history? So when Marx had put forward the above, as the basis of his ostensibly *scientific* hypothesis, how would it have been possible for us not to consider that this hypothesis was perhaps *the* humanly emancipatory *answer* to all our issues? Marx's proposed hypothesis was nothing less than the following: that in all human societies, from their origins, the respective magma of role allocations (together with their genre-specific status-ordering degrees of domination/subordination) had been merely law-likely generated by— thereby as merely a superstructural function of—each such society's material infrastructural base, its mode of economic production. This pari passu with the class struggle, as waged primarily over *the ownership* of each such mode's *means of production* (yet which, rather than being, as it is, de facto, a function of the performative enactment of the Western world system's role-allocating degrees of domination/subordination), was nevertheless itself held out to be *the* principle of causality whose imperative transformation would be the very condition of our progressive human emancipation! That is, the focus is on the expropriation of that ownership, rather than of what that ownership subserves! Who were we, then, to doubt?! Indeed, as many of us were to do for many years, including Marxist feminists, we would attempt to theoretically fit all our existentially experienced issues—in my case, that to which we give the name of *race*—onto the Procrustean bed of Marx's *mode of economic production* paradigm and its all-encompassing "mirror of production."[78]

Furthermore, in the context of the politico-militarily actualized principle of a then overtly Western-imperial colonizing project of global domination/subordination, organized according to an ostensibly immutable "men/native" divide, there is something we must not forget: both before and during the post–World War II global anticolonial and antiapartheid uprisings, fought for and imagined by a multiplicity of colonized "native" peoples, Marx's then prophetic-poetic emancipatory project—its call, for example, that while philosophers have interpreted the world, the point is to change it!—had been, for so long, the *only* ostensibly ecumenically human emancipatory project around![79] One put forward from a seemingly ecumenically human perspective! The result was that, then, many of us had thought that what first had to be transformed, was, above all, our present free-market/free-trade mode of capitalist economic production exploitation system into a new socialist mode of production. The idea was that once this was done, everything else would follow—including our collective human emancipation from what is, for Marxism, merely our present law-likely generated *superstructural relations of production*! What was also expected to automatically change, therefore, was that of the empirical reality of our still ongoing, status-ordered hierarchically structured, world-systemic order of domination/subordination. This change was to automatically follow! It didn't, of course.

Little by little, however, in the wake of the series of anticolonial and antiapartheid uprisings, which were followed by the sixties' uprising movements in the very core of liberal democratic nation-states of North America and Western Europe—all as struggles against the then still overtly imposed imperial world order—my theoretical landscape had begun to shift. Seismically so. I was teaching, from 1977 onward, in one of the earliest black studies programs for which the sixties black students had struggled, at Stanford.[80] I had come to be struck by the in-depth parallels between the black U.S. antiapartheid movement cum civil rights movement and what had been my own direct childhood memories of the anticolonial and "native" labor uprisings that had taken place in British imperial Jamaica. The parallels had led me to see these uprising movements—that in the United States and those not only in Jamaica but also throughout what was then called the British West Indies—as similar movements. With both understood in relation to the major precursor emancipatory projects that began with the founding, by Marcus Garvey, of the Universal Negro Improvement Association and African Communities (Imperial) League (UNIA-ACL) in 1914, his Declaration of Rights of the Negro Peoples of the World (1920) and Back-to-Africa movement, together with their overall revalorization of both Africa and all African-descended peoples, and so on.[81] This legacy was to powerfully fuel the anticolonial and antiapartheid emancipatory struggles and uprisings as they erupted in separate areas of the overall ex-slave-labor archipelago of the post-1492 Caribbean and the Americas—the first in the then British imperial West Indies during the 1930s, the second beginning in the segregated southern United States during the 1950s and 1960s, then spreading out to the inner cities in the rest of the United States (as well as other parts of Europe and North America).

This ex-slave archipelago is one whose first slave labor form (i.e., the Negro/Negra) had been indispensable, as Immanuel Wallerstein points out, to the West's institutionalization of the first form of its "modern world-system" in the post-1492 Caribbean and the Americas.[82] What this makes clear is that when taken together, the respective anticolonial and antiapartheid uprisings of the British West Indies and the United States reveal that while a major component of them was, indeed, *economically driven*—the aftershocks of the great crash of 1929 had been severe in the 1930s British West Indies plantation colonies—nevertheless, this itself was only *one* aspect of the uprisings. These struggles had at a fundamental level been directed overall, by means of their respective *gaze-from-below* uprising acts of moving *out of place*, at the overtly imperial *homo oeconomicus* genre-specific and class-specific capitalist economic system as it was co-relatedly indispensable to the dynamic yet stable replication of the bourgeoisie's genre-specific socially structured and role-allocated status quo order of domination/subordination. With this, these series of uprisings, taken together, had also called into question the following: the hitherto orthodox Marxian presupposition that each society's status system of social relations, together with their respectively role-allocated hierarchies, was merely the superstructural function of the enacting of the infrastructural (i.e., material-economic) base, instituting of each such societal order.

This was the context that had made it possible for me to begin to think that, unlike Soviet Russia's heroic mode/mirror of production Revolution (which was indeed cataclysmic but still *intra-European*), what the range of "native" global uprisings had fundamentally called into question had been, instead, Man2's biocosmogonical and Darwinian-chartered ethno-class descriptive statement. The statement called into question, then, is a biocentric genre of being that carries in it the sociogenic code of symbolic life/death that is actualized by a eugenic/dysgenic *men/native* behavior-regulatory principle of dominion. The "native" challenges to that Man2 "principle of dominion" also brought into focus, therefore, the *mode of auto-institution or of pseudospeciation* central to the institutionalized enactment of liberal monohumanism's Man2 as *homo oeconomicus*. The long-standing and attendant system to this "principal of domination" includes both the socially stratified divisions of labor internal to each bourgeois nation-state, as well as the transnational macro-divisions of labor that are performatively enacted by the dominant/subordinate categories of First/developed, Second/developing, Third/Fourth/underdeveloped so-called worlds. *Both* forms of socially stratified and role-allocated divisions of labor are, thereby *co-relatedly*, indispensable to the overall enactment of *homo oeconomicus* and its genre-specific (ethno-class) world-systemic capitalist free-market economic system in its now globally homogenized—post-Soviet and post-Mao—neoliberal consumer-driven cum politically liberal-democratic, for the main part, modality.[83]

The result here is that, for the first time in our history, we find ourselves having to confront, *as a species*, the overall negative costs now being paid on a planetary level for the continued dynamic enactment, yet stable reproduction, of the above. This as understood with respect to the surplus quantity of these costs, specifically the costs of the single-model free-market competitive capitalist economy in its now, post-1989, homogenizing, transnational/ transreligious and/or transcultural, techno-automated cum mechanized agriculture form: an economy, thereby, all the more fossil fuel *and* consumer driven in its homogenizedly neoliberal globalizing enactment. The large-scale human costs incurred are therefore indispensable—at the level of the societal order enacting of its overall self-organizing, globally incorporating and autopoietic eusocial system—*to that to which that economy gives rise*. Inter alia, that is, the logically induced technologically automated labor process cum large-scale *joblessness* by means of large-scale mechanized agriculture cum peasant farmer landlessness and attendant hunger/poverty/ anxiety cum increasing drug addiction, with the latter's surplus demand, as augmented by the surplus consumer demand by the First World nations' giving origin to, in turn, on the one hand, the large-scale criminalized drug trafficking engaged in by the otherwise now landless/jobless and, on the other hand, to the endless rich/poor divisive conflicts of our post-2001 war-torn, because necessarily unjust, global order.[84] A global order, then, in which secular smart drones vie with religious suicide bombers, the nuclear "haves" (United States/Israel) vie with Islamic Iran's ongoing attempt to join the nuclear club in order to defend itself against the kind of by-proxy regime change now taking place in Syria—just as an also nuclear-armed Russia warns the United States against any overt unilateral intervention in the conflict! So, once again, we find ourselves in a nuclear-threatened world. The fundamental issue is therefore one having to do not only with all of the above costs but also with the species-threatening nature of these negative costs, including that of the relentlessly increasing fossil fuel–driven climate instability's ongoing catastrophe.

Once "we humans" begin to think globally, Gerald Barney proposes, such costs/problems will no longer continue to be thought of as they have hitherto been—within, by implication, the normative terms of our present status quo's "system of learning's" episteme, which inevitably calls for *separate* disciplinary solutions.[85] What at once becomes clear is this: rather than positing that "we humans have a poverty problem, or a habitat problem, or an energy problem, or a trade problem, or a population problem, or an atmosphere problem, or a waste problem or a resource problem," these, on a planetary scale, are understood, together, as "inter-connected problems."[86] Thus, thinking globally, what "we really have is a poverty-hunger-habitat-energy-trade-population-atmosphere-waste-resource problem," none of whose separate parts can be solved on their own.[87] They all interact and are interconnected and thus, together, are constitutive of our species' now seemingly inescapable, hitherto unresolvable "global problematique."[88] The main problem with respect to solving the cognitive contradiction with which we are now confronted is therefore how we can begin not only to draw attention to but also to *mind about* those *outside* our specific and particular *referent-we* perspectives and worldviews. If, as Nicholas Humphrey suggests, the mind is itself a praxis—a praxis by means of which *minds must necessarily be always engaged in minding about* what happens, positively or negatively, *to* a biological species-specific and hybrid (*bios/mythoi*) genre-specific living entity and overall well-being, the following question arises: How can we be enabled to come to *mind about* the well-being or ill-being of those inhabiting worlds *outside* that of our normatively politically liberal democratic *referent-we* of *homo-oeconomicus* rather than to continue, as we reflexly do, to mind about *only* the well-being of the above *referent-we*, as the one to which we, as hegemonically secular middle-class/bourgeois academics belong?[89] Keeping in mind, too, that those "outside" the *referent-we* of *homo oeconomicus* also indicate that they themselves had only been brought into existence as such "outsiders" over the last five hundred years or so, by Western civilization's globally and territorially incorporating planetary imperializing world system. How to envision a system, then, that would no longer follow a biocentric naturally selected/dysselected bioevolutionary teleological logic and necessitates accumulation, but rather engenders a worldview and outlook, reconceptualized, in new meta-Darwinian terms, from the ecumenically human hybrid perspective of our Third Event origin as a species as *homo narrans*?

As Western or Westernized academics and/or public intellectuals and/or creative poets, writers, storytellers, therefore, what we ourselves, as members of the now secular cadre, specific to the Western bourgeoisie's liberal monohumanist Man2, must now recognize is the following: that as such a cadre, our shaman-like role, from our origins until today, has been to elaborate, by means of our genre-specific or culture-specific "system of learning" and our aesthetics, our particular genre-specific auto-speciating, always already storytellingly chartered/encoded "descriptive statement" of being human.[90] This includes a "truth of solidarity" that enacts as well as rigorously conserves our *descriptive statement*, together with the order of consciousness or *mode of mind/minding* to which each such statement's sociogenic code of symbolic life/death, gives origin. The catch has been the following: because we too must continue, together with all other members of our genre-specific (or culture-specific) *referent-we*, to subjectively experience ourselves through the mediation of the same order of consciousness and its mode of mind/minding (thereby reifying the us/not us composed of our inter-altruistic kin-recognizing individual member subjects *of the same symbolic life kind*), this means that we, too, must keep the reality of *our own agency opaque* by attributing that *agency* to extrahumanly mandating entities (sacred Malthusian-Darwinian entities).

So how do we deal with the new reality of the now emergent empirically ecumenically human *referent-we* "in the horizon of humanity"? And how do we grapple with this in relation to the cognitive contradiction that our law-likely correlated genre-specific mode of mind/minding/consciousness, that is necessarily opiate rewarded, in the terms of its genre-specific sociogenic code of symbolic life/death, must law-likely undermine a *species perspective* in favor of a *genre-specific perspective* that honors those of us who are interpellated as "normal subjects" and who thereby constitute the middle-class *referent-we*?[91] How, then, as Thomas Nagel proposes, can we be enabled and empowered "to climb out of our present order of consciousness?"[92] How can we come to know/think/feel/behave and subjectively experience ourselves—doing so for the first time in our human history *consciously now*—in *quite different terms*? How do we *be*, in Fanonian terms, hybridly human?

The Periphery Perspective of the Post-1492 Ex-Slave-Labor Ultimate Human Other Archipelago: W. E. B. DuBois's Double Consciousness, Frantz Fanon's Skins/Masks, and the Reverse Paradox

KM: Turning to the work of W. E. B. DuBois and Frantz Fanon, Wynter draws attention to their respective analyses of their experiential "double consciousness" as it is understood within the context of the post-1492 slave labor archipelago and the fictive and material production of blackness as naturally dysselected. In their delineation of being both *normally* and *abnormally* human, Wynter argues, DuBois's and Fanon's self-reflexive questioning of this "double consciousness" initiated a new Copernican leap: one not with respect to the movements of the planets but with respect to the unsolved—in spite of the best efforts of contemporary neuroscientists—phenomenon of our human consciousness. Fanon's insights on human consciousness create a space to establish his own "double consciousness" as the point of departure both for his *skin/masks* epochal redefinition of our being hybridly human and for what Wynter describes as his transcultural and transcosmogonic "reverse paradox."

SW: To further address the sections above and the struggles ahead, I want us to move back in time. What do we find? We find that the very same Nagel-type problematic not only had been *existentially experienced as fundamental* but also had been agonistically confronted and grappled with, beginning almost a century ago. It is therefore imperative for us to understand the kind of far-reaching mutational leap that W. E. B. DuBois, together with Frantz Fanon, was to initiate. This leap is one that itself could only have been made from the existential ground of the then ex-slave-labor (Negro/Negra) periphery archipelago of the post-1492 New World—a founding politico-statal mercantilist economic system that had called for the institution of a hierarchically stratified triadic system (black enslaved, indentured conquered neo-serf indigenous, white) of labor.[93] With this, as the anthropologist Jacob Pandian documents in his study *Anthropology and Western Tradition* (1985), the above triadic hierarchy of labors was itself one whose principle of domination was inextricably interlinked with the no less hierarchically stratified, triadic classificatory system of ostensibly differential degrees of being human/of humanness (degrees of humanness that, of course, coalesce with the inventions of Man1 and Man2 and bring into focus those black, indigenous enemies of Christ, irrational savages, human-Other(s)-by-nature, with postslave black subject occupying the most subordinated status of nigger/wholly Other).

Yet the West's continued planetary imperializing expansion led to the following paradox: it was only to be in the wake of the West's *abolition* of Negro/Negra slavery—this itself of course as precipitated by, inter alia, the earlier success of the Haitian slave revolution—that all peoples of black African descent were made to embody this most subordinated *wholly human Other* status. Modeled on the natural organism, the Western bourgeoisie's liberal monohumanist self-narrating descriptive statement had therefore, *as the condition of its postslavery enactment*, logically called for all peoples of black African descent to reoccupy the transumptively inherited Man₁'s *symbolic death* role. Thus those of black African descent were cast as the naturally dysselected Native/Nigger figure, ostensibly bioevolutionarily situated between apes and humans. This is a figure barely evolved and wholly subhuman that is Other to the fully evolved, thereby only True Human Self and its genre-specific mode of *symbolic life* that is optimally incarnated in the Western bourgeois liberal monohumanist *homo oeconomicus*. The former, wholly subhuman, together with its black race, is *dysgenically* dysselected to be *racially inferior* cum deficient in intelligence (IQ), in *symbolic death* terms; the latter wholly evolved is, therefore, together with its white race, eugenically selected to be racially superior, proficient in intelligence (in *symbolic life* terms). Furthermore, both premises, together with Man₂'s descriptive statement and that of its biocosmogonically chartered code of *symbolic life/death*, are thereby discursively enacted by the disciplines of the social sciences and the humanities and therefore a status quo "system of learning."

The ultimate periphery slave/ex-slave archipelago's underside of the Western world system, together with its black African–descended men and women (all generically classified as Negroes and/or as colonial *natives*), has thus been made to function, over several centuries, as that of the ultimate embodiment of *symbolic* death—as wholly human Others to *symbolic life*.[94] It is in this context that W. E. B. DuBois wrote, in 1903, from his experience in a then neo-periphery and apartheid U.S. South, about his *double consciousness*. Let's note what he is saying: that to be a professional middle-class American, with a doctorate from Harvard (perhaps the first such), DuBois would have to be anti-Negro! He *cannot* trust his own normative middle class American consciousness, structured as it is by "the tape of a world that looks on in amused contempt and pity."[95] He is therefore saying: I have to wage war against this consciousness. Yet who knows when I will not let my guard down? Then this consciousness—which is not my own, *at the same time as it also is my own*—will reflexly be in command once more! So *The Souls of Black Folk*, in which DuBois published his "double consciousness" essay, "Of Our Spiritual Strivings," is itself the first phase of the war against that (unbeknownst to him then, genre-specific) order of consciousness.[96] This struggle would therefore make apparent to him his reflexly subjective experience of being both *positively* a middle-class American (and implicitly, therefore, of also being *normally* fully human) and negatively a Negro (the abnormal human Other to his normal middle-class self). He experienced this doubleness *in the very terms of his own ostensibly autonomous individual order of consciousness.* This was a war that was to be, therefore, an intellectual, imaginative, and sustained political one. Yet, in passing, let us also note this: DuBois is also implying that the "governing tape of the world" to which he refers, rather than being biologically natural, as it represents itself to be, is instead an *epistemologically and humanly structured one.* This even though the governing tape has been made to be reflexly and subjectively experienced both by him and by all other Americans, white and Negro, as if it were indeed a *bio-instinctually experienced* one, on the part of *each* individual.

Now, the region of the ex-slave periphery archipelago from which Du-Bois was writing at the time was, as earlier noted, that of the pre-1960s racially segregated apartheid U.S. South. But look at this! A century and a half later, when Frantz Fanon writes of the existential reality from another region of the Western world system's periphery ex-slave archipelago—this time from a then French colonial Martinique—he is saying exactly the same thing! In his *Black Skin, White Masks* (1952), Fanon is saying, by implication, that in order to be a middle-class professional as well as a colonial *evolué* Frenchman—and thereby alone being able, in Western terms, to experience himself as fully human—I *have to be* at times reflexly anti-Negro and, therefore, opposed to, averse to, my own ostensibly nonevolved self.[97]

Now let us fast-forward here a minute to the sixties uprisings in the United States. We see Eldridge Cleaver puzzling over another aspect of the same dilemma: Why, he asks, do I find myself, *against my will,* reflexly desiring white women and reflexly being aversive to black women? Then, *against* our orthodox biocentric conceptual grain, he hits on the concept of the *symbolic.* What, Cleaver asks, is *the symbol* of which white women have been made the incarnation *of,* and conversely, black women made the absolute embodied *negation of?*[98] Larry Neal had also noted that his crucial daily struggle was the struggle against "the white thing" within him—at the same time as all other "of color" Americans actively struggled with the same thing reflexly within themselves/ourselves.[99] In the sixties, gays struggling against the no less normative (thereby also opiate-rewarded) "heterosexual thing" within them had started to come out of the closet, as newly minted feminists engaged in *consciousness-raising* sessions against the normatively canonized as the generic sex "male thing" within them. Here I recall one of the more iconic examples of this attempt at "climbing out" of that normative order of consciousness, as it was to take place in the overall dynamic context of the U.S. sixties uprisings: "I have" — here I cite from memory — "sometimes hated myself for being homosexual," the Chicana feminist Rosalie Morales writes. And what's more, Morales continues, "I keep a ten-foot pole to keep myself away from black people."[100] *So the enemy to me* — she's saying, like DuBois, Fanon, and Neal before her — *is also myself*! Are we on the same page here? Because we too are also now struggling to move beyond the knee-jerk limits of the *Us* and the *Them*.

To bring this together, let's return to Fanon. Listen to what he's implicitly saying: I can't trust this order of consciousness — its mode of mind — in whose terms I now subjectively experience myself as a *colonial* middle-class professional evolué Frenchman who is *also* a Negro! I am now in fief to an order of consciousness whose powerfully induced reflex responses of *desire/aversion* impel and induce me not only to desire *against myself* but also to work against the emancipatory interest of the world-systemic subordinated and inferiorized Negro population to which I belong! For these reflex responses of *desire/aversion* are *not* my own! They are only *mimetically* made to be so, through my French imperial/bourgeois education (cum *initiation*) system of French Martinique and through my colonial history lessons that taught me — exactly like a proper member of the French bourgeoisie — that my ancestors, too, were the Gauls (and not the Franks!).[101] This is, of course, because the Gauls had been *storied* as *the* origin-mythic ancestors by the revolutionary French bourgeoisie, over against what had been, pre-Revolution, the ancien régime's privileged hereditary *storied* claim to the Franks and their ruling-caste status as *noblemen, noblewomen*![102] Importantly, the above counterclaim regarding the Gauls is emerging in the wake of the French Revolution's declaration of the ostensibly universally applicable "natural rights of *man*." So you see, one could further read Fanon as thinking: Since my real-life ancestors, then, were slaves (*notres ancêtres, les ésclaves!*) *they* were not Man/human — nor am I, then, human myself. Such 'rights' are therefore neither *natural* nor *universally applicable*! With this being so, and given the interests of my present subjectively experienced middle class order of consciousness and its normative 'tape of the world' — based as it is on such 'natural rights' — do not these laws/rights, *everywhere*, work *against* me? That is, do not these ostensibly universal laws work against my own now consciously, because politically willed, self-emancipatory own?

It is here that Fanon, in 1951 and as a newly qualified psychiatrist, and as

such a "specific intellectual," puts forward what is to be an illuminating—
because *transcultural* and transcosmogonic—comparison.[103] Fanon explains: if I were instead a millennially existing Pygmy, in Africa, and therefore one still "at the center of my own cultural constellation, its rites, and
its myths," *I could never have subjectively experienced myself, negatively, as a
Negro!*[104] As I try to explain to others, this is the neo-Copernican leap that
Fanon, out of this "gaze from below" Western world-systemic, ultimate underside, periphery ex-slave archipelago's liminally deviant, perspective, is
going to make here! A perspective that is, Katherine, a *demonic ground* perspective! This time, however, the leap is not with respect to the Copernican
reality of an also moving earth, a *star like any other*, but instead with respect
to the hitherto unexplored regions of our uniquely hybrid orders of consciousness, their storytellingly genre-specific modes of mind/minding, yet
ones whose hybrid laws of functioning, together with their *non–biologically
determined*, yet biologically *implemented principle of causality*, continue to
be enacted by us outside the (still unfound) *plus ultra* of our cognitively
conscious awareness.

Put in more immediate terms, this is the contradiction that Michel
Foucault had also attempted to come to grips with, from his own self-
questioning perspective: "What I am trying to do is grasp the implicit systems which *determine our most familiar behaviour without our knowing it. I
am trying to find their origin, to show their formation, the constraint they impose upon us*; I am therefore trying to place myself at a distance from them
and to show *how one could escape.*"[105] Without our knowing it! This parallels the self-questioning made earlier by DuBois and Fanon with respect
to their own reflexly subjectively experienced behavior-inducing Western
ethno-class order of "normal" consciousness.[106] In the case of Fanon and
DuBois, however, this questioning had taken on an even more anguished
form: one as a U.S. apartheid subject, the other as a French colonized one,
they would have had to subjectively experience themselves as both *normal*
(thereby in reflexly opiate-rewarded *placebo* terms) middle-class and highly
educated professionals and *abnormal* (thereby in reflexly opiate-rewarded
blocked *nocebo* terms) Negroes. What we nevertheless find is that already,
in 1903, not only had DuBois been anticipating a Foucault-type question—
how can I escape from the burden of my also reflexly experienced double
consciousness of normalcy *and* abnormality—but that he, like Fanon, will
set out to answer it.

In the essay "Of Our Spiritual Strivings," from *The Souls of Black Folk*,

DuBois had put forward his proposed solution. The first thrust of the solution was posed in terms of "a wish," a "longing." His own longing, he tells us, had been "to attain to self-conscious manhood," to do so "by merging" his double self into "a better and truer self."[107] In this "merging," he would wish that "neither of the older selves be lost," but rather to "make it possible for a man to be both a Negro and an American *without* being cursed and spit upon by his fellows, without having the doors of Opportunity closed roughly in his face."[108] In effect, the wish is to attain to "*a better*" because "*truer self*"; one whose reinstituted "tape of the world," its order of consciousness and mode of *mind/minding*, would have to be, because now *consciously* and collectively willed to be so, an ecumenically inclusive one. Nevertheless, the second thrust of his answer had already been identified in his "Forethought" to the *Souls* collection. There he identified the nature of the implacable barrier that *blocked* any such wished-for solution, any such longed-for escape. The barrier of the color line had come to constitute a Problem—one that ensured that 1903 was the dawn of the century that was to be "the bloodiest in human history."[109] This meant that the brutally harsh nature of the postslavery, post–Civil War, post–Reconstruction U.S. South institutionalized white/Negro apartheid system—itself often lynchingly reinforced and having come to govern the everyday lives of U.S. Negroes— was itself nevertheless world-systemically interlinked. Thus, as DuBois was to further write in "Of the Dawn of Freedom," this Problem had come to constitute what was to be *the* Problem of the twentieth century precisely because its global reach was already being enacted by the West's second wave of large-scale imperialism; in its now bourgeois ruling-class articulation, a militarily enforced *colonizer versus colonized* cum *men versus natives* territorially expanding and incorporating project was imposed and was an action that also intersected with what DuBois described as "the *darker* to the *lighter* races of men in Asia and Africa, in America and the islands of the sea."[110]

This meant, for DuBois, that in order for his own wished-for *truer self* to be made possible, the objectively institutionalized Problem of the color line would itself have to be concomitantly solved—and solved by means of a multiplicity of local, small-scale anticolonial, antisettler apartheid, and overall anti-imperial "gaze from below" perspectives and struggles that were as global in their reach as that of the color line itself. The outcome of his wished-for solution was to be this: for the rest of his very long life, DuBois was to be politically and theoretically as actively engaged in the global, world-systemic series of "gaze from below" anti–color line, therefore anticolonial cum antiapartheid struggles, as he was to be in his own "local" U.S. one—a position Fanon would similarly adopt.

Both DuBois and Fanon were, therefore, to uniquely take as their initial point of departure the struggle against the contradictory doubleness that lay at the core of their own reflexly (as if *bio-instinctually*) subjectively experienced order of consciousness. DuBois, in the context of his time, had thereby initiated a self-questioning *heuristics of mistrust* with respect to his own consciousness; a half century later, Fanon, as a young psychiatrist, would find himself engaged in a struggle to provide the explanatory cause that lay behind the reflexly subjectively experienced "doubled" (normal/abnormal) order of consciousness and its mode of mind/minding.[111] In *Black Skin, White Masks*, Fanon's own self-questioning heuristic(s) of mistrust was therefore also to be the springboard for his thinking. It was in doing so that he was to come upon the functioning of what can be recognized, from today's hindsight, as the hitherto unknown, unsuspected, yet law-likely functioning, nonphysically, nonbiologically *determined*, if itself biologically implemented, principle of causality. The principle alone—as I note above—explains the "why" of the phenomenon that underwrites our *genre-specific* and hybridly instituted human orders of consciousness, together with their respective modes of mind/minding.

Fanon too, like DuBois before him, had not wanted to let go of either of his two existentially lived selves. At the same time Fanon also knew that the continued existence of the same color line barrier meant that any merging of his two selves—French, on the one hand, his colonized evolué Negro self, on the other—into a better, because "truer," self would continue to be impossible. It will be precisely on the basis of this parallel recognition that, with Fanon, we shall also see his two selves, including centrally that of his trained professional self as a psychiatrist, jointly dedicated to the war *against* the same formidable metaphysical (because origin-mythic) barrier that Du-Bois identified as the color line. *How do we extricate ourselves?* Fanon writes:

> The white man is sealed in his whiteness.
> The black man in his blackness.
>
> We shall seek to ascertain the direction of this dual narcissism, *and the motivations that inspire it. . . .* I believe that *the fact of the juxtaposition of the White and the black races* has created a massive psychoexistential complex. I hope by analysing it to destroy it.[112]

Fanon's exploration of the explanatory cause that lay behind the above juxtaposition was to lead to the humanly emancipatory breakthrough put forward by him in his *Black Skin, White Masks*. Here, Fanon first identifies the conceptual breakthrough earlier made by Sigmund Freud. "Against the constitutionalist tendency of the nineteenth century," he writes, "Freud insisted that *the individual factor be taken into account*. He substituted for the phylogenetic theory an *ontogenetic perspective*. It will be seen, however," Fanon counterargues, "that the black man's alienation is not an *individual* question."[113] With this, Fanon puts forward (some half century before Godelier), the earlier cited hypothesis with respect to our human agency: as the creators of our societies we must recognize the condition of our being able to live, thereby to *be*, hybridly human: "Beside phylogeny and ontogeny, there stands sociogeny."[114] Society, he further argues, cannot "escape human influences," and *"Man is what brings society into being."*[115] What Fanon meant by this is that the *"sociodiagnostic* prognosis" for the black man's / the black human's collective alienation will—as distinct from an individual *psychoanalytic* one—have to be instead "in the hands of those who are [themselves] willing to get rid of the worm-eaten roots of the structure."[116] This means, by implication, getting rid of the structure of the humanly invented Western world-systemic society whose status quo institutionalized hierarchical order is (also by implication) the cause of their black skins (at the level of ontogeny) having, at the level of sociogeny, to mimetically desire to adopt *white masks*. This mimetic desire and the adoption of white masks uncover an attempt by black subjects to realize themselves / ourselves in non-self-aversive terms as truly human, this reflex, so to speak, an autogenocidal mimeticism, being *the* cause of their / our collective alienation. Fanon therefore concludes:

> The black man must wage his war *on both levels*: Since historically they influence each other, *any unilateral liberation is incomplete*, and the gravest mistake would be to believe *in their automatic interdependence*. Besides, such a systematic tendency is contrary to the facts. This will be proved.
>
> Reality, for once, requires a total understanding. *On the objective level as on the subjective level, a solution has to be supplied.*[117]

Three hypotheses that Fanon puts forward here, taken together, show his conceptual leap to be that of reimagining and redefining the human as a hybrid being. First is his hypothesis that "it is Man" (the human, both men and women) that "brings[s] society into being." Second is his proposal that the black man can only bring his alienation to an end if he, together with his fellows, are also prepared to bring to an end the then still overtly coloniz-ing Western world-systemic societal order, which from its institutionalized origin had led to their collective alienation as a population of black Afri-can and slave descent, both generically classified in racially inferiorized *Ne-gro* and/or *native*, ultimately subhuman Other (i.e., Nigger) terms.[118] Finally, and over against the above, is Fanon's counterhypothesis, which is outlined in his further discussion of the earlier Pygmy/Negro's contradiction, which I deal with later.

What the overall insights of Fanon's work therefore demonstrate is that all of us, too, will also be able to begin to come to grips with the ecumeni-cally human—thereby meta-Freudian *and* meta-Darwinian—implications of our having been, from our species origin, *hybridly* (skins/masks, phylog-eny/ontogeny/sociogeny, *bios/mythoi*, and thereby always hitherto, *rela-tively*) *human*. We might, then, not only learn to think cosmogonically, as Conrad Hyers advises other scholars to do, but also *transcosmogonically*.[119] With this, we will find ourselves, whether white or nonwhite, black or non-black, now cognitively empowered to, as Fanon urges us, "tear off with all [our] strength, the shameful livery put together by centuries of *incompre-hension*."[120]

Through Fanon's insights what we find is this. That it had precisely been on the cognitively empowering basis of his own elaborated cosmogonic, cultural, and transcosmogonic/transcultural perspective that he would develop his counterhypothesis with respect to the Pygmy/Negro contra-diction in the terms of a triadic reverse paradox. To do so, he first puts for-ward in his chapter "The Negro and Psychopathology" a brief but episte-mologically heretical comparative *sociodiagnostic* analysis of the ethnic or *band* societal order of a Pygmy group before "the [homogenizing] flood of civilization" engulfed it.[121] Drawing on Father Trilles's study *L'âme Pygmée d'Afrique*, Fanon emphasizes the fact that, in spite of its author's attempt at a Christian evangelizing interpretation, he had nevertheless given a descrip-tion of the Pygmy society's "whole culture," together with "the [latter's] per-sistence of rites, the survival of myths."[122] *L'âme Pygmée d'Afrique* had there-fore provided him with knowledge of several of the major aspects of a then still *religio-origin-mythically* chartered and *auto-centered* Pygmy society. This knowledge allowed Fanon, by means of a sociodiagnostic analysis, to com-pare and contrast the Pygmy society with that of the no less auto-centered society of France (with which he is already familiar and a society in whose biocosmogonically chartering secular terms, it can be added here, the *psyche* has now transumptively replaced the *soul*). What he is therefore emphasizing, in his reading of the Pygmy and French societies—over against psychoanalysis's privileging of the individual factor—is the sociogenic and its sociodiagnostic perspective. Thus, he writes, that if in France, for example, the family is itself "a miniature of the nation," then in the Pygmy society the family is also, by implication, "a miniature of the 'band,'" or ethnic group.[123] In both cases, therefore, when the French male child and the Pygmy male child grow and are initiated into manhood, through their respective "rites," they will both have come to subjectively experience themselves, reflexly in the respective terms of their own unquestioned, genre-specific, *normalcy of being human*.[124] In both cases, therefore, *normalcy* underwrites their respective societal orders' status quo system of role allocations, as well as that of their also, always already autonomously invented, storytellingly chartered and encoded, thereby auto-centered, genre-specific notions of the Self.

Over against both the Pygmy and the French bourgeois subjects, what Fanon puts forward in now triadic terms, however, is the quite different reality of the Negro subject of France's then still overtly colonized (ex-slave/now "native labor") island of Martinique. This is a status and reality in which, when growing up, the Negro evolué is cast supposedly as a part of the extended "family" of France; the Negro evolué would have thereby been initiated into adulthood in the bosom of a seemingly "normal"/Francophone (Negro middle-class) family. At the same time, however, Fanon, the Negro evolué was taught a colonial curriculum at school, the terms of which would ensure that he would become "*abnormal* on the slightest contact with the white world."[125] This is to say that the colonial variant of the Western bourgeoisie paideia-type initiatory system of education would have taught Fanon, above all, that to be *normally* and acceptably middle-class—and only as such, therefore, as normally, generically human—one must also *normally* perceive Africans as *savage, primitive, wicked*, and, as such, the pre-destined target villains, in French adventure stories, of a range of imperially civilizing French heroes! These heroes—as over against the villains—have as the objects of their heroic deeds the abnormal, primitive, wicked, savage Africans. With this, as is always the case, the Negro evolué schoolboys would have primarily mimetically identified themselves just as the "normal" (non-African) French schoolboys would have (as vicariously and no less mimetically) also identified themselves.

Now in my essay "Towards the Sociogenic Principle" (1995), I attempt, as you may recall, Katherine, to explore in some depth the phenomenological dynamic of Fanon's charting of his own subjectively experienced doubled consciousness of being at one and the same time *normally* and *abnormally* human, that will eventually come to grip him.[126] Upon first arriving in France, he will find that if the French populace's response to him as a phobic object is a *reflex* response—a response often expressed in shouted cries of "dirty nigger" or "mama, the negro is going to eat me up"—all of which are uttered as if bio-instinctually and, indeed, seemingly without their knowing it! This response itself is, nevertheless, in no way simply a phobic and arbitrary response, but is instead a law-likely and collectively formulaic response. A phobic response, therefore, that is uttered in objectively and disciplinarily instituted "tape of the world" terms at the same time as it is subjectively, indeed reflexly experienced by the *referent-we* populace of the then overtly imperial nation-state of France, as if also it were merely, in Western cultural terminology, a *human nature* one.[127]

Fanon, as an evolué Antillean, will thus be forced to recognize that he himself, like the "savage primitive" Negroes of Africa, is also a *Negro!* Indeed, he is a phobia-inducing *Dirty Nigger!* One always already correlated with the genital and whose Reason is nonexistent.[128] As a member of the highly Western-educated bourgeois category to which DuBois before him had belonged, Fanon would thus, from then on, come to be consciously aware of how he was reflexly and subjectively experiencing himself as being at one and the same time *both normally and abnormally human.* Yet this latter, he begins to see, would itself be experienced according to the same white masks or sociogenic code in whose prescriptive terms the French populace of the overtly imperial nation-state of France, at that time, would have also reflexly experienced themselves as being *normally* and indeed *generically* human.

Now, if it had been that traumatic experience that was eventually to make possible the profound irony of Fanon's reverse paradox, one of the major revelations of the latter is the following: that in the everyday run of things—as in the transcosmogonic, transcultural cases of the auto-centered Pygmy and French bourgeois subjects—any *questioning* on their respective parts of their shared *reflexly subjectively experienced normalcy of being human* is law-likely foreclosed. Fanon's transcosmogonic analysis has also centrally revealed, remember, the fact of the empirical functioning of a law-like *continuity* between the family structure and that of the larger societal order.[129]

One that would have further entailed, one can surmise here, the following: that the adult Pygmy subject and the French adult individual bourgeois subject would have *both* reflexly subjectively experienced the normalcy of their being human in the respective genre-specific Bateson-type "descriptive statement" of the self. At the same time, their experiences would, in turn, have been law-likely *mirrored* by those kin-recognizing subjects who, too, were always already experiencing the cosmogonically chartered terms and sociogenic life/death terms underwriting their collective and fictively eusocialized genre-specific *referent-we*. Each respective *referent-we* draws attention to the ways in which subjective experience is *extrahumanly mandated* yet experienced, reflexly, as though it is *normally human*. This is how both the Pygmy and the French bourgeois subjects would, individually, have reflexly subjectively experienced their differential *normalcy of being human*.

If we read the above from today's Western and globally Westernized secular (biocentric liberal/neoliberal and thereby bourgeois monohumanist) perspective, the seemingly vast and unbridgeable differences between the then still noncolonized (ostensibly irredeemably "primitive" and thereby barely evolved darker-skinned, small-statured Pygmy subject) and the highly civilized (ostensibly fully evolved, taller, white-skinned French bourgeois subject), then what becomes apparent here is the following: it is the projected macrocosmic *color line* cum *physiognomic barrier*'s ostensible *nonhomogeneity of genetic substance* (and our divisively markedly different *eugenic/dysgenic* populations) that will now be breached by the identification of what is, *for them both*, a shared, nonnegotiable imperative.[130]

With this, two major questions emerge. First, what is this nonnegotiable imperative? Second, why would this recognition only be made possible by means of the major *reverse paradox* implications of Frantz Fanon's transcosmogonic and transcultural cum triadic comparison/contrast? Regarding the first question, what is made recognizable is this: the respective genre-specific descriptive statements of the Pygmy and French bourgeois subjects, at the sociogenic level of *the self/the soul*—as distinct from the phylogeny/ontogeny descriptive statement at the level of the physiological body—would itself have functioned in starkly different terms.[131] That is, their respective descriptive statements law-likely functioned according to the *same* hybrid (*bios/mythoi*) behavior-regulatory sociogenic *principle of causality* that was enacted in the *genre-specific* and/or *pseudospecies symbolic life/death* terms of their respective *referent-we* and its *us/not us*. Put differently, *both* their nongenetically determined and their encoded sociogenic masks are demonstrative of, as described earlier, a law-likely functioning, nonphysically and nonbiologically determined behavior-regulatory principle of causality that is neurochemically *implemented*. In the terms of my own Fanonianly adapted hindsight hypothesis, therefore, what this entails is that each such mask's origin-mythically chartered sociogenic replicator code of *symbolic life/death*—its second set of instructions—must also therefore law-likely function, in both cases, to *activate*, in positively/negatively marked *semantic (symbolic life/symbolic death)* terms, the opiate-reward (placebo) and opiate-blocking (nocebo) neurochemical system of the Third Event's uniquely evolved human brain.[132] At the same time, however, each such "genre-specific" sociogenic replicator code can only be brought into existence through the chartering storytelling mediation of their respective versions of their *representations of origins*.[133] Thus, and with the second question regarding the triadic comparative frame provided by Fanon: their specific sociogenic replicator codes serve to illuminate both the *religio-centered*—thereby theo-cosmogonically chartering/encoding representation of origins—instituting of the Pygmy subject as well as that of the liberal monohumanist *purely secular*, thereby biocosmogonically coded and Darwinian chartered representation of origins of the French bourgeois subject.

The nonnegotiable imperative result—when understood through Fanon's sociodiagnostic comparison and as earlier noted in an analogical context—is that there can in no way be, on the part of their respective *normal* subjects, any questioning with respect to what is, for them, the *self-evident unchallengeable unassailable truths* of their genre-specific storytelling *representations of origins*. Concomitantly also, there is no questioning with respect to that which the chartering and encoding praxis of each such *representation of origins* can alone bring into existence: the "second set of instructions," which are experienced through the opiate-rewarded conceptions that are determinant of what it is to be *normally human* within the genre-specific terms of their respective *referent-we* and its attendant us/not us theocentric-biocentric scripts.

In the above context, the third major question with respect to the far-reaching aspect of Fanon's reverse paradox—his transcosmogonic sociodiagnostic analysis—now emerges. Why is it, one must ask here, that he, a Western-trained professional and thereby an also Westernized academic middle-class subject *and* a French colonized Negro evolué subject, must find himself irredeemably, indeed irrevocably, excluded from that which, for *both* the Pygmy and French bourgeois subjects, is so assuredly guaranteed to them *as if by birthright*? What now becomes clear in the terms of his reverse paradox is that he is excluded from the always hitherto group-specific auto-centered definitional and storied terms of human normalcy. Put another way, this as a law-like logic which, as a French-colonized Negro evolué subject, would necessarily entail his total exclusion from being able to subjectively experience himself—in opiate placebo-rewarded terms, too—in the analogical terms of the auto-centered, autonomously storied, genre-specific representations of origins he had been able to deduce in the culture-specific cases of the Pygmy and the French bourgeois subjects.

In his own Negro evolué case—as also demonstrated by W. E. B. DuBois—Fanon is *compelled* to reflexly subjectively experience himself in the painfully contradictory terms of being at one and the same time both normally and *abnormally* human. Fanon's nonnegotiable imperative is therefore one that, rather than calling for reflex assent, instead calls upon his Westernized Negro evolué self to agonistically *call into question* his reflexly and subjectively experienced *nonbeing of being normally human* as enacted by the ultimate *symbolic death* (dysgenic) that, together with his population, he is made to embody as a Negro. In addition, importantly, Fanon—as a Western-trained psychiatrist and therefore a *specific intellectual*—is urgently calling into question the very *being* of being human, as incarnated in its globally hegemonic Western bourgeois definition. The above questioning, in turn, calls for the in-depth probing of what is cast and naturalized as a purely biocentric definition of our order of *consciousness*.

Fanon's insights point to the ways in which all Western assimilated and overtly colonized Negro evolué subjects had thus been impelled—as the condition of continuing to reflexly subjectively experience the Westernized colonial world—to realize ourselves as *normally human* in the Western bourgeoisie's always already biocentrically chartered, thereby sociogenically encoded and semantically activated, *symbolic life's* opiate-rewarded (*placebo*) terms. The above experience, however, is law-likely made possible only through the sacrificial *symbolic death* (thereby opiate reward blocked) price, of our Negro/Negra evolué's reflexly subjectively experienced "wrongness of being" of our individual selves; it is also, concomitantly, made possible at the even vaster sacrificial price of the then Western world system's hegemonic bourgeois genre of human normalcy that is enacted by and through the empirically institutionalized ultimate *symbolic death* subhuman status of the Negro (i.e., black African–descended) population as a whole. It is made possible, then, in the ultimate metaphysical color line terms of bourgeois malediction: *Nigger! Don't behave like a nigger!*

The politically activist anticolonial and antiapartheid 1950s and 1960s period that was to witness both the emergence of Fanon's *Black Skin/White Masks* and other similar interrogations of how black selfhood was understood in relation to the normative "tape of the world" also witnessed the emergence of a range of black women's similarly evolué voices that also engaged in the above interrogation of consciousness. An iconic example is that put forth in Toni Morrison's scalpel-like portrayal of the overlapping workings of blackness and gender in her first major classic novel, *The Bluest Eye* (1970). In this work, Morrison discloses the mimetically induced and constant self-rejection of our black selves and those who are like us, not only generically as a population but also specifically as women. Morrison uncovers the terms of being educationally and socially habituated and domesticated in a world where *the bluest eye* is not only iconic of the Western bourgeois liberal monohumanist phenotypically—racially white—aesthetic corporeal standard. In addition, she also gives origin to what can now be seen, in hindsight, as the positive signifiers—the institutionalized and ostensibly universally applicable norm of being *human* and thereby of (white) beauty!—that semantically activate the neurochemical opiate reward process. The color line's range of subjectively experienced *nonnormalcy of being* was therefore to be taken up and further elaborated by a range of black feminists, black lesbians, and black novelists and poets—with this questioning iconically captured not only throughout the work of black/lesbian/feminist sixties activist poet June Jordan but specifically in her wrenching outcry against what she defines as our "unbearable wrongness of being."[134] This as a definition that directly parallels that of Fanon's fellow Martinique and Negro evolué, the negritude poet/intellectual/political activist Aimé Césaire, who uses the poetically powerful term *désêtre*, which translates, in English, as the neologism *dysbeing: symbolic death* as out of place with respect to being human.[135]

Dysbeing, via Fanon's reverse paradox, reveals the quest for a hitherto unknown/unknowable now ecumenically inclusive conception of our human freedom as a species; it will also identify the unique terrain of struggle that had to be waged generically by the overall Negro (i.e., Negro/Negra) populations of black African descent, as well as by individual activists, both against their/our (Negroes/Negro/Negra) reflexly subjectively experienced self-aversive désêtre and wrongness of being, as well as against their/

our imposed mimetic desire to adopt white masks. In the above context, Katherine, nowhere has this "terrain of struggle," together with its historical origin, been more precisely yet at the same time imaginatively portrayed than in your aptly entitled study *Demonic Grounds*.[136] *Demonic Grounds* is, you write,

> in its broadest sense, an interdisciplinary analysis of black women's geographies in the black diaspora. It seeks to consider what kinds of possibilities emerge when black studies encounters human geography. Drawing on creative, conceptual, and material geographies of domination (such as transatlantic slavery and racial-sexual displacement) and black women's geographies (such as their knowledges, negotiations, and experiences). This interplay interests me because it enables a way to think about the place of black subjects in a diasporic context that takes up spatial histories as they constitute our present geographic organization.

This therefore means the following:

> The relationship between black populations and geography—and here I am referring to geography as space, place, and location in their physical materiality and imaginative configurations—allows us to engage with a narrative that locates and draws on black histories and black subjects in order to make visible social lives which are often displaced, rendered ungeographic. . . . Let me give a telling example to outline the ways in which progress and exploration are entwined with a different sense of (black) place. The ships of transatlantic slavery moving across the middle passage, transporting humans for slave labor into "newer worlds" do not only site modern technological progression, which materially moves diasporic subjects through space, that is, on and across the ocean, and on and across landmasses such as Canada, the United States, the Caribbean; these vessels also expose a very meaningful struggle for freedom *in place*. Technologies of transportation, *in this case the ship, while materially and ideologically enclosing black subjects—economic objects inside and often bound to the ship's walls—also contribute to the formation of an oppositional geography: the ship as a location of black subjectivity and human terror, black resistance, and in some cases, black possession.*[137]

Your citation seminally enables us to see, Katherine, two epochally new transformative historico-mutational conceptions of human freedom: one in the process of being empirically actualized, as that of the now increasingly natural-scientifically enabled *technological* mastery over nature, as well as other peoples, and the other to be only potentially realizable over many centuries.[138] Each epochally new historico-mutational conceptions of freedom will be law-likely inseparable from, in both cases, a no less epochally historico-mutational reconception of, in Heidegger's earlier cited guide quote terms, a new answer to the question of who we are *as humans*. Both of which, as you show incisively, were to emerge, inter alia, in the postmedieval dynamic of the politico-statal monarchical and imperializing Western world system's mercantilist transatlantic Negro / Negra slave-trading ships of the Middle Passage from black Africa to the Americas. The latter voyages themselves, therefore, were made possible by the West's postmedieval and increasingly *cognitively open* geographies, these correlatedly with the techno-scientifically applicable physical sciences initiated in the wake of Copernicus's new astronomy. Their mastery over nature, and correlated conception of human freedom, as actualized in the increasing size and power of the Negro / Negra slave-trading ships. At the same time, as you movingly show, it was to be in the holds of the slave ships among the chained-to-the-walls-cum-chained-to-each-other Negro / Negra as commercial cargo, thereby, out of their collective experience of being cast as the total negation of human freedom, as well as, indeed, of being another genus to being human in the West's now monohumanist, secularizing terms, that the dialectical *terrain of struggle* would begin to increasingly emerge. This terrain of struggle — and the holds of the slave ship as origin — identifies what was to be, however eventually and over the long haul, a historico-mutational reconception of a hitherto unknown and unknowable ecumenically inclusive version of our human freedom, together with its now profoundly revalorizing, meta-Western answer to the question as to who we are as humans.

Toward Blombos Cave, the Third Event, a (New) Science of the Word

KM: Wynter's critical reading of DuBois and Fanon foregrounds the imperative need for a new intellectual praxis, one that enables us to now *both consciously* and *communally* re-create ourselves in ecumenically interaltruistically kin-recognizing *species-oriented* terms. Wynter's engagement with and extension of the Martiniquaís poet and political activist Aimé Césaire's "Science of the Word" thereby illuminates what would have to be the complex underpinnings of a now species-oriented perspective — just as that perspective opens us up to an unknown framework through which new beginnings become imaginable. To begin again and open up: Aimé Césaire, ochre, Blombos Cave, and the *plus ultra* of our emancipatory futures.[139]

SW: In the Frantz Fanon guide quote above he puts forth a challenge: *what is to be done is to set man free.*[140] The challenge is one that imperatively calls for our collective and now fully conscious *plus ultra* recognition of our human history as it had veridically begun with our *homo narrans* species—our uniquely hybrid Third Event origin on the continent of black Africa—and to thereby grasp the hitherto *unknowable conception of human freedom that is to be now imperatively realized, this for the first time, in ecumenically human terms.*[141] These are terms that demand a now entirely new (because nonexclusivist) meta-answer to the question of *who we are as human.* This question is, importantly, no longer asked from the biocentric perspective of the human as a natural organism. This task—to set the human free—therefore demands that we must begin, for the first time, to track a complete version of our species' history as it had been performatively enacted from its origins. As such, one conceptualized, as Bruno Latour proposes, from the perspective of our "whole human community."[142] Or perhaps, even more precisely, to set forth a vision of our species' history in Derrida's earlier cited "Ends of Man" terms, doing so therefore from the perspective of the (now emergent referent) "*we . . . in the horizon of humanity.*"[143] The latter "we" itself was brought into being, remember, by a *humanly emancipatory* and homogenizing Western world system that is, *at the same time,* a no less *humanly subjugating* imperial system. "We," as such, is *institutionally* enacted by the storytellingly chartered and sociogenically encoded behavior-regulatory terms prescribed, as noted earlier, by the laws of hybrid auto-speciation. Thereby, with its complementary process—the *emancipatory* and the *subjugating*— having functioned, as they continue to do, *each as the nonnegotiable condition of the enacting of the other.* This entails what can now be recognized as the West's founding aporia of the secular, which has hitherto law-likely remained *irresolvable.*

It is in both of these contexts that Frantz Fanon's former teacher— Martiniquaís-French colonial subject, Negro evolué, negritude poet, and political activist Aimé Césaire—both anticipates and enacts, like Fanon, a meta-Darwinian redefinition of the human as a hybrid being.[144] Consequently, on the basis of this earlier reconception, Césaire was to later emphasize that the imperative struggles of the (still then) physically/militarily colonized subjects of the West could in no way be waged on the basis of a going back to a pre-Europe (to its then, also religious presecular world). By implication, these struggles could only be waged on the basis of a going forward.[145] Going forward, as will become clear, will alone be able to make possible, inter alia, the resolution of the West's hitherto globally hegemonic irresolvable aporia of the secular. In a talk given at a conference held in Haiti in 1946, entitled "Poetry and Knowledge," Césaire had therefore begun with his definition of what to him was the main problem with which the West and the rest of us are confronted: that of the "great silence of [natural] scientific thought."[146] That is, seeing that, in spite of the West's many techno-scientific feats—themselves only dazzlingly made possible by its (natural) scientific thought—this "great silence" has itself to do with nothing less than the causes of our collective human predicament as a species. Now, to be noted here, with respect to the latter, is that at the time Césaire gave his "Poetry and Knowledge" talk, the immensely tragic human suffering of the Second World War had only just ended. Over against the dimensions of the natural sciences and the conspicuous silence with respect to what had been *law-like* causes of the above, Césaire counterproposed a new *human scientific* (rather than only *natural scientific*) order of knowledge. This would be able to deal, for the first time, with the hitherto unsolved phenomenon of human consciousness.[147] His primary hypothesis is therefore worth citing at length here:

> Poetic knowledge is born in the *great silence* of *scientific knowledge*. . . . A view of the world, yes; science affords a view of the world, but a summary and superficial view.
>
> Physics classifies and explains, but the essence of things eludes it. The natural sciences classify, but the *quid proprium of things eludes them.*
>
> But it is not sufficient to state that scientific knowledge is summary. It is necessary to add that it is *poor and half-starved.* . . .
>
> And mankind has gradually become aware that side by side with this half-starved scientific knowledge there is another kind of knowledge. A fulfilling knowledge . . .
>
> *And it is on the word,* a chip off the world, secret and chaste slice of the world, *that he* [the poet] *gambles all our possibilities.* . . . *Our first and last chance.*

More and more the word promises to be an algebraic equation that makes the world intelligible. Just as the new Cartesian algebra permitted the construction of theoretical physics, so too the original handling of the word can make possible at any moment a new theoretical and heedless science that poetry could already give an approximate notion of. Then the time will come again *when the study of the word will condition the study of nature. But at this juncture we are still in the shadows.*[148]

Reading with and through Aimé Césaire's proposed science of the Word is therefore particularly urgent because it demands that we both acknowledge and think *outside* the belief system of a biocentric cosmogony, which, as noted above, gives rise to a *naturally selected/dysselected* bioevolutionary teleological logic that necessitates, above all, the accumulation of capital, with the mandatory imperative of its bottom line, which itself is ostensibly the only solution able to master the Malthusian storytelling trope of *natural scarcity*. As such, this logic is therefore itself law-likely enacted, circularly replicated and reproduced, as well as reflexly behaviorally responded to, by all, according to the Darwinian/neo-Darwinianly storytellingly chartered Word, its liberal (now neoliberal) democratic monohumanist Word/sociogenic code/descriptive statement. This is, too, a sociogenic code of symbolic *life/death* that, while itself *non–biologically* determined (at the level of its mythos, or origin story), is nevertheless *biologically* (i.e., neurochemically) implemented at the level of the *bios*, the brain, its opiate reward/punishment (placebo/nocebo) behavior-regulatory system. This at the same time as that Word/code descriptive statement's "governing principle of causality" is rigorously discursively enacted by its status quo system of learning, together with its no less imperative Rorty-type "truths of solidarity" and overall episteme. The logic of environmental disasters is one itself, which, correlatedly and empirically, *also* enacts the descriptive statement of *homo oeconomicus-on-the-model-of-a-natural-organism*, its codes of a non–biologically determined principle of causality. Hence, the fact that the ever-increasing ratios of economic growth, concomitantly with its also ever-increasing ratios of fossil fuel–driven capital accumulation, are themselves also law-likely equated with ever-increasing ratios of global warming, climate change, and environmental instability. This is an interacting dynamic, therefore, whose ongoing ecosystemic consequences had first been evidenced by the drought-desertification-famine and resultant intergroup conflict in the Horn of Africa, this itself followed by a now vast range of varying, humanly/ecosystemically destructive consequences all over the planet.

It is therefore the above circularly reinforcing—*seemingly no-way-out-Catch-22* situation of our contemporary secular Western and Westernized world system, in its now globally and transnationally *economically homogenized* capitalist neoliberal and corporate financial bourgeoisie ruling class (*homo oeconomicus*) configuration—that we must now all confront. While it is precisely such a way out that Aimé Césaire's proposed hybrid science of the Word (the *mythoi*), in its simultaneous interaction *with* nature (the *bios*, the *brain*), whose new paradigm not only provides a *cognitive opening* onto our Western and Westernized bourgeoisie-Darwinian-chartered word/code/descriptive statement, together with its status quo system of learning, truths of solidarity, and overall genre-specific episteme, but at the same time, also powerfully deconstructs that biocentric word's *homo oeconomicus*'s claim to *the monopoly of humanity*.

With this, I turn to Blombos Cave, South Africa, which I argue is the empirically actualized evidence for the verification of Césaire's proposed way out, as one that—within the context of the above-mentioned fossil fuel–driven ever-increasing ratios of global warming and climate change, as well as their attendant war-torn processes themselves concomitant globally with ever-increasing degrees of human immiseration based on increasing degrees of *racially, socially,* and *religiously* stratified economic inequality—is now ever more urgently sought.

Now Blombos Cave, as described by Guy Gugliotta in his essay "The Great Human Migration" (2008), is situated in a *calcarenite* limestone cliff that overlooks "the rocky coast of what is now the Indian Ocean."[149] At the first level of excavation the archaeologist Christopher Henshilwood and his team had found a 77,000-year-old piece of ochre, on which there is "etched a geometric design . . . with a stone point on the flat polished surface."[150] The design is a "simple crosshatching framed by two parallel lines with a third line down the middle," which therefore means that "the scratchings on this piece of red ochre mudstone are the oldest known example *of an intricate design made by a human being*."[151] As Henshilwood, himself a white South African, further points out with respect to this piece of ochre, for him, "the [very] ability *to create and communicate using such symbols*" is itself "an unambiguous marker" of "modern humans," therefore a marker "of one of the characteristics *that separate us from any other species, living or extinct*."[152] Concurring with this thesis, David Lewis Williams, in his book *The Mind in* the Cave: Consciousness and the Origin of Art (2002), also proposes that because the "piece of ochre" is "carefully engraved with crosses with a central and containing line," this reveals not only that it is the oldest dated "art" in the world but that it also shows "*indisputably modern behavior at an unexpectedly early date*."[153]

In its first excavation, along with the engraved piece of ochre, the Henshilwood team had also found decorative beads made of shells, together with the material technology of bone tools that were dated at eighty thousand years. These, together with the widespread debris of discarded clam-shells, provided evidence of the communal cooking of seafood, as well as of widespread shell-fishing activity.[154] Surpassing all these finds, however, were the results of a further excavation: when digging deeper, they were to discover the even earlier "100,000 year old *workshop* holding the tools and ingredients with which early modern humans mixed some of the first known paints."[155] Specifically, "These *cave artisans* have stones for pounding and grinding colorful dirt, enriched with a kind of iron oxide to a powder, known as ocher," which was then "blended with the binding fat of mammal bone marrow and a dash of charcoal."[156] The special significance here is that the workshop allows us to see the earliest example, to date, of how our emergent species—*homo narrans* in my own proposed meta-Darwinian and meta–*Homo sapiens* terms—"processed ocher . . . its red color apparently *rich in symbolic significance*."[157] A process, therefore, producing materials "for protection or simple decorations" or, as other experts suggest, perhaps used as "their way of making *social and artistic statements on their bodies* or their artifacts."[158]

However, in spite of the above's finely noted other forms of symbolizing recognition, what we find is the following: that both archaeologists and art experts are like ourselves, normally bourgeois and therefore biocentric (and neo-Darwinianly chartered) subjects; what they too—when outside their fields of expertise—must *law-likely overlook*, within the terms of their / our shaman-like genre-specific "truth of solidarity," is the Third Event dimensions of that processed ochre's supraordinate symbolic significance. These are the findings of a heretical anthropologist that were/are nothing less than that of the *symbolic transformation of biological identity*.[159] What his heresy therefore enables us to see is what the findings of the shells, the ochre, and the workshop uncover: the praxis of the ecumenically human ritual of initiation by means of which *individually born biological life* whose macrosymbol and signifier, as Judy Granh argues, is that of *menstrual blood*, is itself transformed into that of the genre-specific communal *referent-we* of *symbolic life*—one whose master symbol and signifier is that of the processed ochre, its *fictive* menstrual blood.[160] The praxis of the ritual initiatory transformation of the first form of life (biologically born individual life) into the second form of life (communal/fictive or *symbolic life*) therefore reveals that the workshop of ochre excavated at the second level can only itself be fully understood in conjunction with the shells and other findings that had been excavated at the first level. This is so not only with respect to the finding of the piece of ochre—itself also *aesthetically transformed* into an engraved symbolic design—but even more so with respect to that of the debris of the discarded seashells, itself as evidence of the analogically also profoundly transformative process of the communal cooking and reciprocal sharing of food.[161]

Materially and symbolically, therefore, Blombos Cave reveals the ritual-initiatory transformation of the biologically born individual subject *into* that of a now fictively chartered and encoded, thereby hybrid, *bios/mythoi* autopoietic form of symbolic life. The ritually initiated individual is thereby now made to reflexly *subjectively experience* themselves as *reborn* in now opiate-rewarded communal *symbolic life* terms. The ritually initiated individual is thus made to reflexly experience themselves as an inter-altruistic kin-recognizing member of an *origin-narratively* chartered, sociogenically encoded, thereby fictive, genre-specific *referent-we*, it's us/not us—with the latter's now institutionalized supraindividual order of consciousness therefore now serving to underwrite each such respective societal order's stable (anti-entropic) communitarian replication. This given that the individual subjects—together with their fellow initiates—*are all now reborn of the same origin story rather than of the womb*. Consequently, each such subject is now enabled to displace/replace, at the reflexly and subjectively experienced level of consciousness, what would have earlier been its *prior-to-initiation-biologically-born*, innately experienced, individual self-interest. Consequently, each such genre-specific displacement/replacement origin narrative would have therefore imperatively functioned—all the more so in traditional *stateless* societies—against their individual subjects, giving priority either to the genetically encoded innate interests of one's (familial) kin or to the even more powerful, genetically encoded imperative interest of one's own Hobbesian bodily self-preservation.

Now because this latter is itself *the* ethical imperative by means of which our first human ancestors would have been alone enabled to communally deal with the then even more formidable constraints of material life, what such an imperative ethics unveils is nothing less than the *why* of the laws of *hybrid* human auto-speciation or pseudospeciation. As such, laws themselves would have been initiatorily enacted in the wake of our *homo narrans's* species uniquely biomutational Third Event, which had itself given origin not only to the faculties of language and storytelling but correlatedly to the mythmaking regions of the brain. This at the same time as the matrix enactment of the Third Event, its mandated ritual-initiatory processes of our *homo narrans* species' hybrid praxis of genre-specific auto-speciation, or pseudospeciation, would have correlatedly had its iconic origin at Blombos Cave (or indeed at any other black African surrogate origin sites, whether already or still to be discovered). This, at the same time, however, as the always genre-specific (i.e., us/not us) enactment of the praxis of our being hybridly human (later described by Fanon in ontogeny/sociogeny terms as that of our skins/masks) had itself been auto-instituted according to the very Third Event laws of whose functioning, even when rigorously behaviorally adhering to them, we ourselves, as earlier noted, have hitherto (until today) necessarily *remained unaware.*

In this way, then, given that it is these very Third Event laws, as they have hitherto hybridly functioned outside our conscious awareness—that now also constitute the domain of Césaire's proposed *hybrid* science of the Word/Nature—the following is revealed: that the *two-level findings* at Blombos Cave can now be seen to validate his proposed new science by providing empirical evidence in support of its epochally new *human scientific* analytical frame and/or paradigm, one whose Word/Nature *hybridity* deductively provides an account of what would have had to have been, as Blombos Cave itself empirically actualizes, our uniquely Third Event origin *as homo narrans.* As such, an analytical frame or paradigm whose metaperspective now allows us to both read and concomitantly *relativize* our still globally hegemonic purely biocentric, Darwinian/neo-Darwinianly chartered and encoded representation of origins. Even further, to read it as one which, because it must law-likely provide a part-myth-part-science storytelling account of our species' origin (i.e., as secular Man2's *Homo sapiens/homo oeconomicus* in genre-specific biocentric bourgeois terms), itself must as law-likely predefine our *homo narrans* species' iconic origin site of Blombos Cave in abductive purely *biological birth* terminology as that of "the cradle of humankind."[162]

On Ends/Beginnings and Giving Humanness a Different Future by Giving It a Different Past

KM: The conversation concludes with a different past; this is a past that knots together the science of the Word, African human-geographic-genetic beginnings, the practice of narratively-experientially-empirically-neurologically knowing and telling our worlds, all of which together illuminate Césaire's remarkable antibiocentric and species-oriented worldview and emancipatory breach.

SW: As noted earlier, with the proposed simultaneity of the hybrid *bios/ mythoi*, articulated through Césaire's science of the Word, the Third Event origin of today's black Africa provides an additional twist. The origin that situates the emergence of the human within the southwest region of Africa has now been proved by Western and Westernized research scholars both in population genetics—in the wake of and due to the techno-scientific feat of cracking the DNA code in 1953—and in archaeology and linguistics.[163] Thus, Africa as *human origin geography* that, simultaneously, signals the birthplace of language, intervenes in and complements the techno-science inherent to genetics. The biocentric origin story, anchored to the *referent-we* of *homo oeconomicus*—which itself has unfolded into discourses of natural scarcity and neo-imperial territorialization—is dislodged by the correlated simultaneity of language-myth-genetics unearthed in southwest Africa. What is further uncovered, with this, is the very belief system that posits genetics and biology alone as the sole origins of biological life (and death)—a belief system that can neither sustain itself nor replicate itself through accumulation, *if the aforementioned co-relatedness is brought into view*.

Why, then, one must ask here, in spite of the above "dislodging," do all of the negative consequences to which that belief system gives origin nevertheless continue to seem "natural" to its global subjects within the terms of the latter's correlatedly institutionalized, bourgeois order of consciousness? Its mode/praxis of mind/minding? It is in this context that Aimé Césaire's proposed hybrid, thereby human-scientific, study of the Word/ Nature (i.e., the brain) can be recognized, first, as one whose primary focus is necessarily that of the hitherto unsolved also hybrid phenomenon of human consciousness; second, and correlatedly, one whose unique domain is therefore also necessarily that of the hitherto nonrecognized, thereby hitherto unsolved, functioning of the Third Event's laws of hybrid human auto-speciation or pseudospeciation. The result is that his proposed study of the Word (i.e., its sociogenic code and / or descriptive statement) is itself, according to those laws, necessarily that of the latter's always hitherto *genre-specific* (or, in contemporary terms, *culture-specific*) respective governing principle of *nonbiological causality*: therefore, of its always already storytellingly, thereby mythically chartered and sociogenically encoded "second set of instructions." These instructions, are ones that, as earlier noted, law-likely co-function at the level of the brain together with our genetic code's "first set of instructions." Thus, it is with respect to the *nonbiological principle* of causality, its second set of instructions, that Césaire's study must begin with an analysis of the way in which that principle must be both discursively enacted and rigorously conserved by means of each genre-specific societal world's correlated status quo system of learning and Rorty-type truths of solidarity.

Both, in turn, thereby give origin to a no less genre-specific (culture-specific) order of consciousness that is itself indispensable to the antientropic integration of each such human world's fictively eusocializing genre-specific or culture-specific *referent-we*. This has the result that each such Word's / Code's descriptive statement's governing principle of non–biologically determined causality comes to be thereby circularly, stably conserved by means of each such world's (i.e., its *referent-we*) integrating, supraindividual order of consciousness together with its genre-specific or culture-specific mode / praxis of mind / minding. It is in this sense, therefore, that consciousness, to draw on Keith Ward, is "a constituent and fundamental element of world *as* we [each *referent-we*] *see* it," and, consequently, "consciousness is not just a by-product of matter as we perceive it. The material world as it appears to us is, at least in part, a *product of consciousness*."[164]

These dynamics, between the outside world, our orders of consciousness, our systems of learning and respective *referent-we* and overall epistemic modes of knowledge, can be therefore understood alongside the proposals put forward by several neuroscientists. For me, the earliest of these, that of J. F. Danielli's heretically pathbreaking paper "Altruism and the Internal Reward System, or the Opium of the People" (1980) can be constructively read alongside Césaire's 1946 human-scientific perspective on the study of the Word. These two texts, together, draw attention to the way in which the non–biologically determined principle of causality would now determine the study of nature, the study of the brain (the study of the brain which, as we know, has hitherto fruitlessly been the exclusive domain of inquiry of the natural sciences).[165] Thus, the study of *nature*/the brain as proposed by Césaire will therefore begin by that of each human world's, to use Fanon's definition of the word, *sociogenic code of symbolic life/death and/or its descriptive statement at the level of the psyche or the soul.*

As such, the discursively enacted governing non–biologically determined principle of causality of each genre-specific or culture-specific *referent-we* is also subjectively experienced at the level of the brain; this reveals that genre-specific narratives of symbolic life/death (us/not us), and their respective positive/negative semantic activations of the opiate-rewarding and opiate-blocking behaviors, are bound up in the regulatory motivating/demotivating neurochemical system of our uniquely human, because storytelling-mythmaking, brain.[166] Put differently, the human's brain's agential implementations of its internal opiate-rewarding and opiate-blocking behavior motivating/demotivating behavior-regulatory neurochemical system are themselves activated by means of the symbolic life/death, their semantically positively/negatively marked terms, thereby biologically implementing the genre-specific and/or culture-specific human world's sociogenic code of *symbolic life/death*—sociogenic and symbolic codes that are specific to each *descriptive statement*'s respective principle of nonphysical and nonbiological causality, thereby, its Word. The Word's sociogenic code of *symbolic life/death* therefore itself functions to *activate* the human brain's internal opiate-rewarding (placebo) and reward-blocking (nocebo) behavior regulatory motivating/demotivating neurochemical system, and always does so in the precisely mediated terms of each such storytellingly chartered *referent-we*, its human world's genre-specific or culture-specific behavior-regulatory principle of non–biologically determined causality.

Understood alongside the earlier discussion of origin myths and origin narratives as always hitherto genre-specific representations of origins, it follows therefore that the human-as-a-*homo-narrans*-species cannot preexist their hitherto always genre-specific or culture-specific representations of origin any more than—at the Second Event level of existence, that based on the emergence of (purely) biological life—*bees can preexist their beehives.* This then enables us to understand what had been the defining characteristics of our hybrid human origin: *the fully completed co-evolution, with the human brain, of the faculties of language and of storytelling.*

It is in the context of the above "nonnegotiable imperative," therefore, that the successful conclusion of our conversation's quest to "give humanity a different future" by giving it a new and species-inclusive account of our meta-Darwinian/neo-Darwinian, therefore hybrid Third Event origins entails the following: that the phenomenological experience of having both conceptually and imaginatively shared what had been the then Blombos Cave–type enactment of our matrix ancestral origins, one that had preceded all later differentiating enactment of origins, can itself be only made possible by the poetic extract as cited from Césaire's "Poetry and Knowledge"—the latter as one in which he had not only put forward his proposal for a new and hybrid science of the Word/Nature but had also insisted, correlatedly, that the latter was also itself a science of which only "poetry can give an approximation of." It is therefore as such a cited extract that it not only seems to bring before our very eyes, but at the same time enables us, within the terms of what had been South Africa's martyred Steven Biko's ecumenically inclusive call for a "new humanity," to vicariously take part in the imagined reality of what would have been, de facto, performatively enacted by the then denizens of South Africa's Blombos Cave. The latter as the quite different enactment of our species' origin, its vastly extended past, that would now make possible for the peoples of contemporary post-Mandela South Africa, as well as our also Western and Westernized global selves, to now collectively give humanness a different future, itself historically chartered by that past.

Thus as Césaire wrote:

And here we are taken back to the first days of humanity. It is an error to believe that knowledge, to be born, had to await the methodical exercise of thought or the scruples of experimentation. I even believe that mankind has never been closer to certain truths than in the first days of the species. At the time when mankind discovered with emotion the first sun, the first rain, the first breath, the first moon. At the time when mankind discovered in fear and rapture the throbbing newness of the world.[167]

Césaire is here reenacting, therefore, in now *antibiocentric* terms, what had been Copernicus's and the lay humanists of Renaissance Europe's then also emancipatory *antinominalist theocentric* poetics of the *propter nos homines*— but now extending their then secularizing *referent-we* poetics to that of a *propter nos homines* remade to the now species-oriented "measure of the world."

Notes

1. Rinaldo Walcott was present at the original interview in 2007, and his contribution to that conversation is greatly appreciated by Wynter and McKittrick. Many of his ideas and questions impacted upon their collaborative dialogue between 2007 and 2014. Many thanks are extended to Mark Campbell, who transcribed and worked closely with the original interview in an earlier iteration. Jack Dresnick and Johanna Fraley have been thoughtful players in this conversation, working closely with Sylvia Wynter as interlocutors and collaborators for more than ten years. The assistance and insights of Nick Mitchell have also been invaluable; his contributions to this conversation—writing, ideas, transcribing, and more—are immeasurably appreciated. We are grateful for the compu-technological facilitation provided by Jack, Johanna, and Nick, too, of course. The work put forth by Wynter here can be understood alongside the 2001 seminar that took place at the Centre for Caribbean Thought at the University of West Indies, Mona, "After Man, towards the Human," which dislodged and unblocked some difficult ideas for her. This was followed up by the edited collection Bogues, *After Man, towards the Human*, an important set of essays that are appreciated by Wynter (and KM!).
2. McKittrick, "The Science of the Word."
3. Wynter, "Unsettling the Coloniality of Being," 257–337.
4. See Douglas and Ney on *homo oeconomicus* in their *Missing Persons*.
5. Danielli, "Altruism and the Internal Reward System," 87–94. See also Goldstein, *Addiction*. See also, for an updated version of the above two, Stein, *The Genius Engine*.
6. "Beside phylogeny and ontogeny stands sociogeny." Fanon, *Black Skin, White Masks*, 11.
7. Wynter is extending the concept of the performative enactment of gender to the performative enactment of all role allocations instituting of each genre of being human. This identifies her thinking on gender-genre, which stems from a long tradition of the relationship between both "gender" and "genre" as terms meaning "kind." Here, "gender" is an indispensable function of our enacting of our "genres" of being human. Etymologically, "gender" and "genre" derive from the same root word (the Middle French *gendre*), which in turn derives from the Latin *genus*, both meaning "kind, sort." On gender performance, see Butler, *Gender Trouble*.
8. Davis, *Planet of Slums*.
9. Césaire, *Discourse on Colonialism*, 73. The links between Wynter's work and that of Césaire's meta-Western project was first put forward by Scott in "The Re-enchantment of Humanism," 119–207. This is also taken up in Eudell, "Afterword," 311–340.
10. Wallace, *Infinite Jest*; Nabokov, *Pale Fire*.

11. Note that Bateson's hybridly dual descriptive statement had been originally put forward in a paper presented under a similar title, "Conscious Purpose vs. Nature," at the July 1967 Congress on the Dialectics of Liberation. The paper was then published as part of the proceedings—themselves all then part of the emancipatory rethinking of the sixties hiatus.

12. On Wynter's use of "descriptive statement," see the Bateson guide quote and Bateson, "The Logical Categories of Learning and Communication," 282–283.

13. Césaire, "Poetry and Knowledge," 134–146. Note that in Césaire's original text, "word" is small case; in her interpretation and extension of his ideas, Wynter capitalizes "Word," drawing attention to its agentive and dynamic relationship with bios/nature while also nodding to the biblical "Word." See also Eudell, "Modernity and the 'Work of History,'" 1–24, for a discussion of Wynter's "Word."

14. Wynter is referring to Robert Bellarmine, an Italian Jesuit and cardinal of the Catholic Church, who demanded in 1616 that Galileo refuse Copernican insights with regard to the moving Earth and the immobile sun, since they called into question the church's original sin/spiritual redemption, behavior-regulatory schema.

15. Chorover, *From Genesis to Genocide*; Blumenberg, *The Legitimacy of the Modern Age*.

16. Hocart, *Kings and Councillors*. See also the guide quote by Mary Douglas and Steven Ney, as well as their discussion of this millennially functioning and ecumenically human modality of thought in Douglas and Ney, *Missing Persons*, 22–23.

17. Cf. Blumenberg, *The Legitimacy of the Modern Age*, 159–163.

18. For this citation by Copernicus, as well as the overall implications of the counterpoetics of the *propter nos* as elaborated by Ficino and other Renaissance figures, see Hallyn, *The Poetic Structure of the World*, 53–57. See also Wynter, "Columbus and the Poetics of the *Propter Nos*," 251–286; Blumenberg, *The Legitimacy of the Modern Age*.

19. In her interview with Joyce King, Wynter writes: "The central point of bio-centrism is that this conception of the human is the first universally applicable conception, which is, since Darwin, that we are biological beings . . . the belief is that we are biological beings who *then* create culture." King, "Race and Our Biocentric Belief System," 361 (emphasis added).

20. Wynter is referring to Aimé Césaire's keynote address, given at a philosophy conference in Port-au-Prince, Haiti, in 1944. It was first published as "Poésie et connaissance" and has been reprinted in English (as "Poetry and Knowledge") and in French numerous times. See also Aimé Césaire, "Poetry and Knowledge," 134–146.

21. McKittrick, *Demonic Grounds*.

22. McKibben, *The End of Nature*.

23. This section should be thought about alongside the phenotypic relativization of concepts of beauty. In the case of the pre-Western Congolese who were, in the nineteenth century, documented by a Christian missionary priest as putting forth that "the one who is of the deepest black color is ... to be the most beautiful. ... [So] we Europeans appear ugly in their eyes." Related, but different, in his 1871 representation of origins, *The Descent of Man*, Darwin draws on travelers' reports from the early to middle nineteenth century to show that almost all human populations continued, precolonially, to take *their own* phenotypic physiognomy as *the* norm of beauty (non-Europeans had therefore also found Europeans ugly from their respective perspectives). Darwin had therefore collected a wide range of travelers' reports in order to validate his own hypothesis with respect to sexual selection/sexual choice (which, with natural selection, could be seen as the cause of differentiation between all species, including, if perhaps less so, the human). Although the above sexual selection hypothesis was to be totally disproved by Mendelian genetics, the material Darwin had collected still provides valuable insight regarding the range of what was then the still origin-mythically, therefore also the aesthetically auto-centered magma of genre-specific precolonial peoples—the majority of whom were to be eventually and forcibly incorporated by the West during its second wave of imperial politico-territorial cum free-trade/economic expansion. With economic expansion, global populations are also folded into the single-model terms, therefore, of the West's genre-specific uniquely secular norm of being and of beauty. The latter norm of beauty is overrepresented as if it were, therefore, the only highly evolved aesthetic norm of being human and underwrites, in Pierre Bourdieu's terms, a "monopoly of humanity." Axelson, *Culture Confrontation in the Lower Congo*; Darwin, *The Descent of Man*; Wynter, "Unsettling the Coloniality of Being," 291–292; Bourdieu, *Distinction*, 491. See also Teruel, "Narrative Description of the Kingdom of the Congo."

24. The *material* underpinnings sustaining the globalized mode of *mimetic* desire began to abruptly come to an end in the wake of our interview (with the Great Crash/credit crisis beginning in 2008). This led directly to, as Wynter pointed out in a different telephonic context, the far-reaching implications of the new "gaze from below" movements such as those of the *Indignados* movement in Spain, or the Occupy movement(s) in the United States, Canada, and elsewhere. Centrally, those of the now *trans-class-trans-race* mode of trade union labor struggles directed, for the first time, at the West's overall *liberal/neoliberal* monohumanist world-systemic societal order and its principle of domination/subordination.

25. At the time of our first interview in 2007, the UN Intergovernmental Panel on Climate Change (IPCC) had released a report that shaped our conversation. See United Nations, "Evidence Is Now 'Unequivocal' That Humans Are Causing Global Warming."

26. Cf. "Skin Bleach Ban Fails."

27. James Dewey Watson codiscovered the structure of DNA, with Francis Crick, in 1953. See also McKibben, *Enough*.

28. These two issues—skin bleaching/whitening/lightening and designer babies—are interlocking and draw attention to the links between climatic-environmental factors and the genetic-hereditary history of our phenotypic/physiognomic differentiation as a species. The climatic-environmental correspondence between high degrees of melanin, on the one hand, and the shutting off of the genes for the production of high degrees of melanin, on the other hand, is meaningful. The latter dynamic, the shutting off of genes for the production of high degrees of melanin, must be understood in relation to the definition of white and whiteness, as the biological norm, *only in the original context of a specific climatic-environmental situation and, indeed, geographic location*. See Juan Luis Arsuaga for an important discussion on race, phenotype, location (i.e., Europe, Africa, European skins, African skins), and vitamin D_3, as this contextualization serves to explode the ostensible link between white skin color (physiognomy) and our contemporary Western-bourgeois origin-mythic belief that the European branch of our species is *the* bioevolutionarily evolved aesthetic norm of being human. Here the long-standing links between racial differentiation/phenotype and intelligence emerge as fictive while also propping up the grounded materiality of race and racism: the Western and Westernized *bourgeois* norms of beauty and the Western bourgeois *single model* of intelligence (or IQ in Herrnstein and Murray's genre-specific eugenic/dysgenic terms) are enjoined. Arsuaga, *The Neanderthal's Necklace*, 75–76; Herrnstein and Murray, *The Bell Curve*.

29. "A Warming Report," explains that "A U.N. climate panel is set to release a smoking gun report soon that confirms human activities are to blame for global warming and that predicts catastrophic global disruptions by 2100."

30. Price-Mars, *So Spoke the Uncle/Ainsi parla l'oncle*.

31. Wynter, "Is 'Development' a Purely Empirical Concept or Also Teleological?," 299–316.

32. Augustine of Hippo, *The City of God*.

33. Wynter further proposes that what we did not realize at the time was this: it was precisely such an alternative, now ecumenically human, thereby post–*homo oeconomicus* mode of material provisioning that was being concomitantly made thinkable. It was made thinkable by what had been the then multiple challenges of the anticolonial struggles, as well as those of the sixties' movements in the imperial centers themselves. The far-reaching anticolonial movements of the sixties, which, when taken together, had been collectively proposing a challenge to the West's prototype of being human in its second reinvented, now hegemonically bourgeois concept of Man2 (in biocentric-liberal mono-humanist terms, *homo oeconomicus*). Frantz Fanon was therefore to precisely diagnose the reasons—especially in the case of the non-Western anticolonial struggles—for our failure to have fully recognized what had then been, as it

still is, and even more urgently so now, the fundamental issue underlying all other issues: that is, the imperative of redefining, thereby of reinstitutionalizing, our being human in now meta-Freudian and meta-Darwinian, thereby meta-*secular* and thereby ecumenically human, profoundly revalorizing hybrid terms, that he himself had earlier put forward in 1952 in *Black Skin, White Masks*. As Fanon later wrote in his anti-imperial manifesto *The Wretched of the Earth* (1963), "Western Bourgeois racial prejudice as regards the nigger and Arab is a racism of contempt; it is a racism which minimizes what it hates. Bourgeois ideology, however, which is the proclamation of an essential quality between men, manages to appear logical in its own eyes by *inviting* the *sub-men to become human, and to take as their prototype Western humanity as incarnated in the Western bourgeoisie.*" Fanon, *The Wretched of the Earth*, (trans. Farrington), 103.

34. See for this Rorty's essay "Solidarity or Objectivity."

35. For example, the ongoing struggle for the San to maintain and/or return to their homeland (currently identified as the Central Kalahari Game Reserve in Botswana). Many San have been forced to resettle in New Xade, an area on the outskirts of the ancestral land, even though their tribal geographies span South Africa, Zimbabwe, Lesotho, Mozambique, Swaziland, Botswana, Namibia, and Angola. Add to this that various Y chromosome studies have demonstrated that the San carry some of the most divergent (oldest) Y chromosome haplogroups (thus, the San have proved to be a rich bioscientific resource for biologists, if not as yet a humanly culture/historical resource for anthropologists). For the biologists, these haplogroups are specific subgroups of haplogroups A and B, the two earliest branches on the human Y chromosome tree. The Masai, a semimigratory group located in Kenya and northern Tanzania, have also been pressured to settle rather than maintain their migratory lifestyle and nomadic farming techniques; they also continue the practice of circumcision, biocentrically defined as *genital cutting* by the West. Other initiatory rites of passage within Masai culture have also generated further controversy for Western and Westernized subjects. Both the San and the Masai have resisted the government demands to settle/resettle in the terms of their ruling Westernized elites' mimetically adopted plans for so-called human/economic development.

36. Wynter is here paraphrasing the following quotation from Frantz Fanon (also presented in the guide quote above): "Having reflected on that, I grasp my narcissism with both hands and I turn my back on the degradation of those who would make man a mere mechanism." (*Black Skin, White Masks*, 23).

37. Wynter refers here to Heidegger's 1946 essay "Letter on Humanism," 239–276.

38. Wynter was to further develop this hypothesis in an unpublished paper made available to the editor entitled "Human Being as Noun."

39. Wynter credits Carole Boyce Davies and Elaine Savory Fido for initiating her early discussion of correlated "isms." In their contributions to their edited col-

lection *Out of the Kumbla*, both Boyce Davies and Fido avoid the trap of the separating identity categories (individual "isms") by calling for a triadic perspectival approach (i.e., race, class, and gender), which had then made possible Wynter's own essay "Afterword: Beyond Miranda's Meanings," as well as the kind of thinking that went into it. See Boyce Davies and Fido, "Preface," ix–xx; Boyce Davies and Fido, "Introduction," 1–24; Wynter, "Beyond Miranda's Meanings," 355–372.

40. Derrida, "The Ends of Man," 31–57.
41. Erikson, *Life History and the Historical Moment*; Maturana and Varela, *Autopoiesis and Cognition*.
42. Erikson, *Life History and the Historical Moment*; Maturana and Varela, *Autopoiesis and Cognition*.
43. Arsuaga, *The Neanderthal's Necklace*.
44. Newberg, D'Aquili, and Rause, *Why God Won't Go Away*.
45. Grassi, *Rhetoric as Philosophy*, 102–103. Grassi writes that religion "is defined as man's endeavor to construct a holy and intact cosmos which he conceives to be an overpowering reality other than himself. . . . [the cosmos] surrounds men and encloses him in its order of reality."
46. Gauchet, *The Disenchantment of the World*.
47. Nelson, *Economics as Religion*, xv. Here, as Nelson writes, "Another basic role of economists is to serve as the priesthood of a modern secular religion of economic progress that serves many of the same functions in contemporary society as earlier Christian and other religions did in their time."
48. Girardot, *Myth and Meaning in Early Taoism*, 6–8.
49. Stackhouse, "Foreword," ix.
50. Cf. Ward, *The Big Questions in Science and Religion*.
51. Maturana and Varela, *Autopoiesis and Cognition*.
52. Maturana, "Introduction," xvi.
53. For example, Maturana and Varela, *The Tree of Knowledge*; Maturana and Poerksen, *From Being to Doing*; Varela, *Principles of Biological Autonomy*.
54. Wynter, "'Genital Mutilation' or 'Symbolic Birth'?," 501–522.
55. Heidegger, "Letter on Humanism," 239–276.
56. Prigogine, "Foreword," 16.
57. Cf. Rolston, *Three Big Bangs*.
58. Wynter put forward this hypothesis, revolving around "gender" and "genre," in the paper "Gender or the Genre of the Human?," presented at a symposium held in honor of Sherley Anne Williams. A writer, poet, and professor of literature at UC San Diego, Williams first invited Wynter to join the faculty in the Department of Literature there.
59. Wynter, "Rethinking 'Aesthetics,'" 237–279.
60. Butler, *Gender Trouble*.
61. Herrnstein and Murray, *The Bell Curve*.
62. Sahlins, *Apologies to Thucydides*.

63. On the functioning of the brain's endogenous opiate-reward (placebo) and opiate-blocking (nocebo) neurochemical system, see Stein, *The Genius Engine*.

64. Ward, *The Big Questions in Science and Religion*.

65. See, in this context, Hans Blumenberg's citation of Darwin's admission that it had been the clergyman cum economist Thomas Malthus whose seminal *Essay on Population* (1798) had given him "a theory with which to work," the result of which was to lead to far-reaching negative consequences. See for this Blumenberg, *The Legitimacy of the Modern Age*, 224–225.

66. Isaac, "Aspects of Human Evolution," 509–543 (emphasis added).

67. The innovative proposal that we should see all origin accounts, including both those to which we give the name "origin myths" and those, like Darwin's, to which we give the name "science," as being functions of each human society's "representation of origins" is also put forth in Yanagisako and Delaney, "Naturalizing Power," 1–22.

68. Godelier, *The Enigma of the Gift*, 171–175.

69. The biblical monotheistic theo-cosmogony of Genesis, in its Christian variant, reveals this with its sociogenic code of symbolic life/death (redeemed spirit/fallen flesh) and its invented extrahumanly mandating agent—the sole creator God (himself portrayed with the redemptive figure of his Son, Christ, the Messiah. This, too, is seen in Islam with its sole creator god, Allah, absolutized by a sociogenic code of symbolic life (that adheres to the central *tawhid* doctrine of the faith and the belief "that there is no god but God and Muhammad is God's messenger") and the code of *symbolic death* (that adheres to shirk, the practice of "obscuring God's oneness in any way"). In Islam, too, the sociogenic code recognizes the sin of greed, of not paying the tithe or *zakat* and eschewing the *divine obligation* to care for and protect the poor (and any other grave sin that keeps the believer apart from God, *One* God). In Judaism the first Abrahamic monotheism is the theo-cosmogony where the sole creator god Yahweh is the extrahumanly mandating forerunner analogue—when seen transcosmogonically, in relation to Christianity's Jehovah and Islam's Allah. Here the sociogenic code of *symbolic life* requires being religiously adherent to the covenant that Yahweh had made with his chosen people; *symbolic death* is that of a turning away from any such adherence. This because, as in the other two later Abrahamic theo-cosmogonies, their respective codes of *symbolic life/death* would have also had to be enacted in subjectively experienced terms, by means of the semantically, positively/negatively marked terms able to activate the opiate-reward (*placebo*) effect (defining of *symbolic life*) and the opiate reward-blocking (*nocebo*) effect (defining of *symbolic death*). In all three cases, therefore, this would have enabled the three monotheisms, their positively/negatively marked *symbolic life/death* terms, to be chartered by their respective theo-cosmogonically chartered theologies and therefore co-function at the *bios* level with the storytelling cum mythmaking mechanisms unique to the

human brain See Aslan, *No God but God*; Newberg, D'Aquili, and Rause, *Why God Won't Go Away*, especially 54–76.

70. Cf. Yanagisako and Delaney, "Naturalizing Power," 1–22. For an in-depth critique of Darwin's projected agency of natural selection/dysselection in relation to artificial breeding/artificial selection, see Fodor and Piatelli-Palmarini, *What Darwin Got Wrong*, as well as Lewontin, "Not So Natural Selection."

71. Cf. Michel Foucault, who writes: "The configuration that defines their positivity and gives them their roots in the modern episteme at the same time *makes it impossible for them to be sciences*; and if it is then asked why they assumed that title, it is sufficient to recall that it pertains to the *archaeological* definition of their roots that they summon and receive the *transference of models borrowed from the sciences*. It is therefore not man's irreducibility, what is designated as his invincible transcendence, nor even his excessively great complexity, that prevents him from becoming an object of sciences. Western culture has constituted, under the name of *man*, a being who, by one and the same interplay of reasons, must be a positive domain of *knowledge* and cannot be *an object of science*." Foucault, *The Order of Things*, 400 (emphasis added).

72. Erikson, *Toys and Reason*.

73. For an up-to-date yet precise post-the-fall-of-the-Berlin-Wall description of the scale of these now globally incorporated systemic injustices, see Badiou, "The Communist Hypothesis," 38.

74. Derrida, "The Ends of Man," 35.

75. Pagden, "Human Rights, Natural Rights, and Europe's Imperial Legacy," 171–197; Williams, *The Divided World*.

76. For example, and as so often presently tackled, the climate problem is discrete from the poverty problem, which is discrete from the addiction problem, and so forth. Wynter's insights here thus also point to the limits of disciplinary boundaries (i.e., only economists can define economic well-being and "solve" the problem of economic crises).

77. Pocock, "Civic Humanism and Its Role in Anglo-American Thought," 80–103.

78. See, for this concept, Baudrillard, *The Mirror of Production*.

79. On the men/native divide, Jean-Paul Sartre wrote: "The earth numbered two thousand million inhabitants, *five* hundred million *men* and one thousand five hundred million *natives*. The former had the Word; the others had the use of it." Sartre, "Preface," 7. To be noted here also is C. L. R. James's proposal that a more adequate translation of Fanon's 1961 text title would be, literally, *The Condemned of the World*—that is, condemned to their/our overall subordinated status according to the *principle of dominion* (i.e., that of the governing sociogenic principle enacting of our present Western bourgeois genre of being human). See James, "C. L. R. James on the Origins," 29. Many thanks to Aaron Kamugisha for his archival assistance with the James reference. Wynter also asks us to note that Fanon's call, at the end of *Les damnés*, to set forth a "new man," is usually interpreted in Marxian terms: as that of instituting

a new mode of production that itself will bring forth a new man. In his first chapter, "Concerning Violence," however, what he emphasizes is the issue of *decolonization*—and, one can add, de-settler apartheidization, and indeed, de-imperializing—as instituting a new *species* of man.

80. Wynter also notes: This program, then entitled African and Afro-American studies, had the good fortune to have been first headed by Professor St. Clair Drake, who was a distinguished full professor of anthropology and sociology. St. Clair Drake had no hesitation in helping to initiate as well as teach in the new program, since, as he was to later argue, the black students who called for the program were asking new questions that could not be answered in any of the available disciplinary fields. His own involvement in African studies, as well as that of his fellow anthropologist Professor James Lowell Gibbs, ensured that the program's intellectual focus also drew attention to the ways in which the Afro-American historico-cultural tradition had uniquely crossed the Atlantic from Africa to the New World, traveling with the Negro/Negra slaves in the holds of the Middle Passage slave ships to be then rerooted in the New World, thereby giving origin to what is one of the now hegemonic popular-political musical cultures of the globe. This program was to be later reduced—fortunately for me, just prior to my own already planned retirement from Stanford—to being merely one aspect of the Stanford history department's intellectual Counter-Reformation Program, entitled Comparative Studies in Race and Ethnicity!

81. See also Jacques-Garvey, ed., *Philosophy and Opinions of Marcus Garvey*, Hill, ed., *Marcus Garvey, Life and Lessons*, Lewis, *Marcus Garvey*.

82. Wallerstein, *The Modern World-System*, vol. 1; Wallerstein, *The Modern World-System*, vol. 2.

83. Cf. Polanyi, *The Great Transformation*; Heilbroner, *Behind the Veil of Economics*; Badiou, "The Emblem of Democracy," especially 6–8.

84. Maté, *In the Realm of Hungry Ghosts*. In a recent talk, Gabor Maté stressed the systemically induced nature of the epidemic of drug addiction; however, he attributed it only to the capitalist *economy*, rather than to the overall world system's enacting of *homo oeconomicus* and its attendant ethno-class genre of being human that is overrepresented—in liberal monohumanist terms—as if its *member class* were isomorphic with the *class of classes* of being human. Maté, "Capitalism Makes Us Crazy."

85. Barney, cited in Rue, *Everybody's Story*, 3. See also Barney, *Global 2000 Revisited*.

86. Barney, cited in Rue, *Everybody's Story*, 3.

87. Barney, cited in Rue, *Everybody's Story*, 3.

88. Barney, cited in Rue, *Everybody's Story*, 3.

89. Cf. Humphrey, *A History of the Mind*.

90. On our shaman-like roles from our origin until today, see Bauman, *Legislators and Interpreters*, 8–21. Note also his further revelation that in all human societies, the self-definition of their respective intellectual cadres involves, often

unknowingly, "the reproduction and reinforcement of a given social configuration and—with it, a given (or claimed) status for the group" (8–9).

91. Notably, while we may not all occupy the 1 percent of the upper bourgeoisie's corporate financial oligarchy, we are, in the context of, inter alia, our status quo system of initiatory learning, at the symbolic life core of our own now globally hegemonic Western and Westernized ethno-class, national, and transnational world-systemic order.

92. Nagel, *The View from Nowhere*, 11. John Davis gives an illuminating example of this auto-instituting, pseudospeciating, behavior-inducing imperative. In *Exchange*, he writes of Trobrianders: those "who wished to be considered *good of his kind* had to participate in urigubu and *youlo*, in kula and kovisi, and to do so fairly and honestly with some success. We expect our acquaintances to try to be rounded people with a reasonable personal repertoire, then we may call them good of their kind—good men, good women, good shopkeepers, good Registrars. In my view, *it is the notion we have of what a full life and what a whole rounded person should* be that leads us to attempt to play a number of different pieces from the repertoire available." Davis, *Exchange*, 46 (emphasis added). Davis outlines what is, in effect, a *bios/mythoi* law of auto-institution; therefore, a Trobriand man *cannot preexist* the cosmogonically chartered sociogenic code of symbolic *life/death*, by means of whose "second set of instructions" alone he can performatively enact himself as being human in the *genre-specific terms* of being a "good man" of his Trobiander *kind*. Nor, indeed, with respect to our contemporary, now purely secular, therefore Western/Westernized bourgeois (i.e., Man2) own, can we.

93. For a discussion of the ways in which transatlantic slavery interconnected with Man1 and Man2, see Wynter, "1492," 5–57; Wynter, "Unsettling the Coloniality of Being," 257–337; Mudimbe, *The Invention of Africa*; Mudimbe, "Romanus Pontifex (1454) and the Expansion of Europe," 58–65.

94. For the role of the Negro/Negra archipelago's embodiment of ultimate human Otherness to the West's now secularizing self-conceptions, see, for example, Césaire, *La Tragédie du Roi Christophe*; Césaire, *Aimé Césaire*.

95. DuBois, *The Souls of Black Folk*, 8. W. E. B. DuBois was the first black graduate to receive a PhD from Harvard, in 1895.

96. DuBois, *The Souls of Black Folk*, 7–15.

97. Fanon, *Black Skin, White Masks*, 30.

98. Cleaver, *Soul on Ice*. It is therefore important to also note that the issue of "double consciousness," as raised by Cleaver, enabled him to pose such a question only in the context of his own self-awakening, which had been made possible by the then ongoing 1960s range of uprisings. This awakening, therefore, enabled him to pose questions regarding the then nonconscious drives that had led to his earlier brutal rape assaults on white women, while preparing for doing so by "practicing on black women" as merely, so to speak, their *stand-ins*.

99. Neal, "The Black Arts Movement," 36.

100. Wynter is referring to Rosalie Morales's poem "We're All in the Same Boat," 91–93.

101. The process and enactment of *initiation*, as originally invented by the so-called primitive peoples of the first *nomadic* human societies of black Africa, is *the* institution specific to all human societies, whether given the Greek name of *paideia*, articulated through Christian baptism or Jewish bar mitzvahs, or enacted vis-à-vis secular societies' *education systems*. Anne Solomon's description of the rock paintings of the ancient San of the Kalahari, some of whose groups have been proved to be genetically nearest to our real-life empirical human ancestors—that is, not Adam and Eve—are meaningful in this respect. On the rock paintings, she found depicted what seemed to be initiation ceremonies, many of which were specific to the women. Solomon, "Rock Art in Southern Africa," 42–51. We can extend this hypothesis to notice the fictively eusocializing institution of initiation, as the founding institution of our being human (itself enacting of the Third Event origin of our hybrid human-level existence both biological and metabiological). With respect to the variant pseudospeciating origin myths of Franks, Gauls, Britons (from Brutus), and a range of others, see the extraordinarily brilliant study of Richard Waswo, *The Founding Legend of Western Civilization*. Waswo investigates the multiple ramifications of the founding origin myth, or legend of descent, on whose basis post-Renaissance Western civilization was to institute itself from then on until today, as the first planetarily extended, globally incorporated empire in our human history. See also Eudell, "Modernity and the 'Work of History,'" 1–24. On Frantz Fanon and the Gauls, see Fanon, *Black Skin, White Masks*, 147.

102. For both the claim and the counterclaim's wider context, as that of the West's chartering Renaissance literary-poetic origin-mythic or *Legend of Descent*, see Waswo, *The Founding Legend of Western Civilization*.

103. Michel Foucault discusses the "specific intellectual" in the essay "Truth and Power." See Foucault, *Power/Knowledge*, 109–133. Mikhail Epstein's thinking on "transcultural" can be found in Berry, Johnson, and Miller-Pogcagar, "An Interview with Mikhail Epstein," 103–118. In this interview Epstein proposes that while the institution of *culture* freed the human species from subordination to nature, only a *transcultural* perspective can free us from our subordination to any *one* culture.

104. Fanon, *Black Skin, White Masks*, 142.

105. Simon, "A Conversation with Michel Foucault," 201 (emphasis added).

106. There is another parallel here, however. Foucault—although a "normal" French/Western bourgeois subject—would, with respect to his sexual orientation, have also experienced the "double consciousness" of being. On the one hand, he was a *"normal"* middle-class professional subject, and as such—if only potentially so—was also a French colonizer, to be entrusted, if now only in neo-imperial terms, with France's "civilizing mission." On the other hand, within the same ethno-class "governing tape of the world," he would have also

had to experience himself as being "abnormal" as nonheterosexual. Thus, in Darwin's implicit terms—at the end of *The Descent of Man*—Foucault would be cast as *naturally dysselected*, because he is a *nonbiological procreator* of "the fittest" progeny. Darwin, *The Descent of Man*, 310–311.

107. DuBois, *The Souls of Black Folk*, 9.

108. DuBois, *The Souls of Black Folk*, 9.

109. Arsuaga, *The Neanderthal's Necklace*, 304.

110. DuBois, *The Souls of Black Folk*, 16.

111. Note, too, that Fanon—born out of the same objectively instituted contradictory, subjectively experienced situation as DuBois—had himself gone on to fight as a Frenchman (*evolué* or not) when France was invaded by a then intra-European imperializing Nazi-Aryan Germany. This occurred in spite of what was to be his later relentless indictment of French settler imperialism and its ruthlessly deployed militarized force against the indigenous anticolonial struggle of the Algerian Arabs. As we know, Fanon was to actively take part in this anticolonial struggle on the side of the Algerians. To be noted here, therefore is that the telos of all his struggles was against the institution of *empire* itself, whether that of totalitarian Nazi Germany or that of liberal-democratic France. Empire, then, is an institution whose destructive effects he was determined to bring to an end. His joining the Algerian anticolonial struggle was therefore the result of what had been his own personal experience when fighting for the French and of the reality, nevertheless, that its imperial attitudes with respect to non-European peoples were themselves a variant of the Nazis' with respect to other European peoples.

112. Fanon, *Black Skin, White Masks*, 9–10 (emphasis added). On the generic and gendered uses of Man—albeit through a normative white and middle-class feminist thought lens—see Gallop, *Reading Lacan*. Fanon's use of "he" and "man" as universal, of course, reflects his discursive-historical context, although the many debates on his privileging of masculinity are also informative. For an overview, see Sharpley-Whiting, *Frantz Fanon*.

113. Fanon, *Black Skin, White Masks*, 11 (emphasis added).

114. Fanon, *Black Skin, White Masks*, 11 (emphasis added).

115. Fanon, *Black Skin, White Masks*, 11 (emphasis added).

116. Fanon, *Black Skin, White Masks*, 11 (emphasis added).

117. Fanon, *Black Skin, White Masks*, 9–12 (emphasis added).

118. As the historian Peter Green points out, before the Industrial Revolution, all imperial world civilizations, including that of the West, had to be slaveholding ones. Green, *The Hellenistic Age*, 77. This, however, had also been the case *before* the West, of the "even more" large-scale slaveholding civilization of a religio-imperial Islam. In this context, slaves had been composed of many pagan peoples or races, including pagan Europeans. This was an extensive slave trade, emerging out of a largely decentralized stateless black Africa and coexisting with several large, even imperial states and kingdoms. The pagan slaves,

however, were to be both classified respectively as *abd* rather than as *mamluk*, and thereby treated as the most stigmatized and inferiorized of all slaves. While given that, from the eighth century onward, Islam had also conquered the Iberian Peninsula (i.e., Spain and Portugal), with this only ending with the final reconquest of the peninsula by Portugal and Spain in 1492, this tradition of the stigmatization of black slaves, both in Ham's curse biblical terms and in *by nature irrational ones*—a stigma that Islam itself had also inherited from the Greco-Roman imperial slaveholding cum philosophical tradition of Aristotle—had then been passed on from Islam to Christian Spain and Portugal. See, in this respect, Segal, *The Other Black Diaspora*. See also Sweet, "The Iberian Roots of American Racist Thought," 143–166.

119. Hyers, *The Meaning of Creation*.
120. Fanon, *Black Skin, White Masks*, 12 (emphasis added).
121. Fanon, *Black Skin, White Masks*, 142.
122. Fanon, *Black Skin, White Masks*, 142.
123. Fanon, *Black Skin, White Masks*, 142. The terms "band" or "ethnic" to describe the groupings of the foraging/hunter/gathering Pygmy peoples are themselves merely provisional ones, seeing that, as the ethnographer Colin Turnbull emphasizes, the Mbuti (Pygmy) people whom he studied "frequently changed the groups to which they belonged, through a process of 'fission and fusion,'" and were therefore not "subject *to the clan system* of the agricultural peoples of Africa with whom they had millennially coexisted and exchanged services." Turnbull, cited in Ichikawa, "The Japanese Tradition in Central African Hunter-Gatherer Studies," 105.
124. Regarding these initiation rites in the case of the French bourgeois subject, see Louis Althusser on teachers, teaching, and the role of school, where he represents it as a transumptively inherited ideological state apparatus (thereby, Wynter proposes, the state's *initiatory apparatus*). Althusser writes, "So little do [teachers] suspect . . . that their own devotion contributes to the maintenance and nourishment of this ideological representation of the School, which makes the School today as 'natural,' indispensable, useful and even beneficial for our contemporaries as the Church was 'natural,' indispensable and generous for our ancestors a few centuries ago." Althusser, "Ideology and Ideological State Apparatuses," 85–126. For the initiation rites of the Pygmy, see Turnbull, *The Forest People*.
125. Fanon, *Black Skin, White Masks*, 143 (emphasis added).
126. The most powerfully illuminating pages of Fanon's *Black Skin, White Masks* are those that chronicle his own personal experience of the above trauma in the wake of his arrival as an adult in France. Fanon, *Black Skin, White Masks*, 109–140. See also Wynter, "Towards the Sociogenic Principle," 30–66.
127. See, for this *relativizing* identification of the West's concept of *human nature* as if an ecumenically human one, Rorty, "Solidarity or Objectivity?"
128. Fanon, *Black Skin, White Masks*, 157–163; cf. Gordon, *Fanon and the Crisis of European Man*.

129. This emphasis on cultural continuity between the familial and the societal points to Fanon's residency under radical François de Tosquelles, who emphasized the role of culture in psychopathology.

130. Wynter's discussion of the Pygmy is to be read alongside Colin Turnbull's research on the Pygmy, who, when understood through the religio-centered world of Egypt's pharaonic civilization, were defined as a "tiny people who sing and dance to their gods, a dance that had never been seen before," and therefore as *Dancers of God*. At the beginning of the modern world, however, the English anatomist Edward Tyson had classified the Pygmy in "Chain of Being" terms—which is apparent in the title of his treatise "The Anatomy of a Pygmie Compared with That of a Monkey and a Man." As it turned out, however, the skeleton he had thought was that of a Pygmy had been that of a chimpanzee! See Turnbull, *The Forest People*, 15–16. The latter classification was to live on, however, as part of the popular folklore superstitions of the West, if no longer as part of what had long been its natural-scientific racism, in the wake of the cracking of our species' DNA code. Wynter's discussion of the color line and the eugenic/dysgenic divide can be read in Wynter, "Columbus, the Ocean Blue and 'Fables That Stir the Mind,'" 141–164.

131. See for the above process as distinct from Darwin's ostensible purely top-down natural selection, the following, as now identified by the new field of *evo-devo*: "Genes and phenotypes still count, of course; but the evo-devo revolution has stressed that evolution is essentially the evolution of the arrow that connects them. The slogan is: evolution is the evolution of ontogenies. In other words, the whole process of development, from the fertilized egg to the adult, modulates the phenotypic effects of genotypic changes, and thus 'filters' the phenotypic options that ecological variables ever have a chance to select from." See Fodor and Piatelli-Palmarini, *What Darwin Got Wrong*, 27.

132. Newberg, D'Aquili, and Rause, *Why God Won't Go Away*.

133. Cf. Yanagisako and Delaney, "Naturalizing Power," 1–22.

134. Cf. Jordan, "Poem about My Rights," 309–311. See also Audre Lorde, Nikki Giovanni, the Combahee River Collective, Dionne Brand, Angela Davis, and Jayne Cortez.

135. See also Wynter, "On How We Mistook the Map for the Territory," 108.

136. McKittrick, *Demonic Grounds*, 38. The concept "terrain of struggle"—as discussed in *Demonic Grounds*—is borrowed from Scott, *Refashioning Futures*, 31.

137. McKittrick, *Demonic Grounds*, x–xi (emphasis added).

138. Cf. Headrick, *Power over Peoples*.

139. In our discussions of Blombos, we returned again and again to the 1960 Sharpeville Massacre (which Wynter wrote an elegiac poem about while residing in the United Kingdom, which was read on a BBC program and beamed to South Africa) and the 2011 Marikana Massacre. Wynter's reading of Blombos here is thought about alongside these specific geopolitical contexts of *les*

damnés—and the practice reinvention in relation to Steven Biko's call, before his death in a prison cell, for a new humanity. Biko, *I Write What I Like*.

140. Fanon, *Black Skin, White Masks*, 23.

141. See, for an insightful analogy, Sahlins, *Apologies to Thucydides*.

142. Latour, *We Have Never Been Modern*, 68.

143. Derrida, "The Ends of Man," 35.

144. The shared existential experiences of Césaire and Fanon, although of different generations, had led to the shared quality of their thought. While Fanon is partly dismissive of the movement of negritude, which had been spearheaded by Césaire as well as by Leopold Senghor of Senegal, in an interview with Marie-Line Sephocle, Césaire had stressed that there would have been no need for the counter-self-assertion of negritude (the normal humanness of being black) had there been no *Blanchitude* (i.e., the West's imperializing assertion of its hereditary variation or *race's* generic claim to be the *only* incarnation of "civilized," thereby of highly evolved, human normalcy). Thus, as Césaire further argued, while for him "Negritude is simply the state of being Black," one should not forget that there had been a time when "alienation prevailed among Black people," to such an extent that "there were men whose ideal was to make people *forget that they were Black.*" Indeed, in the Paris of his student days, there were Antilleans who wanted "to pass for South Americans. It was a very serious problem!" This "problem" was to be central to Fanon's *Black Skin, White Masks* (1952). Sephocle, "Interview with Aimé Césaire," 369 (emphasis added).

145. Césaire, *Discourse on Colonialism*, 23. Césaire writes: "It seems that in certain circles they pretend to have discovered in me an 'enemy of Europe' and a prophet of the return to the ante-European past. For my part, I search in vain for the place where I could have expressed such views; where I ever underestimated the importance of Europe in the history of human thought; where I ever preached a *return* of any kind; where I ever claimed that there could be a *return*. What I have said was something quite different."

146. This talk, written by Césaire in French as well as in the highly poetic prose, whose form was thereby intended to emphasize the quite different dimensions of his new proposal, is one whose most successful English translation is that by A. J. Arnold, published in Césaire, *Lyric and Dramatic Poetry*, xlii–lvi. Also cited above as Césaire, "Poésie et connaissance," 158–170; Césaire, "Poetry and Knowledge," 134–146.

147. Keith Ward's insights are important to note here as he explores the phenomenon of human consciousness, with respect both to quantum physics and to religion and its theological Word, functioning at the level of consciousness of a uniquely *non–biologically determined*, if biologically implemented (i.e., at the level of the brain by the "laws of nature"), behavior-regulatory *principle of causality*. See Ward, *The Big Questions in Science and Religion*. See also Rosenblum and Kuttner, *Quantum Enigma*.

148. Césaire, *Lyric and Dramatic Poetry*, xliii–xlix (emphasis added).

149. Gugliotta, "The Great Human Migration."

150. Gugliotta, "The Great Human Migration." See also Henshilwood, d'Errico, and Watts, "Engraved Ochres from the Middle Stone Age," 27–47.

151. Gugliotta, "The Great Human Migration," (emphasis added).

152. Gugliotta, "The Great Human Migration," (emphasis added).

153. Williams, *The Mind in the Cave*, 98 (emphasis added).

154. Gugliotta, "The Great Human Migration."

155. Wilfred, "In African Cave," A14 (emphasis added).

156. Wilfred, "In African Cave," A14 (emphasis added).

157. Wilfred, "In African Cave," A14 (emphasis added).

158. Wilfred, "In African Cave," A14 (emphasis added).

159. Cf. Pandian, *Culture, Religion, and the Sacred Self*.

160. See, for this, Granh, *Blood, Bread, and Roses*.

161. Cf. Lévi-Strauss, *Mythologiques*.

162. The Blombos/southern African region was deemed a world heritage site—and officially named "the cradle of humankind"—by UNESCO in 1999. See UNESCO, "Fossil Hominid Sites of South Africa." See also Wayman, "Evolution World Tour."

163. On the origin of humans (where today's Angola and Namibia meet), see Wade, "Eden Maybe," A6. On genetic diversity and genetic drift within and beyond southwest Africa, see Tishkoff and Kidd, "Implications of Biogeography," 21–27; Destro-Bisol, "Interview with Sarah Tishkoff," 637–644. On the correlation of language and genetic diversity in Africa, see Ehret, *The Civilizations of Africa*. On language diversity, genetic diversity, and the origin of human language in Africa, see Atkinson, "Phonemic Diversity," 346–349. Atkinson studied the phonemes—or the perceptually distinctive sounds that differentiate words used in 504 languages—and found that the number of phonemes is highest in Africa, *and decreases with increasing distance from Africa*. Atkinson also notes that "*the pattern of phoneme usage around the world mirrors the pattern of human genetic diversity*, which also declines as humans *expanded to colonize* [i.e., *humanize*] other regions."

164. Ward, *The Big Questions in Science and Religion*, 267 (emphasis added).

165. Danielli, "Altruism and the Internal Reward System," 87–94. Note Danielli's brilliant universalizing of Marx's seminal "opium of the people" concept—itself originally applied only to religion and its order of discourse—which he connects to all orders of discourse, including that of our now purely secular biocentric (rather than theocentric) own.

166. Briggs and Peat, "Interview," 69–74; Goldstein, *Addiction*; Stein, *The Genius Engine*; Newberg, D'Aquili, and Rause, *Why God Won't Go Away*.

167. Césaire, *Lyric and Dramatic Poetry*, xliii–xlix (emphasis added).

3   BEFORE *MAN*

Sylvia Wynter's Rewriting of the Modern Episteme

This world divided into compartments, this world cut in two is inhabited
by two different species. The originality of the colonial context is that
economic reality, inequality, and the immense difference of ways of life
never come to mask the human reality. When we examine at close quar-
ters the colonial context, it is evident that what parcels out the world is
to begin with the fact of belonging to or not belonging to a given race, a
given species. In the colonies the economic substructure is also super-
structure. The cause is the consequence; you are rich because you are
white, you are white because you are rich. This is why Marxist analysis
should always be slightly stretched every time we have to do with the
colonial problem.

FRANTZ FANON, *THE WRETCHED OF THE EARTH*

Indeed I wonder whether, before one poses the question of ideology, it
wouldn't be more materialist to study first the question of the body and
the effects of power on it. Because what troubles me with these analyses
which prioritize ideology is that there is always presupposed a human
subject on the lines of the model provided by classical philosophy, endowed with a consciousness which power then thought to seize on.

MICHEL FOUCAULT, "BODY/POWER"

When describing how European (Spanish and Portuguese) colonial projects participate in the institution of racial difference as a human signifier,
Sylvia Wynter adds a crucial dimension to Latin American and Caribbean
framings of coloniality. Much like Frantz Fanon, Aimé Césaire, Anibal Qui-

jano, and Enrique Dussel—to name a few—she reads coloniality as the juridical-economic referent of racial difference, thus suggesting the latter as a political signifier. Wynter is interested in exposing the ethical implications of the European colonial project by locating the Iberian colonial venture as the edging of two distinct "descriptive statements of the human" and their corresponding ethics: the religious ethics of Scholastic thought; and, the civic ethics of early programmatic and philosophical accounts of the modern juridical-political region, namely, the register of the state and law. My task here is to read Sylvia Wynter's description of the conditions that accompanied the emergence of the "space of Otherness"—"the order of race" or racial difference. I read her thinking as an excavation of the modern onto-ethical field, one that corrects Michel Foucault's description of the post-Enlightenment onto-epistemological ascension of man, as an empirico-transcendental figure.

In reading Wynter's project against Foucault's argument that the modern episteme (here renamed post-Enlightenment thought) always already resolves difference as a moment of the (transcendental, pure, or teleological) Same, I track how Wynter recuperates what remains illegible in Foucault's critique of Man: "the idea of race." What she offers to the critique of modern thought, I argue, is an analysis of how in the Renaissance and post-Enlightenment epochs, two moves of naturalization—the secularization of rationality and the representation of the human through the workings of natural selection, respectively—would position Man in such a way as to disavow other, coexisting modes of being human. I therefore illuminate the ways in which racial difference performs its role as an ethico-political signifier. The chapter is divided into three sections. The first section briefly summarizes Wynter's arguments, specifically her deployment of the colonial to rewrite the classical order as a political grid, in which rationality guides the writing of the human difference; and the Darwinian rearticulation of the rational/irrational pair (which was recast as the naturally "selected"/ naturally "dysselected" by evolution) as representations of difference that inform colonial juridical-economic architectures. In the second section, I draw attention to her ontological argument regarding post-Renaissance and post-Enlightenment knowledge. I use this to guide a reading of Foucault's description of the modern episteme (in which Man rules as the transcendental-empirical king). Because it fissures Foucault's account of the modern episteme, Wynter's critique allows us to appreciate the ethico-political significance of Man's being as an empirical thing and how it would become the signifier of European difference. The chapter closes with a comment on the ways in which Wynter's destabilization of the two central modern ethical themes, the transcendental and the human, demands a discussion of the notion of *humanity* itself.

Sylvia Wynter's analysis of modern thought, then, is precisely the delineation of that critical juncture engulfed by the concept of the racial, when read as a refiguring of the colonial.[1] This refiguring, anchored by "the idea of race," uncovers a shift of registers from the juridical to the symbolic, thus making possible a post-Enlightenment writing of Man that produces the "natural man" *as the effect of the productive tools of transcendental reason.* If this reading of her work can contribute to the formulation of critical projects that address the pressing political matters of the global present, I hope this discussion encourages analyses centered on the notion of humanity and the colonial project to engage Wynter's subtle but profound writing of the colonial at the center of the Kingdom of Man.

The Naturalization of Man

In "Unsettling the Coloniality of Being/Power/Truth/Freedom: Toward the Human, after Man, Its Overrepresentation—An Argument," Sylvia Wynter outlines the potential retrieval of the human (us, all of us, the "human species") from the bowels of the oversized figure of the human subject produced by modern philosophical and scientific projects, namely, Man. In doing so, she centers the colonial in the examination of the modalities of subjugation at work in the global present. What Wynter brings to the table is a version of the epistemological transformations that constituted modern thought—in the Renaissance and the Enlightenment, respectively—which follows very closely Michel Foucault's chronology. She adds to this the critical question of how, as Anibal Quijano states, "the idea of race" does the work of the "naturalization of colonial relations between Europeans and non-Europeans."[2] Importantly, Wynter does not seek an answer to the question of how "the idea of race" has served as an ideological excuse for colonial domination. Rather, she proposes an account of the relationship between juridical, economic, and symbolic moments of power that is very faithful to the early tenets of historical materialism. Both the Renaissance and Enlightenment epistemological transformations, she argues, were "made possible only on the basis of the dynamics of a colonizer/colonized relation that the West was to discursively constitute and empirically institutionalize on the islands of the Caribbean and, later, on the mainlands of the Americas."[3]

For Wynter, as for Marx and Engels, the dominant ideas of a *civitas* reflect the conditions of economic production. Hence her path differs radically from the conventional liberal critique, which sees "the idea of race" as a mistaken, false scientific apprehension of the human body. Similarly, her thinking differs from the conventional historical-materialist critique, which sees "the idea of race" as an ascriptive sign without direct correspondence to economic production. What is her radical move here? She begins with the ontological question—that which ponders human existence and who/ what we are—*alongside* "the idea of race." Specifically, she focuses on the ways in which the architectures of colonial juridical-economic power are encoded, and thus sustain, what it means to be human while also offering a *refiguring* of humanness that is produced *in relation to* the monumental history of race itself. "Race," she states, "was therefore to be, in effect, the nonsupernatural but no less extrahuman ground (in the reoccupied place of the traditional ancestors/gods, God, ground) of the answer that the secularizing West would now give to the Heideggerian question as to the who, and the what we are."[4]

How does Wynter articulate her version of the secular ontological argument? In the first description of Man (referred to as Man1), she links the epistemological transformation of the Renaissance to the reconfiguring of *civitas*—a reconfiguring that was underwritten by conquest and the architectures and procedures of colonial power it engendered. How did conquest perform this feat? Citing Jacques Le Goff, Wynter reminds us that the medieval, Spirit/Flesh pair established two distinctions, a nonhomogeneity between "the spiritual perfection of the heavens . . . as opposed to the sublunar realm of Earth."[5] With this, "the geography of the earth" is also "being divided up between . . . its temperate regions centered on Jerusalem . . . and those realms that, because outside this Grace, had to be uninhabitable."[6] This spatial and ideological narrative would be disproved by the Portuguese travels to the Americas, as those geographies "outside Grace" were, in fact, inhabited. The emergence of a *new* framework of political (juridical-economic) power set in place in the Americas and the Caribbean yielded an "epochal rupture." Wynter argues, then, that this rupture "was to lead to the gradual development of physical sciences . . . made possible only by the no less epochal reinvention of Western Europe's matrix Judeo-Christian genre of the human, in its first secularizing if still hybrid religio-secular terms as Man as the Rational self and political subject of the state, in the reoccupied place of the True Christian Self."[7] This is to say that travels of colonial conquest were entwined with the ideological shift away from medieval Christian man and the shift toward secularized rational man as the inhabitants of the Americas, those residing in what was formerly considered to be "outside Grace," were rendered irrational. From then on, the rational/irrational pair would then remap the "space of otherness" and, significantly, be represented by the bodies and territories subjected to colonial power.[8] As such this distinction—irrational/rational—is always already written *as* political, "civic-humanist," and the theory of sovereignty.[9]

In linking the emergence of a secular ontological account of Man to the "voyages of discovery" that instituted the colonial modality of power, Wynter fractures the glassy depiction of the classical thought Foucault has offered. She does so in two moves. On the one hand, she recalls the link between Hobbes's and Locke's accounts of the *civitas* as the Empire of Reason (even if still in a conception of nature as the domain of the divine, and a conception of the "natural man" as both effects and tools of secular universal reason). On the other hand, she argues that Man, posited as a *natural* thing, would also be elevated in such a way that all other modes of being human would be symbolically disavowed. This naturalization of Man, positioning one mode of human as *naturally* rational and good (a purely *natural*-biological thing), negates the ability to distinguish the human from other natural things. The production of the human, Man, and nature draws attention to Wynter's reconceptualization of the classical order. Specifically, her thinking recasts the formal table/ruler and the tools for classification and measurement Foucault describes as being introduced in the colonial juridical-economic context. That is, in Wynter's description of the mode of thought governed by the "table of identities and difference," she shows us how Necessity ("laws of nature") would serve Freedom ("the laws of society"). In this context, emancipated reason (Wynter calls it "degodded") is both subjected to the demands of European-colonial *societates* and to its economic needs and also put forward and calcified as the sovereign, final determinant—the final cause—of everything social. With this, she deploys the colonial to fissure Foucault's glassy classical order, reproducing at the level of the symbolic, the colonial juridical-economic grid, thereby inviting a return to the kind of critique of ideology Foucault dismisses.

The postmedieval secularization of Man is followed by a second descriptive statement of man (Man2), framed with the evolution paradigm and put forth in Charles Darwin's insights on natural selection and science. This ideological shift revised humanness, according to Wynter, to *differentially* categorize "all the colonized darker-skinned natives of the world and the darker-skinned poorer European peoples themselves."[10] The "new master code," a purely scientific one, divided the world into the "selected" and "dysselected." Within this Darwinian context, the figure of Man is over-represented as human according to a "principle of nonhomogenity," which is "embodied in the new line W. E. B. DuBois was to identify as the color line: that is, as a line drawn between the lighter and the darker peoples of the earth, and enforced at the level of social reality by the law-likely in-stituted relations of socioeconomic dominance / subordination between them."[11] The color line would replace the previous codes (medieval and classical) "in order to enable the selected / dysselected, and thus deserving / undeserving status organizing principle that it encoded to function for the nation-state as well as the imperial orders of the Western bourgeoisie."[12] She adds that the paradox of the Darwinian descriptive statement that "defines the human as a purely biological being on the model of a natural organism" derives from the fact that it must sustain "strategic mechanisms that can repress all knowledge of the fact that its biocentric descriptive statement is a descriptive statement."[13] That is, the biocentric descriptive statement, which casts some as naturally selected and most of the world as naturally dysselected, reflects a particular collective *self-representation* and *not* an eter-nal (extrahuman) truth determined by the immutable, objective, and neces-sary "laws" and "forms" of nature. For Wynter, the distinctions found in the global space—the Negro, the native, the colonial, or Third / Fourth World question—result not from our present mode of economic production but rather from the ongoing production and reproduction of "the bourgeois answer to the question of what is human and the present techno-industrial, capitalist mode of production [that] is an indispensable and irreplaceable, but only proximate function of it."[14]

What is important in this argument, then, are the ways in which the re-lationship between the economic and the symbolic, between material pro-duction and ideological production, are inverted, with the latter (symbolic / ideological production) rendered determinant. More crucially, and through an anti-Foucauldian move, Wynter couches her analysis of modern thought on the promise of an answer to the ontological question that does not rep-resent a particular version of the human as the Human as such. For her, the shifts in episteme described above—medieval, classical, biocentric—"were not only shifts with respect to each episteme specific order of knowledge / truth, but were also shifts in what can now be identified as the 'politics of being'; that is, as a politics that is everywhere fought over what is to be the descriptive statement, the governing sociogenic principles, instituting of each genre of the human."[15] What her formulation of the ontological question also does is to unearth a struggle (rewriting Marx's class struggle) between *different* "descriptive statements of the human . . . about whose master code of symbolic life and death each human order organizes itself."[16]

While Wynter and Foucault agree on the selection of the markers of the epistemological transformations that constituted modern thought, what accounts for the fact that Wynter finds Man emerging much earlier than Foucault? Elsewhere I describe how Foucault's Man, the self-determined (interior/temporal) thing, would only emerge when transcendentality was manufactured to describe Europe's particularity, to distinguish the mode of being human found in Europe from those encountered in other regions of the globe.[17] For Wynter, however, Man, as the selected ontological signifier for Europeans and the Human in general, makes its appearance before Formal Transcendental (universal/pure) reason became the Living Transcendental (universal/teleological) subject, and also before Hegel's correction of Kant's soulless mapping of the modern onto-epistemological grounds. Now Wynter's critical move is to conceive of the classical order, and the rational grids (measurement and taxonomy) organizing it, as a transmutation (juridical-economic → symbolic) of colonial power. Such a move unsettles modern onto-epistemological assumptions precisely because she subsumes formalization, the distinguishing feature of classical order, to desire. When doing so, she troubles, deeply, Foucault's separation between the order of knowledge and the rules of power.

The A Priori Rule of Domination

> The Classical episteme can be defined in its most general arrangement in terms of the articulated system of mathesis, a taxinomia, and a genetic analysis. The sciences always carry within themselves the project . . . of an exhaustive ordering of the world; they are always directed, too, towards the discovery of simple elements and their progressive combination; and at their centre they form a table on which knowledge is displayed in a system contemporary with itself.
> —Michel Foucault, *The Order of Things*

Wynter's attention to the links between the "voyages of discovery," the colonial formation, and the formal re-presentation of Man allows her to read the lines of Foucault's classical table as a political grid that refigures European colonial mapping of the global. Why does Foucault's description of the same transformations, and his "theory of domination" as understood in relation to modern thought, miss the connection?[18] Wynter uncovers that a "theory of domination" can engender the critical project (ideological or otherwise) as one that locates the conditions of possibility for modern representation (its onto-epistemological grounds) outside, exterior to, the self-determined mind and thus contingent upon the relationships of power that organize global-historical moments. Wynter calls into question Foucault's thesis on modern thought precisely because her critique of modern ontology is interested in the tracing of the effects of colonial power beyond its juridical-economic architectures. That is, in her privileging of *exteriority* at the ontological level, her insistence in highlighting the material conditions of possibility for onto-epistemological transformation enables a feat, specifically the unsettling of freedom, that Foucault has never quite successfully performed because of, I suggest, his own investment in Kantian interiority. Nevertheless, even a lack of interest in ideological critique does not fully explain a portrait of modern thought that does not even contemplate the question of whether or not colonial power may have played a role in setting up the epistemological arrangements that compose modern representation. In what follows, I think about Wynter and Foucault together in order to demonstrate that the latter's glassy depiction of classical order is related to how he formulated a view of power as a "theory of domination" without systematically considering colonial domination.

Thinking this through will require the same kind of misreading of Western self-narratives Spivak performs in her delineation of the figure of the "native informant"—with the only difference here being the fact that, in this case, the "native informant" is the Western intellectual himself, Foucault.[19] In Foucault's description of the classical order and the discourse on race, despite the brief reference to "European colonialism," I locate a double dismissal of the colonial context. First, his portrait of the classical order does not ask the question of whether or not the colonial context, which necessarily situates Europe as the subject of juridical-economic subjugation of other peoples and places, played any role in a writing of difference that precludes any external reference. Here is where Wynter's reading of the first "degodded" secularized version of Man, overrepresented as *the* Human in/ and Nature, cracks open Foucault's classical order. She shows that, *beyond* providing the grounds for the abstract mode of comparison (measurement or classification that resolves difference in a glassy text as taxonomy or mathesis), *universal reason*, precisely because it is the ground for the rational/irrational pair, refigures the medieval Spirit/Flesh divide and *sustains* the writing of European particularity.

"The projected 'space of otherness,'" she argues, "was now to be mapped on phenotypical and religio-cultural differences between human variations and/or population groups, while the new idea of order was now to be defined in terms of degrees of rational perfection/imperfection, as ... that of the 'law of nature,' 'natural law': as a 'law' that allegedly functioned to order human societies in the same way as the newly discovered laws of nature served to regulate the processes of functioning of physical and organic levels of reality."[20]

Second, Foucault's reading of the "discourse on race," even if not explicitly and systematically, operates within the European space (though subjugated by the hegemonic "theory of sovereignty" and its "principle of right"). This further forecloses an investigation of the relationships of force that marks the colonial context. This is evident because Foucault introduces a critique of the dialectic (the Hegelian version) as a philosophical resolution of the discourse on race that empties its historical import because it takes it over and displaces it "into the old form of philosophical juridical discourse."[21] The dialectic finally, he continues, "ensures the historical constitution of a universal subject, a reconciled truth, and a right in which all particularities have their ordained place. The Hegelian dialectic ... must be understood as philosophy and right's colonization and authoritarian colonization of a historico-political discourse that was both a statement of fact, a proclamation, and a practice of social warfare."[22] Had Foucault asked the question of whether there were other determinants, extra-European processes enabling the Hegelian resolution, he might have had to consider that *the articulation of the Transcendental performed in the Hegelian dialectic resolves the discourse on race only because it writes the universal subject as a particular world-historical figuring of reason, one that is exclusive to post-Enlightenment Europe.*[23] Consequently, he would not have been able to write the deployment of the discourse on race in "European colonization" as an after the (historical) event, the result of its comprehension by philosophy, which lead to the two "transcriptions of race" he identifies. Instead, he would have to trace the parallel unfolding of the discourse of race in the regional (European) context and the rationality/irrationality code Wynter identifies in the global (colonial) context.

This epistemological and theoretical pathway would have led him to ask *why* the classical order could describe itself without any reference to either the colonial or the European context and, finally, whether or not the table/ruler of mathesis might have played any role in the writing of Man *as the* empirico-transcendental figure he finds emerging in the post-Enlightenment period. To engage this pathway, as Wynter's framework shows, Foucault would have had to conceive of Man as *one version* of the broader ethico-political figure at stake, namely, the Human. This would have meant a different tracing of "subjugated knowledges"; it would have meant taking up a critique of ideology that targets the symbolic itself and returning to a serious consideration of the juridical-economic dimensions of the political existence, but one which, as in Wynter's critique, poses the latter as a consequence and not as the ultimate determinant of the ideological production of subject.

To be sure, Wynter demonstrates that the Foucauldian framework can aid in a critique of the symbolic moment of power, of representation, without reducing it to an epiphenomenon. Yet, her unsettling of Man fissures Foucault's classical order when it unveils how the "first encounter" shook the basis of medieval thinking and in the process rescued Man from the entrails of the Fallen Flesh (the dregs of the Spirit/Flesh pairing) while also apprehending the world through a disavowal that casts alternative/non-European modes of being human (the newly dysselected inhabitants of the Americas) as the Other of the secularized rational mind. What Wynter uncovers is that the conditions of possibility—the context of emergence of the refiguring of the "discourse of race" Foucault locates in the nineteenth century—in fact resides in the division of the Human into the rational European and its irrational (American, African, Asian, Australian, etc.) Others.[24]

From opposite but parallel directions the critical projects of Wynter and Foucault meet; both recognize the productivity intrinsic to modern (post-Renaissance and post-Enlightenment) representation, and both presuppose and announce a different modality of representation, which will release the subject, the political thing, from the armatures of disciplinary power/knowledge and, to use Wynter's vocabulary, refigure the "biocentric" master code.[25] They part ways, however, in two moments. First, each locates the place of disassemblage at distinct levels: in Foucault's technology of self (and theory of domination), the task is to be performed at the level of the *singular* human being's self-refashioning; in Wynter's project, the critical task requires the refashioning at the *collective* level, one that necessitates an acknowledgment of human beings' ability to "auto-institute ourselves as human through symbolic, representational processes that have, hitherto, included those mechanisms of occultation by means of which we have been able to make opaque to ourselves the fact that we so do."[26] Second, while Foucault hopes that, along with the theory of sovereignty, the grip of disciplinary power would also be dissolved—and the refashioning of the singular being would be possible—Wynter invests in and recasts scientific knowledge. Following Aimé Césaire, and as Katherine McKittrick also argues in this volume, Wynter enmeshes science, *scientia*, and logos in order to shatter the mechanisms of occultation. She thus writes that the "natural sciences . . . are, in spite of all their dazzling triumphs with respect to knowledge of the natural world, half-starved. They are half-starved because they remain incapable of giving us any knowledge of our uniquely human domain."[27] What would this new science do, then? Wynter continues:

> Only the elaboration of a new science, beyond the limits of the natural sciences . . . will offer us our last chance to avoid the large-scale dilemmas that we must now confront as a species. This would be a science in which the "study of the Word" . . . [a study] of the neurophysiological circuits/mechanisms of the brain that, when activated by the semantic system of each such principle/statement, lead to the specific order of consciousness or modes of mind in whose terms we then come to experience ourselves as this or that genre/mode of being human. Yet, with this process taking place hitherto outside our conscious awareness, and thereby leading us to be governed by the "imagined ends" or postulates of being, truth, freedom that we law-likely put and keep in place, without realizing that it is we ourselves, and not extrahuman entities, who prescribe them.[28]

Instead of remaining within the limits of modern representation, by setting up one answer (*universal poesis* or *universal nomos*) to the truth of the Human, Wynter, along with Césaire, places her bets on the *universal nomos*'s (in the guise of scientific reason) unveiling powers. In that, she remains faithful to the trust of classic historical materialism and thus the view that material conditions of existence, in this case the body (brain) itself, respond to the ideological representations governing our collective existence. I will not engage in an assessment of Wynter's particular choice—again, see McKittrick's essay in this volume—and elsewhere I have made it clear that I consider that neither the field of history (the domain of *universal poesis*) nor the field of science (the domain *of universal nomos*) provides helpful sites or useful analytical tools for the production of critiques of modern representation that would aid in the disassembling of disciplinary and biopolitical mechanisms of subjection and raciality.[29] I am more interested in whether and how the fissures Wynter identifies might, for the time being, help the critique of the Human—overrepresented as Man—that is now ruling the global symbolic reservoir and humanity.

Of-the-World

> Knowing is a mode of being of Dasein as being-in-the-world, and has its ontic foundation in this constitution of being. But if, as we suggest, we thus find phenomenally that knowing is a kind of being-in-the-world, one might object that with such an interpretation of knowing the problem of knowledge is annihilated.
>
> —Martin Heidegger, *Being and Time*

Two ethico-political questions can be posed vis-à-vis Sylvia Wynter's account of the Human as always already an effect of coloniality, particularly for those invested in the project of displacing the Transcendental, in its Kantian or Hegelian rendering, as the privileged basis for ethical accounts. More successfully than Hegel's first formulation, perhaps, is Heidegger's version of phenomenology—the writing of the being of Man as the Human in the world—that resolves exteriority into interiority, space into time, by enveloping the whole domain of existence as the moment of Dasein, or the being whose particularity resides in the fact that it asks the question of being that is concerned with what and who we are.[30] This resolution is indicated in the always already there, in the world, of Dasein. To be sure, it is almost impossible not to read twentieth-century versions of phenomenology as a response to the Darwinian "descriptive statement of the human." Explicitly and implicitly, Heidegger, for instance, casts the field of science as the proper site for the production of the truth of Man when he recuperates existence—and all things external to existence—within the confines of anthropological and sociological investigations of human conditions. Nevertheless, as with other writers who posit and think through Man as the subject of *universal poesis* and a self-representing being, Heidegger only attributes to the human being a particular, protected kind of contingency, that is, the interior determination of temporality. He writes that the "articulated structural totality of the being of Dasein as care first becomes existentially intelligible in terms of temporality," which constitutes "the primordial meaning of being of Dasein,"[31] and thus puts forth a being whose meaning lies in the horizon of time.[32] In Wynter's reformulation of the ontological argument, her framing of the question of being—in particular the argument concerning the political nature of the modern universal answers, that is, the descriptive statements that overrepresent Man as *the* sole/full Human—emerges out of the possibility that any answer to the question of who and what we are, especially but not only scientific ones, may be unable to avoid recolonizing, via naturalization, all and any other possible modes of being Human.

This point raises the two aforementioned ethico-political questions. First, Heidegger's reversal of the Kantian statement on the possibility of knowledge, that is, the submission of the pure intuitions of time and space to metaphysics itself, promises an account of the Human that leaves open space for a difference that is not resolved in the glassy table/ruler social categories refigure. Significantly, the thinking of difference this formulation opens up was already being explored by other modern thinkers (in particular Herder, in what was also a rejection of the Kantian transcendental reason). It is precisely this thinking of difference that would be recuperated—even if resolved through a scientific arsenal—by twentieth-century anthropology and Lévi-Strauss's rejection of the scientific writing of the human, which celebrated human diversity. Nevertheless, even these celebrations of human diversity, as a testimony to the rule of *universal poesis, could not but engulf other modes of being human,* now *objects* of anthropological knowledge, into categories of human beings with their own foundational dichotomies.[33] That is, the tools of raciality, racial and cultural difference, have been, as Wynter intimates and I argue, an effect of the second secular descriptive statement, the Darwinian biocentric version of Man. However, that does not render them less effective and productive political/symbolic weapons: they are inscribed in the global political landscape, constituting the ontological referent to the juridical architectures, such as the human rights framework, humanitarian (military) occupation, and the International Criminal Tribunal, to name a few. Hence, the ethico-political question becomes whether or not critical projects toward global justice, and the images of justice they carry, should work toward dissembling the subjects of raciality to institute a Human universal, but one which, as Wynter hopes, will not be just a refiguring of one particular "descriptive statement of the human" as the global norm and thus a replication of the present role played by the notion of humanity, as overrepresented by Man, in the global present.

Second, if knowing—either as a precondition for representing or as the effect of representation—is so fundamental to the defining of the Human as a political subject (as Foucault, Wynter, and many other have argued), the ethico-political question becomes whether or not justice can be imagined from within the available modalities of knowledge, which includes Foucault's archaeological and genealogical tools along with the already known historical and scientific tools, with all the necessary erasures and engulfments they presuppose and entail. As we saw earlier, for Wynter, scientific knowledge, specifically the natural sciences, may play an important role by unveiling the nonhistorical or extrahuman (natural/biological) structurings of cultural or ideological mechanisms. Foucault, however, conceives of knowledge, the modern versions of it, as sites of exercise of domination, which produce the very subjects it subjugates.

As far as the documents orienting the "global contract" are concerned (specifically the texts that guide the framing and working of the current political juridical-economic figures such as nation-states, multinational corporations, international nongovernmental organizations, multilateral bodies, and so forth), the products of the "biocentric code" (the social categories that are aligned with racial, gender, and sexual difference) have been integrated into the political text, as proper political signifiers whose inclusion would/will fulfill modern democratic claims.[34] That is, these power/knowledge effects are here to stay insofar as they are encoded in juridical texts. The problem is that these very global juridical architectures also deploy a particular thread of humanity as a moral signifier that is also *the* ethical gauge for the members of the global polity. Curiously, the conception of humanity circulating—privileging dignity and diversity as descriptors of the Human, tags that are added to the already operating attributes of freedom and equality—remains the same one articulated in post-Enlightenment knowledge. That is, and as the issue of female genital cutting most dramatically shows, this thread of humanity cannot comprehend—in fact, it actually disallows—the contemplation of difference in the establishment of the proper principles guiding political decisions.[35] Certainly, the critique of deployments of such conception of humanity consistently recalls the social categories, the political context of their emergence and the ones they have produced, and demands the recognition of their effects in political decisions. Nevertheless, as Foucault has suggested, disciplinary power and biopower have not displaced and will not displace the principle of right; that is, the critique of humanity based on arguments that disciplinary power is productive, and that the very deployment of humanity functions as a juridical-political device, precisely because it ignores the effects of the category. If knowledge will provide us with any way into advancing a critique of the political effects of humanity in the global present, it will take more than merely bringing scientific knowledge to speak truth to power, as Wynter hopes; and it will take more than individual self-fashioning and the disrobing of the clothing of disciplinary power, as Foucault suggests. Furthermore, it will most certainly not be accomplished through a recitation of the very philosophical texts that produced this figure to begin with. What will help us to open up the path? I think it should begin with asking different questions, methodological rather than ontological ones: instead of the question of who and what we are, we need to go deeper into the investigation of how we come up with answers to the questions. That is, our approach to humanness and social justice will take systematic investigations of knowing—along the lines that Wynter and Foucault have undertaken, but without the substitutes they provide—but extricate knowing from the constitution of Dasein, to indicate how it is possible to avoid continuously rewriting it in self-determination, thus hiding the very violence that delineates its place.

Notes

1. For a discussion of the notion of engulfment, as a political-symbolic strategy, and of how the concept of the racial functions as such, see Silva, *Toward a Global Idea of Race*.
2. Quijano, "Coloniality of Power, Eurocentrism and Latin America," 534–535.
3. Wynter, "Unsettling the Coloniality of Being," 264.
4. Wynter, "Unsettling the Coloniality of Being," 264
5. Wynter, "Unsettling the Coloniality of Being," 278.
6. Wynter, "Unsettling the Coloniality of Being," 278–279.
7. Wynter, "Unsettling the Coloniality of Being," 281.
8. Wynter, "Unsettling the Coloniality of Being," 281.
9. In fact, others have pointed to how the rewriting of these bodies and territories—under the dominant discourse of sovereignty—would operate as a justification for colonial domination. Fitzpatrick shows how rationality is also deployed in writings of modern law and how it is contingent upon constructions of non-Europeans as savage. See Fitzpatrick, *The Mythology of Modern Law*.
10. Fitzpatrick, *The Mythology of Modern Law*, 310.
11. Fitzpatrick, *The Mythology of Modern Law*, 310.
12. Fitzpatrick, *The Mythology of Modern Law*, 322.
13. Wynter, "Unsettling the Coloniality of Being," 326.

14. Wynter, "Unsettling the Coloniality of Being," 317.
15. Wynter, "Unsettling the Coloniality of Being," 319.
16. Wynter, "Unsettling the Coloniality of Being," 317.
17. Silva, *Toward a Global Idea of Race.*
18. Foucault, *The Order of Things.*
19. Spivak, *A Critique of Postcolonial Reason.*
20. Wynter, "Unsettling the Coloniality of Being," 296–297.
21. Foucault, *Society Must Be Defended*, 58.
22. Foucault, *Society Must Be Defended*, 58.
23. For the full development of this argument, see Silva, *Toward a Global Idea of Race.*
24. That division would haunt the European space and culminate in the Nazi project of obliteration makes sense because of the ways in which—as Giorgio Agamben shows—those killed in Hitler's concentration camps had to first be dehumanized, disavowed, or, to use Agamben's vocabulary, banned, transformed into a life without law and morality (i.e., into bare life). See Agamben, *Homo Sacer.*
25. Wynter, "Unsettling the Coloniality of Being," 313.
26. Wynter, "Unsettling the Coloniality of Being," 328.
27. Wynter, "Unsettling the Coloniality of Being," 328.
28. Wynter, "Unsettling the Coloniality of Being," 328–329.
29. Silva, *Toward a Global Idea of Race.*
30. Heidegger, *Being and Time.*
31. Heidegger, *Being and Time*, 216–217.
32. The disavowal of spatiality (exteriority), which usually accompanies this kind of statement, is performed earlier in the book when Heidegger rejects the idea of insidedness as defining Dasein's mode of being in the world. He does so precisely because it necessarily institutes the possibility that exterior things may have any role in the determination of being. To prevent this effect—which has haunted modern representation since the Cartesian inaugural statement—he moves on to describe the "kind of spatiality which is constitutive to Dasein," which begins with the acknowledgment that the world itself is not "objectively present in space" (Heidegger, *Being and Time*, 94). "The spatiality of Dasein," he states, "is essentially not objective presence" but, rather, "in the sense of a familiar and heedful association with the beings encountered within the world" (95). It is therefore defined in terms of *already* being-in the world, *as* "de-distancing" and "directionality" (97). That is, it is the fundamental *distinguishing intentionality* of Dasein, which renders the world its playing ground; *it never exists as the other beings/things that are found there.*
33. Lévi-Strauss, *Tristes Tropiques.*
34. Silva, "No-Bodies," 212–236.
35. Silva, "Mapping Territories of Legality," 203–222.

4 SYLVIA WYNTER

What Does It Mean to Be Human?

The Issues

Following in the steps of Frantz Fanon, Humberto Maturana, and Francisco Varela, Sylvia Wynter's works have been pursuing a cognitive shift that in this essay I characterize as decolonial. Why decolonial? Why not postmodern or postcolonial? Wynter's work has consistently called into question whether the "post"—in poststructural, postmodernity, postcolonial—is a useful conceptual frame, thus putting it aside in order to understand, instead, how particular epistemologies are unthinkable and/or unarticulated within hegemonic Western categories of knowledge and philosophy of knowing. Wynter is a radical thinker. She powerfully explores the roots of Western and colonial knowledge systems and uncovers the otherwise veiled link between racial, gendered, and sexual belonging, differential ways of knowing and imagining the world, and the overarching governing codes that have created, maintained, and normalized practices of exclusion. She is not looking to change or supersede epistemic categories and established knowledge, but rather seeks to undo the systems through which knowledge and knowing are constituted. At the same time, Wynter is not proposing to contribute to and comfortably participate in a system of knowledge that left her out of humanity (as a black/Caribbean woman), but rather delink herself from this very system of knowledge in order to engage in epistemic disobedience. Under the rules of the epistemic canon, and according to its racial mandates, if you have been classified in/as difference, then you are required to submit and assimilate to the canon *or* remain outside. Wynter does not follow either of these pathways. She instead engages what I call the decolonial option, a practice of rethinking and unraveling dominant worldviews that have been opened up by Indigenous and black and Caribbean thinkers since the sixteenth century in América (with accent) and the Caribbean. The decolonial option does not simply protest the contents of imperial coloniality; it demands a delinking of oneself from the knowledge systems we take for granted (and can profit from) and practicing epistemic disobedience.

Wynter's decolonial project calls into question the concept of the Human and its epistemological underpinnings.[1] Her work draws on the research of Chilean scientist, philosopher, and intellectual Humberto Maturana (in collaboration in an early stage with Francisco Varela) and black and Caribbean intellectuals and social theorists. Wynter draws on Maturana's insights, in particular his work on autopoiesis, which uncovers the interconnectedness of "seeing" the world and "knowing" the world: specifically, he shows that what is seen with the eyes does not represent the world outside the living organism; rather, it is the living organism that fabricates an image of the world through the internal/neurological processing of information. Thus, Maturana made the connection between the ways in which human beings construct their world and their criteria of truth and objectivity and noticed how their/our nervous system processes and responds to information.

It is across both neurobiological cognition and decolonial practices that Sylvia Wynter's work and her intellectual disobedience emerge. Wynter suggests that if we accept that epistemology gives us the *principles and rules of knowing* through which the Human and Humanity are understood, we are trapped in a knowledge system that fails to notice that the stories of what it means to be Human—specifically origin stories that explain who/what we are—are, in fact, narratively constructed. Wynter's commentaries on Man1, Man2, and the making of the Human should thus be understood alongside historical and epistemological epochs (medieval, classical) that present humanness through intelligible cosmogonies that, as Denise da Silva argues in this collection, require a juridical-economic colonial presence. To study "Man" or "Humanity" is therefore to study a narrativization that has been produced with the very instruments (or categories) that we study *with*. In short, it is precisely the practice of *accepting* the *principles and rules of knowing* that produces narratives that naturalize, for example, evolution and dysselection and thus biocentric Human origin stories. It follows that we fail to notice that evolution, dysselection, and biocentricity are *origin stories with an ontological effect*. Put simply: we tend to believe our cosmogonies as natural truth(s); this belief system is calcified by our *commitment* to this belief system; the schema self-replicates, as we continually invest in its systemic belief qualities. In this way, Wynter's writings on the Human and who/what we are are reflective of Maturana's autopoietics.

Wynter refuses to embrace the entity of the Human independently of the epistemic categories and concepts that created it by suggesting instead that our conceptualizations of the Human are produced within an autopoietic system. The problem of the Human is thus not identity-based per se but in the *enunciations* of what it means to be Human—enunciations that are concocted and circulated by those who most convincingly (and powerfully) imagine the "right" or "noble" or "moral" characteristics of Human and in this project their *own* image-experience of the Human into the sphere of Universal Humanness. The Human is therefore the product of a particular epistemology, yet it appears to be (and is accepted as) a naturally independent entity existing in the world.

Implicit in this epistemological framework are the worldviews of those who have been cast as non-Human or less-than-Human: Frantz Fanon's *les damnés*, imperial constructs who can only be understood as the difference outside. Les damnés are the *anthropos* in relation to *humanitas* as *humanitas* is defined by those who conceive of themselves as Human. Here, clearly, imperial epistemologies emerge alongside the widespread coloniality of knowledge: Christian theology, secular philosophy, and sciences that were formed and shaped under European geographic monarchies and nation-states (which also provided the unification of Western knowledge systems in six modern/imperial languages grounded in Greek and Latin). This is the belief system that Wynter's work unveils: the naturalization of and thus a steadfast belief in modes of thinking—the principles and rules of knowing—that calcify a commitment to an epistemological tract that profits from replicating itself. By unveiling this system, she draws attention to the conditions through which the epistemologies of les damnés are made. The epistemologies of les damnés do not seek to arrive at a perfect or true definition of the Human, for there is no Human "out there" beyond the Western imperial concept of Man/Human from the Renaissance on.

Vitruvian Man and 1492

Sylvia Wynter's decolonial project understands that the European Renaissance stamped a concept of Man that brought together the colonization of time, the colonization of space, and the perfection of geometric forms that have been immortalized in the famous *Vitruvian Man*, drawn by Leonardo de Vinci circa 1487–1490. The correlations in this image between the Human body and the universe hide the fact that the body depicted and the experience upon which Leonardo was relying was a Greco-Roman concept of the human figure. The complicity between colonization of time (specifically detaching Man/Human from a Christian medieval idea of human dependency from God) and the colonization of space (specifically the emergence of "Indians" in the European consciousness coupled with the image of Africans, as descendants of Ham, already embedded in the consciousness of European Christians) prompted a system of categories to emerge: derived from Greek and Latin, this system disqualified Africans from Humanness (thus rendering them appropriate for enslavement) and excluded Indians from the proportions, rationality, and knowledge of God.

Wynter's writings demonstrate that Western epistemology built itself on a concept of Human and Humanity that, in turn, served to legitimate the epistemic foundation that created it. That is, Human and Humanity were created as the enunciated *that projects and propels to universality the local image* of the enunciator. The enunciator assumes, and thus postulates, that his concept of Human and Humanity is valid for every human being on the planet. However, once the universality of the Human has been postulated— and we encounter this formulation in many official documents telling us that humans are "all born equal"—hierarchies are needed and put into place to establish differences between all who were "born equal." Indeed, after we are born, we inhabit a world made of inequality. The discourse that "we are all born equal" is inflected with practices of inequity that shape how we live in the world differentially. The mirage of totality—of epistemic totality that is laden with seeming egalitarian open-mindedness entrenched in our various birthrights—is the trap that Wynter has not only recognized but also struggled against.

Columbus's arrival in the Americas in 1492 and other voyages outside of Europe are landmarks of the moment in which the concepts of Man and of Human became one and the same and, at the same time, came to be understood in relation to race and racism. The epistemology from which Indians were observed and described was, of course, not the epistemology of the Indians. And, given that the arrival of Columbus and his contemporaries did not, in fact, correspond to the worldview of the Indians (and the rest of the non-European world), New World subjects did not imagine that they were being classified by a structure of knowledge that will soon become both hegemonic and dominant. With this in mind, racism and epistemology become part of the package whose point of reference is Man-as-Human—a reference point that corresponds to Wynter's project to move "beyond Man, toward the Human," which can be found across her works. By uncoupling Man (the Vitruvian Man) as a model of Humanity, the point is not to find the true and objective definition of "what is Human," but to show that such projects are filled with an imperial bend, a will to objectivity and truth—a truth that, as Maturana explains, bolsters the belief system that supports such an epistemology.

The year 1492 is, for many, a turning point in the history of the world. Sylvia Wynter and many black intellectuals (such as C. L. R. James, George Lamming, Wilson Harris, Aimé Césaire, Frantz Fanon, and so forth) draw attention to the significance of plantations and *palenques* and *kilombos*, colonization, nationalism and independence, gender, and the state in relation to fifteenth-century global processes. The fundamental issue underlying this intellectual tradition of rereading European encounters in the Americas is not class or hegemony or subalternity but rather the question, What does it mean to be human? The year 1492 is also a turning point for the Indigenous populations of the Americas and for South American Jews—as has been recently strongly and convincingly argued by Santiago Slabodsky.[2] Indeed, Jewish history intersecting with 1492 underlines the significance of this fracture in world history. Indians and Africans were, so to speak, absent from written, printed, and distributed history at the time—certainly, toward the end of fifteenth century, each coexisting civilization had its own ways of documenting and dealing with the past. But "history" (Greek *istorein* translated into Latin as *historia*) became an anchor word of Western civilizations, including the narrative of the origins told in the Old and New Testaments. Thus, the triad of *istorein*, translated into *historia*, was coupled with the origin narrative embedded in the Bible *and* the consequent secularization of knowledge. In other words, both the sacred and secular, in Hegel's canonical lesson in the philosophy of history, set the stage for the belief that the *facts* narrated were ontologically independent of the narrative itself.[3]

Why is this important? Because in 1492 there is a bifurcation of history that is particularly clear in the case of enslaved Africans, aboriginals (named "Indians"), and Jews. It is the moment, as Carl Schmitt explains, in which "global linear thinking" is defined and linked to the creation of international law.[4] This moment also created and implemented external and internal colonial differences: Indians and blacks were cast as inferior beings outside of

Europe; they were deemed without religion and at the mercy of the Devil. "Global linear thinking" traced the lines in land and sea *and* racial lines. Within these geographic and racial paradigms, and due to the logic of internal colonization within Christian Europe, Jews were portrayed as suspicious beings with the wrong religion. In 1492, Jewish history took a detour and became entangled with the history of Indians and enslaved Africans in the New World: in 1492, Spanish Jewish communities were forced to convert, were expelled, or were killed under the Edict of Expulsion, enacted by Ferdinand and Isabella. Thousands of Jewish exiles fled to South America. This is a point that Slabodsky clearly understood and that, surprisingly, Jonathan Boyarin—in a concerted effort to undermine the turning point that 1492 was for Indians (who described it as *Pachacuti*/the world turned upside down)—failed to see.[5] For these populations, including the populations of European descent in South and Central America and the Caribbean, 1492 is the date that marks history, memory, and being in the modern/colonial world order. While such narratives and experiences are certainly diverse, given the very different homelands of Europe, Africa, the Caribbean, and so forth, 1492 unfolds into a series of meaningful and interlocking moments: it is the date that marked the expulsion from paradise, it is the date that prompted the advent and the formation of coloniality or the colonial matrix of power and modern/colonial racism and contemporary articulations of race and racism, and it is the date through which the invention of the modern/colonial Other ascended.[6]

Wynter's contribution to the rethinking of 1492, coloniality, race, and humanness is radical in that her work demonstrates how one can perceive the world with one's eyes (a Western imperial weapon) as one feels the weight of the modern-colonial world in the body as that body dwells in the legacies of colonial histories. If Wynter took from Maturana his radical epistemic shift, and called into question the aims and scaffolding of philosophy and science, she turned to C. L. R. James to meet him in the same struggle: the Afro-Caribbean epistemic revolution against the Eurocentric concept of "Man" and its role in the construction of racism.

Wynter's Epistemic Shift through James's Counterdoctrine

Sylvia Wynter's long, well-researched, and highly insightful articles form a network, wherein her ideas and writings are in conversation with and refer back (and forth) to one another. You can enter the network through engaging with any of her articles and essays, and I will enter through her article on C. L. R. James, "Beyond the Categories of the Master Conception: The Counterdoctrine of Jamesian Poiesis."[7] One of the reasons I am interested in this work is that C. L. R. James has been read, particularly in the United States, as primarily a Marxist thinker due to his *Notes on Dialectics* (1948) and his *State Capitalism and World Revolution* (1950)—even though his allegiance to Marxism is only partial.[8] Wynter unravels the complexity of the ways in which James's thought is anchored in the history and experience of the slave trade—and thus the fifteenth and sixteenth centuries—noticing that his sole preoccupation is not with the emergence of the proletarian consciousness and the Commune and the coup of 18 Brumaire. Wynter puts it in this way:

> The starting point for James's displacement/incorporation of the labor conceptual framework is his insistence on the seminal importance of the trade in African slaves. In particular, he wants to end its repression in normative Western conceptual frames . . . what Wallerstein has called the world system was constituted by James as above all a single network of accumulation. This network can be divided into three phases: (1) circulation for accumulation; (2) production for accumulation; and (3) consumption for accumulation. In each of these phases . . . the source of extractive value . . . [are] different. In the first, it was the African slave, in the second, the working class, and in the third and current phase, it has been the consumer.[9]

These three stages are the core of what Wynter describes as James's counterdoctrine. Yet James's counterdoctrine, she argues, also emerges from his willingness to view and think theoretics and aesthetics *together*. A Jamesian aesthetic and theoretic doctrine emerges, then, in the questioning of "the dictatorship of the master conceptions of Liberalism and Marxism."[10] To understand the Jamesian doctrine, "it is necessary to look at the semiotic foundations of bourgeois thought, the monarchical system of power it delegitimated, and the liberal state it helped to establish."[11]

Wynter's analysis of the Jamesian doctrine runs parallel to the arguments advanced by the collective workings of modernity/coloniality/decoloniality.[12] Wynter argues that in order for power to be effective, it has to have, within it, discursive legitimization. As we have learned from Michel Foucault, and Wynter follows suit, discursive formations go hand in hand with institution-building: "Cultural conceptions, encoded in language and other signifying systems, shape the development of political structures and are also shaped by them. *The cultural aspects of power* are as original as the structural aspects; each serves as a code for the other's development. *It is from these elementary cultural conceptions that complex legitimating discourses are constructed.*"[13] Thus, the complicity between institution-building and legitimizing discourses allowed an ethno-class (Wynter's term), the European bourgeoisie, to displace the monarchy and the hegemony of aristocratic classes. And Wynter explains: "It was not enough to gain politico-economic dominance. It was also necessary to replace the formal monarchical system of signification with a cultural model that 'selected' its values as normative. The elementary cultural conceptions upon which the monarchical system of signification rested can be designated as 'the symbolics of blood.'"[14]

Wynter focuses on the paradigmatic change, in the internal history of Europe, between the monarchic and the bourgeois ethno-classes, and brings into focus the ways in which broad intellectual, social, and geographic shifts—during the Renaissance, between the European Middle Ages and the Renaissance monarchic system—are due, in great part, to the emergence of sixteenth-century Atlantic commercial circuits and the changes this generated in Europe itself. More specifically, she underscores the first moment of accumulation as it is tied to the exploitation of labor and the initiation of the modern/colonial slave trade Atlantic triangle. Here Wynter's argument recognizes the ways in which the massive exploitation of labor corresponds to the massive appropriation of land. The colonization, expropriation, and violence directed at lands and peoples engendered a new type of economy based on the reinvestments of gain and the impulse to increase production that would create and satisfy a global market. In Wynter's analyses, "capitalism," as we know it, is revealed to be *one* economic *aspect* of the emerging colonial matrix of power; this framework, in turn, challenges analyses that focus solely on the capitalist underpinnings of the slave trade and land exploitation by delineating features, particularly those brought into view by non-Europeans, that are not simply driven by economic matters (cultural practices, social exchanges, political shifts).

Wynter's analysis thus seeks to think through the nuances of colonial encounter with and beyond a capitalist frame. Indeed, she reveals that the economy of colonialism, alone, analytically belies a much broader narrative of coloniality and encounter. This framework lends to her reading of C. L. R. James. Wynter removes James from Marxists' co-option and describes his thinking by reading his life through a "pieza conceptual frame."[15] But what is the "pieza conceptual frame"? The "pieza," Wynter tells us, was the name given by the Portuguese during the slave trade to the African who functioned as the standard measure. A pieza "was a man of twenty-five years, approximately, in good health, calculated to give a certain amount of physical labor value against which all the others could be measured—with for example, three teenagers equaling one pieza and older men and women thrown in a job lot as refuse."[16] Wynter suggests that in the "Jamesian system, the pieza becomes an ever-more general category of value, establishing equivalences between a wider variety of oppressed labor power."[17]

The "pieza," then, can be seen as the anchor, the reference point for a sensibility that emerged in the sixteenth century alongside the conquest of the Caribbean islands, Anáhuac and Tawantinsuyu; it is a measure, furthermore, that did not exist before conquest and that set in motion what today we call "capitalism." This specific sensibility was the facility through which the ruling class, the merchant class, and conquistadores could build an institution and a legitimating discourse that made certain human lives were dispensable vis-à-vis differential categories of value—from the symbolic of blood (the monarchic moment) to the symbolic of skin color (the secular moment whose foundation was established in the Spanish colonies in the sixteenth and seventeenth centuries).[18]

The metaphoric and methodological uses of "pieza" trouble Marxist-oriented analyses that suggest that slavery and racism play a secondary role in the constitution of capitalism. For this reason, Wynter argues that "the pieza frame" requires a repositioning of the mode of production in relation to the mode of domination in which the former becomes a subset of the latter. Connecting this framework to James's theoretics—noticing James's system as a remark on the significance of the pieza system—is a way of rethinking European analyses of capitalism. As Wynter writes, "economic exploitation only follows on, and does not precede, the mode of domination set in motion by the *imaginaire social* of the bourgeoisie. Consequently, the capitalist mode of production is a subset of the bourgeois mode of accumulation which constitutes the basis of the middle-class hegemony."[19]

Here is precisely where the Afro-Caribbean analysis set in motion by C. L. R. James and the modernity/coloniality perspective set in motion by Anibal Quijano join forces, with both outlooks maintaining their respective local histories in the modern/colonial world *with* the broader singular experiencing of the colonial wound. A black in the Caribbean and a mestizo in the Andes are not the same "rank" in the modern/racial classification, yet they are sensitive to and aware of the colonial wound; they are cognizant of the simple fact that one does not see and feel capitalism in the same way across time and space and thus across different colonial settings. Instead, what you see and feel from different and differential colonial places is the colonial matrix of power of which the economy is only one component: domination precedes accumulation, and domination needs a cultural model or a colonial matrix that legitimizes and naturalizes exploitation. The mode of production is a subset of the mode of domination. And, the mode of domination has been set, transformed, and maintained in the colonial matrix. In the colonial matrix, the legitimizing discourse encompasses authority, gender and sexuality, knowledge and subjectivity, authority and economic organization. In short, Wynter shows us that the Marxist analysis focuses on economic organization, while the pieza frame and the colonial matrix focus on the layered workings of colonial praxis—with the "cultural model" of Europeanness overriding (although not erasing) the perspective of those it marginalizes.

Wynter's Epistemic Shift through Fanon's Sociogenesis

To delink and decolonize means to adumbrate what was hidden and ignored—and to do this is to recognize, extend, and invent new concepts. In nineteenth-century Europe, where the "capitalist" economy was dominant, Marx's "surplus value" and Freud's "unconscious" became concepts that were firmly embedded in the internal organization of Europe itself. While both proved to be inadequate descriptive statements, Frantz Fanon utilized them concomitantly to work through the complexities of coloniality, subjectivity, and liberation. It is through Fanon—and his now much cited statement that "beside phylogeny and ontogeny stands sociogeny"— that Wynter develops the sociogenic principle.[20] The sociogenic principle is the process of languaging and knowing. It uncovers the differential workings of power embedded in the ranking of languages in the modern/colonial world order. As Fanon writes: "To speak means to be in a position to use a certain syntax, to grasp the morphology of this or that language, but it means above all to assume a culture, to support the weight of a civilization. . . . The Negro of the Antilles will be proportionately whiter—that is, he will be closer to being a real human being—in direct ratio with his mastery of the French language. A man who has a language consequently possesses the world expressed and implied in that language. . . . Mastery of language affords remarkable power."[21]

Sylvia Wynter extends and enhances Fanon's sociogenic principle by envisioning a *scientia* (and I write it in the Renaissance style to distinguish it from the concept of *science* that unfolded from Galileo to Newton and from Newton to Einstein; and from Buffon and Linnaeus to Darwin). Or, more aptly, this area of her work can be posited as *decolonial scientia* based on Fanon's sociogenic principle. Fanon's hypothesis, Wynter argues, is groundbreaking because it is derived from his awareness of reporting in the *third* person, his own experience in the *first* person ("Look, a Negro"!).[22] The experience he tracks, in other words, is of *Being* through the eyes of the imperial Other. Here he uncovers the *experience* of *knowing* that he is being perceived, in the eyes of the imperial Other, as not quite human. Thus, the *decolonial scientia* is the *scientia* needed not simply for progress or development but for liberating the actual and future victims of knowledge for progress and development. This does not reveal a case for *studying the Negro problem* from the perspective of any of the already established social sciences or humanities — for, if that were the case, sociogenesis would become an *object* of study rather than *being the historical foundation and constitution of future and global loci of enunciation*. This *scientia*, built upon the sociogenic principle (in this case the lived experience of the black man, although this is not the only colonial experience or colonial wound that would sustain the emerging *scientia*), makes clear from the start that the mind/body problem (or the soul/body if we take a step back from secularism to Christian theology) *only makes sense in the domain of ontogenesis*. Put differently, the sociogenic principle reveals what the ontogenesis principle hides: that race is not in the body but rather is built in the social imaginary grounded on colonial differences. Wynter follows Fanon by setting the limits of ontogenesis: ontogenesis is an imperial category while sociogenesis introduces the perspective of the subject that ontogenesis classifies as object.[23] It is from sociogenesis that concepts such as "double consciousness" and "border epistemology" come into clear view. The concept of sociogenesis underlines that: I am who I am in relation to the other who sees me as such; and, in a society structured upon racial hierarchies, becoming black is bound up with being perceived as black by a white person (as Fanon understood that he *was* black, according to the child's and the mother's eyes, in the oft cited train scene in "The Fact of Blackness"). This process of being seen and seeing oneself is sociogenesis or DuBoisian double consciousness. The sociogenic principle is not introduced as an object of knowledge but rather as a locus of enunciation that links knowledge with decolonial subjective formations.

If modern/imperial epistemology (in its diversity, but always imperial diversity) and *scientia* were spatially, chronologically, and subjectively located vis-à-vis the sociogenic principle, the project of *decolonial scientia* would emerge and recontextualize our global nodes of space, time, and subjectivity. To recast space, chronology, and subjectivity through sociogeny and think about *decolonial scientia* can be imagined as follows:

a) Spatially: *decolonial scientia* is located at the borders (territorial as well as linguistic, subjective, epistemic, ontological) and created by the consolidation and expansion of the modern/colonial epistemic matrix. This matrix emerged in the sixteenth century and was guided by theology and attendant imperial/colonial connections between Atlantic Europe and the Americas. These processes folded and unfolded, in the hands of England and France, and were projected into/onto Asia and Africa, from the late seventeenth century to the mid-twentieth century. This framework was later taken up by the United States and evidenced the ways in which the basic principles and structures of knowledge were expanded by the use of the English language and the meteoric enlargement of scientific knowledge and technology. Consequently, *decolonial scientia* is literally all over the globe, in the same way that modern/imperial science is, and it moves constantly from the "third" to the "first" world, and from the latest Western imperial countries to the "emerging empires."[24]

b) Chronologically: *decolonial scientia* regionalizes—on the one hand—the chronological line of the imperial matrix of knowledge. This reveals the ways in which Europeans themselves conceived, narrated, and practiced their own conception of knowledge. And, *decolonial scientia* reorganizes—on the other hand—chronology into global space. In imperial scientia connections through time, including epistemic breaks and paradigmatic changes, followed one another in a linear fashion. *Decolonial scientia* links the space of colonial and decolonial struggles around the world to recent large-scale migrations of the "barbarians" to the "civilized regions."

c) Subjectively: *decolonial scientia* draws attention to colonial subjects or modern subjects that detach themselves from imperial knowledge and subjectivity. Contrary to the male, Christian, and Eurocentric subjects and subjectivities that dominated the structure of modern/imperial knowledge systems, the decolonial subject is at the border of non-European languages, religions, epistemologies (and thus subjects that have been categorized, through imperial knowledge, as racially subordinate, sexually deviant, economically disadvantaged, and so forth), and imperial subjects who, instead of "saving the colonial Other" through themselves, join and accept the guidance of the decolonial subjectivity.

Decolonial scientia puts forth three types of tasks. First, it reimagines rather than denies the links between geo-history and knowledge and between biography and knowledge. Second, it explores the consequences that Western expansion (today called "globalization") had and continues to have for the population and the environment (exploitation of natural resources, for example, as *needed* by imperial economy). This emphasizes the ways in which both particular lands and peoples have been and are targeted for conversion to Christianity, conversion to civilization, to development models, and, most recently, *for* human rights and democracy. With this in mind, it is necessary to look at responses globally and avoid the imperial trap that looks at *local responses* to *global designs*. Third, *decolonial scientia* generates knowledge to build communities in which life (in general) has priority over economic gains, economic growth, and economic development. This is knowledge that will subject economic growth to human needs rather than submit human needs to economic growth and development.

What Is It Like to Be Human? Sociogenesis and Coloniality of Being

In her rehistorization of the human, Wynter distinguishes between two kinds of histories. One is the history of the emergence and spread, on planet earth, of living organisms (and, with this, the overrepresentation of Man-as-Human in postmedieval and modern epochs). The second history is that of the sociohistorical *conditions* that made it possible for the elite of European Man to construct such an idea — of Man-as-Human — and to be successful in implementing it. As she notes, the *idea* of Man at a particular moment of world history, the European Renaissance, was also the foundational step for building racism as we sense and know it today.[25] This rehistorization of the human shifted the geography of reason. Instead of accepting that there is a universal perspective provided by Man's consciousness and imploring it to be recognized in the house of Humanity, Wynter shifts the perspective, thus rehistorizing what it means to be human from within the perspective of sociogenesis, double consciousness, and, I would add, *la conciencia de la mestiza*. In her work there is not a claim for recognition *within* the hegemonic concept of Humanity but a claim for recognition that the imperial (racist and patriarchal) concept of Man/Human is no longer sustainable. In Wynter's words, outlining the inventions of Man should be accompanied by the history of living organisms of the human species and alternative stories:

> It is the story in which the idea of humanism, of its de-godding of our modes of self-inscription first erupts, where Man and its human Others—that is, Indians, Negros, Natives (and I would add, Jews and Muslims)—are first invented. And this history is the history of the expansion of the West from the fifteenth century onwards, and an expansion that is carried out within the terms of its own cultural conception of its own origins. And you see, it is this ethnoculturally coded narrated history that is taught both in a now global academia as well as in all our schools, while it is this history in whose now purely secular terms we are all led to imagine ourselves as Man, as purely biological and economic beings. The *history* for Man, therefore, narrated and existentially lived as if it were the *history-for* the human itself.[26]

Crucial in Wynter's statement is her concept of *history-for*. It is through this concept that she is able to show the ways in which the local concept of Man/Human and its imperial universality puts out of consideration any other self-conceptualization in languages and civilizations that were not Greek and Latin and thus based in Western Christendom. What Wynter calls "human" (without capitals) and the attendant story of the spread of the human species around the planet from their originary site of becoming—what is now known as Africa—are complemented by Iranian philosopher Ali Shari'ati's assertion that in the Qur'an a distinction is made between *Bashar* (being) and *Ensan* (becoming). In this conceptualization we (humans in noncapitals) are all Bashar; we are collectively that species of living organisms that spread around the planet from times immemorial, thousands of years ago, many centuries before the elite of the European Renaissance classified themselves as Man/Human and disregarded those who fell outside of this category. Bashar (being) and Ensan (becoming) are explained by Shari'ati as this: "The difference between Ensan, Bashar and all the other natural phenomena such as animals, trees, etc., is that all are 'beings' except Ensan who is 'becoming.' . . . But man in the sense of the exalting truth, towards whom we must constantly strive and struggle in becoming, consists of divine characteristics that we must work for as our ideal characteristics. . . . Mind you that becoming Ensan is not a stationary event, rather, it is a perpetual process of becoming and an everlasting evolution towards infinity."[27]

I am not offering this definition as a replacement for the Christian humanist definitions. I am just noting that Shari'ati has the same right to be wrong as the European humanists. In other words, I am underscoring that each definition is *truth-for* and moving toward pluriversality and thus seeks to delink from the belief and expectation of universality. And this assertion cannot be made from the perspective of *humanitas* if it is maintained as the point of reference to which one has to aspire. Decolonial thinking and living are not to assimilate but to deny the universal pretense of *humanitas*.

The problem Wynter and all of us face is that we (and I mean all those who are not fully incorporated in the Western construction of Man/Human, that is, all of the "we" who do not identify as Human because "we" have been placed outside of it) have to work through, confront, and engage the concept of Man/Human in order to crack the Vitruvian circle in which Leonardo has depicted the visual image of Man/Human. This working through, confrontation, and engagement require border thinking or border epistemology. Now we (you, reader, and me) must be ready to go into Wynter's *truth-for* and its theoretical, political, and ethical implications. Notice first the Western conditions in which Man/Human emerged. Wynter puts it as follows:

> The issue of race as the issue of the Colonial Question, the Nonwhite-Native Question, the Negro Question, yet as one that has hitherto had no name, was and is fundamentally the issue of the genre of human, Man, in its two variants. The clash between Las Casas and Sepúlveda was a clash over this issue—the clash as to whether the primary generic identity should continue to be that of Las Casas's theocentric Christian, or that of the newly invented Man of the humanists, as the rational (or ratiocentric) political subject of the state. . . . And this clash was to be all the more deep-seated in that the humanists, while going back to the classics and to other pre-Christian sources in order to find a model of being human alternative to the one in whose terms the lay world was necessarily subordinated, had effected their now new conception and its related "formulation of a general order of existence" only by transuming that of the Church's matrix Judeo-Christian conception, thereby carrying over the latter's schematic structure, as well as many of its residual meanings.[28]

Truth-for is a crucial piece of Wynter's argument, and it is the hinge that connects the two stories through the racial contours of colonialism: the global story of the human species and the local story of the European Renaissance Man/Human that appropriated and universalized the first. The starting assumption in her thinking is that "every form of life, every living species would now be able to know its reality only in terms of its specific truth-for."[29] This premise *already* questions the assumption that there is a truth-for someone who can know the truth-for everyone else. For Wynter the premise that every living species has its own *truth-for* applies to the particular species we are now referring to as humans: the species that can semiotize, that is, translate into audible or visible signs, its own conception of its own being as a species and its place among other species:

> For example, before the voyages of the Portuguese and Columbus we can say that all geographies, whatever their great success in serving human needs, had been ethnogeographies—geographical *truth-for* a genre of human. Before Copernicus, the same—all astronomies by means of which humans had regulated and legitimated their societies had been, in their last instance, ethnoastronomies. Before Darwin, again, the same thing. Knowledge of biological forms of life had been, in spite of their great value for human needs, ethnobiologies. And now the rupture with these forms of *truth-for* is going to be made possible only by means of the two intellectual revolutions of humanism, the first which took place in the Renaissance Europe, the second which took place at the end of the eighteenth century in Great Britain. . . . Or to put it more precisely, in our case, an ethno-class or Western bourgeois form of humanism, whose *truth-for* at the level of social reality is truth for Man cannot be truth for the human.[30]

The main task of Sylvia Wynter during the past thirty or more years, at least since the publication of "Ethno or Socio Poetics" (1976), has been to erode the foundation of the Western imperial (racial and patriarchal) concept of Man/Human.[31] Two pillars in her conceptual genealogy of thoughts that clearly stand out are her analyses, rethinking, and utilization of the ideas advanced by C. L. R. James and Humberto Maturana. From James, and the black and Caribbean intellectual tradition (see also Eudell in this volume), she calls into question the white, post-Renaissance concept of Man/Human. From Maturana, she posits that "creation" of the image of the world is the result of autopoietic (self-generating) processes and links this to the work of Frantz Fanon and the repetitive constitution of Man-as-Human. What she proposes, overall, is a shattering of the imperial concept of Humanity based on the ideal of White Man, and to reconceptualize it not by providing a new definition or image but by starting with the question: What does it mean to be Human? Wynter follows this by thinking through that which we have inherited from imperial Europe, the possibilities and limitations of purely Western science and knowledge systems, and how humanness can be recognized as connective and interhuman. With this, it is crucial to take away the right that an ethno-class attributed to itself to "possess" or embody the truth of what Human is and means. Wynter's argument calls for a radical delinking from that myth and the urgent need to move in a different direction. Wynter summarizes this project in a famous sentence: "Towards the Human, after Man."[32]

Notes

1. I have capitalized "Human" and "Humanity" here to draw attention to what Wynter refers to as the descriptive statement that reinvented Man-as-Human under the colonial-biocentric model. See Wynter, "Unsettling the Coloniality of Being," 263–264.
2. Slabodsky, "De-colonial Jewish Thought and the Americas," 269–290.
3. Hegel, *Philosophy of Right.*
4. Schmitt, *The Nomos of the Earth in the International Law of the Ius Publicum Europaeum.*
5. Boyarin, *The Unconverted Self.*
6. Murena, *El pecado original de América*; Quijano and Wallerstein, "Americanity as a Concept," 549–557; Dussel, *The Invention of the Americas.* In terms of racism and its contemporary articulations, I suggest along with others that "racism" as we sense it today emerged in 1492. Greek and Aztec cultures differentiated between themselves and "foreigners" (the barbarians, the Chichimecas) for example, thus drawing attention to ethnic classifications. But racism, as we sense it today, goes hand in hand with the historical foundation of capitalism (which neither Greeks nor Aztecs knew). See Mignolo, "Racism as We Sense It Today," 1737–1742.
7. Wynter, "Beyond the Categories of the Master Conception," 63–91.
8. James, *Notes on Dialectics*; James, *State Capitalism and World Revolution.* It would be helpful for the reader to also remember Antonio Gramsci's work. It is clear that the problems that James and Gramsci have with Marxism—rather than with Marx—are related to their respective embodied histories: a white from southern Italy who writes about "the Southern Question" and a Black Caribbean for whom "the Human Question" and racism are of primary concern. Both kinds of experience were off the Marxists' radar.
9. Wynter, "Beyond the Categories of the Master Conception," 81–82.
10. Wynter, "Beyond the Categories of the Master Conception," 65.
11. Wynter, "Beyond the Categories of the Master Conception," 65.

12. For an overview, see Mignolo and Escobar, *Globalization and the Decolonial Option.*

13. Wynter, "Beyond the Categories of the Master Conception," 65 (emphasis added).

14. Wynter, "Beyond the Categories of the Master Conception," 65.

15. James, *C. L. R. James and Revolutionary Marxism*; Wynter, "Beyond the Categories of the Master Conception," 73.

16. Wynter, "Beyond the Categories of the Master Conception," 81

17. Wynter, "Beyond the Categories of the Master Conception," 81.

18. Castro-Gómez, *La Hybris del Punto Cero*; Mignolo, *The Idea of Latin America,* chapter 2.

19. Wynter, "Beyond the Categories of the Master Conception," 81 (emphasis added).

20. Fanon, *Black Skin, White Masks,* 11.

21. Fanon, *Black Skin, White Masks,* 17–18.

22. Fanon, *Black Skin, White Masks,* 109.

23. Wynter, "Towards the Sociogenic Principle," 30–66.

24. Such as China, Russia, and perhaps in the near future, India and the Islamic Middle East; further in the future, one can see that in the Andes, under the leadership of Bolivia, the model of Tawantinsuyu will interact with the model of the liberal/colonial state as well.

25. Mignolo, *"Racism as We Sense It Today,"* 1737–1742.

26. Scott, "The Re-enchantment of Humanism," 198.

27. Shari'ati, "Modern Man and His Prisons," 47.

28. Wynter, "Unsettling the Coloniality of Being," 288.

29. Scott, "The Re-enchantment of Humanism," 196.

30. Scott, "The Re-enchantment of Humanism," 196 (emphasis added).

31. Wynter, "Ethno or Socio Poetics," 78–94.

32. Taken from Wynter's article title "Unsettling the Coloniality of Being," 257–337.

5 STILL SUBMERGED
The Uninhabitability of Urban Redevelopment

Sylvia Wynter's genuinely heretical essay "1492: A New World View" maps, unsettles, and pushes us beyond the geo-racial syntax undergirding post-Enlightenment configurations of humanness.[1] In this essay, Wynter chronicles how Columbus's voyages unraveled Europe's pre-1492 geographic schemas (which rested upon an ostensible bifurcation between the European temperate zone and the *other* torrid zone and between what constituted a geographic site of habitability as opposed to an "ungeographic" site of uninhabitability). This geographic reconfiguration prompted by "discoveries" of 1492 also produced new corporeal codes and ways of knowing that Wynter captures in the simple term "Man."[2] Wynter argues that Columbus's insistence on geographic homogeneity—the capacity for all lands to be inhabited, subjugated, and rationally known by the feudal European "we" of Western European, Christian, heterosexual, aristocratic (and soon bourgeois) men—arose only through ontological compromise: the cross-application of now obsolete geographic distinctions (temperate/torrid) onto racialized human classificatory models in the production and meaning of self/other.

In this essay, I extend Wynter's metacartography of Man and *les damnés de la terre*/the wretched of the earth, and thus the now normalized Cartesian production of and development of space, by looking toward contemporary debates over the urban.[3] Taking as my focus the teleological parade known as urban redevelopment and renewal, I interrogate the current "epistemological resignation"[4] that marks far too much scholarly research on urbanity. Given the overwhelming academic consensus in favor of "deconcentration of poverty" campaigns and urban renaissance initiatives, my aim is to confront and denaturalize these central premises of urban studies. Noting the epistemological illegibility and silence enshrouding the forced displacement, mass imprisonment, and state and epistemic violence facing urban, low-capital communities of color, I turn to Wynter's meditations on the intersections between notions of habitability and gauges of humanness.[5]

I situate this line of inquiry in and around post-Katrina New Orleans, drawing upon notions of contamination, deluge, and purification. I argue that the always already defiled status of black geographies and corporealities within scholarly literature (and far beyond) sustains the synaptic workings of the dominant episteme that was ushered in by the encounters of 1492. My aim is to explore the ways in which narratives of contamination serve as an auto-instituting trope for knowing and regulating this postdisaster city. It is important to note here that I am intentionally noticing a thread, anchored by discourses that link blackness to dispossession, across different eras and notable historic moments: feudal spatial organization, 1492/conquest, Victorian ethicality, 1960s struggles, 1980s responses to supply-side economics, Katrina and neoliberal recovery projects, and post-Obama poverty. This is not to conflate these particular moments and suggest that black dispossession and other modes of living remain the same across time and space, but rather to bring into focus how the narratives that collide with the (pure and impure) economics of city life—and Katrina/New Orleans—can, from one view, offer a useful/workable generalization about black geographies that, as we grapple with race, sheds light on a curious consistency grounded in black contamination.

The Katrina event was fodder to a discourse of contamination already written into the foundations of New Orleans. With racial and sexual transgression constitutive of the historical-geographic workings of New Orleans, the city has long been as threatened and enlivened by the defilement of the body politic as it has by the cyclical depositing of effluvium by an outraged and unwieldy Mississippi.[6] Katrina's floodwaters unlocked these meanings, buoying not only bodies, cars, and homes but also a matrix of multiple and contradictory understandings of disaster reflected by a question posed repeatedly and apprehensively by the media: What is in the water? The answer was laden with the polluted confirmation of oil dependencies, climate change, and centuries of precarious city expansion and marshland depletion, yes, but it also gnawed at contradictions that delve deeper than these often depoliticized narratives of green (un)sustainability might suggest. Images of a water-blanketed city consolidated memories of the past's forced migrations and extirpations, calling forth the biblical Flood along-side slave ships, Emmett Till's corpse being dragged out of the neighboring Tallahatchie River alongside Hurricane Betsy's obliteration of the Ninth Ward in 1965. Katrina's water figured as a substance of sojourn, alienation, and death in a space whose bedrock was cast out of black bodies as slaves. This meaning was produced contemporaneously with reincarnations of bourgeois Victorian hysterics over cholera and other waterborne diseases, anxieties that conveyed racialized, apocalyptic visions of a disordered urban void.[7] Contaminating floodwater merged with tainting body, prompting the unasked questions: Are black bodies and spaces really vulnerable to tox-ins? Can a black body—the raw material for dysgenic narratives of racial apocalypse—be further contaminated?

The Katrina moment thus symbolized a dreadful and alarming contra-vention of the optimal status criterion of disciplined, gridded urbanity. Accordingly, this dreaded and racially coded understanding of the event shaped popular responses. Relief and reconstruction efforts over the next few weeks and years operated and pronounced their legitimacy through the tangible and metaphoric meanings now owned by this shocking and anar-chic Muck. Contamination not only became and remains a keyword of the post-Katrina era, but contamination is itself constitutive of the technologies and ideologies that characterize the ongoing social and geographic struggles within New Orleans. Deployed by a multiplicity of positionalities, contam-ination is the common discursive ground for conflicts over the state and future of the city.

Not at all particular to New Orleans, this semiotics of blight and purity is a foundational trope of dominant urban knowledges. The first overriding apriorism of contemporary urban studies (as well as geographic, anthro-pological, and sociological research on urbanity), whether emanating from liberal or conservative positions, is that "concentrated poverty" is an uncon-ditional evil of the cityscape.[8] Most often associated with the language of contamination—"blight," "pollution," "disease," "weeds"—concentrations of poverty invoke some of the most vilified images within the urban imagi-nary. The dominant mode of subjective understanding knows these spaces and their residents as simultaneously contaminated and contaminant. A no-tion that dates back at least to late nineteenth-century, Victorian concerns about city purity in an age of cholera, tuberculosis, typhoid, and smallpox, the employment of metaphors of contamination remains a central operat-ing mechanism for the contemporary city. Urban "homeplaces" define—

geographically, corporeally, and metaphorically—what it is to be impure and liminal.[9] Most frequently, dominant debates around concentrated poverty assume as self-evident the despicable nature of these geographies and the *inhuman* ("ghetto-specific") behaviors that are naturalized to them.[10] These assumptions are rarely challenged; instead, they serve as the self-evident foundations of any scholarly investigation. Out of these naturalized doxa spring forth an abundance of scholarly arguments surrounding the origins, implications, and nature of concentrated poverty.

The relatively uncontested epistemological constructions surrounding concentrated poverty carry tremendous ramifications in the realm of urban policy. Since geographies of concentrated poverty are by definition *uninhabitable*, it follows that poverty should be "deconcentrated." This ubiquitous trope of urban studies represents the second major premise of most scholarly research conducted around urban homeplaces. Deconcentration of poverty is not only the preferred treatment for what is often naturalized as a *disease* afflicting the "inner city," it is posited as the only imaginable treatment. Scholarly and political consensus around this avowedly deracialized initiative borders on absolute; the debate occurs not over this particular modus but rather over its methodology and ramifications.

Referred to here as the *deconcentration paradigm*, this set of theoretical and practical components constitutes a system of symbolic representations through which urban spaces and bodies are understood and contextualized. I argue that deconcentration of poverty is nothing other than spatial and bodily *purification of blackness* and the environmental conditions associated with this racial classification.[11] This geo-racial motion is, in many ways, in direct lineage with auto-instituting premises that have marked dominant European conceptions of American land since the events of and following 1492. The urban homeplace is painted as the new American frontier, the potentially profitable and undoubtedly treacherous landscape whose every street corner gains its meaning from specific modes of racialized thinking derivative of American conquest and subjugation / dismemberment of people of color. Yet within the logic of twenty-first-century multicultural doxa, these highly racialized spaces—landscape known by phenotype and phenotype known by landscape, to paraphrase Katherine McKittrick—can only be represented by race-blind language. In this post-1960s Obama moment, the language of poverty has usurped all resonance from the language of race, enabling vigorously deracialized concepts—"concentrated poverty," the "underclass"—to acquire their "unimaginably black"[12] racial signification only through what is unpronounced and whispered in scholarly or political discourses, or sirened in the mass media.

Once understood as a racial project, the deconcentration of poverty can be more appropriately conceptualized as an exercise in spatial and bodily *purification* than an exercise of *gentrification*. The latter often presumes that market logics alone govern the postmodern city. Yet the new trends in population geography and cultural phenomenology that characterize postmodern urban space—a reversal of white and middle-class flight back into the urban core, principles of new urbanism, sustainability, and self-help, and a revival of hipness, spectacle, and culture as signifying tropes of city life—are not isolated forces disengaged from images of U.S. urbanity as the new racial frontier. The postmodern city, that hypersexualized, creative core identified as much by its exotic imagery as by its commerce, is fashioned out of the blackness that embodies these same constructions.[13] The cultural footprint of a "ghetto-specific" black presence now displaced (in order to generate pure[r] communities) renders this space trendy and alluring. Hypervisibilized and celebrated in the form of commodified culture, low-capital blackness is only tolerable when its physical threat is erased, deconcentrated, regulated, and invisibilized.

Redevelopment schemes have recurrently precipitated widespread displacement of the lowest-capital black residents living in sites deemed concentrations of poverty. And they must. Residents' bodies and places serve as the ground for visions of a *rehabilitated* space: the purification and redemption of entire geographies rest upon their erasure. Hegemonic debate over deconcentration seldom hinges on the issue of forced dispersal/migration, which has become a naturalized occurrence in the urban landscape; rather, dominant frameworks, having fully affirmed the uninhabitability of concentrations of poverty (and, by extension, the inhumanity of those who do indeed inhabit those spaces), often celebrate as urban redevelopment and progress the phenomenon known as gentrification.[14]

Sylvia Wynter's cartography of humanness is critical in locating the source of the "epistemological resignation" that underlies uneven geographies. Following Wynter's lead, I argue that the imagination and execution of deconcentration derive from the interplay between humanness and habitability. To imagine the urban homeplace within the narrow terms of dispossession, what Michael Dear and Jennifer Wolch describe as "landscapes of despair," is to borrow from narratives that originated in the context of the 1492 event, which splintered preexisting feudal geographic schemas.[15]

As Wynter illuminates, the feudal, pre-fifteenth-century conception of the world was shaped by a "binary opposition . . . inscribed in an ostensibly un-bridgeable separation between the *habitable* areas of the earth (which were within the redemptive grace of the Scholastics' God and His only 'partial providence for mankind'), and the *uninhabitable* areas of the earth (which were outside His grace)."[16] The earth was nonhomogeneously conceptualized: only the geographies under God's grace were habitable, and no human action could disrupt this providential spatial binary. Europe constituted the "temperate" zone, for it was capable of sustaining human life, while all geographies peripheral to these blessed and redeemed lands were considered too hot or incompatible for human habitation. According to the feudal cosmological understanding of the earth, these peripheral geographies constituted the "torrid zones" and were thought to be wholly submerged underwater. This geographic dichotomy arose from interpretations of the biblical Flood, the aftermath of which was understood to have determined the areas suitable for habitability. Within this schema, the uninhabitable areas (or all spaces surrounding the island of habitable land whose center was Jerusalem) were left as a depository for the waters of the Flood and "in the terms of Christian-Aristotelian physics, the more spiritually degraded and heavier element of earth, *had* to be submerged in its *natural place* under the element of the lighter element of water."[17] In sharp contradistinction to these areas, the lands composing the "temperate zones" and containing European peoples were redeemed by godly intervention to rise above their "natural" place under the water. This providential redemption enabled these areas to contain land and support human life.

With Columbus's voyages, geographies previously known only by their uninhabitability (by lying west of Europe) were "discovered," and, through a series of transformations in the European cosmogony, the Americas were deemed potentially habitable. The condition for this ontological transformation in geography—the Americas' categorical shift from the "torrid" zone, underwater and too hot for habitation, to the "temperate" zone, landed and capable of sustaining human life—was an epistemological revolution that could support such a rupture in the dominant mode of feudal European knowing. This lay humanist revolution, which coincided with Copernicus's challenges to the astronomical foundations of feudal European spatial thought (removing the earth from the center of the universe, positing its mobility, and, in so doing, nullifying discourses of human helplessness and lack of agency before the Christian God), sought to impose humanist notions of utopian geographies and systems of being onto the earth through homogenization of land. Wynter writes: "There could be no longer *habitable* and *uninhabitable, inside* the sheepfold, or *out*. All was now one sheepfold, and if not, was intended to be *made so*."[18] Within this revised system of symbolic representations, the Americas were *not* endlessly uninhabitable, for they could be transformed to sustain European habitation. Yet as they stood—unkempt, wild, savage—they took on all the meanings of chaos that haunted the humanist imagination.

A crucial vulnerability in Columbus's schema, the negotiation of which has determined the way in which colonization has been imagined and rationalized, was the unmistakable empiricism that these lands were indeed inhabited. Columbus's reaction to the existence of Tainos and Arawaks on the island soon named Hispaniola was to "see the New World peoples in the way his earlier learned antagonists had 'seen' the 'uninhabitable' torrid zones," as *idolators*, non-Christians, antihumans.[19] In this way, the European project of homogenizing land and rendering it inhabitable was conceptualized and legitimized through the ontological certainty that no humans were previously occupying it. Such certainty derived from now-outmoded spatial schemas that dichotomized the torrid and the temperate. As the torrid found corporeal signification in the idolatrous indigenous populations (and the temperate in the European body), ideas of racial difference emerged as a critical index of humanness.

Wynter follows this classificatory model through the Enlightenment, the rise of the bourgeoisie, and Darwin's bioevolutionary revolt, when secular principles served to reinscribe these hierarchies in the discourse of objective rationality, thus articulating the question of the human in the new language of eugenics and racial-cum-national progress: "This premise is that of a bioevolutionarily determined difference of genetic value substance between *one* evolutionarily selected *human hereditary variation* and therefore *eugenic* line of descent . . . and a series, to varying degrees, of its nonselected and therefore dysgenic Others."[20] This, remarks Wynter, is W. E. B. DuBois's color line, which makes

> conceptualizable the representation . . . of a bioevolutionarily selected
> line of eugenic hereditary descent, the symbolic construct of "race"
> mapped onto the color line has served to enact a new status criterion of
> *eugenicity* on whose basis the global bourgeoisie legitimates its ostensibly bioevolutionarily selected dominance—as the alleged global bear-

ers of a transracial line of eugenic hereditary descent—*over* the global nonmiddle (or "working") classes, with its extreme Other being that of the "jobless" and "homeless" underclass, who have been supposedly discarded by reason of their genetic defectivity by the Malthusian "iron laws of nature."[21]

The poetics of purity and taint, already a central symbolism in feudal Christian thought, merged almost seamlessly with the discourse of eugenics and biological determinism that was encoded onto secularized, Enlightenment conceptions of humanness. Accordingly, the embodied nature of filth became a mainstay of this new discourse, inspiring an entire politico-scientific apparatus whose aim was to diagnose, categorize, and act upon bodies and bodily behaviors known as filthy. There was no way to speak of filth without speaking of tainted/tainting bodies, just as there was no way to understand these same bodies outside the poetics of filth. Nineteenth-century racial thinking took shape from this epistemological link, finding its deepest popular resonance in the language of hygiene, cleanness, and filth.[22]

This tainted state of alterity delivered meaning and urgency onto a new model of being, an optimal status criterion under constant threat of contagion. Out of bourgeois fears of racial impurity, disease, moral degradation, and pollution was born a new mode of humanness realizable only through proper bourgeois behavior, status, and the embodiment of whiteness. Anne McClintock alludes to the emergence of this status in her discussion of Victorian fetishism of soap. She outlines how the purifying symbolism evoked by soap—having become highly commodified during this era—was informed by the cultivation of emergent middle-class values, including, "monogamy ('clean' sex, which has value), industrial capital ('clean' money, which has value), Christianity ('being washed in the blood of the lamb'), class control ('cleansing the great unwashed'), and the imperial civilizing mission ('washing and clothing the savage')."[23] Soap became the mark of the white bourgeois subject, a necessary consumptive tool for pursuing the fulfillment of bourgeois selfhood. In the sense that cleansing oneself in the appropriate fashion was the mark of humanness, soap, and more generally the hygienic regime, served as a disciplinary and regulatory mechanism, instilling in the body politic a mode of subjective understanding in which the discourse of purity configured which thoughts and actions were deemed normative or transgressive.

The complexities of late eighteenth-century and early nineteenth-century urbanization permeated this racialized poetics of embodied cleanliness and taint. The city often haunted Enlightenment thinkers, symbolizing an anarchic, indefinable, and uncontrollable mesh of bodies and structures. Typically represented as antithetical to the natural realm, the city was seen as all that nature was not: toxic, human, degraded, fallen.[24] Yet even in its hazardous fluidity and unruly rapidity, the city represented a fundamental achievement of Man: domination over an equally treacherous nature and implementation of human knowledge models onto a physical landscape. The city typified the promise and perils of the Enlightenment episteme. To subdue and organize the city and its constituents was to translate Enlightenment modes of rationality over a social and physical landscape, a task that was forced to come to terms with the patently chaotic motions of Victorian urbanity. New models of governmentality idealized an arrangement of Victorian space that reflected Enlightenment ideals. Like Foucault's panopticon, the city grid was to be calculated and standardized, a geographic form that would most effectively facilitate and regulate the behavior of urban residents. This environmental determinism supposed that behavioral norms would take form in harmony with spatial organization.[25] Inversely, behavioral deviance began to be traced to substandard living conditions and spatial malfunction.

Locating the origins of vice in the physical surroundings of impropriety, the environmentalist position departed from pre-Enlightenment understandings of vice as a result of fallen nature, of an ingrained, cursed disposition. As this metamorphizing epistemology opened up new possibilities for the human subject, it simultaneously reinscribed genetic difference as a primary mode of understanding the body and its continence. It is crucial to note that the environmentalist thesis did not do away with genetico-behavioral causality for social transgression. In its most extreme versions, it obscured it; in its more typical manifestations it aligned environmental determinism alongside biological and ethical determinisms.

This geo-racial poetics of filth continues to shape dominant conceptions of subaltern spaces and bodies. It is this enduring cartographic exercise — the mapping of concentrations of poverty as sites of uninhabitability and deviance within the liberal environmental thesis — that ensures that black pathology remains fixed and immutable within the dominant mode of subjective understanding. Black pathology is invoked by the liberal environmental thesis by employing resurrected and refined discourses of alterity that have historically shrouded representations of black bodies.[26] The deployment of these discourses in urban studies, even when understood to be transformable and structurally induced, confirms the base *inhumanity* of residents. The liberal penchant for structural musings, while attempting to locate the origins of this pathology outside of the individual residents themselves, nevertheless accepts black deviance as the defining characteristic of entire geographies. Furthermore, this preoccupation with pinpointing the structural roots of "ghetto-specific" pathology understands the question of the city as a question of materiality—that is, in terms of access to employment, schools, housing, and other "opportunities"—and in so doing ignores the systems of thought that operate within and through these material considerations. Left uninterrogated are the ontological schemas that guarantee the material status of "impoverished" inner-city dwellings and dwellers, as well as the epistemological systems that govern the modes through which this status is interpreted, named, and known. Few prominent analyses of the urban take into account the symbolic, concerned as they are over the material. In turn, this epistemological resignation relegates liberal analyses to base acceptance of post-Enlightenment conceptions of what constitutes humanness and what sites stand capable of supporting human habitation.

Geographic considerations are paramount in understanding how this naturalization process occurs despite the ostensible liberal efforts to escape genetic/biological determinisms characteristic of eugenic discourse. In marking the urban homeplace as uninhabitable, the bodies occupying it are, in turn, rendered inhuman in the bioevolutionary poetics of dysgenic human status. This relationship ensures schematic consistency in the sense that the essential condition for the spatial status *uninhabitable* is the occupier's inhumanity, and conversely, the implication of the occupier's inhumanity is the production of an uninhabitable place. McKittrick explicates this correlation: "Post-1492, what the uninhabitable tells us, then, is that populations who occupy the 'nonexistent' are *living* in what has been previously conceptualized as unlivable and unimaginable. If identity and place are mutually constructed, the uninhabitable spatializes a human Other category of the unimaginable/native/black."[27]

Because space attains meaning from body, and body from space, the widespread engagement of discourses on behavioral pathology complements the liberal/humanitarian concern for spatial unlivability, thus reinscribing the naturalness of both and, in so doing, creating the requisite ontological atmosphere for the reproduction of bioevolutionary narratives that render low-capital black subjects genetically inferior, deviant, and other. It is within these narratives that the deconcentration paradigm arose and continues to reassert its legitimacy as the contemporary rearticulation of the frontier scenario. It is within these narratives that the displacement of thousands of blacks across the United States becomes an inevitable, unremarkable fact.

Liberal/leftist theorists have been unsuccessful in offering an emancipatory analysis of the urban question precisely because the emblem of their discourse—concentrated poverty—is overwhelmingly complicit with and immersed in dominant modes of knowing. The copious pages dedicated to enumerating the causes or effects of concentrations of poverty are wholly incapable of breaking out of the epistemological covenants that mold and regulate the geographic, corporeal, as well as the hermeneutic and metaphoric borders of the urban homeplace. There can be no structural indictment without a pathological subject, no pathological subject without state structures that can be located for critique. In other words, the deviant resident of the black homeplace (and the black homeplace of the deviant resident) serves as the ground for a liberal assessment of the state. The paternalistic logics of concentrated poverty discourse flow through the concentration of poverty, the perverse black body, reaffirming the atrophy of both. In so doing, these formulas preserve the episteme that generates the state policies and attitudes they seek to critique.

A constitutive trope in this semiotic process, contagion figures as the mucilage between the physical geographies and bodies of the urban homeplace. The two are set next to each other, indistinguishable, as this adhesive set of meanings surges toxicity fluidly between them. Contagious and contaminated black geographies are pitted as the inevitable product of black behavior/genetics, inequitable political economy, historical discrimination, and an assortment of other formulations that naturalize and totalize bodies and geographies according to a dysgenic logic. A faceless and placeless topography materializes where this inevitable space of defiled inhabitance meets putative uninhabitability. Unavoidable yet unnatural, produced but monstrous, predetermined and at the same time out of place, concentrations of poverty imperil the purity of dominant logics, bodies, and spaces. By definition, they must be excised.

In post-Katrina New Orleans, the deconcentration paradigm draws on the tropes of contagion and purification in a context that is already ripe with such poetics. To a significant degree, this assemblage of symbolic representations delivers to Katrina its resonance within popular discourse. In locating this event within a continuum of purity politics and poetics, understandings of Hurricane Katrina are locked into a central site of signification within the present episteme. The Katrina moment becomes an exercise in sociospatial purity, pursued through discourses on contaminated bodies and urban space.

The who, where, and why of contagion give meaning to the liberal/reformist/humanitarian understanding of urban renaissance. Although the poetics of contamination is common to deconcentration projects nationwide, its deployment in New Orleans carries a particular salience and logic, as the imagery of the floodwaters left a profound metaphoric residue even after the streets were drained. Toxicity has entered the realm of fetish, becoming the terrain in which reconstruction policies and languages attain meaning. When, in a particularly spectacular manifestation of this phenomenon, a Louisiana Department of Environmental Quality inspector publicly consumes a spoonful of dirt to prove its innocuous qualities, there remains little doubt that notions of toxicity and purity, taint and decontamination, shape the contours of competing discourses on the state and future of post-Katrina New Orleans.[28]

The reconstruction of New Orleans since August 2005 has been molded around a "racially hygienic collective fantasy"—a redemptive motion away from the city's seemingly magnetic attraction to all things defiled.[29] Dylan Rodríguez collapses this enterprise: "The fundamental logic governing the discrete geographic and human drowning of a post-segregation, though effectively apartheid, New Orleans is animated by the sturdy symbiosis between black disposability and American nation building."[30] For Rodríguez, black "social death" or "black bodily and geographic liquidation" is "an epochal articulation of democracy, state-building, and nationalist well-being."[31] Preservation/restoration of the "sanctity of white bodily integrity" relies upon black expendability (in the forms of containment and erasure) to excise tainting blood, spaces, images, behaviors, and sex out of geo-racial fantasies.[32] Performed through a multicultural syntax, this spectacle of "death and dying" prompts Joy James to ask, "Can there be lynching without a formalized lynch party?"[33]

Spatial concerns figure centrally in this "racially hygienic collective fantasy." Recalling Wynter's explanation of the geo-racial restructuring that occurred at the end of the fifteenth century ("there could be no longer *habitable* and *uninhabitable*, *inside* the sheepfold, or *out*. All was now one sheepfold, and if not, was intended to be *made* so"),[34] I submit that efforts to regulate and purify post-Katrina New Orleans operate through understandings of humanness.[35] Within the dominant system of symbolic representations, defiled geographies holding and containing contagious bodies are *terra nullius*/no-man's-land. Uninhabitable and ontologically uninhabited, these spaces define and are defined by the antihumans who are located in or mapped to them.

Exploring the tension between the abstract impossibility of an uninhabitable space (for, paraphrasing Wynter, all can be *made* into one sheepfold) and the epistemological indispensability of such uninhabitability (for it correlates to the autopoietic truth of different grades of humanness), McKittrick proposes the existence of "different degrees of inhabitability." Elaborating upon Wynter's premise of a 1492 geo-racial restructuring, she writes, "This geographic transformation . . . does not fully erase the category of 'uninhabitable,' but rather re-presents it through spatial processes as a sign of social difference."[36]

Gradations of inhabitability are negotiated through regimes of spatial and bodily discipline, which regulate different spaces and bodies in contiguous and divergent ways. Geographies of humanness (i.e., the French Quarter and Garden District of New Orleans), exhibiting optimal status criteria for livability, are marked as provisionally pure spaces even as they may harbor bacchanalia and sexual perversity. The protective borders of pure spaces — police, "tipping" discourse, property values, freeways, parks, other physical barriers, and so forth — are erected from within and without these enclaves, guarding from both internal and external taint. Geographies of antihumanness and uninhabitability — in our case black geographies as urban homeplaces — are regulated according to the logics of containment and erasure. Post-Katrina, with the taint of these spaces now derived from the memory of those killed or bused away (instead of their corporeal presence), *containment becomes erasure.* This "racially hygienic collective fantasy"[37] imagines an expungement of uninhabitability and the bodies that designate spaces as such.

Wynter instructs that it is precisely this nexus of abjecting signification that enables the proper functioning of the dominant episteme through its legitimation of the auto-instituting premises upon which all that is pure is defined. As Wynter notes of the liminal other, "such a category, because it served to 'trigger' and motivate each order's subjects' behavioral adherence to the pathway or the 'cure' prescribed by the supraordinate telos and 'sense of right' generated from the mode of lack that it empirically incarnates, is the indispensable condition of the autopoietic functioning of each system. It is also the indispensable condition . . . of the truth of its order of knowledge."[38] Adapting Wynter's argument, I suggest that the integrity not only of white bodies and white spaces (as understood to be metonymical with *pure* bodies and spaces) but also of the dominant order of knowledge and power is held in the semiotic balance. Thus, the self-evident defilement besmirching black geographies and corporealities sustains the synaptic workings of the dominant episteme by fueling the teleological parade I have termed the deconcentration paradigm. It is therefore the very act of conceptualizing geo-racial taint/pathology/contagion/dysgenics that upholds the telos of purity and the necessitated purification rituals (and, as an extension, the sanctity of the epistemological order), even as it ensures the failure (and consequently the recycling) of this purifying exercise. Wynter's cartographic project thus opens up and pushes us toward the cracks in these epistemological currents. Her mapping unravels the self-evident logics that generate Man even as it boldly outlines the task before us—the elaboration of a new mode of humanness first forged in the epistemological tumult initiated by 1950s and 1960s anticolonial and black civil rights struggles.

McKittrick extends Wynter's injunction by calling for the recognition and production of "more humanly workable geographies."[39] For McKittrick, this dismantling of traditional, dominant geographies entails "recognizing both 'the where' of alterity *and* the geographical imperatives in the struggle for social justice."[40] In post-Katrina New Orleans, such an undertaking is particularly fraught. Low-capital black residents have been forced into a discursive pit. Because they themselves carry the contamination the reconstruction effort seeks to abate in the creation of a "safer, stronger, smarter City,"[41] their continued erasure is the cornerstone of the rebuilding of the city. Accordingly, the language of reconstruction and return is so readily collapsed into the project of geo-racial purification that there exists little room for a counter-discursive maneuvering. At the same time, with residents hastily bused away all over the country, the idea of reconstruction and return is a critical one. Thus they are told to choose between, on the one hand, a New Orleans that does not want them, one that is still suffering from the infrastructural effects of Katrina and the whirlwind of privatization that followed it, and on the other, a life in diaspora from the city where their communities were ripped apart by death, trauma, forced migration, and imprisonment. Residents must stake a position between the state-sanctioned brutality marking their homes (trans-Katrina), the violence of mass displacement (post-Katrina), and the liberal, paternalistic discourse of opportunity, rebirth, and health (the deconcentration paradigm) that professes to resolve the foregoing issues.

The resident-led struggles that have emerged over the last four years under the banner "The Right to Return" have navigated these discursive sand traps by advancing alternative geographic frameworks that situate black communities and struggles at the center of the New Orleans landscape. During the highly publicized struggles in 2007 against the eventual demolition of the city's few remaining public housing structures, the question of habitability became the locus around which antidemolition campaigns organized. Habitability claims served as points of departure for the counterhegemonic project of transmuting notions of humanness. In asserting the right to return to their homes, antidemolition residents challenged matrices of knowledge and power that render them permanently out of place, antihuman, and geographically peripheral. At stake in the struggles surrounding public housing was not only residents' capacity to inhabit and therefore regulate space, but their license to live at all. If public housing geographies and residents' bodies are normatively defined through their reciprocal abjection, both are also tied up in "cartographies of struggle" as sites for reimagining knowledge, agency, and power.[42] Wynter addresses this creative potentiality in terms of the ocular: "The liminal category is the systemic category from whose perspective alone, as the perspective of those forcibly made to embody and signify lack-of-being, whose members, in seeking to escape their condemned statuses, are able to call into question the closure instituting the order and, therefore, the necessary 'blindness' of its normative . . . subjects."[43] Deviation from and confrontation with the self-negation assumed and mandated by the dominant mode of subjective understanding is thus both an act of self-making and space-making, as well as an unlacing of the operative logics of the dominant order.

The discursive hazards facing New Orleans's reconstruction struggles foreground the indispensability of Sylvia Wynter's meditations on the interplay between geography, habitability, and humanness. Wynter points toward a humanness unmoored from the violent limitations of Man and, in so doing, serves as a contributor and guide in the critical project of recognizing, envisioning, and fashioning "more humanly workable geographies."[44]

Notes

I am tremendously indebted to Demetrius Eudell, Gayle Pemberton, and David Stein for their editorial insight with early versions of this chapter.

1. Wynter, "1492," 5–57.
2. I borrow the term "ungeographic" from Katherine McKittrick. McKittrick, *Demonic Grounds*, x–xiii.

3. I ground this inquiry in an understanding of geography that, following Wynter's lead, interrogates and then unsettles a Cartesian production of space. Wynter illustrates how the traditional geographic project of partitioning the world into grades of habitability concomitantly practices a politics of humanness that differentiates Man from his human Others. In exploring how this geo-racial imagination flows in and out of the contours of a tangible, physical landscape, and in so doing is called into question by the very existence of bodies "out of place," I draw upon McKittrick's reading of Wynter's geographies as interhuman: "While geography, space, and place are useful to thinking about ways in which we are differently 'in place' and implicated in the production of space, they are also useful in signaling the alterability of the 'ground beneath our feet.'" McKittrick, *Demonic Grounds*, 146. *Les damnés de la terre*/the wretched of the earth is taken from Fanon, *The Wretched of the Earth* (trans. Philcox).

4. Wynter, "Unsettling the Coloniality of Being," 278. She takes this concept from Hallyn, *The Poetic Structure of the World*.

5. Here one might also review Mike Davis's *Planet of Slums* in light of my thinking, as this work details (in a different fashion and from a different perspective than I do here) the interlocking workings of global urbanization, discourses of "progress" and "change," accumulation, and the naturalization of regional poverty and death.

6. Since its acquisition by the United States in the 1803 Louisiana Purchase, New Orleans has been positioned as an outlier among the nation's cities. Maintaining its sui generis reputation for its topography, racial makeup, sexual (un)conventions, architecture, colonial past, economy, music, and gastronomy, New Orleans has long vexed U.S. fantasies of homogeneity and regulated difference. New Orleans has been an emblem of nationalist fears of racial and sexual deviance for as long as it has been a U.S. city. Branded a space of decadence and freedom, it has touted its singular libratory appeal since the mid-nineteenth century, when local elites first actively sought to stimulate a tourist industry. Its notorious reputation as a "bastion of commercial sexuality and sex across the color line" was first nurtured in the years preceding the Civil War, and by Emancipation its sex worker districts had become institutionalized matrices of racial/sexual surveillance and deviance, as well as state-sanctioned projects in the new technology of bioevolutionary race-making. Grey, "(Re)Imagining Ethnicity in the City of New Orleans," 134; Long, *The Great Southern Babylon*, 1–2.

7. Declaring cholera a "master trope for urban existence," Erin O'Connor proposes that the disease was metonymical for the unruly by-products of a radically transforming urban and epistemological landscape. Classifying cholera as a production of the working class, English sanitary reformist critics pathologized poor bodies as atrophied and designated their neighborhoods as the breeding ground for the epidemic. O'Connor also explores how cholera sym-

bolically reflected Victorian distress over racial purity amid heightened immigration and involvement in contaminating colonial archipelagoes, a symbolism infused with the exigencies of industrial pollution: "Depicting Asiatic cholera as a kind of biological warfare, medical and popular accounts of infection emphasize the transformative violence of the disease with a metaphorics of miscegenation, a penetrative model of pathology that saw victims as infected with blackness itself." O'Connor, *Raw Material*, 6–7, 26, 43.

8. By "contemporary," I point to urban studies scholarship that begins around the mid-1980s, although the continuities with earlier modes of scholarly knowledge are clearly discernible.

9. "Homeplace," which is borrowed from bell hooks's essay of the same name, signifies the spaces inhabited by communities and residents engaged in real struggle against systemic forces that render them conceptually other. Residents of homeplaces are neither figures of dispossession, devoid of agency, nor romanticized effigies of resistance against oppression. Neither of these constructions recognizes the humanity of residents, who struggle for selfhood and community in contexts that deem both their bodies (vis-à-vis race, gender, class, and sexuality) and their environments as antithetical to dominant understandings of humanity and land. hooks, "Homeplace," 41–50.

10. Wilson, *The Truly Disadvantaged*, 14.

11. The parameters of my argument, shaped by research about New Orleans's public housing (wholly composed of black residents), are necessarily focused around black communities. The notion of purification, as imagined here, might be analogous to deconcentration efforts in areas that are home to other communities of color or white populations. These comparisons are not the focus of this work.

12. McKittrick, *Demonic Grounds*, 5.

13. For a thorough examination of the postmodern city, see Cross and Keith, *Racism, the City and the State*.

14. This conceptual and rhetorical formulation traces back to 1960s concerns over urban renewal programs. Glass, *London*.

15. Dear and Wolch, *Landscapes of Despair*.

16. Wynter, "1492," 21.

17. Wynter, "1492," 22.

18. Wynter, "1492," 28.

19. Wynter, "1492," 29.

20. Wynter, "1492," 39.

21. Wynter, "1492," 40.

22. Dyer, *White*, 72–81.

23. McClintock, *Imperial Leather*, 208.

24. Reed, "Toward an Environmental Justice Ecocriticism," 150.

25. Poovey, *Making a Social Body*, 25–54.

26. This argument, the liberal response to the aforementioned tension, has been

an active theoretical supposition in contemporary debates since William Julius Wilson's book *The Truly Disadvantaged* (1987). Wilson asserts that although "pathological" or, more precisely, "ghetto-specific" behaviors are definitive markings of the urban homeplace, they are not its innate characteristics. Constructing an argument around the structural causations of "social isolation"—his central theoretical concept for representing the problems of the urban homeplace—he depicts the behavioral pathologies resulting from "social isolation" not as fixed and immutable but rather as specific to the environment in which they arise. He writes that social isolation, a result of structural inequalities, "magnified the effects of living in highly concentrated urban poverty areas—effects that are manifested in ghetto-specific culture and behavior." Distancing himself from "culture of poverty" formulations derivative from Oscar Lewis's 1965 essay by the same name, he goes on to qualify his contention by introducing the potential for cultural/behavioral transformation: "It would be dogmatic to rule out this possibility, however . . . as economic and social situations change, cultural traits, created by previous situations, likewise *eventually* change even though it is possible that some will linger on and influence behavior for a period of time." Wilson, *The Truly Disadvantaged*, 138.

27. McKittrick, *Demonic Grounds*, 130.
28. Bullard, "Let Them Eat Dirt."
29. Sexton, "The Obscurity of Black Suffering," 126.
30. Rodríguez, "The Meaning of 'Disaster' under the Dominant of White Life," 134.
31. Rodríguez, "The Meaning of 'Disaster' under the Dominant of White Life," 135.
32. Rodríguez, "The Meaning of 'Disaster' under the Dominant of White Life," 136.
33. James, "Afterword," 160–161.
34. Wynter, "1492," 28.
35. See Sibley, "Purification of Space," 409–421.
36. McKittrick, *Demonic Grounds*, 131.
37. Sexton, "The Obscurity of Black Suffering," 126.
38. Wynter, "Is 'Development' a Purely Empirical Concept or Also Teleological?," 305–306.
39. McKittrick, *Demonic Grounds*, 145.
40. Wynter, "1492," xix (emphasis in the original).
41. Unified New Orleans Plan, "City Wide Plan."
42. I borrow this phrase from both Chandra Mohanty and Katherine McKittrick: Mohanty, *Feminism without Borders*, 43; McKittrick, *Demonic Grounds*.
43. Wynter, "Is 'Development' a Purely Empirical Concept or Also Teleological?," 305.
44. McKittrick, *Demonic Grounds*, xii.

6   AXIS, BOLD AS LOVE

On Sylvia Wynter, Jimi Hendrix, and the Promise of Science

Scientists inspired by the legendary improv of Miles Davis and John Coltrane are peering inside the brains of today's jazz musicians to learn where creativity comes from.

ASSOCIATED PRESS, "SCIENCE LOOKS AT BRAIN ON JAZZ"

Private Hendrix plays a musical instrument during his off duty hours, or so he says. This is one of his faults, because his mind apparently cannot function while performing duties and thinking about his guitar.

DEPONENT L. J. HOESKSTRA, STATEMENT ON THE MENTAL AND PHYSICAL INVESTIGATION OF PRIVATE JAMES M. HENDRIX, FORT CAMPBELL, KENTUCKY, 1962

Preamble and Plot

This chapter explores the ways in which scientific knowledge is mobilized in the writings of Sylvia Wynter. The first section briefly outlines Wynter's intellectual project, followed by a discussion of how science and *scientia* emerge in her writings and enable her conceptualization of the human. The second section explores, broadly, why science matters—with specific reference to how race and racism inform the conveyance and transmission of scientific knowledge. The third section examines how our contemporary scientific framings—biocentric, Darwinian—inform our academic positionalities and foreclose cross-disciplinary conversations. The final section of the discussion brings these areas together, looking specifically at the ways in which the creative labor of Jimi Hendrix is demonstrative of Wynter's *scientia* project.

The Scientific Project

The intellectual project of Sylvia Wynter is a vast rethinking of the ways in which the human is constituted. Wynter's research draws attention to how the sociospatial expressions of Western modernity—colonial encounters during and after the fifteenth and sixteenth centuries, the Copernican leap and the ascent of astronomy, physics, and physical geography, the secularization of Man and his human others within a Judeo-Christian setting, territorial expansion and transatlantic slavery, industrialization, the rise of the biological sciences—accumulated and formed overlapping governing codes (Man1 and Man2) as overrepresentations of the human.[1] These governing codes produced racialized/non-European/nonwhite/New World/ Indigenous/African peoples as first, fallen untrue Christians (in the fifteenth and sixteenth centuries) and, later, as biologically defective and damned (in the nineteenth century). I want to highlight Wynter's assertion of the ways in which our present conception of the human—and what it means to *be* human—delineates how colonial encounters, and thus the fallen and the damned, were *central to* the rise of meaningful cognitively emancipatory breaches and thus the reinventions of humanness. This is to say that at the nexus of theological punishment, colonial brutality, and imperial greed, underpinning the new sciences that recast how we perceive our physiology and our sociocultural systems—physics, astronomy, cartography, biology, and so forth—are the fallen and defective who put immense pressure on European ways of knowing the world. As particular local-indigenous-black-diasporic knowledges are encountered and circulated, the conditions through which local-indigenous-black-diasporic knowledges must be vanquished and a "universally applicable law of human identification," with Man-as-human identificatory figure, are nurtured.[2] Colonial encounters incited "discoveries" and violence, as well as social, economic, and political exchanges between local (indigenous, black) and European cultures—a practice that increasingly took place in relation to "one single criterion" (Man) and also brought into being "our present single world order and single world history."[3]

Indeed, one of the many reasons Wynter's work is so provocative is that she fully integrates the impact racial encounters, non-European worldviews, and practices of subjugation have had, and continue to have, on our global worldview—which is now firmly harnessed to a Western bourgeois tenet— and how the making of humanness is necessitated by said racial encounters that, in fact, inform and/or make possible meaningful emancipatory moments that radically alter humanness itself. In her work, the racial-Other does not *haunt*, but rather is a fully present figure who *enables* emancipatory cognitive leaps. This presence *necessarily*, as noted, brought a challenge to the ascendant mode of thinking through asserting local-indigenous-black-diasporic as well as shared (European-and-nonwhite/creolized/hybrid) perspectives on the state of being human—perspectives that culminated in the 1960s anticolonial and civil rights movements and opened up new claims to the category of human. If we trust these knotted provocations, the human changes, although not in the popular linear evolutionary fashion wherein we collectively (yet differentially) ascend and biologically grow toward the fittest (and phylogeny reigns). Instead, what emerges is a co-relational figure that Wynter (this volume) describes as articulating both bios and mythoi: a figure who is a physiologically organic *and* cognitive *and* creative being that *authors* the aesthetic script of humanness. Turned around and put slightly differently, a co-relational human being is the *flesh-and-blood* cognitive figure who is *at once* physiologically organic, cognitively responsive, and creatively inventive and, *in this simultaneity*, provides the origin stories through which we make sense of our flesh-and-blood and neurological and cultural claims to humanness.

With this vast project in mind, I am interested in the ways in which science functions to advance Wynter's wager and how the physiology of what it means to be human—our flesh and blood and brain matter—is woven into her ideas to unsettle and enmesh the otherwise bifurcated and dichotomized epistemological clusters of science and creativity. When reading Wynter's theoretical work, then, from her early writings in *Jamaica Journal* to her more recent research on being human as praxis, one can plot out how she integrates the writings from a range of scientific and philosophical theories that attend to areas such as (but not limited to) Copernican theory and theories of naturalism; questions of physics and neurobiology; and computer science and environmental science. These areas of thought and writings, in addition to the other sources she integrates from the humanities and the social sciences, delineate that the question of science emerges in three ways in Wynter's work. First are the ways in which the question of scientific thought ushered in broad cognitive ruptures, with the aforementioned Copernican leap pointing to the ways in which new conceptions of the physical cosmos boldly exemplified how particular "discoveries" led to a radical, albeit gradual, shift in how we collectively perceive the world and its inhabitants. Second, science is noted for being produced as an objective system of knowledge that enumerates and classifies "difference," with the codes developed from about the nineteenth century on being especially pertinent—botanical difference, racial-sexual difference, spatial difference, linguistic difference, and so forth. Here the scientific expressions of modernity—newly rational Man, cartographies of colonialism and the plantation, the metrics of nonwhite/enslaved/gendered bodies, the mathematics of nature, the economy of labor, the biological sorting—disclose the ways in which the question of human life is mapped out by scientific imperatives that increasingly profit from positing that we, humans, are fundamentally biocentric and natural beings.[4] Third, Wynter explores what I want to call the science of our living—the physiological and neurological processes through which humans organize their environments. This thread in Wynter's research looks closely at "the puzzle of conscious experience."[5] Here she thinks through what Humberto R. Maturana and Francisco J. Varela call "the realization of the living" by addressing the ways in which governing codes impact upon neurological activities.[6] Specifically, Wynter reads biological theory to claim that autopoiesis—the consensual circular (not teleological-evolutionary) organization of human life through which we scientifically live and die as a species—draws attention to "a new frame of meaning, not only of *natural* history, but also of a newly conceived *cultural* history specific to and unique to our species, because the history of those 'forms of life' gives expression to [a] . . . hybridly organic and . . . *languaging* existence."[7] With this in mind, Wynter thinks through our life and death narratives and laws and, extending the writings of Frantz Fanon, notes that our investment of a biocentric version of the human (our present organization of human life) fails to attend to the enmeshment of consciousness and neurology, or the mind and the brain, precisely because it is underwritten by a social coding that reduces the workings of mind, brain, consciousness, and neurology to purely and naturally scientific activities. Wynter thinks about, then, how consciousness and experience are neurochemically determined by our social systems, a viewpoint that noticeably asserts that who/what we are and how we survive are not driven by genetics and extrahuman laws of naturalism. The prevalent subsuming of our social perception (consciousness/experience) to our physiological labor (neurobiology) unravels in two ways: first, it disregards the ways in which human beings are simultaneously biological and cultural (bios-mythoi) and thus presents an obscured narrative of purely biological Western life stories; and second, it imparts, quite strikingly, the ways in which our present biocentric narrative unevenly imbues the science of the body and the science of knowledge with race, with the black/nigger cast out and dysselected and neurologically responding to a system that rewards racial hatred.

Closely related, Wynter thus posits that the practice of representing the human follows governing codes that divide science and creativity (or, put crudely, the natural sciences and the humanities). This process closely follows nineteenth-century "half-scientific, half-mythic"[8] Darwinian origin narratives that represent the human as a purely biological being that has "evolved" differentially according to phenotype, economic status, and region, with the vanquished representing the dysselected; here science functions to produce the human as a mere biological mechanism, which, in turn, differentiates itself from extrabiological creativity and reifies the "nonhomogeneity of genetic substance between the category of those selected by evolution and the category of those dysselected-by-Evolution."[9] Or, our scholastic and disciplinary divides, like our differential biological ethnic divides, are genetically and naturally pregiven. At the heart of Wynter's project, then, stands the organization of academic knowledge into discrete disciplines that replicate the us-them *and* biocentric-social-geographic divides—here the color line surfaces—while also gesturing to our intellectual imperative:

> The prescriptive guidelines of how we are to set about this challenge lie in the paradox of the new Darwinian descriptive statement of the human: Man in its second, purely secular, biocentric, and overrepresented modality of being human. What then had been the contradiction at the heart of the Darwinian Revolution, at the core of its paradigm of Evolution that was to give rise to, on the one hand, the continuing dazzling successes of the biological sciences and, on the other, not only to the obsessive ethno-biological beliefs in the genetic inferiority of nonwhite natives, in the barely evolved near-primate status of black-skinned peoples (as matrix beliefs that would logically make possible the "life unworthy of life" extermination credo of the Nazis), but also at the same time to C. P. Snow's "Two Cultures" division of knowledge? That is, to the natural-scientific disciplines on the one hand, and to the rigorous yet adaptive, and therefore ethno-disciplines of the humanities and social sciences on the other?[10]

Wynter's scientific challenge, then, is threefold: to explore how the governing code of Man-as-human is implicit to how the human *organism* biologically feels and experiences and creates; to think through how questions of physiology, neurobiology, physics, math, and other areas allocated to the natural sciences can be conceptualized *in relation to* human activities (rather than as naturally pregiven); and to denaturalize biocentricity and its attendant fallen/dysselected castoffs while honoring the science of functioning living systems.

Race matters in this formulation, and Wynter, elaborating on Frantz Fanon's assertion that alongside the living, growing, and dying biological human (ontogeny, phylogeny) stands sociogeny (our social production of our world), posits that

> it is as "native" colonial subjects, as black subjects, in a normatively Western and white world, that we experience ourselves in terms of the specific order of consciousness that makes it possible for us to be, at times, aversive to ourselves. Now were that consciousness genetically determined, as that of any purely organic species, it could *not* have been a purely narcissistic, self-validating one. . . . In the case of humans, [Fanon] says besides the genetically programmed processes of ontogenesis, there is the, so to speak, symbolically encoded processes of sociogenesis. So what is this going to mean with respect to consciousness in the case of the human? It means that besides the neural firings which physiologically implement our reflex responses of aversion or attraction, there must be something else which determines *the terms in which* those neural firings will be activated, and, therefore, the phenomenological experience.[11]

It follows that, given our origin narratives of the biological survival of the fittest—which secure a normative worldview that is inhabited by the logically fallen indigenous/nonwhite/black/African—we replicate our present world order, ensconce our selfhood in that order and governing logics, because it appears to be the *natural* thing to do. *Believing* this system (perhaps) precludes self-expendability and/or community expendability. With our neural firings activated by biocentric logic, we invest in a script that profits from biocentricity and unsurvival of the vanquished with the hopes of surviving!

Before moving on, it is important to reemphasize here that scientific knowledge is not posited by Wynter as an emancipatory antidote; the natural sciences do not stand alone, conveying authoritative corrections to practices of injustice and racial-sexual violence. And, perhaps most significantly, the science she integrates into her project *traces*, but does not endorse, the scientific objectivity we are familiar with and proposes a *new* science of being human—a new science that unsettles our familiar (Darwinian, objective, racist, sexist) governing codes of scientific thought and honors what she calls, borrowing from Aimé Césaire, a science of the word, a science "of our dual descriptive statements [bios-mythoi] and thereby of our modes/genres of being human."[12] Wynter's project thus encourages noticing very specific and meaningful cognitive leaps—that are underwritten by colonial encounters—that uncover the knotted interconnections between scientific thought, colonialism, race and racism, cognition, identity, time, and space. Indeed, following Walter Mignolo (this volume), it is perhaps useful to cast Wynter's "science" as a *scientia*—the Latin word for knowledge—to distinguish it from the concept of *science* that unfolded from Galileo to Newton, from Newton to Einstein, from Linnaeus to Darwin: toward, *scientia* then.

Why Science and *Scientia* Matter

In the social sciences and the humanities, three overlapping research themes delineate why science matters and, consequently, why we might turn to Wynter's intellectual contributions: some analyses address the ways in which the racial underpinnings of science have long informed analyses of social inequities, poverty, racial and sexual discrimination, citizenship, and belonging (scientific research leans in favor of racially and economically privileged groups); research on genomes, blood quantum, miscegenation, the bell curve, evolution, familial ties, intelligence testing, reproductive technologies that brings into focus meaningful racial formations (racial/ethnic groupings are differentially knotted to scientific research, testing, and resulting conclusions); investigations that take up the body, phenotype, skulls, height, hair, racial passing, and gender comportment reveal biological differences among humans (the "kind" of sexual body matters). In each of these areas of study, two important themes arise: that race is socially produced yet differentially lived vis-à-vis structural inequalities; that the application of science can, and in some cases has, condemned particular communities to racial and sexual subjugation. Put differently, although science is a knowledge system that socially produces what it means to be biologically human, it is also the epistemological grounds through which racial and sexual essentialism is registered and lived. These research foci and themes, for the most part, tend to underscore the long-standing prominence of scientific "facts" developed between the eighteenth and nineteenth centuries, the racial workings of Charles Darwin's "survival of the fittest" hypothesis, the dominance of the patriarchal Western knowledge systems and scientific racisms, and undoing these histories.[13]

Biologists, geneticists, physicians, and anatomists, as well as specialists in related fields such as biochemistry, microbiology, and neurology, examine race and racial difference in relation to genetic variants, health disparities, neurological "recognition," drug therapy, diet, mental illness, and other factors that impact upon human/living systems. In applying the findings and theoretical queries developed in the natural sciences to human agents, while noticing the widely accepted "social construction of race," differences between bodies continue to matter: race, class, gender, sexuality, location, and age impact upon the conditions through which life and living are made possible.[14] Indeed, the political outcome of scientific research is to ethically mend, care for, study, improve, and alter our collective human and environmental worlds. Yet, when race makes itself known in the natural sciences, historical and social prejudices arise: the making of the racial nation and promoting national well-being are underpinned by neurological exams, collected statistics, cytology, and medical procedures (e.g., sterilization) that can be linked to eugenics projects, which then unfold into contemporary genetic engineering; or, the promises of genetic maps and biodiversity— the science and stories of bloodlines and blood histories—are met with both caution and skepticism rooted in racial experiments conducted during and after transatlantic slavery, the Holocaust, and colonial apartheids.[15]

Noticeably, these scholarly contexts reveal that, depending on perspective, scientific research continues to be haunted by a racial past and contemporary expressions of this past. I want to suggest, then, that the racial underpinnings of scientific knowledge and the application of this knowledge to black bodies have foreclosed interdisciplinary conversations and what Sylvia Wynter describes as a "hybridly organic" and "*languaging* existence."[16] Put differently, the racial workings of science always already subjugate and/or exclude marginalized communities, thus bifurcating our *analytical approaches* to race, science, knowledge, and collaboration. It follows, then, that the creative works of black musicians, writers, and artists are distanced from, or simply unimaginable, in science studies and in the production of scientific knowledge. Yet in black studies, in addition to the research of Sylvia Wynter, the work of M. NourbeSe Philip, Aimé Césaire, Houston Baker Jr., Simone Browne, and Paul Gilroy, among others, explores such tangled scientific perspectives: black holes, DNA, infrahuman categories, genomes, bloodlines, and poetic sciences are analytical sites these thinkers utilize to work through racial politics and questions of emancipation.[17] Following Wynter, I suggest, then, that scientific racism cannot have the last word because this analytical frame refuses collaborative insights. While the natural sciences are certainly informed by monumental racial histories—and this is not to be dismissed—noticing conversations and connections between black creative texts and scientific knowledge will reveal important scholarly challenges: to breach analytical barriers and open up meaningful ways of imagining and honoring "a new contestatory image of the human" and therefore disclose otherwise unacknowledged political and intellectual narratives that *differently* imagine the scientific workings of emancipatory knowledge.[18]

The Axis and Our Left-Center-Right Intellectual Work

In what follows, I suggest that our present political spectrum, left-center-right, forecloses the potential of a new science of being human. I look to the writings of Sylvia Wynter to draw attention to an intellectual imperative that can (and does) provide a route to noticing, as Rinaldo Walcott explains, a "new opening up and opening out of the category of human, meant to re-cuperate a different kind of planetary life."[19] I offer that within the academy, our political imaginary is produced within a self-referencing system that is underwritten by normative and biocentric conceptions of the human. Here, normal-biologically-and-economically-politically-right-on-Man inhabits the center or origin of our geopolitical systems, representing, embodying, and *defining* full humanness and emancipation, while Man's human Others, in particular those coded as racially-sexually condemned, are variously (dis) placed within this system.

Given this context, there are two interlocking themes that I will high-light in relation to Wynter's project. First are the ways in which the "left" of the spectrum plays out in our Western academic worlds. I am using "left" in an intentionally crude sense, to include such academic projects as feminism, antiracism, ethnic studies, left studies—those hopeful intellectual projects that have, since about the 1960s, become increasingly institutionalized. Second are the geographic contours of politics, for the left-center-right spectrum takes place and has a place—in institutions, offices, streets, and homes. Indeed, these political geographies are multiscalar and bordered as much as they are changing ideological expressions and/or calcified sites of human activity.

The worldview Wynter enables hinges on her ability to turn a hopeful intellectual project invested in emancipation in on itself. To paraphrase Wynter, as she reflects on the promise of civil rights, black is beautiful, feminism, and other "left-leaning" social movements of the 1960s and 1970s: these political projects might be analyzed not though the profits and successes of various "identity" studies—African American studies, for example—that often (but not always) effectively territorialize and identify that the study of (and thus the success of) "race" is one working toward or meeting the standards of Man in patriarchal, economic, and ethnic absolutist terms (we might also think of this as the Cosby-Poussain *code noir*, their invitation to submen/black men to become human).[20] Instead, we might see these movements as the *incomplete challenge to* the conception of Man itself and thus unfinished.[21] More clearly, her critique of our institutional-intellectual work suggests that a project such as African American studies, which initially challenged the making and meaning of Man-as-human, has increasingly abandoned this endeavor in favor of valorizing a project through which Man-as-human is axiomatically preconceptualized as the marker of emancipation.[22] Within our intellectual history and the terrain of the academy, particular antiracist, antisexist, and anticolonial challenges fell into—in fact utilize(d)—a biocentric model (racial-anatomical difference) to resist the overrepresentation of Man as they simultaneously scripted this as a "normal" way of life (racial-anatomical difference is coded as normally and differently human and profitable as such).[23]

Wynter therefore unveils the political work of our institutional-intellectual and emancipatory projects—Marxism, civil rights, left studies, feminism, antiracism, humanism, and so on—turning them in on themselves to reveal the ways in which they are framed vis-à-vis bourgeois values that are underpinned by biological scripts (of which race and racism are natural outcomes). What is uncovered are the ways in which Darwinian "survival of the fittest" narratives seep into our intellectual struggles and consequently render particular academics and their projects more likely to *naturally* (read: economically) survive the world than those of their nonconforming counterparts. Or, even more crudely, and put in spatial terms, particular kinds of antiracists have bigger offices—so what does this say about liberation, exclusion, territory, and racial justice? This is not a project of simply identifying scientific racism and biological determinism; nor is it a project of pointing to our present disappointments with the unmet (and met) achievements of civil rights, feminism, and other liberation struggles.

It is a project that understands our order of knowledge as repetitively instituting a mode of humanness that projects a bioeconomic being (Man) as the centered and healthy purveyor of reality/truth/emancipation and thus, through practices of exclusion as it is coupled with the desire to become healthy, centered, bioeconomic beings, reifies particular intellectual projects as logically and comfortably profitable.

Wynter refuses a horizontal (left-center-right) political framework. The consequence of turning the left and other left-leaning social movements in on themselves, while resulting in important critiques, has also resulted in Wynter's commitment to what she terms a "new world view."[24] This worldview points to two interlocking analytical processes: first, it identifies our present conception of the human as defined in (recurring) biocentric terms. Put crudely, a Cartesian axis is formed, with vertical/biocentric/top-down (Man/native/nigger/nigger woman) and horizontal/political (left-center-right) coordinates (see figure 6.1). These social and political classifications offer limited options—up and down, left and right—with particular communities barely moving at all. These coordinate options also, as we know, function to reify us/them, margin/center, right/left, right/wrong, human/Other categories. Wynter brings into focus how particular intellectual and emancipatory projects—the left, civil rights, feminism—while historically promising, have in fact failed to radically unsettle, or call into question, the pivot point and definer of this Cartesian axis—Man-as-white-heterosexual-breadwinner-and-measuring-stick-of-human-normalcy, or Man-as-human. Man is situated firmly as the centralized anchor of the Cartesian axis, a position that in mathematics is incidentally referred to as "the origin." The result is a *closed* system, a sliding up and down, between Man-as-human and nigger woman as they are differentially positioned between right, center, and left.

Wynter's political vision thinks outside the defining terms of Man, and thus outside racially informed (x-axis) genres of being human and left-center-right (y-axis), because, if we *trust* her argument, our political coordinates are determined by the pivot point (Man-as-human) and its attendant assumption that humans are differentially valued based on biological markers such as race. This is significant because it is in the coming together of these two points, *from* the point of origin, that freedom makes its appearance within our intellectual communities. It is therefore in Man's terms that we tend to conceptualize freedom *as* historically bound to a *Western* conception of freedom, slavery, and abolition. Or, to put it another way,

A bio-politico system, identifying the origin and definer of freedom (Man, 0, 0) as the pivot point. Here are also the classificatory hierarchies of humanness: bios-vertical, x axis, (man-to-jobless nigger woman), and the horizontal political y axis (left-center-right). x, y, are connected with a squiggly curve, closing the system, yet idintifying that x, y, are also sliding scales. You are right if you have noticed that figure 6.1 is inverted and incomplete. Most axes look like this:

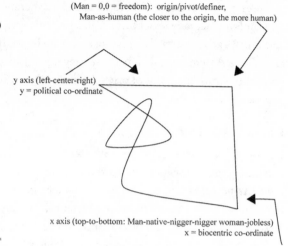

(Man = 0,0 = freedom): origin/pivot/definer, Man-as-human (the closer to the origin, the more human)

y axis (left-center-right)
y = political co-ordinate

x axis (top-to-bottom: Man-native-nigger-nigger woman-jobless)
x = biocentric co-ordinate

And within coordinates of most axes, x = vertical and y = horizontal. The partial inverted axis in figure 6.1 perhaps then points to the uncompleted challenges to Man and the limits of geometric positivism, too, and therefore points us towards the more interesting Axis: Bold as Love

Figure 6.1. Axis line drawing by Katherine McKittrick, prepared by Ray Zilli.

our social struggles in the academy are whirling around in a closed system wherein freedom, liberty, power to the people, and equal rights continue to be informed by plantation-colonial mentality wherein Man is overrepresented as fully human and all others are defective/dysslected humans who, in their political struggles, identify the biocentric, economic, and political model of Man-as-human—the bigger office—as the final frontier/a normal way of life.

What I am trying to underline is Wynter's wager, which is to veer us away from inadvertently or intentionally overrepresenting Man-as-human, precisely because, in many of our struggles to reimagine the world, Man remains *the* oppositional category—something we resist, the conceptual enemy—and is therefore positioned as the definer of and central to our emancipatory strategies, and thus the purveyor of the origin story and belief system through which the full/true human self is reinstituted as, Wynter writes, the "we" of "the breadwinning/investing/capital accumulating/consuming/middle classes."[25] This means that the left and other political positionalities, whether battling or embracing Man, often stage this within our present liberal humanist model as *classed* members of this social system, and thus actually profit from replicating this system, rather than being co-human and existentially *with* those who are logically excluded from this knowledge system (excluded because they inhabit spaces conceptually imperceptible from the point of origin, reside at the bottom of the barrel, are too alien to comprehend).[26]

Scientia Bold as Love

How might we embrace, as Sylvia Wynter puts it, "being human as praxis"[27] and think outside the logic of coordinated exclusion and profitable conformity? As noted earlier, part of Sylvia Wynter's intellectual challenge asks: How do we attend to the promise of science—we are, after all, cognitive, neurolinguistic, flesh-and-blood, and thus "science-y" beings—without reifying a biocentric left-center-right worldview? Following Wynter, it is useful to turn to Aimé Césaire's "science of the word" to think through alterability of the human.

Deploying "the science of the word" is the act of representing our human condition through poetics and language. It emphasizes how we symbolically attend to, and *feel*, our genetic and biological world. The science of the word does not *describe* our surroundings, our flesh and bones, and our experiences; rather, it emphasizes how the emergence of the human was accompanied by, rather than preceded by, the word, or mythos. This is a significant point to keep in mind, for Wynter is suggesting that our cognitive understanding of the world and our selves is *simultaneously* biological and cultural (bios/mythoi)—biochemistry, neurons, matter here, not as essential racial-genetic truths but as indicators of the ways in which human consciousness is crucial to undoing our present order of life. This simultaneity provides the "demonic grounds" of being human and a vision of *scientia* rather than science as we know it, precisely because it refuses to privilege biocentricity—of which race and racism are outcomes—as the natural, pregiven order of things *as* it recognizes the "neurophysiological circuits/mechanisms of the brain" that contribute to, alongside the word, "introducing [human] *invention* into existence."[28] The science of the word, then, points to creative labor as recoding science through representational and biological feelings—it is, as noted earlier, a project *scientia*.[29] This is an interdisciplinary and collaborative task, one that allows us to think about how the creative narrative can and does contribute to what is otherwise understood as "the laws of nature," thus creating an intellectual space to explore the worlds of those communities who are otherwise considered unscientific, scientifically inferior, endangered, and/or too alien to comprehend. This framework also points to relational and connective knowledges rather than positioning, say, science first and resistance later.

In the wake of our commitment to a social constructionist perspective that tends to *follow* biological categorization, Wynter insists that we take seriously the workings of neurology, blood, flesh, bones, and muscles, as biological life and death are languaged into existence: the key is, then, to think about the meaning of a biological organism—or more generally what is otherwise considered objective scientific knowledge (the jobless nigger woman; see figure 6.1)—as it is implicit to the creative text. Here, M. NourbeSe Philip is instructive: she writes, for example, that the language of the black diaspora is wounded due to Eurocentric discourses that denigrate certain phrases such as "thick lips" and "kinky hair."[30] Philip wonders, then, how to write herself and her community anew, given the black struggle with racial hatred as it is tied to thick lips, kinky hair—the biological data difference, the scripts that make promises of despising this biological data of difference. What she suggests is a collaborative language, one spoken creatively "with the whole body ... gestures, arms akimbo" as this living body becomes a communicative image *and* a speakable subject. Like Wynter, Philip suggests that the artist solders together self, flesh, physiology, and the word—bios-mythoi, cognition-neurology-creativity, phylogeny-ontogeny-sociogeny—to newly describe an ongoing, but hopeful, struggle.[31]

Here, the indexical, the measurable, the death-dealing workings of scientific racism might not be understood through a discourse that clings to the "rightness" of the "pure sciences"; instead, the cognitive rupture of linear phylogenic narratives unveils the ways in which creative narratives point to the neurological, flesh, blood, and bones of humanness as these biologics are entwined with a racially structured discourse of condemnation. Here I think of, among others, hip-hop artist Nas's commentary on his dysselected/defective masculinity, the *"pain* in his brain."[32] Nas employs the science of the word as a worldview that neurologically and physiologically *feels* flesh, blood, gender, race, class, and politics as co-humanly connective rather than systemically organized from top to bottom and left to right. Here, Man-as-human-and-origin fades away not to be *replaced* by an alternative perspective/figure who occupies that defining position, but rather to bring a challenge to *where* humanness takes place. It is precisely the pain in the brain, the poetics of science, and the conditions of being human that give form to the complex feelings of diaspora existences and geographies, and thus a value system that imagines a version of being human that cannot be contained—and by no means emancipated—by our present social system and biocentric governing codes. Put differently, the science of the word *feels and questions* the unsurvival of the condemned, thus dislodging black diasporic denigration from its "natural" place through *wording* the biological conditions of being human. Or, Nas's "pain in the brain" is not simply *descriptive* of blackness/racism, it *is* physiological-neurolinguistic-diasporic-ontology *as* human life.

This imagining a human *scientia*, and linking it to diasporic practices, is best exemplified, for me, through music and music making—here the science of the word is writ large, with the physiological/neurological human being assembling creative texts that understand and perceive the world as necessarily connective (due to the call-and-response, the audience participation and desire, sharing intellectual narrative, the subversive expression of diasporic histories that narrate slow, fast, danceable, sorrowful stories). In a study done by Maryland medical researchers Charles Limb and Allen Braun, the two hypothesized that "spontaneous musical improvisation would be associated with discrete changes in prefrontal [brain] activity that provide a biological substrate for actions that are characterized by creative self-expression in the absence of conscious self-monitoring."[33] In other words, Limb and Braun wondered about and analyzed how improvisational music and music making might be acts that are creatively scripted outside governing codes, and thus evidence of unbounded or ungoverned brain activity. Their research indirectly, at least for me, parallels the kind of biological-intellectual creativity enacted through the science of the word. This is to say that Limb and Braun provide a pathway for us to think about how black diasporic creative texts are bios-mythoi/neurological-intellectual assertions of humanness. This attention to the scientific contours of the arts—which takes very seriously the physiological and neurological—challenges us, as intellectuals, to rethink how we take up racial-sexual justice precisely because it locates knowledge making as connective to flesh, blood, bones, muscles, and brain matter while also forcing us to notice new forms of scientific life in the arts.

Creative texts are simultaneously lived and assembled (rather than lived *and then* socially produced), with creative brain activity opening the door to rethinking how humanness might be imagined, for it is here, alongside the MRI, the neurological activity, and the creative text, that the conditions of being human are described in terms that refuse biocentricity without eschewing our physiological data. This, in turn, does something to the axis coordinates described in the previous section, for it not only discloses a closed system through which we self-monitor our behaviors and thus reinstitute Man-as-human (conscious awareness and/or routine living and naturalization of governing codes), but also identifies another system that poetically attends to the pain in the brain, the fact of blackness, the poems of illness and incarceration. This reconfiguration of being reveals, Wynter explains, a level of human existence "defined by the fact of its being regulated in its behaviors by the discursive neuronal patterns of its culture-specific modes of the 'mind' or systemic consciousness, by, in effect, the hybrid correlation between the *ordo naturae* of our neurological brain states and the *ordo verborum* of our systems of meanings, necessarily impels . . . the human subject beyond our present 'order of discourse' and episteme into 'realms' beyond 'conventional reason.'"[34]

Enter, then, composer, songwriter, and guitarist Jimi Hendrix—a return to the 1960s, a return to premature black death. Hendrix is known for his live performances, his innovative electrical-technological compositions, his "radical use of his Stratocaster's tremolo bar, shifting between high-pitched screams and dive-bomber bursts of low-end crunch," and particular portions of his black masculinity (hair curled and puffed out, clothing style, "authentic" corporeal gestures, sexual parts/phallus).[35] Additionally, Hendrix sonically draws our attention to an Ellisonian jazz moment—that different sense of time and space the Invisible Man alerted us to as he abandoned the left/communism and took residency underground.[36] Hendrix thus draws attention to the governing musical codes, the overrepresentation of Man and the science of the fittest, creative labor, diasporic maps, improvised musical arrangements, and innovative studio albums, all of which unfolded into a series of creative texts, sounds, and insights that bear "witness to specificities of black life while gesturing toward a more general condition of Western modernity."[37] The musical geopolitics Hendrix asserts, vis-à-vis the personified "axis" who institutes a "bold as love" black figure/ Hendrix into our worlds, provides a context through which the science of the word, a bios-mythoi worldview, invokes a different place from which to articulate the stakes and politics of being human. Put simply: bold as love, Hendrix does not make sense within a belief system that is invested in the overrepresentation of Man. Indeed, I suggest that Hendrix's creative labor, his improvisational skills, his technical, engineering and songwriting expertise, as well as the narratives and sounds that emerge from the song "Bold as Love" illuminate a mathematically-affective, bios-mythoi, data set—an "axis bold as love." Here new axis coordinates are produced and the old coordinates (the original crude axis sketched above) are both recognizable and changed. Hendrix's vision combines structures of feeling (bold as love) with a scientifically familiar configuration (axis); the mathematical is rendered implicit to love, boldness, his lyrical critique of the uninhabitable and the imperial militarization of place, and his artistic imagining of, as Paul Gilroy notes, "not-yet" planetary futures.[38]

Gilroy writes that Jimi Hendrix was a complex figure who wrote "immortal articulations of the slave sublime, transposed into futuristic genre-defying statements of human suffering, yearning and hope."[39] Hendrix creatively negotiated race, racism, and masculinity as he impressed himself upon—and was inserted into—many diasporic political geographies. Celebrated guitar genius, gypsy, discharged paratrooper, black-Cherokee-Mexican, Hendrix has, during his musical career and after his death, become a central figure in popular culture and rock-and-roll/blues/jazz and global guitar debates. Notably, as Gilroy points out, Hendrix is often cast as a primal musician—so celebrated is his talent that many (although certainly not all) of his fans, biographers, and colleagues suggest that he did not have to work or practice to achieve genius.[40] Add to this Greil Marcus's observation that Hendrix, unlike Bob Dylan, Paul Simon, and Neil Young, has never been regarded as a serious poet.[41] Hendrix: primal unpoetic biological fact? Gilroy refuses this absolutist perception by contextualizing Hendrix's worldly, diasporic, anticolonial vision as it was/is underscored by a complex ontological bid for embodying and imagining post-Fanonian human.[42] I want to further suggest that Hendrix provides a poetics-politics that is scientifically diasporic and thus, if thought about alongside Sylvia Wynter's *scientia*, provides a way to unthink the auto-instituting geographic constraints that structure our sense of place. More specifically, the title of his second album with the Jimi Hendrix Experience, *Axis: Bold as Love*, as well as its final track, "Bold as Love," point to a useful poetic-scientific-mathematical promise that is creatively expressed, imagined, written by a black diasporic figure vis-à-vis humanness. Rather than solely attending to the literary-symbolic work of his song(s), or returning to Hendrix's blues-jazz-psychedelic genius, I look to how Hendrix—specifically his practiced techniques of creative labor and the "axis bold as love"—presents the science of being human.

If we think about music and music making as *scientia*, the conceptual stakes of "axis bold as love" are intensified. Notably, of course, Hendrix practiced guitar day and night and was meticulous with studio technologies.[43] As with many excellent guitarists, his live performances did not transparently map out the studio versions of songs; rather, the governing structure of the studio music was overlaid and interrupted by improvisational techniques. This combining of structure and ungoverned musical possibilities draws attention to the simultaneity of physiological, neurological, and creative labor implicit to his work. Importantly, the *work* of practice is always coupled with improvised sound—for one cannot improvise without practicing and arranging and rearranging memory patterns developed through partly unconscious repetition and creative innovation. The brain and consciousness express, physiologically, creative *scientia*.

Hendrix's "axis bold as love" is thus as much measurable as it is not. In addition to being structured through and physiologically expressing improvised mathematical creative human labor, the live version of the song can serve as an auditory palimpsest to its textual codes. Specifically, consider that chord structure, the time and beat, and the lyrics have all been documented in a score, which guides the musician or reader through the song: there are treble clef, time signature (4/4) and tempo markings, a suggested "feel" and "genre" (moderately slow rock), and notes (play A, then E, then F-sharp minor, then D; then play A, E, F-sharp minor, D; then play D, A, B minor, G, G-sharp, and so on). The notations are complemented with hints, tempo changes, and other musical matters such as "hammer on to E sharp without picking and slide up to F sharp" or "2nd string sounds unintentionally."[44]

If, as noted earlier, the textual complements the physiological, neurological, mathematical, and creative contours of the axis, the audio of the song itself invites another layer of technological labor. In addition to engineer Eddie Kramer using a reel flange in the "outro" of "Bold as Love"— wherein one uses one's hands to sync up two identical tape recordings and then manually manipulates one of the tapes to alter the audio output— Hendrix played the Mellotron, an early sampler keyboard that played back and remixed prerecorded sounds.[45] The sonic and auditory innovations that underlie Hendrix's music making invoke a long-standing *technological* relationality that is implicit to black musics—between and across humans, instruments (including instruments such as oil drums, plastic bottles), politics, desires, and geography. Yet when coupled with the *scientia* of imagining and expressing an "axis: bold as love," his creative labor also draws attention to a human "coming into existence through the participation in the reconstruction/redefinition of sound and sound-making activities" as it articulates the limits of our present governing codes.[46]

The "axis bold as love" is a knotted invitation to reimagine the science of being human. It not only invokes Earth's axis and a Cartesian axis, and hopeful futures of the "not yet,"[47] but it draws attention to a different system of knowledge that cannot function through self-referencing biocentric modes of humanness precisely because this framing would counter the mathematical-scientific workings of bold love and neurological creative output. As I read Hendrix's axis, with Wynter in mind, political (left-center-right) geographies are thrown into disarray as they are identified as dichotomized locations of violence and privilege (to return to Hendrix's lyrics: "waters are taken for granted, trophies of war"), while the "axis bold as love" institutes a global world from a different perspective, a newly tilted axis, a labored radically nonconformist-jazz-blues-rock narrative with scientific promise. This is to say that Hendrix's practiced, labored, musical "genius" provides a poetics-politics of future love — more humanly workable due to the crisscrossing of science and poetics that emerges out of a critique of a closed system — coming from the neurological-spontaneous-creative-activity and thus a flesh-and-blood worldview.

It is through such creative acts that we might find the scientific poetics of our future: in this challenge to disciplinary and epistemological bifurcation — symbolized here by a crude Cartesian axis — black cultural production writes scientific and disciplinary knowledge anew, as necessarily a human project. Here the "axis bold as love" is projected through an aural communicative act, which in turn mediates the history of subjugation in a new context. This new context is not a space of absolute otherness, it does not identify diasporic/subaltern subjects as "outcasts" to nature, it does not seek to understand blackness by "saving" and therefore simultaneously preserving and erasing racial difference, and, it does not assume a purely primal unpoetic black narrative. Rather, this new context forces us to think about the alterability of humanness as it is insisted upon through creative acts that map out the relational workings of science. All of this is to say that in poetically "science-ing" the biological contours of the human, the creative text can, and here I paraphrase Wynter, move us toward the transformation of our present purely biologized understanding of what it means to be human and toward the redefining of the human as praxis, perhaps looking to and reexamining those cosmic sounds, the neural substrates that underlie musical performance, internally motivated, stimulus-independent behaviors that unfold in the absence of social processes, political options, and intellectual imperatives that typically mediate self-monitoring: an axis as bold as love.[48]

Notes

1. See the introduction to this volume and McKittrick, *Demonic Grounds*, 124.
2. Wynter, "New Seville and the Conversion Experience of Bartolomé de Las Casas," 54.
3. Wynter, "1492," 12–13.
4. A biocentric conception of the human refers to the law-like order of knowledge that posits a Darwinian conception of the human—that we are purely biological beings—as universal. It assumes, then, that we are bioevolutionary humans *that do not* author a racially coded bioevolutionary script; rather, a biocentric narrative posits human beings as inherently natural (produced by nature). See King, "Race and Our Biocentric Belief System," 361–366.
5. Wynter, "Towards the Sociogenic Principle," 30–66.
6. Maturana and Varela, *Autopoiesis and Cognition*.
7. Wynter, "1492," 7 (emphasis in the original).
8. Wynter, "Unsettling the Coloniality of Being," 319.
9. Wynter, "Unsettling the Coloniality of Being," 322.
10. Wynter, "Unsettling the Coloniality of Being," 318.
11. Scott, "The Re-enchantment of Humanism," 189 (emphasis in the original); see also Fanon, *Black Skin, White Masks*, 11.
12. Wynter, "Unsettling the Coloniality of Being," 331.
13. For an overview, see Subramaniam, "Moored Metamorphoses," 951–980; and Harding, *The "Racial" Economy of Science*.
14. Krieger, "Refiguring 'Race,'" 211–216.
15. Kevles, *In the Name of Eugenics*; Jackson, "African-American Responses to the Human Genome Project," 181–191; Dodson and Williamson, "Indigenous Peoples and the Morality of the Human Genome Project," 204–208.
16. Wynter, "1492," 7.
17. Browne, "Digital Epidermalization," 1–20; Césaire, "Poetry and Knowledge," 134–146; Gilroy, *Against Race*; Philip, *A Genealogy of Resistance*; Baker, *Blues Ideology and Afro-American Literature*.
18. Wynter, "1492," 50.
19. Walcott, "Reconstructing Manhood," 89.
20. Fanon, *The Wretched of the Earth* (trans. Farrington), 163. It is worth recalling Fanon's full sentence in light of Bill Cosby and Alvin F. Poussain's *Come On People*. Fanon writes: "Bourgeois ideology, however, which is the proclamation

of an essential equality between men, manages to appear logical in its own eyes by inviting the sub-men to become human, and to take as their prototype Western humanity as incarnated in the Western bourgeoisie."

21. Wynter, "On How We Mistook the Map for the Territory," 107–169.

22. Wynter, "On How We Mistook the Map for the Territory," 107–169.

23. The history of institutionalized feminism also clearly maps out the profits of embracing Man-made politics, with liberal feminism dominating definitions of equality: equality with men, on Man's terms, with Man's paycheck, and Man's standards of beauty. Disguised as "progress," the economic project of feminism financially benefits from asking subwomen (non-Western, nonwhite, poor, incarcerated) to become "real" women without identifying the ways in which white-woman-human was produced alongside colonial violence and encounter and reinstitutes a biocentric worldview (through which the death of nonwhite womanhood continues to be cast as natural, through which the life stories of nonwhite women continue to be cast as primitively "different"). In our academic worlds, we need to only consider the glaring absence of African feminism (and thus the assumed *profitability* of an African-less/evolved collection) from the *Norton Anthology of Feminist Theory and Criticism*. See Pius Adesanmi's letter, "Disappearing Me Softly."

24. Wynter, "1492," 5–57.

25. Wynter, "Human Being as Noun, Or Being Human as Praxis? Towards the Autopoetic Turn/Overturn: A Manifesto," (quoted with permission).

26. "Too alien to comprehend" is taken from Lorde, *Sister Outsider*, 117.

27. Wynter, "Human Being as Noun."

28. Wynter, "Unsettling the Coloniality of Being," 328–329 (emphasis added).

29. Wynter, "The Pope Must Have Been Drunk," 17–41.

30. Philip, *A Genealogy of Resistance*, 53.

31. Philip, *A Genealogy of Resistance*, 25, 41–56; Wynter, "Rethinking 'Aesthetics,'" 237–279.

32. Nas, "Life's a B****," from *Illmatic* (Sony, 1994); see also Carole Boyce Davies's discussion of the illness and poetics of Claudia Jones in her *Left of Karl Marx*, 99–129. Here I also draw attention to the work of Ruth Wilson Gilmore, whose discussions of premature death and mortal urgency in *Golden Gulag* disclose what I call prison-*life*; from the outset, the text references, relies on, and infuses prison expansion with human life, kinship, and survival in the face of human condemnation. Gilmore, *Golden Gulag*; McKittrick, "On Plantations, Prisons, and a Black Sense of Place," 947–963.

33. Limb and Braun, "Neural Substrates of Spontaneous Musical Performance," 1.

34. Wynter, "Beyond the Word of Man," 645–646.

35. Waksman, "Black Sound, Black Body," 79, 103; Gilroy, *The Black Atlantic*, 93; Lawrence, *Jimi Hendrix*, 32, 51–52.

36. Ellison, *Invisible Man*. See also Weheliye, *Phonographies*, 46–72.

37. Weheliye, *Phonographies*, 47.

38. Gilroy, "Bold as Love?," 112–125.

39. Gilroy, "Bold as Love?," 112.

40. Gilroy, "Bold as Love?," 112.

41. Marcus, *Mystery Train*, 79.

42. Gilroy, "Bold as Love?," 112–125.

43. See Redding and Appleby, *Are You Experienced?*; Cross, *Room Full of Mirrors*.

44. "Bold as Love" score interpretations are taken from Aledort and Jones, *Hendrix—Axis: Bold as Love*, 124–135.

45. Many thanks to Ray Zilli for assisting with my reading of the musical score of "Bold as Love," as well as with clarification on the reel flange, the Mellotron, the engineering work of Eddie Kramer, and Jimi Hendrix's guitar techniques. Any musical mismeasurements or misunderstandings on the technicalities of "Bold as Love" are, of course, mine.

46. Campbell, "Remixing Relationality," 300–301.

47. In addition to Hendrix's lyrics in "Bold as Love," see Gwyneth Jones's science fiction novel *Bold as Love*.

48. Wynter, "Unsettling the Coloniality of Being," 257–337; Wynter, "Human Being as Noun."

7   STRATEGIC ANTI-ESSENTIALISM
Decolonizing Decolonization

> A New World view of 1492 should seek to reconceptualize the past in
> terms of the existential reality specific to our [American] continent. It
> must recognize, as Cuban novelist Alejo Carpentier (1976) indicates,
> that all the major and hitherto-separated races of the world have been
> brought together in the new world to work out a common destiny. This
> destiny would entail the transformation of our original dominant /
> subordinate social structure and its attendant perceptual and cognitive
> matrices into new ones founded on reciprocal relations.
> SYLVIA WYNTER, "1492: A NEW WORLD VIEW"

In her essay "1492: A New World View," Sylvia Wynter addresses an issue of
great urgency: the ongoing, "world-fateful," effects of the Columbian "exchange."[1] Initiated with Christopher Columbus's 1492 voyage to the Caribbean, the enormous movement of plants, people, animals, communicable
diseases, and ideas across space — and the kind of ties that such movements
engendered — gave rise to what can truly be described as a *new world*. I argue that it was new in many senses of the word, the least of which is Columbus's own "new discovery," that is, a view that was both Eurocentric and
geographically limited to the Americas. Rather, the New World was one in
which people across continents and oceans were brought together into *a
single field of power*. This is the world we have collectively inherited, a world
organized by social relations that are, to say the least, grossly uneven. There
is no doubt, of course, that this coming together was asymmetrical, but it
was a process that led to the creation of a world where the lives of its human
inhabitants came to be (and remain) intimately connected.

All those moving people, plants, animals, and ideas were brought together into a global arena of capitalist relationships. People in what we now know as the Caribbean and mainland of the Americas were brought into this new world through the force of "blood and fire," as Karl Marx put it.[2] No amount of blood and fire was spared for people in places now known as Africa and, not much later, Asia and the Pacific, as they too found themselves enclosed within a globalizing system of rule. And, of course, terror, immiseration, and death were visited upon great numbers of people in Europe as well, even as some of the wealthiest and most powerful people and nodes of vast empires were entrenched there. What was left in Columbus's wake, then, was a world of deep, often violent, sometimes cooperative, but always connected human relationships.

In the making of a new world, new social bodies and new social imaginaries were made as well. Indeed, many (most?) of the identifications through which people across the world now see themselves would have been unrecognizable prior to 1492 (and, in many cases, much later). Certainly, our "races" and "nations," the oppositional binaries through which we imagine "gender," the existence of "homosexuals" and "heterosexuals," indeed, the very existence of "Europeans," "Americans," "Africans," "Asians," "Pacific Islanders," and so forth, are "modes of representation," as Wynter puts it, that would have been incomprehensible to humans five hundred years ago (and less). Certainly, none of the people enmeshed within the relationships of empire in 1492 would have understood themselves through any of these categories.

In short, much has changed since Columbus's initial voyage. While this may seem far too obvious or even trite to say, it is, nonetheless, a point that is often forgotten, even disavowed, by those Wynter describes as falling on either side of a dualism of "celebrants" and "dissidents" of the events of 1492.[3] Celebrants see in the Columbian exchange only a "glorious achievement," while dissidents see in it only an unending disaster. Paradoxically, though focused on the *consequences* of 1492, both celebrants and dissidents presume that the exchange did not irrevocably *change* the lives—and futures—of everyone concerned. This is, in part, due to the disconnected or, as Wynter puts it, *particularistic*, sense of the "we" that both celebrants and dissidents recognize themselves as belonging to. Each particularistic "we" is racialized, ethnicized, and, increasingly, nationalized. Celebrants in the United States, for example, continue to imagine the nation as a simple extension of a "European" or "White" society *as if* this is actually so, while dissidents imagine native societies *as if* the category of native was not, itself, borne from a colonizing desire for power and the strategic need to foster hierarchical difference. Both celebrants and dissidents refuse to acknowledge that something other than either glory or devastation was also wrought from the events following 1492, something that can possibly point to ways of being connected to one another as humans without the hierarchies and homogenizations developed in the process of the Columbian exchange.

Wynter argues for another way of analyzing the making of a new world, one that recognizes its horrors, its *newness*, and its potentialities. Her "new world view" is a recognition of the *transversal* character of the Columbian exchange, a recognition that invites people to deviate from the hierarchicalizing and homogenizing "accumulation of differences" emblematic of Columbus's own limited view of the new world he helped to bring into being.[4] In rejecting the dualism advanced by celebrants and dissidents, Wynter asks whether "a new and ecumenically human view" of the events following 1492 can emerge, one that expands our sense of who "we" are, one that will allow us to co-identify and coexist as interaltruistic co-humans.[5] This "new world view," she argues, is one that most closely reflects our actually, already existing interrelationality, a form of connectivity to each other that has long manifested itself ecologically as well as "sociosystemically."[6] Indeed, Wynter believes that our new world, *precisely because of the exchanges that brought it into existence*, has given us the option to form new social relationships with one another based on our shared humanity. Subjectively aligning ourselves through nonhierarchical relations of co-specificity, Wynter argues, is ethically "the *only* possible commemoration of 1492."[7]

In this essay, I begin with an examination of Sylvia Wynter's argument regarding what she, after Robert Pirsig, calls Columbus's "root expansion of thought."[8] Columbus's challenge to the prevailing Christian views of his time concerning the earth's geography and its habitability, she shows, allowed him to expand then-existing ideas of humanity. For Columbus, *all* of humanity was—or could/must be made to be—part of the (still very much Christian) fold. Such an expansion in the meaning of the *propter nos*—the "us" for whom the world exists—*if* taken to its fullest potential *and* denuded of its hierarchical rankings can provide us, Wynter maintains, with the cognitive framework to end the most nefarious effects of the initial Columbian exchange.

I follow by examining some of the ways in which we have, so far, been mostly unable to recognize either that a new world was indeed forged in the aftermath of 1492 or that this new world has provided us with potential escape routes away from its devastating consequences. The failure to take up the possibilities of this new world is, perhaps, most clearly evident in recent efforts to posit a Manichaean relationship of people and place where one is either native or not. In this simultaneously expanding and narrowing dualism of belonging, it is all those who are constituted as migrants who are said to *colonize* those constituted as natives. I show how this deep hostility toward *mobility* is one of the more nefarious outcomes of the unevenness of the Columbian exchange. It is a view that refuses to see persons constituted into putative groupings of natives and migrants as coexisting in a *shared* field of colonial (and now postcolonial) power. Situating my discussion in the Americas, I argue that to undo this dualism, we need to take the necessary step of bringing both natives and migrants into the *same field of analysis*.[9] I conclude with a discussion of how efforts to expand our sense of co-specificity have always coexisted alongside efforts to narrow them so that we can see that espousing particularistic senses of "we" is only one choice among many, a choice that we can and, I would argue, we should reject.

The basis of the rejection of a particularistic *propter nos* rests, I believe, on a rejection of territorialized senses of self and, thus, other. Part of the consequence of expanding capitalist social property relations to the Americas (which began in earnest in the late sixteenth and early seventeenth centuries) was the *territorialization of* land, place, subjectivity, and belonging. Control over land and control over a sense of place and who "belonged" there and who did not were absolutely crucial to gaining control over people.[10] This process of territorialization was significant in the ushering in of a "new world order" of both constituting and partitioning putative "races," genders, and later "nations," and later natives and "migrants."

Wynter's "Poetics of a New *Propter Nos*"

For Wynter, there is a paradoxical relationship between the ruthlessly violent making of the New World and the potentially liberating conceptual shifts that the first voyage of Christopher Columbus set into play. Columbus's personal victory—the vindication of his insistence on sailing west to India, his newfound social elevation—led to a world-shattering level of destruction against the inhabitants of the places that Spain's monarchs claimed during their imperial conquests. At the same time, Wynter notes, this led to a "root expansion in thought" concerning ideas of self, other, and space.[11]

Wynter reminds us that not only did Columbus successfully challenge prevailing ideas of the navigability of the earth; his voyages also shattered existing ideas of the *human habitability* of the earth and the *connectedness* of its geographically dispersed humanity. Columbus's millenarian fervor over what he believed was the imminent Second Coming of Christ combined with his belief in the earth being created *for* the "life and the creation of souls" led to the generalization of the then marginal idea of *propter nos*: the belief that the earth was *for us*. Columbus's "discovery" that this *human* "us" inhabited regions previously thought of as nonexistent brought people across the planet into *relationship* with each other.[12] In this sense, the New World was not simply a mistaken formulation of Columbus imagining himself as having landed in India but one that brought the Eastern and Western Hemispheres *together* in a single field of imagination—and, of course, imperial power.

What Wynter refers to as the Janus-faced nature of 1492, therefore, lies in the simultaneous expansion in thought that led to the discovery that there was a geographically dispersed but still *shared* humanity across the planet *and* the genocidal elimination of much of that humanity as empires in Europe extended both their territorial claims and their exploitation of people's labor. Wynter contends that this paradox stems from the *incomplete* character of the new subjective understanding of human co-specificity.

Calamitously, the new, ruling mode of subjective understanding contained a distinction *between* humans. Although still imagined *as human*, some were more or less so. Unsurprisingly, those granted higher *existential* standing were the same elites who also gained privileged *material* status within expanding European empires. A *propter nos* limited by Christendom, Wynter shows, fundamentally shaped the "encounter" between European voyagers and the inhabitants of the Caribbean and Americas.[13] Columbus behaved toward the people he first encountered in the Caribbean in ways that maintained his distinction between his Christian *propter nos* and its oppositional referent of idolaters. Although Columbus believed that all of humanity *could* be made into a single Christian flock, by positioning his Christianity in binary terms, the people he encountered were viewed as occupying a legitimately subjugated place in the social order. As far as Columbus was concerned, he had not only the right but the duty to remake the Lucayan, Tainos, or Arawaks *in his own image*. Most of the people represented as lesser humans in Columbus's Christian *propter nos*, as we know, paid for his system of subjective understanding with their lives.

Wynter's insistence that an examination of people's modes of subjective understanding tells us something very useful about how to end practices of colonization, specifically her understanding of humans as being "hybridly" organic *and* "languaging" life forms. All humans, she argues, have "culture-specific system[s] of symbolic representation," which alone influence our "modes of conspecificity."[14] It "is on the basis of that mode [of subjective understanding]," she adds, "that the subjects of each human order are enabled to experience themselves as symbolic kin or interaltruistic conspecifics."[15] *Particularistic* modes of essentialist subjective understandings inherently create a *limited* sense of conspecificity, one that continuously creates the conditions for the subjugation of others. This is because any particularistic *propter nos* is practically "impervious to philosophical attack" and "impervious also to empirical counterevidence."[16] Hence, those within it are often unable to *see* the shared humanity of those imagined as outsiders.

Therefore, Wynter proposes that "the central mechanism at work" in processes of colonization—and even decolonization—"was and is that of *representation*."[17] It is through strategies of representation "that each human order and its culture-specific mode of empirical reality can be brought into being as a 'form of life."[18] And, importantly, who we think *we* are—be it "Spanish" or "European" or "Aztec" or native—and who our co-specifics are (those with/for whom we feel we have a connection) has significant effects on our actions. Wynter shows, for example, how the "Spanish" conquistadores were as incapable of imagining the "Aztecs" as their co-specifics as the "Aztecs" were in their view of other groups in (what is now) Mexico. The actions of both the Spanish and the Aztecs were limited by their partial, subjective understanding of themselves. The problem of partial perspectives on being human, then, is one that is shared across the line of colonizer/colonized.

Hence, Wynter calls for *another* root expansion in thought, one that can imagine the *propter nos* as one encompassing *all humans as a species*. This possibility exists not in the abstract but in the acknowledgment that human beings *are* deeply interconnected with one another and with the environment of which we are a part (although, unfortunately, Wynter's call does not extend to nonhuman life).[19] This connectivity remains real even as the groups and territories we are said to belong to are ideologically rendered as being particularistic (e.g., the United States as a "white" space) or as our connections to each other *across* spaces are denied (e.g., we are "American"). Indeed, as a result of the global expansion of ruling relations, life on the planet and thus our diverse planetary lives and ties are perhaps more connected to each other than ever before. This, along with the threat of nuclear destruction hanging over all of our heads for the last sixty-odd years, shows us that our futures are also intimately related. It is the reality of these connections and our shared need to secure the conditions of continued life that may, Wynter argues, make it possible for us to accept each other in toto, as a truly co-identified species.

In Wynter's proposed "human view" of 1492, the possibility of aligning our subjective understanding of ourselves with our social reality of interconnectivity is ours, *if we want it*. If the opportunity to do so is taken, we may be able to win, Wynter argues, the "true victory" promised by past expansions in our understanding of our co-humanity that remain incomplete.[20] To do so, we both need to transform the systems of symbolic representations we use and make an equally transformative change in our relationships to each other, relationships that, today, continue to hierarchically value people so that our ability to live a healthy, peaceful, and dignified life remains as unequal as the terms of the initial Columbian exchange.[21] I turn now to an examination of attempts at expanding our imagination of *propter nos* as well as current attempts to narrow it. This, I believe will help us clarify the *political* choices that we currently face and which are ours to make.

Subjected: Autochthony and Its Others

The very real possibility of thinking and acting *outside* the limits of any specific culture's self-understanding by expanding people's sense of *nos* is evident in countless attempts over the past five hundred years to broaden the circle of those with whom we hold affective ties. Significantly, this is a process that has been engaged in both by dominant groups and by those they rule over. To use an example given by Wynter, while the Aztecs in the early sixteenth century were unable to imagine others living in what is now "Mexico" as their co-specifics—and thereby enabling Hernán Cortés to successfully ally himself with other groups to destroy the Aztecs—there now exists a subjective understanding of being "indigenous."

Emerging in the post–World War II era, indigeneity is a relatively recent mode of representation, one that encompasses very diverse people across the Americas, indeed across the world, often under a single, shared subjective understanding of being the "first" to live in any particular place.[22] Being indigenous is a form of co-identification among people who previously did not see any connection with one another. It is also a way of laying claim to particular lands (or, more accurately, *territories*) on the basis of having (or having once had) specialized knowledge of that place. Yet, this mode of representation, however new or potentially expansive, remains particularistic. Indigeneity is a form of subjectivity that emerged *because of* the devastation wrought in the aftermath of 1492. Moreover, it is a form of subjectivity that interpellates people into efforts to gain national sovereignty within the global system of national states. Indigenous, then, as a mode of representation includes the often unacknowledged elision between native as a colonial state category of subjugation and indigenous as a category of resistance.

Indigenous conceptualized as such retains two interrelated problems that ensure that the kinds of unequal relationships organized in the aftermath of 1492 are reproduced. First, by denying the *social constitution* of the category of indigenous, it disavows people's now-long history of *connectivity* across (and sometimes against) this category. Because this connectivity challenges the particularistic nature of indigeneity, recognition of interrelationality is itself represented as a threat. Second, by continuing to limit the criteria of membership of each *nos*, each is unable to accept as co-specifics those who are rendered as always-already oppositional others. Indeed, in making any particularistic *nos*, the significance of omitting certain others cannot be underestimated.

The category of indigenous, thus, does a sort of political work. It produces a particular *nos* (and thus a particular Other-to-indigenous *nos*).[23] For some (though certainly not all) of those currently constituted as indigenous, it seems that one of the consequences of the enormously uneven Columbian exchange is the denunciation of the *process of exchange* itself. Today, the *movement* of life, plants, humans, and other animals is often cited as the *cause* for the devastation wrought on their native equivalent.[24] Rather than focus on the hierarchical and exploitative *relations* of the Columbian exchange, some assume that the cause of the problem was/is *mobility* itself. Within such a worldview, that which moves is consequently denounced as inherently polluting, and, in an idiom that is gaining in popularity, movement and migration are posited as inherently *colonizing*.

An understanding of mobility as always colonizing is evident in the expansion of the term "settler colonist" to include *all* those deemed nonnative in any given space. Recently, within both indigenous studies and social movements for indigenous rights, the historical distinctions between the voyages of Columbus (and other colonizers) and those of slaves who survived the Middle Passage, indentured workers recruited in the wake of slavery's abolition, and present-day migrants captured in a variety of state categories ranging from illegal to immigrant, have been collapsed. All, it is claimed, are *agents* of colonialism. It seems, then, that as there has been an expansion in the subjective understanding of people as indigenous, there has been a subsequent expansion in their other. Put differently, within some indigenous systems of belonging, all past and present people constituted as migrants are situated as colonizers.

In our present "great age" of migration, how did "colonizer" become a meaningful way to describe people who move across space?[25] Indeed, how did "colonizer" come to be an increasingly dominant mode of representing indigenous people's others, others who were once understood as co-colonized people or, at least, not as an *oppositional* other? Is there a relationship between these particularistic modes of representation and the false separation and hierarchical ranking of different but related experiences of colonization, such as the processes of expropriation and people's displacement across space?

The answers to these questions lie *within* the logics of autochthonous systems of representation and the ways in which claims to indigeneity *bring to life* discourses of alienness or foreignness. Jean Comaroff and John Comaroff argue, by "elevating to a first-principle the ineffable interests and connections, at once material and moral, that flow from 'native' rootedness, and special rights, in a place of birth," autochthonous discourses place those constituted as natives at the top of a hierarchy of the exploited, oppressed, and colonized and insist on the centrality of the claims of natives for the realization of either decolonization or justice.[26] Within the negative duality of natives and nonnatives that such discourses put into play, origins (and, in some contexts, claims of *original*, versus later, human discovery or inhabitation) become the key determinant of who belongs in any given space today—and who does not.

The *quintessential* alien or foreigner within autochthonous discourses is the figure of the migrant. This is because the hegemonic understanding of what it means to be a migrant in today's world is one where migration is seen as *movement away from one's native land*. Thus, migrants come to stand as the ultimate nonnative. Such a move works to shift the focus from a dialectics of colonialism—where the key historical dynamic is one of expropriation and exploitation, and the key relationship is one between the colonizers and the colonized—to one where the dichotomy between native and nonnative becomes central to both analysis and politics. Patrick Wolfe, a historian of Australia, captures this perspective well in his claim that "the fundamental social divide is not the color line. It is not ethnicity, minority status, or even class. The primary line is the one distinguishing Natives from settlers—that is, from everyone else. Only the Native is not a settler. Only the Native is truly local. Only the Native will free the Native. One is either native or not."[27]

From such an autochthonous perspective, being native is both *spatially* and *temporally* dependent. Temporally, migrants may be identified as natives at some point in time and in some given space, but once having moved away from the spaces where such representations may be claimed, they become *nonnatives*. Spatially, migrants remain native but only to the places they no longer live in. Thus, some argue that migrants can continue to claim native rights to places they have moved from *if* they are able to show genealogical descendance from those with native status in that space.[28] Candace Fujikane, in dismissing Asian claims to belong in the United States, puts it this way: "Indigenous people are differentiated from settlers by their genealogical, familial relationship with specific land bases that are ancestors to them. One is either indigenous to a particular land base or one is not. Asian Americans are undeniably settlers in the United States because we cannot claim any genealogy to the land we occupy, no matter how many lifetimes Asian settlers work on the land, or how many Asian immigrants have been killed through racist persecution and hate crimes, or how brutal the political or colonial regimes that occasioned Asians' exodus from their homelands."[29]

In this logic, indigeneity is racialized/ethnicized, and in the process, *land*—or more accurately, *territory*—is as well. Natives, it is assumed, belong in "their" native land and *only* there. Further, who can be recognized as native is dependent upon ancestry, thereby adding blood to the discourse of soil. Descent becomes of further importance in this distinction, for many indigenous people are, of course, also Asian (and European and African and so on) as well as vice versa. It is one's ability to claim some indigenous ancestor that *can* allow one to be seen as indigenous today. While such claims can be social and not biological, many indigenous groups, following from certain governments' own categorical recognition of indigeneity, rely on some form of blood quantum rule that requires a minimal indigenous lineage. Not surprisingly, such criteria for belonging (and for the rights and entitlements of membership) have not always worked for those subordinated through other axes of oppression and exploitation. Thus, many women have found that their claims to native status are often the first to be discounted.[30]

In this, there is an ironic historical continuity of autochthonous ideas and practices of belonging and the underlying logics of the colonial (and, in some places, postcolonial) state. Indeed, the meaning of native was one that was used to *distinguish* the colonized from the colonizer so that the natives could be represented as less human and, therefore, as legitimately colonized. Being native, then, was a signifier of being colonized and the ultimate signifier of abjectness. Nativeness as a mode of representation, then, was designed to institutionalize the new racist orders implemented by different colonial empires. Importantly, all colonized people were variously identified as "the" natives in order to signal their *lack of membership* in the *propter nos* of the colonizers.[31]

In the post–World War II era of postcolonialism, when, through much struggle, colonial empires were removed from the list of legitimate forms of political rule, the right to claim rights within and to any given space came, increasingly, to be seen as belonging to "the" natives. After all, we were told, the anticolonial project was often posited as fighting for the rule *of* the natives *for* the natives. Not surprisingly, then, the battle over resources and over place has, thus, increasingly become one about the meaning of nativeness.

In this way, autochthonous modes of belonging are significant in advancing particular *nationalized* regimes of rights, for the national subject is often defined through an exclusive racialized/ethnicized criteria through which political rights and rights to property, especially social property rights in land and natural resources, are to be apportioned within any claimed national space. Contemporary, postcolonial forms of racism are often based on ideas of autochthony. All those who are said to have *migrated* to the places where they live (or who cannot prove their prior inhabitance) are increasingly viewed as *agents* of (instead of *co-victims* of) colonial projects. The ruling ideology of nationalism has provided an explanation for belonging and has come to be a key way to distinguish between *who* is properly native to any given place and who is not. Today, the rhetoric of autochthony is evident throughout the world, including diverse sites in Europe, southern Africa, Central Africa, Latin America, North America, and the Pacific. Significantly, such a discourse spans the political spectrum from the Right to the Left. Here, I focus on the emergence of autochthonous discourses in indigenous nationalist politics (engaged in by both natives and nonnatives) in the territories claimed by Canada and the United States, with a particular focus on the Hawaiian archipelago, where this discourse is well rehearsed.

The position that all migrants are settler colonists has been advanced in a number of recent scholarly works in Canada and the United States. In the context of Hawai'i, it has been argued that "Asians" in Hawai'i (most of whom are the descendants of contractually indentured plantation laborers who began arriving in the mid-1800s) are "settler colonists," *active* in the colonization of native Hawaiians due to their nonnative status.[32] The main distinction between the two groups, they argue, is that native Hawaiian claims are based on rights of *national sovereignty* over "their land, water, and other economic and legal rights," while Asians, because they are not native, have no right to make such claims.[33]

In a Canadian context, Bonita Lawrence's and Enakshi Dua's article "Decolonizing Antiracism" (2005) in *Social Justice* makes some of the same arguments made by the contributors to the special issue of *Amerasia Journal* on "Asian Settler Colonialism in Hawai'i."[34] Like them, Lawrence and Dua also focus on those nonnatives who are nonwhite. They contend that the *antiracist praxis* of nonwhites has "contribute[d] to the active colonization of Aboriginal peoples."[35] Indeed, they contend that "antiracism is premised on an ongoing colonial project" and on "a colonizing social formation."[36] Postcolonial critiques of national liberation strategies, social constructivist critiques of the naturalness of races or nations, and arguments against ethnic absolutism, such as those made by Stuart Hall, become, for them, examples of how antiracism is a *colonial* practice.[37] Lawrence and Dua maintain that these kinds of analyses *colonize* indigenous people by "contribut[ing] to the ongoing delegitimization of Indigenous nationhood."[38]

In these essays, then, *critiques* of nationalisms or of the naturalization of social categories are tantamount to attacks against indigenous people. It is in such assertions that we can find the *ideological* character of autochthonous discourses. In arguing for the theoretical and political *centrality* of nativeness, there is an effort to depoliticize native nationalisms. By insisting that any critique of nationalism is tantamount to a colonial practice, the nationalist assumptions and politics of native nationalisms are taken out of the realm of that which can be contested. Consequently, native nationalisms are posited as the *only* strategy for decolonization.

It is precisely the *nationalism* inherent within autochthonous discourses that helps to explain not only why all nonnatives are conceptualized as colonizers but also why the (varied) *critics* of nationalism (or those who argue for the *social* basis for ideas of race and ethnic purity, or those who uncover a politics of solidarity across such lines) are also *colonizers*. Negatively racialized persons, in this logic of *nationalized* self-determinacy, are relegated to being mere *minorities* of various nations and their existing or hoped-for national sovereign states. Thus, because they are not *a* people/nation as defined by hegemonic doctrines of self-determinancy, Asians, for example, in Hawai'i, or elsewhere in the United States and Canada, are represented as *not*-colonized and, therefore, in the dualistic mode of autochthonous representations, as *colonizers*.

Within autochthonous discourses one can only be colonized if they "belong" or are indigeneous to that space itself. In this view, the colonization that people experience supposedly ends once one *moves away* from the colony (or, now, the postcolony). Instead, these migrants come to be represented as colonizers. Because a key aspect of the subjective understanding of indigenous is being a colonized person, only other colonized persons can be seen to be co-specifics. Neither those constituted as migrants nor their struggles can be perceived as part of anticolonial struggles. As such, they cannot be included as *commensurate* human beings within any colonial or postcolonial space.

This view imagines the space of colonialism as finite. It fails to see the broader field of power that processes of colonialism opened up. More specifically, it fails to see migration as a part of the colonial experience. The world as seen through an autochthonous lens is one of discrete, disconnected spaces, each belonging to its native people. This is the autochthonous view of the world *prior* to colonization and of the ideal *decolonized* space. It thus appears that as borders and relationships begin to realign to allow for new forms of subjective understanding and conspecificity, some scholars and activists are actively working to *re-fix* borders and territories through particularistic strategies of identification. The new mode of representation of indigeneity, which, ostensibly, appears to be an *expansion* in subjective understanding, creates a Manichaean dualism of native and nonnative. Such a logics of representation assumes that all past and present processes of exchange are *inherently destructive*. Colonialism, from such a view, was (and remains) about people *moving* about and that it was/is in this process of moving away from where they are native to places where they are not that has caused the enormous destruction of life. By casting all human mobility as colonial acts, autochthonous modes of representation, ironically, *empty* out from the meaning of colonialism the enormous violence that has been done by colonizers. It also minimalizes—or even denies—the violence done to people who moved and who move today.

Borders, including the borders between natives and nonnatives, although seemingly about the physical separation of those in the national *nos* from its foreign others, then, are primarily concerned with making differences *within* the same space that the *nos* and its others *both* live in. Because we—and, with Sylvia Wynter, I use "we" in all the fullness of the term "humans"—have long lived in a world that is connected *across* now-demarcated spaces, making claims to land, to livelihoods, and to belonging *on the basis of particularistic claims*, such as a racialized national membership, only works to ensure that the oppressions and exploitations wrought in the aftermath of 1492 are maintained, albeit in new guises.

Conclusion

Autochthonous discourses present the Columbian exchange as a zero-sum game between putative "groups" of natives and nonnatives. Neglected within such discursive modes of representation is the fact that the gross inequalities engendered by this exchange were structured not by some *inherent* struggle between natives and nonnatives but by a set of struggles between expropriators and the expropriated, the exploiters and the exploited, the oppressors and the oppressed. Tragically, these struggles were won by those who cemented their victory in a set of social relations that institutionalized private property, an ever-expanding capitalist mode of production, colonial, and then national, state power, and an interlocking web of ranked hierarchies formed around ideologies of the noncommensurability of humans through ideas of "race," gender, "nation," and citizenship. Each of these has been normalized to the extent that even (some of) the expropriated, exploited, and oppressed people on earth have come to identify with these ideologies instead of with each other.

However, if we understand the New World not simply as a mistaken formulation of Columbus imagining himself in the western part of India but one that brought the four hemispheres *together* in a global field of power, we come to see that the New World was made in and across multiple geographic sites. The moments of New World invention necessarily involved people across the planet and came into being not suddenly, in 1492, but over a longer period through which "European" elites expanded the territories they controlled and responded to the incredible consolidation and spread of capitalism. Indeed, as Sylvia Wynter well shows, the shorthand of "1492" does not capture the fact that the processes leading to the colonization of people in the Caribbean and Americas were begun by much earlier imperial ventures in the Middle East, western Mediterranean, eastern Atlantic and West Africa.[39] Encounters here established a specific pattern of relations that

were to be extended not only to the Caribbean and Americas but, importantly, *within* the space of what we now call Europe.

The New World, then, was forged through processes that people across
space and time would be able to recognize. Marcus Rediker calls these
processes the "four violences": the expropriation of the commons both in
Europe and in the Americas; African slavery and the Middle Passage; the
exploitation and the institution of wage labor; and the repression organized
through prisons and the criminal justice system.[40] Silvia Federici adds to our
understanding of these shared experiences by showing that the persecution
of women and the containment of their liberty (especially during various
and ongoing hunts for witches) were crucial elements in the Columbian
exchange.[41]

People's shared experience of the terror of expropriation, exploitation,
and oppression led to their shared *resistance*, something, unfortunately, left
unexamined within Wynter's oeuvre.[42] Neither the ruling-class version of
colonization-as-progress nor the autochthonous view that colonization
was caused by "foreigners" entering native spaces tells us *this* story. Recent
work by social historians, such as Peter Linebaugh and Marcus Rediker,
or political theorists such as Michael Hardt and Antonio Negri, however,
show that there was indeed a serious struggle over the terms of what is now
(too ahistorically and uniformly) often called "modernity."[43] That capitalists
were victorious in this struggle should not blind us to the fact that they did
not instigate the revolution (or the "root expansion in thought" that Sylvia
Wynter discusses in relation to Columbus's challenging of medieval European notions of space). The bourgeoisie, instead, were part of the *counterrev-
olution* against those actively challenging extant forms of ruling in Europe,
including challenges to the medieval idea of transcendent power of all sorts
(church, God, king/queen).

The *actual* revolutionaries were derisively called the multitude or the
motley crew and were composed of the rural commoners, urban rioters,
fishers, market women, weavers, and many others who mobilized countless
rebellions to realize their *immanent* demand that producers fully realize the
fruits of their labor, and do so on earth.[44] As the spread of ruling relations
moved across the planet, so too did communities committed to revolution.
When the imperial elites in Europe expanded their territorial claims—and
processes of expropriation and exploitation to the Caribbean, the Americas, and the rest of the planet—new communities of resistance across these
spaces were formed on the basis of radical solidarities. Revolutionaries from

spaces now imagined *separately* as Europe, Africa, the Caribbean, the Americas, Asia, and the Pacific encountered one another and, in many cases, saw in each other's experiences a desire for their own common emancipation.

The motley crew, then, was very much a cluster of new world formations—new world because they stretched across the entire global field of power of expanding imperial states. They explicitly challenged emergent discourses of their innate noncommensurability, be it racialized, nationalized, or gendered lines of difference. As a result, as Linebaugh and Rediker uncover, these solidarities were considered as the *greatest* threat against the aspirations of the newly emerging elites—the traders, ship owners, slave owners, plantation owners, and leaders of imperial states. Significantly, it was ideas—and *subjective identifications*—of nation, race, and gender that severely weakened this "many-headed hydra" and set back *its* revolution.

It is precisely *this* revolution, *this* "root expansion in thought," that Sylvia Wynter ignites with her call for a human species–wide sense of conspecificity. In her essay "1492: A New World View," Sylvia Wynter creates an imaginative space for a new and expansive subjective understanding of who "we" are so that we can undo the continued exclusionary, uneven, and purposefully divisive legacy of 1492. While those who shamelessly celebrate the aftermath of 1492 continue to believe that they can act unilaterally and with impunity against groups they have identified as native *and* migrants with no consequence to their own lives, and while some native nationalists believe that the *nos* of natives is a liberatory one that will lead to a postcolonial state of their own, Wynter's "new world view" allows us to see that both partial perspectives are ideological. Neither reflects the lived experiences of people the world over, which are organized through both shared experience and tangible connection. As a result, neither is able to seize the revolutionary promise of an expansion in our empathic and affective ties with those with whom we live our lives.

Wynter, by defining humanness as a social, historical, and discursive co-production rather than merely a biological one, urges us to become cognitive revolutionaries, to see our potential to forge social relationships with one another—relationships that recognize not only the massive changes wrought by the events following Columbus's voyage of 1492 but also the possibility of what we can *do* with these changes. The New World produced new social formations, and it is *within* these social formations that struggles for decolonization have taken place and continue to and need to take place. This does not mean that we must make a choice between the celebrants' universality, which is little but a parochial concern of elites, or the alternative of dissidents that romanticizes an essentialized "community" set in battle against its others. Rather, we can, if we choose, reject both views and reorient ourselves—and *respatialize* ourselves—with one afforded to us by the *world* that we have inherited, a world wrought with strife and inequality but a single world, nonetheless. This project is and always has been, by necessity, a shared one. Indeed, the making of new social bodies is not an epistemological problem but an ontological one. It is in the ontological unity of our human intra-actions that we can come into being what we already are: a species of humans, one, no less, that is intimately involved with *all other life* on our shared planet.

Notes

1. Wynter, "1492," 5–57.
2. Marx, *Capital*, 786.
3. Wynter, "1492," 5.
4. Federici, *Caliban and the Witch*.
5. Wynter, "1492," 8.
6. Wynter, "1492," 8.
7. Wynter, "1492," 40.
8. Wynter, "1492," 19.
9. The primary location of my discussion here is, broadly, the Americas (with a specific focus later in the essay on debates in Canada and the United States). Wynter's discussion of 1492 brings into focus the significance of the Americas in relation to global flows and struggles. As Bench Ansfield notes in this volume, formerly conceptualized by Columbus and his contemporaries as uninhabitable, the Americas invited, upon "discovery," new corporeal significations (specific to this region) where ideas of racialized difference were significantly reconfigured and intensified as a critical register of global humanness. This is the context I am working through. While I do touch on questions of nation, nationalism, and migratory struggles outside the Americas in my discussion of autochthony, these different contexts raise a set of questions I am unable to address in this essay.
10. See Nevins, *Operation Gatekeeper and Beyond*.
11. McKittrick, *Demonic Grounds*, 124.
12. Wynter, "1492," 25.
13. Wynter, "1492," 25.
14. Wynter, "1492," 31.
15. Wynter, "1492," 20.
16. Wynter, "1492," 31.
17. Wynter, "1492," 45.

18. Wynter, "1492," 45.
19. There are, however, increasing demands for an understanding of we-ness that cuts across species. In June 2008, the Spanish parliamentary committee on the environment approved resolutions urging Spain to comply with the Great Apes Project, which argues that apes and chimpanzees, the close genetic relatives to humans, be granted rights to liberty and life once seen as legitimately limited to humans. This resolution may lead to legislation that, if approved, will ban harmful experiments on apes and make illegal, under Spain's penal code, their use in circuses, television commercials, or filming. See Roberts, "Spanish Parliament to Extend Rights to Apes."
20. Wynter, "1492," 49.
21. Wynter, "1492," 47.
22. Niezen, *The Origins of Indigenism*. A different reading of black indigeneity, as a representation, predates World War II; it has been argued, for example, the plantation draws attention to a narrative of blackness that is implicit to modernity and indigenous to the Americas; and, as Carole Boyce Davies notes (this volume), Jean Price-Mars argued that African-based cultures *claimed* the environment they had been forced to inhabit through transatlantic slavery and created a cultural resistance that can also be identified as indigenous in that it was harmonized with the land. In addition to Boyce Davies, see Wynter, "Novel and History, Plot and Plantation," 95–102; and Wynter, "Jonkonnu in Jamaica," 34–48. However, today, such claims are increasingly rendered as suspect and, in and of themselves, *as colonial acts* against "the" *original* indigenous inhabitants.
23. Sharma and Wright, "Decolonizing Resistance, Challenging Colonial States," 120–138.
24. For an interesting discussion on the concept of "invasive species," see Comaroff and Comaroff, "Naturing the Nation," 120–147.
25. By 2005, an estimated 190 million people were engaged in international migration (United Nations, 2008). United Nations, *Statistical Yearbook for Asia and the Pacific*. This is more than a doubling from the number of migrants in the mid-1980s. Importantly, in contrast to the great "age of mass migration" of the late nineteenth and early twentieth centuries, when migration was mainly out of Europe, most cross-border migrants today are from the Global South. See Hatton and Williamson, *The Age of Mass Migration*; and Sutcliffe, "Migration and Citizenship," 66–82. In stark contrast to the experience of people out of Europe a century or more ago, today's international migrants, particularly those from the Global South, face intense restrictions on and increasing criminalization of their mobility to and within the national spaces they try to make home.
26. Comaroff and Comaroff, "Naturing the Nation," 128.
27. Patrick Wolfe, back jacket comment for Fujikane and Okamura, *Asian Settler Colonialism*.

28. Kauanui, "Colonial in Equality," 637.

29. Fujikane, "Foregrounding Native Nationalisms," 77.

30. For a recent discussion of this, see Kauanui, *Hawaiian Blood*.

31. Wynter, "1492," 37.

32. Fujikane and Okamura, "Whose Vision?" This special issue of *Amerasia Journal* has been reconstituted as a book with some additional essays. See Fujikane and Okamura, *Asian Settler Colonialism*.

33. Fujikane and Okamura, introduction to "Whose Vision?," vii.

34. Lawrence and Dua, "Decolonizing Antiracism," 120–143. For a critique of Lawrence's and Dua's arguments, see Sharma and Wright, "Decolonizing Resistance, Challenging Colonial States," 120–138.

35. Lawrence and Dua, "Decolonizing Antiracism," 122–123.

36. Lawrence and Dua, "Decolonizing Antiracism," 123, 129–130.

37. For an Aboriginal scholar who takes on board Stuart Hall to theorize indigenous identities, see Valaskakis, *Indian Country*, especially chapter 8.

38. Lawrence and Dua, "Decolonizing Antiracism," 128.

39. Indeed, prior colonizations were crucial for the success of Columbus's (and subsequent conquistadores') journeys: Columbus's first stop on his initial 1492 voyage was the Canary Islands, which had been previously claimed by the Castilian monarchy.

40. Rediker, "The Red Atlantic," 111–130. Thanks to Cynthia Wright for drawing my attention to this essay.

41. Federici, *Caliban and the Witch*, 12.

42. Wynter tends to portray the battles over "modernity" within Europe as a contest only between the elites of the old feudal order and the emerging mercantile elite. It is the latter's "new ethic" of imperial statehood and their discourse of civic humanism, she contends, that replaced the feudal order's theological absolutism (see Wynter, "1492," 14). She does not recognize the enormous efforts made by nonelites in challenging the power of the clergy and the institutionalized church and the elites' reactionary efforts to quell these.

43. Linebaugh and Rediker, *The Many-Headed Hydra*. Hardt and Negri, *Empire*. For a comprehensive critique of the ahistorical use of the term "modernity," see Cooper, *Colonialism in Question*.

44. Linebaugh and Rediker, *The Many-Headed Hydra*.

8   GENRES OF HUMAN

Multiculturalism, Cosmo-politics, and the Caribbean Basin

It would be necessary to interrogate from this point of view what is
called globalization, and which I elsewhere call *globalatinisation*—
to take into account the effect of Roman Christianity which today
overdetermines all language of law, of politics, and even the interpretation of what is called the "return of the religions." No alleged
disenchantment, no secularization comes to interrupt it. On the
contrary.

JACQUES DERRIDA, *ON COSMOPOLITANISM AND FORGIVENESS*

I find myself suddenly in the world and I recognize that I have one right
alone: That of demanding human behavior from the other.

FRANTZ FANON, *BLACK SKIN WHITE MASKS*

But tolerance as a political discourse concerned with designated modalities of diversity, identity, justice, and civic cohabitation is another matter.
It involves not simply the withholding of speech or action in response to
contingent individual dislikes or violations of taste but the enactment of
social, political, religious, and cultural norms; certain practices of licens-
ing and regulation; the marking of subjects of tolerance as inferior, deviant, or marginal vis-à-vis those practicing tolerance; and a justification
for sometimes dire or even deadly action when the limits of tolerance
are considered breached. Tolerance of this sort does not simply address
identity but abets its production; it also abets in the conflation of culture
with ethnicity or race and the conflation of belief or consciousness

with phenotype. And it naturalizes as it depoliticizes these processes to render identity itself an object of tolerance.

WENDY BROWN, *REGULATING AVERSION: TOLERANCE IN THE AGE OF IDENTITY AND EMPIRE*

Every science is necessarily based upon a few inarticulate, elementary, and axiomatic assumptions which are exposed and exploded only when confronted with altogether unexpected phenomena which can no longer be understood within the framework of its categories. The social sciences and the techniques which they have developed during the past one hundred years are no exception to this rule. It is the contention of this paper that the institution of concentration and extermination camps, that is, the social conditions within them as well as their function in the larger terror apparatus to totalitarian regimes, may very likely become that unexpected phenomenon, that stumbling block on the road toward the proper understanding of contemporary politics and society which must cause social scientists and historical scholars to reconsider their hitherto unquestioned fundamental preconceptions regarding the course of the world and human behavior.

HANNAH ARENDT, "SOCIAL SCIENCE TECHNIQUES AND THE STUDY OF CONCENTRATION CAMPS"

In the last scenes of Isaac Julien's feature-length film *Young Soul Rebels* (1991), the audience is given a glimpse of a community "to come": the white, the black, the male, the female, the gay, the heterosexual all come together, dancing in the same space to African American music, having formed a new and more hopeful affiliation within the context of racism and British nationalism of the 1970s. The moment is representative of a deeper struggle by the filmmaker to reveal attempts to transcend the social classifications that allocate human worth according to differential racial markers and sexual practices. *Young Soul Rebels* points to two overlapping contexts: first, Julien's decision to set the film in the 1970s draws attention to the tail end of the civil rights movement, and the production of new identificatory categories and social identities that, while somewhat tempered extensions of the struggles of 1960s, engaged with and pushed against post–civil rights racism, sexism, homophobia, and so forth; second, the release of the film in 1991, and the final scene, played out against the culture wars, identity politics, and the ruling categories of Enlightenment modernity—all of which calcified a politics that thrived on a self-commitment to one's own historical experience as discrete and uniquely individual. Julien's film refused the seduction of an identity politics rooted in individualism; the refusal he offers in *Young Soul Rebels*, circulating some ten years prior to the traumatic events of 9/11—which has launched the globe into new heights of chaos—might seem nostalgic, ethereal, utopic, and even a bit surprising from our contemporary vantage point.

In the 1990s, and within the context of the viciousness of the culture wars and the divisiveness of identity politics, the affiliation presented by Julien—the final scene, the dancing together, the glimpse of the community "to come"—seems, all at once, necessary, possible, and having already occurred. The moment of affiliation in the film comes out of the recognition of differences and a political solidarity based upon a "poetics of relation" that materializes within and across national and psychic boundaries.[1] At that historical moment Julien captured the *changing* relations of race, nation, gender, and sexuality and narrated what Stuart Hall would later term "new ethnicities."[2] The moment of new ethnicities that Julien cinematically represented and symbolized is what I call, along with Himani Bannerji, everyday or popular multiculturalism.[3] It is a multiculturalism that occurs from below, driven by the intimacies of contemporary life; but it is also a multiculturalism that is unfolding into creolization, en route to new indigenisms, and asserting new ways of coming into the world.

While *Young Soul Rebels* uttered the imagined and material context of multicultural London at a particular moment in history, the images of a new and differently racialized and ethnicized London in the post–July 7, 2005, moment utters yet another one. The aftermath of the 2007 bombings in Britain drew attention to the Creole children[4] produced in and by the racisms, nationalisms, and xenophobias that Julien's film called into question and wished we might move forward from—thus revealing the ways in which failures of the nation (ongoing racial anxieties and violences) have, in fact, both produced these newer Creoles of London and tagged them as fundamentalists of all sorts. I have begun with Julien's film for a number of reasons. The last scene of *Young Soul Rebels* was and is a poignant hope and a wish for London, for Britain, and maybe even the world. At the same time, I would also argue that the very substance of the hope and the wish echoes the traces of Julien's own complicated British-Caribbean relationalities and thus gives way to an upbringing that draws attention to how the brutal constitution of the nation and colony allowed for the colonial and ex-colonial to arrive in London and claim Britain as their own. Implicit in this diasporic arrival and claim are the formerly colonized giving birth to children who further negotiated and renegotiated the complicated arrangements of mother-country politics, whiteness, nation, and citizenship. I am suggesting here, then, that a trace of the Caribbean is evident in Julien's hope and wish and that a Caribbean consciousness or unconsciousness is etched into the film's narrative.

This essay grapples with the Caribbean basin as multicultural and Creole and therefore a cosmopolitan geopolitical entity that is mobile and sits at the center of Enlightenment modernity.[5] The Caribbean basin also draws attention to the Enlightenment invention of what Sylvia Wynter calls the overrepresentation of Man-as-human.[6] I suggest that looking to the Caribbean can help scholars in the humanities and social sciences (and even the natural sciences) assess and reformulate what might be at stake in the radical incompletion of the project of modernity and what might be necessary to reanimate the promises of modernity in order to differently imagine, and live, the human as an alterable species-subject. Thus, I am thinking about the human as an authorizing subject that holds in it a "descriptive statement" that can/does assert a *new* human self that exceeds the category of Man-as-human. Locating the Caribbean within and against discourses of European Enlightenment modernity, I seek to articulate a cosmo-political ethics of reading and interpretation that troubles contemporary articulations of cosmopolitanism that position it as fundamentally opposed to discourses of multiculturalism and a multiculture.

In this essay I worry about the ways in which cosmopolitanism has been cast as a higher order of Man, and I seek to dethrone it by suggesting its vernacular forms. In doing so, I suggest thinking about a cosmopolitanism from below in which the "archipelago of poverty," as Sylvia Wynter has termed it, becomes the place now where genres of the human proliferate and thus offer us insight into the work of "culture."[7] The utter unique and brutal place of the Caribbean as a place of invention, as an extension of Europe, Africa, Asia, and beyond, as amputation and incubator of the modern, as overseas department, as site of import and export, as housing the enslaved, the free, the indentured, and all those situated in between, as the contemporary backyard of the United States and the playground of Europe, makes it a place where the cosmo-political takes root/route in all the messiness that ethnicity and raciological thinking engender. Thus in this essay I posit the Caribbean as a space of unique invention in the colonial and modern world.

I stake this claim being fully aware of critiques of exceptionalism. This essay will work with the history of ideas produced in and beyond the Caribbean basin but also influenced by it, in order to initiate different and even better conversations about the ways in which genres of humanness inform our troubled times.

Developing Creole Society and the Question of Culture

A Creole society, as Kamau Braithwaite termed it in his book *The Development of Creole Society*, is "caught up in some kind of colonial arrangement with a metropolitan European power."[8] Brathwaite was writing about the Anglo-Caribbean—in particular Jamaica—when he offered that definition of Creole society. He ventured to suggest that Creole society was a complex situation where external metropolitan forces pressured the colonial polity, forcing constant internal adjustments between master and slave, elite and laborer, and so on, to incite "a culturally heterogeneous relationship."[9]

Many of Brathwaite's terms for the conditions of Creole society not only continue to exist in the Caribbean today but also manifest themselves in the metropolitan spaces outside the Caribbean, informing mid-twentieth-century migrations that produced a more globally intimate world. In particular, his discussions concerning cohabitation and uneven acts of power can be detected in colonial and postcolonial Caribbean contexts, and in contemporary neoliberal global contexts as well. Thus, while Brathwaithe's definition requires a bit of fine-tuning when relocated beyond Jamaica and the Caribbean—which I will consider later vis-à-vis Edouard Glissant—it provides an initial description of contemporary human life. Let me be clear here, however, that creolization takes place in the context of unequal and brutal power arrangements alongside forms of severe cultural dominance. But, as Stuart Hall points out, creolization could not take place "without extensive transculturation" in the context of "brutal cultural dominance and incorporation between the different cultural elements."[10] Thus, creolization is that which arises out of the brutal context and unequal power relations through which differing cultures come into contact and engagement with each other. I thus do not read creolization as simply assimilation/integration; nor do I understand it as a process through which hybridity emerges. Rather, I am drawing attention to the ways in which creolization must bring into focus the violent process of becoming through/in modernity.[11] Thus, during and after transatlantic slavery, the early state (plantation society, for example) or the state (in our contemporary moment) has been the arbiter of uneven power and its brutalizing qualities. The importance of creolization, conceptually, is that it locates our lives, histories, and experiences between brutality and something different—something more possible, if I can use such a phrase. The brutality of the fusing and mixing of diasporic cultures into hybrid forms in the Americas is, as Hall reminds us, a precise historical specificity that "we should be careful of infinitely extending" as it is a process that also uncovers those new brutalities being done to those whom we are currently forced to cohabit with in a world reorganized around planned and unplanned migrations.[12] It is in this context that creolization also offers something altogether more possible—including innovative ways for those in the humanities and social sciences to think through historical, empirical, and imaginary evidence and narratives (and thus debates over the public sphere) as they are informed by our Creole present.

In *Caribbean Discourse*, Edouard Glissant explains that "creolization is, first, the unknown awareness of the creolized."[13] Thus, unlike some conceptions of hybridity, which consciously reach for fusion and mixture in their accounts, the process of creolization is inflected with brutality, produced by the excess of relation, and evidences living a life in the context of intimate and contradictory relations of domination and subjection. Creolization is an altering of the human that concerns itself with surviving a process of "mutual mutations."[14] In this fashion, then, creolization is not contained only within the Caribbean basin, despite Hall's caution that the term not be proliferated too much beyond the brutal history of the region. What I am suggesting is that we live in brutal times, reminiscent of the colonization of the Americas and plantation slavery, and that the making of the modern nation-state, as we now live it, accentuates an "unknown creolization" that we cannot name but must struggle to recognize.

I am inferring that the brutalities which produce the Caribbean, and by extension the Americas, also generate the production of new modes of human life, even today. In this regard, the social conditions that frame our current brutalities—security certificates, antiterrorism acts, prison industrial complexes, wasted/impoverished populations, diseases, and so forth—require that we ask new questions. I turn to Caribbean thought and Caribbean thinkers because I find this work pays close attention to modernity in all its forms, and it does not pedagogically signal an "end of man" discourse but instead grapples with the inability to seriously consider other worldviews. The delegitimation of other worldviews means that other conceptions of the human remain just beyond our reach. These submerged and discredited conceptions of the world offer meaningful nonsovereign positions—which challenge modernity's assertion of sovereignty *as* land, nation, and state— and demand new approaches to culture and multiculturalism.

In both *Refashioning Futures: Criticism after Postcoloniality* and *Conscripts of Modernity: The Tragedy of Colonial Enlightenment*, David Scott writes of the problem-space as "an ensemble of questions and answers around which a horizon of identifiable stakes (conceptual as well as ideological-political stakes) hangs. . . . Notice, then, that a problem-space is very much a context of dispute, a context of rival views, a context, if you like, of knowledge and power. But from within the terms of any given problem-space what is in dispute, what the argument is effectively about, is not itself being argued over."[15] Scott's deployment of the concept of problem-space allows him to reassess the critiques of postcolonial theorists who, he argues, in their antiessentialist scholarly moves, actually essentialize the colonial/anticolonial period by focusing on how this historical moment *answered* particular questions about colonialism, decolonization, and emancipation; this focus on answers fails to think through the ways in which the *questions* asked in that moment reflected a very particular context. Scott argues that to better understand the colonial/anticolonial period, the questions asked of the anticolonial moment need understanding and thought—not the answers— and that such a method would allow us to ask different and better questions of our present-future. In Scott's quarrel with postcolonial theorizing, he offers a pedagogy of reading that requires intellectuals to think more carefully about the questions than about the answers. I find Scott both provocative and instructive because his framework opens up the possibility for thinking about the present-future in a manner that has too often stifled the political and intellectual Left. Thus, if Stuart Hall is correct, that migration is the joker in the globalization pack of cards, then I would suggest that multiculture and multiculturalism might be the ace or the problem-space within the context of global migrations.

What kinds of new questions might we ask of multiculturalism? What kinds of new vistas can we imagine for living with intensified and constantly shifting forms of difference? How might we think about resistances from below that challenge political-ideological formations from above? Finally, how might the questions of multiculturalism both become complicit with and continually alter "the categories brought into play by European modernity," and the resulting genres of the human that practices of modernity have produced?[16] To do this work I now turn to Sylvia Wynter.

Sylvia Wynter's Unsettling Provocations:
Genres of Man and Its Overrepresentations

In a project that takes its most potent intellectual force in the moment leading up to and after the quincentenary of Christopher Columbus's voyages
and "discovery" of the Americas, Sylvia Wynter sets out to articulate a pathway that offers a "third perspective" on how we might remember 1492—and
thus thinks outside the two prevailing approaches (denunciation/celebra-
tion) to this narrative.[17] In a series of essays, Wynter addresses the ways in
which the colonial project and thus "the coloniality of being" have come
to define our present sociopolitical and epistemological order. Wynter offers a reading of how the white, the red, and the black as "types," "kinds,"
"modes," or "genres" come to be. Reading each category as an invention—a
very complicated invention of domination, subjection, and complicity—
Wynter argues that these categories of humanness were designed alongside
a hybrid religio-secular European domination that produced "the Indio/
Negro complex," in the Middle Ages, which unfolded into "the nigger/na-
tive complex" in (and for) a degodded eighteenth- and nineteenth-century
Europe.[18] Schooled and describing herself as an Occidentalist as opposed
to a Europeanist, Wynter is interested in demonstrating how Europe's conception of Man "overrepresents itself as if it were the human itself."[19] Her
project, then, comprehensively attends to the ways in which we have come
to and produced our contemporary conditions of being human—wherein
Man is the measuring stick of normalcy and Man's human Others are excluded from this category of being—and how we might unsettle and undo
this conception of humanness.

Wynter's discussions of the post-1492 world system are important for any
conversation that centralizes the ways in which questions of culture inform
humanness. In her contribution to the study of the human, Wynter demonstrates that the human—as a physiologically and narratively constituted
being—is simultaneously bios (biological) and logos (worded/cultural).
While she places an emphasis on culture—arguing in a number of essays
that the last five hundred years (and we might add plus) have been "culturally and not historically determined"—Wynter is very attentive to biology
as both a known and unknown quality of what it means to be human.[20] Her
writings evidence the ways in which culture and knowledge are implicit to
producing scientific descriptive statements of humanness, as well as disclos-
ing the very scientific underpinnings of a flesh-and-blood worldview.

In our times, European domination has meant that European knowledges define and thus discipline what the Human means and might mean. Related to the question of domination is Wynter's claim, and I follow that claim, that the Caribbean basin, or "the archipelagos of poverty," is the incubator wherein the European tested out and invented modes of being human. In enacting modernity, European knowledge systems posited the representation of European bourgeois Man as the only just mode of being human, thus also spatializing the Caribbean as a viable site where the overrepresentation of Man-as-human thrives. To repeat, the Caribbean was and in many instances remains a site of modernist experimentation and invention, making it different from other colonial spaces. In many ways the Anglo-Caribbean might be understood as invented from scratch.

As Wynter traces how European conceptions of the world evolved from religious and supernatural, to religious and secular, to biological and secular, she draws attention to the production of new modes of being human and new modes of governance. In each systemic transition from ecclesiastical to monarchial, from landed gentry to industrial / entrepreneurial to neoliberal / overconsumptive West, new modes took shape while producing human Others for whom degradation, subjection, and now "wasted life," in Zygmunt Bauman's terms, have become the normalized governing codes of rule.[21] In this context Wynter identifies the 1960s as a pivotal element in the story and our contemporary time because the subgenres of humanness—in particular nonwhite, queer, and feminine modes of humanness—were unleashed and pushed against the overrepresentation of Man and the ethno-class of the West through the civil rights movement, anticolonial struggles, feminism, and gay and lesbian liberation struggles.[22] Her attention to genres of the human conveys the ways in which a specific and overrepresented ethno-class produces knowledge that is, for example, "normally" antiblack and antigay, and which is then internalized as "normal" by the subgenres of the human who inhabit that knowledge system. The 1960s produced a fundamental challenge to the overrepresentation of Man-as-human. Indeed, Wynter further suggests that the challenges initiated in the 1960s have since been co-opted and refashioned, and in fact replicate a governing system that profits from "wasted lives."[23]

From the vantage point of the 1960s, and in the context of the last five hundred years of European expansion and domination of the globe, Wynter argues for a new form of human life from the perspective of the species. As Katherine McKittrick articulates it, "Specifically, Wynter asks that we recognize that the making of the Americas was/is an (often dangerously geno-cidal and ecocidal) interhuman and environmental project through which 'new forms of life' can be conceptualized. Recognizing that new forms of life, occupying interhuman grounds (beneath *all* our feet), can perhaps put forward a new world view from the perspective of the species—that is, from outside the logic of biocentric models: not as a *genre* or *mode* of human but as human."[24]

The co-optation of the 1960s challenge has reproduced—for most of the second half of the twentieth century and into the beginning of the twenty-first century—Enlightenment modernity's genres of the human that are hierarchically categorized and organized according to the webbing of social differences (class, locale, race, gender, sexuality, and so forth) as they are represented and located in relation to middle-class-ideals-and-Man-as-human. Consequently, the aftermath of the 1960s reveals a kind of stalemate; our desires to renarrativize and rescientize what it means to be human and a human species have languished. I want to suggest that this kind of thinking discloses the ways in which contemporary conversations of cosmopolitanism do very little to unsettle the present coloniality of our being. In fact, I argue that beneath many of the conversations of cosmopolitanism are pedagogies that are built upon—and not even in opposition to—raciological subgenres of humanness. In what follows I turn to the problem of the unsaid pedagogies of cosmopolitanism's appeal as a way to begin opening up questions that might frame new forms of human life.

Against Cosmopolitanism: Dethroning Man and Uttering New Forms of Human Life

In the wake of the brutalities that have followed in the shock of 9/11 globally, Jacques Derrida's engagements with cosmopolitanism, hospitality, forgiveness, and friendship stand out as ideas and insights necessary for engagement. With the new urgencies of war, and further threats of terrorism in the West, alongside a serious commitment by many of the genres of the human that European coloniality has unleashed, scholars in the humanities and social sciences have been searching for, rehabilitating, and resuscitating concepts of all kinds to think through these new conditions. Paul Gilroy has turned to conviviality, but more have turned to cosmopolitanism as the favored conceptual term to attend to our present moment and its various impasses.[25] Indeed, no other concept has made a firmer return than cosmopolitanism in a post-9/11 scholarly Western world. Cosmopolitanism has been resuscitated and, as Seyla Benhabib points out, signifies "for some . . . an attitude of enlightened morality that does not place 'love of country' ahead of 'love of mankind' . . . for others, cosmopolitanism signifies hybridity, fluidity, and recognizing the fractured and internally riven character of human selves and citizens, whose complex aspirations cannot be circumscribed by national fantasies and primordial communities."[26]

Benhabib offers an additional option, which is a conception of cosmopolitanism that comes into being in the aftermath of the Universal Declaration of Human Rights, which as we all know is in part a response to brutality. Thus, I want to suggest that such a conception of cosmopolitanism sits more closely in relation to what I have been suggesting is creolization; this is to say that this version of cosmopolitanism is, in fact, anticipating a cosmopolitanism that is vernacular in form and thus also gesturing to a different kind of human existence. These forms of being come into focus through brutality, through resistance, and through struggle.

Out of my engagements with Jacques Derrida, I have developed the term "cosmo-political ethics" in an attempt to capture the ways in which cosmopolitanism is en route "to a democracy to come," to borrow his phrase, but one that is only possible if we take seriously our multicultural present.[27] Such a requirement would necessitate a grappling with the vernacular cosmopolitanisms that, I suggest, constitute the Caribbean basin and many other colonial places in varying degrees. This position is strongly influenced by Stuart Hall's insistence that "the term multiculturalism is now universally deployed. However, this proliferation has neither stabilized nor clarified its meaning. . . . multiculturalism is now so discursively entangled that it can only be used 'under erasure.' . . . Nevertheless, since we have no less implicated concepts to think this problem with, we have no alternative but to go on using and interrogating it."[28]

The struggle to think about cultural differences outside of conceptions of multiculturalism is a significant denial of our present order of knowledge and modes of being human. To make this claim is not to suggest that multiculturalism as an idea is singular in what it can achieve for human good, but rather to think seriously about how a multiculture functions to produce genres of the human for which our only hope of an engagement beyond those categories is to ethically recognize them as meaningful to all.

It is from such a position that contemporary discussions of cosmopolitanism are lacking—they seek a better story through its redeployment by sidestepping the messiness of what Wynter would call "its culturally coded mode of subjectivity" when the story is one of brutality for which, as Derrida states, "forgiveness forgives only the unforgivable."[29] Derrida extends his insights to state: "That is to say that forgiveness must announce itself as impossibility itself."[30] Such is the space of the Caribbean basin. Both its history and its culture, and the ways in which the region is underpinned by modernity, reveal that it is a site that marks the impossibility of forgiveness. Viewed from the brutality that birthed the Caribbean, a vernacular cosmo-politics of the region raises difficult ethical dilemmas for thinkers who seek to bypass multiculturalism and a multiculture and move toward a higher order of Man called the cosmopolitan. The Caribbean region symbolizes how various cultures amalgamate not into one—despite Jamaica's motto "Out of Many One"—but rather inhabit and live with the constant negotiation of human difference, the ethno-political, all the while articulating a humanness yet "to come." These failed nation-states of the archipelago of misery—with Haiti as the beacon of the Enlightenment's dark excess—forged out of modernity's brutality and a plantation ecosystem, should constantly remind us of both the limits of European humanism and the possibilities of living a human life. In fact, it is the brutal and yet simultaneously life-affirming, constantly renewing cultures of the Caribbean that make it a unique space of colonial invention, resistance, and reinvention. The conceit of my argument is that the region has much to offer contemporary global culture on living difference as central to humanness.

It is the still "to come" of the region—now globally situated—that sits at the foundation of the ongoing narratives of threat and fear that continue to shape our world today. One of the central apprehensions of that which is still "to come" is the place of the postcolonial migrant within the walls of the metropolitan city; this migratory presence signals the repeated limits of European humanism and the failure to reach beyond its limited conceptions of Man. This fear and threat have been most loudly proclaimed as an end to multiculturalism and a call for something else. I want to argue, however, that the task for scholars working in the humanities and social sciences and spaces in between is that we need to struggle with the idea of multiculturalism—as Stuart Hall explains, "we have no better terms to think the situation with."[31] I also want to suggest that we need to up the ante in our struggles to grapple with the idea of multiculturalism and offer something more—something simultaneously empirical and imaginary and "to come"—all of which, I argue, arise in a vernacular cosmopolitanism.

Let us take as our example Kwame Anthony Appiah, who in two books has tackled the issues I have been grappling with thus far in this essay. In *The Ethics of Identity*, Appiah offers engagements with cosmopolitanism that are closer to those of hybridity, fluidity, and cross-cultural sharing and borrowing than of conceptions of cosmopolitanism that take justice, duty of hospitality, and obligation as their source—Appiah develops a Kantian-influenced cosmopolitanism. In this book he engages what he calls "globalizing human rights" and its Kantian influence briefly, but the bulk of his argument is not concerned with that particular understanding of cosmopolitanism. Instead, Appiah is concerned with a cosmopolitanism that travels as people and objects and things travel, and he provides the groundwork for conversations among groups that share and debate their common and diverse experiences; he writes, "We learn about the extraordinary diversity of human responses to our world and the myriad points of intersection of those various responses," providing us the pedagogical guide I mentioned earlier.[32] Finally, in his critique of the Enlightenment philosophers, he notes that they lack imagination in terms of what we share in common; Appiah reasserts a position of "universalistic and antiuniversalitic" as his understanding of cosmopolitanism.[33] The chapter "Rooted Cosmopolitanism" concludes Appiah's book and is preceded by a chapter on the state, "Soul Making," that pays attention to the work the state can do for the soul. In that chapter he is concerned with when the state should intervene into issues of culture and identity and when it should not intervene, and how the role of the state can be understood in relation to culture-specific and identity truth-claims.

In his more recent general audience text, *Cosmopolitanism: Ethics in a World of Strangers*, Appiah asks how we might proceed in our contemporary moment. He replies, "not globalization" and "not multiculturalism," as both terms are, he remarks, "shape shifters."[34] For Appiah, cosmopolitanism concerns difference both in its singularity and in its universalism—and sometimes the two clash. Appiah, as I read it, creates a false separation between the idea of multiculturalism and the idea of cosmopolitanism. In my view each idea inflects the other, and thus it is not possible to have one without the other. What Appiah fails to do in *Cosmopolitanism*, which he does haltingly better in *The Ethics of Identity*, is to think about the state and state practices. While he is prepared to dismiss the idea of multiculturalism for being entangled with state and corporate discourses of marketing and other state seductions, he finds energy to work around the difficult colonial history of cosmopolitanism's conceptual birth.

Kobena Mercer has reminded us that cosmopolitanism's history is one of "wealthy elites who seemed to exist 'everywhere and nowhere' with little or no loyalty to the nation-state."[35] Mercer further points out that the term was also used by Karl Marx to point to "the international dimensions of a market economy constantly expanding its search for raw materials and new consumers across the world."[36] Marx's use of the term seems prophetic and echoes some of our contemporary global and neoliberal propositions and circumstances. Mercer's intervention demonstrates that the work we call on cosmopolitanism to do today has been done, under another name, in the past.

So why not multiculturalism for Appiah? His intervention is anchored in an inability to seriously grapple with state power explicitly; he reduces the idea of multiculturalism to state and corporate multiculturalism, but finds in the history of cosmopolitanism more to work with. He also does not seem to recognize the state and corporatist reduction of some conceptions of cosmopolitanism to the language of "global citizen," with its attendant pedagogical trends in the neoliberal university and other educational institutions. What is most significant for me about Appiah's arguments in *Cosmopolitanism* is that his examples approach what I have been calling creolization, but I would argue that his fear of ethnicity does not allow him to go there as fully as he should (of which I shall say more later).

So while the resuscitation of cosmopolitanism has been proffered in opposition to multiculturalism, and I am not in immediate suspicion of the ideals of cosmopolitanism, I do believe that a caution is warranted. Much of the discourse of cosmopolitanism is regrouped under the rubric of internationalism, a rubric that places the West in the position of achieving internationalism at the expense of the rest, who are not ushered into a higher order of Man. Similarly, one becomes international as a result of an engagement with recognizable Western practices, ideologies, and positions—cultural-orienting behavior—whatever those shifting terms might signal in terms of dominant circulating conditions of the time.

What is most significant for me about Appiah's arguments in *Cosmopolitanism* is that his examples keep returning to questions of ethnicity even though he wants to erase ethnicity from the conversation. Appiah's inability to unmake ethnicity as a recurring cultural phenomenon and problem alongside the workings of global capital tells me that, following David Scott's method, the question being asked—of how to live better together—is not the question to be asking. Thus I return us to the problem-space of freedom and unfreedom, to signal once again the terms under which European modernity continues to shape all of humanity. Therefore, an assumed uncomplicatedness of belonging, identity, and nation becomes the grounds of regulation, containment, and refusal. But when one troubles those grounds of regulation and containment, there can be no doubt that something called identity comes to the fore again and again.

Because much of the discourse of cosmopolitanism is based in the simple but not simplistic idea of how to live better together, it requires that we ask the question that precedes it, of why we do not live well together in the first instance. When we attempt to answer why we do not live well together in the first instance, questions of identity, culture, and ethnicity return to haunt cosmopolitanism's desire for better living. Embedded in the haunting are the conditions of unfreedom that are the very conditions that proponents of cosmopolitanism in the most generous sense would seek to ameliorate by a desire for living better together. However, what remains unclear is that the claims to difference for which cosmopolitanism would have us live better with are grounded in the very same conditions that produced them as differences that matter in terms of a range of disadvantaged positions. Thus cosmopolitanism's conceptual terrain must indeed begin with and accept those differences as somewhat immutable and therefore meaningful to a degree, making it clear that the idea of cosmopolitanism owes its debt to an already deeply racialized modernity. This racialized modernity requires both a politics and an ethics that might help us to think about its limits and its possibilities while never forgetting the brutal disadvantages which its naming (that is, cosmopolitanism) necessitates and therefore from which many of us seek collective relief.

Conclusion: On Ethno-Politicality and the Undoing of Freedom

The Caribbean basin is a place and space of cosmo-political ethicality. By that I mean the ways in which different identities and cultures have been pitted against each other, or at least in tension with each other, while simultaneously living intimately with each other and sharing across those differences have produced "new" modes of being human in the region. The range of different ways of naming various cross-cultural presences and resonances in, for example, skin color is one mode of the cosmo-political at work. Such sharing is not necessarily utopic or egalitarian; in fact, much of it recalls the brutality of previous encounters, but much of it also speaks to the politicality of life and the stakes of living lives in which claims to and from identity sometimes do matter and matter powerfully in terms of questions of ethics and justice. Thus it is in part my argument that the Caribbean basin as a space of cultural and identity experimentation has much to offer our thinking on how questions of identity, culture, ethics, and justice might inform ideas and practices of freedom.

The brutality of the founding of the Caribbean makes identity and ethnicity crucial to its constitution. Therefore, in the Caribbean, identity and ethnicity are not dissolved or resolved, but in many places identity and ethnicity are the site of the making and remaking of the human category as one of possibility—and thus a vernacular cosmopolitanism forged in an unknown creolization. I call this remaking ethno-politicality or ethno-politics. By this I mean to signal that one does not get out of the mess of Enlightenment modernity by sidestepping its inventions, but rather by grappling with them.

I am suggesting that the ethno-political is important because we must confront the ways in which our colonial present and imperialism continue to make identity a locus of control, containment, and regulation. Therefore, the recent past of a reflexive identity politics critique has reached its nadir. Past critiques of identity politics too easily dismissed appeals to identity in an effort to mobilize a politics that might move beyond self-recognition into one that might activate a practice of care for those with whom we did not have anything in common. These critiques of identity politics that many of us so quickly fell victim to shifted the politics of the dispossessed and questions of justice, hospitality, and obligation. Many of these questions require the state, not individual taste and appreciation. There is then a curious moment, for clearly in the context of Julien's film in 1991 that I began with, we did not do the work to make the interventionist politics of various identity groups garner real traction as a fundamental rethinking of the work of the state.

The ethno-political is not an appeal to essentialize identity, and in this case ethnicity, but rather to highlight the ways in which identity and particularly ethnicity matter in our colonial present. Thus, as Diana Fuss stated back in the heady days of the essentialist/constructionist argument: "To insist that essentialism is always and everywhere reactionary is, for the constructionists, to buy into essentialism in the very act of making the charge; *it is to act as if essentialism has an essence.*"[37] Thus, I am not arguing for ethno-politicality as the *only* ground of a renewed collective politics, but I am arguing for the language of ethnicity as a central element for how we approach a collective politics of the possible and thus a postcolonial to come, out of our present Creole but submerged multicultural present on the way to a possible freedom.

In an essay titled "On Disenchanting Discourse," Wynter throws the critical gauntlet down when she suggests:

> The unifying goal of *minority* discourse, if the term *minority* and its related discourse is to constitute itself as the "institutional" (and therefore the ontological) fact that it is rather than as the "brute" or empirical fact that it is strategically projected to be within the coercive analogic of our present onto-episteme, will necessarily be to accelerate the conceptual "erasing" of the figure of Man. If it is to effect a rupture, minority discourse must set out to bring closure to our present order of discourse, as the nineteenth-century Western European bourgeoisie did from their parallel ontologically subordinated status *vis à vis* the "enchanted" discourse of the landed gentry.[38]

Is it possible to have sovereignty without land? Most, not all, Caribbean people are people who must make themselves native to a place they are not from, as Jamaica Kincaid once put it.[39] Such a conception begs for different ideas of sovereignty, nation, and citizenship. At the same time, this is to say nothing of giving up on land, since it is coterminous with human existence, especially if we understand the human as bios and logos in our globally troubled environmental times. At the same time, Dionne Brand offers a challenge to modern forms of sovereignty when those forms get tied to land, as it is conceptualized vis-à-vis nation and country: "I don't want no fucking country, here / or there or all the way back, I don't like it, none of it."[40]

This is how Wynter dares to formulate the project of a future beyond cosmopolitanism, even its vernacular kind. Writing about C. L. R. James, she argues that his work provides "a vision of life that unfurls new vistas on a livable future."[41] She continues: "With its ease and certainty of phrase, its refusal at whatever price to fake the game, it establishes the new identity of Caliban. The region is not only new. It evokes a shared 'Ah'! of recognition and delight."[42] In this rather brilliant essay on the corpus of James's work, Wynter reads James both flatteringly and against himself to demonstrate that the region of the Caribbean is the foundation that drove the engines of his thinking. Out of James's oeuvre she formulates the project of a future beyond European conceptions of Man: "Consequently, for fundamental change to take place, it must take place both in the conception and in the pattern of relations. Such changes must therefore call into question both the structure of social reality and the structure of its analogical epistemology." To do this "we must pass through the threat of that chaos where thought becomes impossible."[43] We all know from the sites of the conscious and the unconscious that wherever identity enters, the impossible follows, terror follows; avoiding it does not dissolve or resolve its hold on the human, but engaging it can remind us of the need to endlessly alter the human beyond Man.

Notes

1. Glissant, *Poetics of Relation*.
2. Hall, "New Ethnicities," 441–449.
3. Bannerji, *The Dark Side of the Nation*.
4. These children are Creole for many reasons. As the first- and second-generation British children of parents who are from the former British colonies, these children live a claim to the "mother country" that is radically different from their parents' claims. These children are not "immigrants," but their experiences can sometimes mirror those of "immigrants." These children also live their parents' nostalgia for another home, and sometimes they live the very real evidence of that home as well. Additionally, they live a displacement from Britain that is one shared with their parents, but also different from it, yet informed and shaped by their parents' displacement as well. A complex web of relationalities and disconnections frame their sense of self and thus their sensibilities, both conscious and unconscious, are Creole.
5. While is not within the purview of this essay to list the theoretical genealogies of the key terms used throughout—"cosmopolitanism," "multiculturalism," and "creolization"—the following texts provide overviews: Gilroy, "Multiculture, Double Consciousness and the 'War on Terror,'" 431–443; Walcott, "Caribbean Pop Culture in Canada," 123–139; Mercer, "Introduction"; Balutansky and Sourieau, *Caribbean Creolization*; Crichlow, *Globalization and the Post-Creole Imagination*.
6. Wynter, "Unsettling the Coloniality of Being," 257–337.
7. Wynter, "Rethinking 'Aesthetics,'" 243.
8. Braithwaite, *The Development of Creole Society in Jamaica*, xv. Wynter's position on creolization is in fact not that different from Braithwaite's. As Carole Boyce Davies outlines in her essay on *Maskarade* in this volume, Wynter, drawing on the writings of Jean Price-Mars, underscores the ways in the practice of plantation slavery produced the conditions through which black subjects became intimately tied to (and perhaps indigenous to) the land—a position that does not cast aside creolization but rather understands it as limiting the black experience (specifically displaced rootedness) to assimilation and Eurocentrism. Braithwaite's attempt to theorize the Caribbean through using its land-

scape to form a language that is both descriptive and abstract—for example, his use of tidelectics—speaks to his own assertions of what both Wynter and Braithwaite call "indigenism."

9. Braithwaite, *The Development of a Creole Society*, xvi.

10. Hall, "Creolization, Diaspora and Hybridity," 186.

11. I am thus working with a specific conceptualization of creolization (drawing on, as noted earlier, Braithwaite, Hall, and the ideas in note 8) rather than iterations that are preoccupied with the analytic limits of the term. These stakes have also been explored and rehearsed in my earlier work, Walcott, "Pedagogy and Trauma," 135–151. For a slightly different take, see Khan, "Journey to the Center of the Earth," 271–302.

12. Hall, "Creolization, Diaspora and Hybridity," 193.

13. Glissant, *Caribbean Discourse*, 3.

14. Glissant, *Poetics of Relation*, 89.

15. Scott, *Conscripts of Modernity*, 4. See also Scott, *Refashioning Futures*, 8.

16. Scott, *Conscripts of Modernity*, 9.

17. Wynter, "1492," 5–57.

18. Wynter, "The Pope Must Have Been Drunk," 27.

19. Thomas, "ProudFlesh Inter/Views Sylvia Wynter"; Wynter, "Unsettling the Coloniality of Being," 260.

20. Wynter, "The Pope Must Have Been Drunk," 35.

21. Bauman, *Wasted Lives*.

22. Notably, Wynter explains: the Black situation and the homosexual situation are parallel. We are the only ones who are socialized in such a way that we cannot trust our own "consciousness." Thomas, "ProudFlesh Inter/Views Sylvia Wynter."

23. Wynter, "On How We Mistook the Map for the Territory," 107–169.

24. McKittrick, *Demonic Grounds*, 135 (emphasis in the original).

25. Gilroy, *Postcolonial Melancholia*.

26. Benhabib, *Another Cosmopolitanism*, 17–18.

27. Derrida, *Spectres of Marx*, 65.

28. Hall, "Conclusion," 209.

29. Wynter, "Columbus, the Ocean Blue and 'Fables That Stir the Mind,'" 156; Derrida, *On Cosmopolitanism and Forgiveness*, 32.

30. Derrida, *On Cosmopolitanism and Forgiveness*, 33.

31. Hall, "Conclusion," 209.

32. Appiah, *The Ethics of Identity*, 258.

33. Appiah, *The Ethics of Identity*, 258.

34. Appiah, *Cosmopolitanism*, xiii. This is really a rewriting of the chapter "Rooted Cosmopolitanism" from his *Ethics of Identity*.

35. Mercer, "Introduction," 10.

36. Mercer, "Introduction," 10.

37. Fuss, *Essentially Speaking*, 21 (emphasis in the original).

38. Wynter, "On Disenchanting Discourse," 208–209 (emphasis in the original).
39. Kincaid, "The Flowers of Empire," 28–31.
40. Brand, *Land to Light On*, 48.
41. Wynter, "Beyond the Categories of the Master Conception," 89.
42. Wynter, "Beyond the Categories of the Master Conception," 89.
43. Wynter, "Beyond the Categories of the Master Conception," 67. See also Walter Mignolo's discussion of Wynter and C. L. R. James in this volume.

9   FROM MASQUERADE TO *MASKARADE*
Caribbean Cultural Resistance and the Rehumanizing Project

> It is this mask which links the "creolization" process of Jonkonnu with
> the second process the "indigenization" process. . . . The Jonkonnu as the
> cultural manifestation of African religious beliefs was therefore involved
> in this resistance.
>
> **SYLVIA WYNTER, "JONKONNU IN JAMAICA: TOWARDS THE INTERPRETATION OF**
> **FOLK DANCE AS A CULTURAL PROCESS"**

Maskarade, a play by Sylvia Wynter, was written in 1973 as part of a larger
project to claim Caribbean culture as rooted and therefore indigenized in
the Caribbean landscape. With this, the play allows us to locate the early
versions of what has become Wynter's primary project of removing our
analyses from more local and singular arguments and theoretical lines, to a
larger critique of the entire Western bourgeois social order that has erected
itself as normative. *Maskarade* allows us to see the ways in which such questions fit into Wynter's early creative work, among which is her dramatic
writing, which is not as widely known as her more substantial body of analytical writing.

    In an amazingly comprehensive interview with David Scott, Sylvia Wyn-
ter recalls that she saw herself first of all as a dancer and actress (indeed,
there are wonderful photographs of a youthful Sylvia as dancer throughout)
and then as a playwright, in that order, and later in life as a novelist and
theorist. She remembers: "I began by writing plays. . . . I did a translation
[into Jamacian creole] of Garcia Lorca's play, *Yerma*.[1] In fact, she continues:
"I wrote *The Hills of Hebron* originally as a play for the BBC called *Under the
Sun*. Then I decided to try and rewrite it as a novel."[2] She also identifies the

movement of the play *Maskarade* from a television play to a more expanded play produced and with music added by Jim Nelson (a television producer in Jamaica at the time), staged in Kingston and then taken to Cuba for Carifesta. According to Wynter, *Maskarade* was staged a decade later by Sandra Richards, first at Northwestern University and then by the Stanford University drama department in collaboration with Black Performing Arts in the spring of 1983.[3] It was also given a more public staging at the Tricycle Theatre in London, in the 1990s, but no full analyses are available. However, in this play one can identify some of the early ideas that would be developed, elaborated, and re-elaborated in Wynter's later work. Issues of gender, history, culture, and ethical/political choices surface throughout *Maskarade*. In the unpublished version of the play, for example, which was used for the Stanford production, the narrative closes with a beginning articulation of the theory of the human that would preoccupy her later theoretical work: "Let us dance clan by clan / In the maskarade of man."[4]

We are thereby able to link *Maskarade* (1973) to this larger dramatic oeuvre as one of several plays she has written and, more deliberately, to her novel, *The Hills of Hebron* (1962).[5] Wynter was also commissioned by the Jamaican government to write the play *1865 — Ballad for a Rebellion*. So, significantly, *Maskarade* locates Wynter squarely within a generation of Caribbean creative and radical intellectuals who were engaged in a process of challenging Eurocentric readings of Caribbean and larger African Diaspora cultures, with more informed understandings of what was unfolding in the postenslavement/colonial period and projecting the kind of new Caribbean societies they were imagining and hoped to create. Through her dramatic interventions we are also able to delineate a body of Wynter's creative and analytical materials that specifically target the Caribbean — even though all of her work would, at some level, engage the meaning of the Caribbean in the grander scheme(s) of European modernity.[6]

Maskarade: Advancing the Creative/Theoretical and the Resemanticizing of Blackness

The play *Maskarade* has remained outside of the frames of analysis of the Wynter intellectual trajectory for too long, largely because it has not been published in European/North American or other mainstream contexts. But in many ways the play is central to understanding what has unfolded as the larger theoretical contributions and interventions for which Wyn-

ter is now primarily known. I have suggested elsewhere that the creative/
theoretical split, often assigned to writers in the Western canon, is perhaps
less useful when we begin to evaluate some of the writers who come out of
the Caribbean region and whose "theoretical work is intimately connected
to the imaginative."[7] In addition to Sylvia Wynter, with whose work we are
concerned here, we can therefore almost automatically identify NourbeSe
Philip, Derek Walcott, George Lamming, C. L. R. James, Erna Brodber, Kamau Brathwaite, Aimé Césaire, and Edouard Glissant as some of the most
recognizable black thinkers who enmesh the theoretical and the imaginative.

Produced for telecast by the Jamaica Broadcasting Corporation in December 1973, *Maskarade* was one of three plays published in Jamaica in 1979
in the collection *West Indian Plays for Schools*.[8] In the production notes, we
are told that the spelling "MASKARADE" is "intentional—it conveys the ca-
dence of the Jamaican pronunciation of masquerade."[9] Thus, in its title, there
was a move into a specific usage of local Caribbean language forms. Wynter addresses this as not wanting to limit the use of "dialect" to the comic
or the trivialized, but to understand how language could be reinvented. As
she notes in her essay "One Love—Rhetoric or Reality? Aspects of Afro-
Jamaicanism," for the enslaved/colonized/African, "language became the
area of the plantation where he negated his Being. His response was to
assimilate this language to his own structure of thought; of imagination.
Recreating its essence through the trauma of his new existence."[10] She sees
Rastafari, though, as offering a cultural praxis that "re-semanticizes blackness" away from the abjection with which European people and black
middle classes locate African-descended people, including themselves. In
her words, Rastafari would call into question the "negation of our being
as a population whose New World origin had been as slave labor/slaves."[11]

The production notes also point intertextually to Wynter's essay "Jonkonnu in Jamaica: Towards the Interpretation of Folk Dance as a Cultural
Process,"[12] suggesting that the idea of the play had been "inspired" by this
essay and that before "any attempt is made to produce the play—or even
read it, in drama class—drama teachers and drama students would do well
to read the article."[13] Wynter also indicates another type of intertextuality,
making connections with the work of Jean Price-Mars and his *Ainsi parla
l'oncle (So Spoke the Uncle)*.[14] The essay "Jonkonnu" begins with an epigraph
from Price-Mars on the particulars of revalorization of Caribbean cultures.
Price-Mars, she indicates, deliberately claimed a revalorization of what had

been "the totally stigmatized history of our ancestors" before, especially during, and after Middle Passage constructions. Therein lies our continued struggle for "full human status as a population."[15]

In "Jonkonnu in Jamaica," Wynter had proposed a two-part focus for her essay in order to do the following:

a) Offer a thesis with regards to, and attempt an interpretation of, the Jonkonnu folkdance as an *agent* and *product* of a cultural process which we shall identify and explore as a process of *indigenization*.

b) Tabulate the survivals of folkdance in Jamaica, briefly relating them to the cultural process.[16]

The essay itself mounts a defense of the utility of culture for full emancipation and, similar to the work of other scholars of that generation, takes apart the misreadings of colonial and other Western scholars who attempted to form conclusions about black cultures, "under western eyes."[17] The point of the scholars who identified with movements such as negritude and *indigenismo* was how to claim African/Caribbean cultures. The discussion seemed to center on a debate about "creolization" and its relation to "indigenization" (not the singular discourse that "creolization" itself has become under Glissant and others).[18] Using Price-Mars, Wynter argued: "The cultural resistance to colonialism in this new land was an indigenous resistance. The history of the Caribbean islands is, in large part, the history of the indigenization of the black man. And this history is a cultural history—not in 'writing,' but of those *homunculi* who humanize the landscape by peopling it with gods and spirits, with demons and duppies, with all the rich panoply of man's imagination."[19] Price-Mars had basically reinstated the idea that African-based cultures claimed the environment they had been forced to inhabit through transatlantic slavery; in that way, just as Europeans following de Sepulveda had used culture as a weapon of domination and defined their posture of European civilization in relation to native cultures, Africans had created a cultural resistance that can also be identified as indigenous in that it was harmonized with the land.[20] Importantly, Wynter suggests that both negritude and *indigenismo* would begin with the rehabilitation of African and Amerindian cultures, both of which are understood as claiming different modes of indigeneity.[21] The use of culture as resistance would permeate black decolonization struggles across Africa and the Caribbean, with scholars like Frantz Fanon, Amílcar Lopes Cabral, Ngũgĩ wa Thiong'o, and

Claudia Jones offering leading analyses of the use of culture to combat the colonizing of the mind.

It is within the context of histories of servitude and colonialism, decolonization struggles, and strategies of cultural resistance that *Maskarade* exists—it is a space of rehumanizing the landscape with culture created in the Caribbean. *Maskarade* operates, then, to give Jonkonnu a cultural and historical meaning as both resistance and affirmation, a re-creation of African culture in the Caribbean landscape deriving elements from European, Amerindian, and African cultural forms, particularly masquerade traditions, from which it created its own pathway.[22] But internal to the play are several other human dramas that have to do with gender, youth, and age. Particularly notable is the Miss Gatha narrative. Miss Gatha on the surface heralds an older woman's resistance to being moved aside to favor a younger woman; her story is also presented as a metaphor for the injustice of being used for years only to be discarded. It is clear that the model for Miss Gatha in both *Maskarade* and *The Hills of Hebron* was someone of the power of Amy Ashwood Garvey[23]—and in *Maskarade* we begin to see that depth at work in her studied revelation in the final moments of the play:

GATHA: Is me
After all these years
Driver writes me out of the play:
Blot out my part, my scene:
So I write a different end, Brainsy
To a different play.[24]

It is significant, as Keshia Abraham notes in her introduction to *The Caribbean Woman Writer as Scholar*, that Miss Gatha continues to reappear in other texts—such as Wynter's *Hills of Hebron* and in Erna Brodber's work. She is imagined, Abraham suggests, like a "kumina mother, responsible for spiritual preparation and transformation."[25] Wynter, for her part, sees Miss Gatha in a much more complex light; she struggled with the television producer not to make Miss Gatha comic but to have her reflect and represent the ethics of an older order not founded upon exploiting and discarding a series of "expendable peoples" (and consequently the post-1492 disrespecting of a range of earlier more prominent actors). So Miss Gatha is not just a gendered figure—indeed, at the end of the play she dresses as a male figure, the executioner, which draws attention to Wynter's complex creative decision to have her embody a range of meanings and tendencies that bring together the gender/genre split affected via European liberal feminism.[26]

In *Maskarade* there is also the tragic unfolding of consequences in what is identified as the "European Doctor Play," also indigenized and made to serve a role within the Jonkonnu performance.[27] Wynter, however, in her contextualization and theorization of Jonkonnu, offers a doubled reading: one that leans more toward "prettification," and a more "underground" version that leads to indigenization: "The 'creolized jonkonnu' of the Set-Girls patterned the power structure of the society. Slave society was hierarchical. The hierarchy was based on the biological concept of race. The room at the top was spacious and white; that at the bottom cramped and black. In between, on the middle rungs of the ladder one was graded according to shade. Culture, too, was reduced to a racial concept. European culture was white; African culture was black. In this concept the Jonkonnu dance became mere 'antics'; and grotesque."[28]

Related, in terms of cultural history, there is also within the play the re-enactment of the banishing of Jonkonnu by the colonial powers, relegating it to the rural areas due to fears of violence. Jonkonnu was banned in Kingston in 1841 until a century later, in 1950, when it was brought back as part of the beginning cultural decolonization search for local cultural forms. Here is the mayor's declaration as articulated within the universe of the play:

> I did warn you! I did warn you!
> Now I declare war on Jonkonnu:
> I am going to stamp out Jonkonnu
> Stamp it out!
> I am the Mayor of Kingston:
> A tough man, a no-nonsense man:
> Hereby, by fiat. I Man, I
> Abolish Jonkonnu in the environs of Kingston
> I ban it! I banish it![29]

Alongside potential erasure there is room for a new interpretation and cultural resistance: "Since Jonkonnu ban in Kingstown Town / Jonkonnu take to the hills" and "Jonkonnu Maskarade hide in the shadows."[30]

One of the few essays to discuss this play is Sandra Richards's piece "Horned Ancestral Masks, Shakespearean Actor Boys, and Scotch-Inspired Set Girls: Social Relations in Nineteenth Century Jamaican Jonkonnu."[31] Richards's project was not to study Jonkonnu in depth, but she does use it to offer a reading of the social relations being enacted in the nineteenth century and provides a brief history of the horned ancestral mask.[32] She also references the unpublished essay by Wynter titled "Behind 'Maskarade'" and indicates that as masquerades and Jonkonnu moved through time, there was a shift from a "horned mask to a human configuration."[33] And the horned mask disappeared briefly when it was banned along with the other deliberate colonial de-maskings (bans, restraints, and censorships) across the Caribbean, because of the governmental fear of the amassing of African power bases.

One sees, therefore, a parallel unfolding with other African-based carnival forms across the Caribbean from Crop Over in Barbados to Gumbay in Bahamas and Carnival in Trinidad: attempts by the colonial state to ban these African-derived forms and practices of resistance and re-creation. Thus one still finds in 2010 the reenactment of the Canboulay Riots in Trinidad. Critical elements like stick fighting, dance, drumming, and costuming become workable and central to this carnival-as-street theater-play.[34] Under the leadership of Eintou Pearl Springer, the Canboulay reenactment became an essential ritual opening point of the annual carnival, with its history described in the following terms: "Enslaved in this new land, their freedom had finally been won in 1838. The Canboulay celebrated that freedom, in remembered masking traditions, cultural retention and creativity engendered by their recent history. In February of 1881 the people faced the might of the Colonial powers represented by the police under Captain Baker. That day represented a great victory for the people."[35]

"Jonkonnu play over? / Jonkonnu play just begin" is how the Wynter play *Maskarade* ends, signaling that the reenactment is hardly over.[36] Wynter had assured this logic of re-creation of culture and imagined the humanization of nature for the benefit of the people and not that of European colonial order. Note that the full cast of characters, who also appear in *The Hills of Hebron*, all occupy the category of "native labor"—low-wage, no-wage, lowly skilled, no-skilled, those called *les damnés* by Fanon. The play draws attention to an assortment of working-class, jobless, and poor folk: the mayor's driver, shoemaker, traditional artists and puppeteer, all peasants and urban poor, people who are just eking out a living and raising enough money to keep a roof over their heads. This is the underclass—not even proletarian— the condemned, who Wynter explains were produced and marginalized for the benefit of the colonial order.[37] Still for her it is this same "African presence [which] *rehumanized nature* and helped to save his own humanity against the constant onslaught of the plantation system by the creation of a folklore and folk-culture."[38]

Wynter is at pains here, given the time the essay and play were written in the early 1970s, to provide explanations and tracings for some of these Jamaican cultural forms. Reflecting on that era of scholarship now, we recognize that the earlier tracing of retentions and survivals had a particular role within the logic of the reclamation of African history, a certain "use value" of diaspora activism and scholarship, as Brent Edwards Hayes argues.[39] The tabulating of the survivals of folk dance practices in Jamaica, and briefly relating them to the cultural process, which Wynter identifies in her early writings, is but one stream of a larger scholarly project (such as that outlined by Larry Neal in his "Some Reflections on the Black Aesthetic").[40] Wynter suggests that not being an anthropologist or an ethnologist, she could only work with the research material available in order to arrive at her own creative thinking on what was developing as Caribbean culture.[41]

The articulation of the black radical tradition has been addressed by a number of scholars. One of the best summaries is provided by Robin D. G. Kelley, who identifies it as the work of several scholars and activists with the essential ideological orientation being "some kind of diaspora sensibility, shaped by anti-racist and anti-imperialist politics of the nineteenth and twentieth centuries and deeply ensconced in black intellectual and historical traditions, profoundly shaped historical scholarship on black people in the new world."[42] In the Caribbean radical intellectual tradition, a cadre of scholars and artists created a series of political and artistic movements on each island and in the Caribbean Diaspora. Writers, artists, and activists include, among others, J. D. Elder and Beryl McBurnie in Trinidad; Derek Walcott in St. Lucia; and Hubert Harrison, Marcus Garvey, and artists like Claude McKay and others who would form the New Negro Movement and the Harlem Renaissance in the United States. Caribbean intellectuals like Aimé Césaire and Leon Damas, who formed the negritude movement and would influence the writings of Frantz Fanon, Kamau Brathwaite, and members of the Caribbean Artists Movement, Una Marson and the BBC Caribbean Voices in London, Claudia Jones and her *West Indian Gazette and Afro-Asian Caribbean News,* and a series of subsequent political and artistic movements such as that of John La Rose in London are also part of this radical tradition.

Thus, a project like *Maskarade* was a component of generational and ongoing creative activism. This is the same task to which African American

writers and thinkers of the Harlem Renaissance—such as those noted by
Alain Locke in "The Legacy of the Ancestral Arts"[43] who occupied both artistic and philosophical fields, as well as figures like Amiri Baraka in the Black
Arts Movement—would be oriented. Wynter's creative work also spoke
to the political/organizational sphere of those like Hubert Harrison who
defined the New Negro Movement and subsequently influenced Marcus
and Amy Ashwood Garvey, who would take the revindication movement of
the black subject much further and, as Wynter puts it, build a politics that
"nourished on a constant stream of African cultural survival."[44] For many,
work on cultural survival closes off and "ends" just after the civil rights and
anticolonial struggles; the practice of thinking about how we might return
to and honor those cultural histories remains frozen and cast as dated intellectual work. Wynter, however, sees the ethnologists as providing the raw
data or evidentiary material with which one can work.

For Wynter, then, the second aspect of the project is important: to "offer a thesis with regards to, and attempt an interpretation of, the Jonkonnu
folkdance as *agent* and *product* of a cultural process which we shall identify
and explore as a process of *indigenization*."[45] It is here that Wynter begins,
then, to chart a theory of Caribbean cultural process. Jonkonnu, as festival,
aligns with African and other world festivals as reenacting the process by
which human societies held themselves together; it became the integrating
mechanism in the social order outside of official policing structures and the
invention of fake kinships.[46] Festivals overturn hierarchies of order but are,
as well, a series of conflicting tendencies either aligned with or critical of
dominant culture. The essay "Jonkonnu and Jamaica" and the play *Maskarade*, then, allowed Wynter to continue into a more advanced theoretical
enquiry. This is the concern of the following section.

Theorizing Caribbean Cultural Process: Indigenization and/or Creolization?

One of the historical themes that Wynter addresses in the "Jonkonnu in
Jamaica" essay is the spatial division into plantation and provision grounds.
The provision grounds were plots of land and spaces that the Africans were
able to work, sustain, and cultivate when they were away from the demands
of the plantation. Taking off from Leopold Senghor's "Essay on the Problem
of Culture," which had recognized that Western man had effected an economic transformation of the world by making us believe that the transformation of nature by man is the very essence of culture, she was able to move
to another argument that is at the basis of her subsequent theorizations of

the human: "We propose that this break in thought, attitude and relation by which a dual and oscillatory process was replaced by the single-minded conquest of Nature by Western Man, began with the discovery of the New World. Or, if it did not begin, a qualitative change brought a qualitative change in emphasis. For it is with the discovery of the New World and its vast exploitable lands that the process has been termed, 'The reduction of Man to Labour and of Nature to Land under the impulsion of the market economy.'"[47]

She also quotes Karl Polanyi on this new economic relation, and there is an aspect of Marxist analysis here as the identification of this "new relation" meant that "Nature became land and land if it were to be exploited needed not men essentially, but so many units of labour power."[48] But her take, while informed by Marxist analyses of labor relations, is not wholly Marxist. In her interview with David Scott, Wynter explains that like many of her generation, up until her Guyana experience—working for Cheddi Jagan among the violent ethnic divisions, labor strikes, the burning of Georgetown, riots inspired by the CIA—she was a Marxist. She notes that "Marxism gave you a key which said look, you can understand the reality of which you're a part. . . . [After the riots in Guyana in 1961,] I said no, there is something important that this paradigm cannot deal with. . . . It was not a matter of negating the Marxian paradigm but of realizing that it was *one* aspect of something that was larger."[49]

It is the kind of twist that has shaped the thinking of C. L. R. James and several other Caribbean intellectuals and activists. They had arrived at an allied argument: that these New World societies were created only for market purposes and that in many ways the Caribbean became the place where this land-labor-capital process was refined and allowed European modernity to take place. Eric Williams had worked out the "capitalism and slavery" piece of the analysis in his 1944 work with the same title.[50] Wynter's extension of this argument begins as follows:

Out of this relation, in which the land was always the *Earth*, the centre of a core of beliefs and attitudes, would come the central pattern which held together the social order. In this aspect of the relation, the African slave represented an opposing process to that of the European, who achieved great technical progress based on the primary accumulation of capital which came from the dehumanization of Man and Nature. In general he remained a transient, a frequent absentee, his society without roots in the new soil. The African presence, on the other hand, *"rehumanized Nature"* and helped to save his own humanity against the constant onslaught of the plantation system by the creation of a folklore and folk culture.[51]

Wynter sees the Caribbean subject as caught in a "dual role, ambivalent between two contradictory processes."[52] Thus culture develops in the attempt to make sense of the Caribbean landscape, this environment, this new place, in which black subjects had to "root" themselves—and in several cases, as in the Maroon communities, created replicas of the social relations that existed in Africa.

The "provision grounds" argument becomes critical here for Wynter: by these means, the African in the Caribbean rescued Caribbean culture from plantation debasement. The provision grounds fed its people but importantly created the basis for a Caribbean cuisine and an entire Caribbean cultural life. "The relation of slave to provision ground was a relation of man to the Earth," Wynter argues.[53] Dance, then, was a way of strengthening and reestablishing that relation of human to the earth. Using a range of available scholarship for the period on dance, religion, festival, and music cultures in Africa and the New World, Wynter was able to conclude that "Jonkonnu as the cultural manifestation of African religious beliefs was therefore involved in this resistance. It was also the more 'public,' 'secular' manifestation of a syncretic cult religion which played and was to play an important part both in the Jamaican religion and folk culture."[54]

A debate was being waged in that period about the articulation of *indigenization* as opposed to *creolization*. In this piece, Wynter comes out on the side of *indigenization*. Her argument pushes against what would now become the more settled discourse of creolization, which she did not see then (or now) as an end point.[55] In "Jonkonnu in Jamaica" she puts into play the link she sees taking place *between* creolization and indigenization: "Whilst the 'creolization' process represents what Kerr has termed as a more or less 'false assimilation' in which the dominated people adopt elements from the dominant one in order to obtain prestige of status, the 'indigenization' process represents the more secretive process by which the dominated culture survives; and resists."[56] In this early piece, Wynter provides a very hard critique of creolization and anticipates the discomfort that some have felt with the popularity of its articulation.[57] For her, creolization is the process of the house slaves approximating the white dominant culture; it is always lodged because of its terminology and meaning discursively and historically to Europeanization outside of Europe.[58] Thus even Michel-Rolph Trouillot, in his "Culture on the Edges: Creolization in the Plantation Context,"[59] ends with the "Plantation as Cultural Matrix," thus returning those who identify with creolization (even as opposed to *créolité*) to the plantation: "For a majority of enslaved Africans and Afro-Americans, prior to the mid-nineteenth century, creolization did not happen away from the plantation system, but within it."[60] While he sees "grand marronage" (large-scale slave rebellions) as the "privileged example" often given for Caribbean resistance, he draws attention to the importance of "petit marronage" (small-scale opportunistic flight from plantations, slave theft, malingering) as it emphasizes how the majority of the enslaved conducted their lives and their daily departures and returns through which they were able to create creole societies.[61] Trouillot returns to the idea of the provision grounds that Wynter had initially asserted but does not give it the weight and separate theoretical articulation that she does. He asserts only that it was on the provision grounds that the slaves learned how to survive on the plantations and follows her in concluding that it was in this space that they developed and created cultural practices. For Wynter it is the "provision grounds" that allowed the indigenization process to take place and the full development of a Caribbean cultural process; and, it is the variety of Maroon contexts that began the basis of indigenization and being rooted in the Caribbean landscape. Thus "Jonkunnu take to the hills / Jonkunnu maskarade hide in the shadows."[62]

In light of our consideration of *Maskarade*, it is interesting that Wynter began *The Hills of Hebron* as a play, which she rewrote for publication as a novel in 1962, in that it indicates a range of figurations and ways to creatively articulate the meaning of nationhood in the context of the Caribbean independence movements. Thus, while she was capable of experimenting with the theatrical form, she saw the novel as able to, in Kelly Baker's words, find the "space to imagine the newly independent Jamaica."[63] Elizabeth De-Loughrey more directly uses the "provision grounds" metaphor to examine the "spatial geographies of Caribbean culture" and thus the ways in which the "violence of modernity alienated humans from nature and the implications for the Caribbean novel."[64] DeLoughrey's project looks at how the logic of provision grounds serves as a "symbol of the roots of creolization in Caribbean literature."[65] I need to add here that the argument forwarded by DeLoughrey is definitely not Wynter's project, as Wynter is, as noted earlier, very critical of the entire concept of creolization, identifying it as coming out of and therefore inextricably linked to the plantation. This is how Wynter describes the basis for her version of Caribbean "indigenization":

> The relation of the slave to the provision ground was a relation of a man to the Earth. While the Plantation ideology, the official ideology, would develop as the ideology of property, and the rights to property, the provision ground ideology would remain based on a man's relation to the Earth, which linked a man to his community. The first would give rise to the superstructure of civilization in the Caribbean; the second to the roots of culture. . . . The technical power of the Earth is universal and all men show this in the ritual observances by which they show respect. The dance plays a central part in all these ritual observances.[66]

It is interesting that while she wants to move beyond Marxism as a master discourse (as noted earlier vis-à-vis her interview with David Scott, Marx was only partially right for her), some Marxist categories inevitably remain: Marxism provides/provided an analytical tool.[67] The Caribbean Left presents various permutations on this problematic, often seeing what Althusser refers to as "Marx at his Limits."[68]

Wynter's position is perhaps even more clarified in her critique of "Creole Criticism," which challenges the constant creation of what she calls a "middle-colored" (middle-class colored) identity in which Africa is measured and cast as debased and/or decoration.[69] Her essay "Novel and History, Plot and Plantation" provides the relevant analyses of this aesthetic choice, though in a much later work Wynter would engage and support at some level Clyde Taylor's critique of the aesthetic itself.[70] In "Novel and History, Plot and Plantation," she wrote, "The novel form, a product of the market economy, its exchange structure, and its individual here set free, to realize his individuality by the 'liberal' values of individualism, linked to the very existence of the market system, nevertheless, instead of expressing the values of the market society, develops and expands as a form of resistance to the very market society. In effect, the novel form and the novel is the critique of the very historical process which has brought it to such heights of fulfillment."[71] There is an interesting relationship, then, between *Maskarade* and *The Hills of Hebron*, that underscores not a hierarchy of forms but rather Wynter's experimentations with various forms, all leading to the creative/ theoretical formation of her ideas on the nature of the human condition as it pertains to the Caribbean/black/working poor subject. Wynter identifies herself as growing up poor in Kingston, in what would now be identified as the ghetto, and with a peasant grandmother from whose community her *Hills of Hebron* comes.[72] Thus Kelly Baker concludes that "Wynter's later theoretical writings on Caribbean culture, gender and the reinvention of humanism help to illustrate the tensions evident in her novel between old European paradigms and new Caribbean situations."[73]

"Novel and History, Plot and Plantation" expands and develops in more detail the earlier argument that had begun in the "Jonkonnu" essay, providing a more comprehensive elaboration of the process that she calls the "plantation-plot dichotomy."[74] Her argument is that our relationships with the plot and the plantation—as historical and creative narratives that shape, inform, and *represent* social systems—are not discrete, but rather that we are caught in that ambivalent relation between these two poles, and in effect Caribbean society, during struggles for independence and the movement toward nationhood, had to choose one system over the other. *Maskarade* then operates right at that intersection—between plot and plantation—as it presents a range of these struggles, between an ethics of fairness. Miss Gatha represents that principle of fairness, against exploitation and the discarding of people who are no longer useful, a kind of female principle that is able to execute justice.[75] As Miss Gatha recostumes herself in the role of the executioner, the play continues:

LOVEY:
Real life catch up with the play . . .

. . .

[Widen spot as the EXECUTIONER hands the axe to CUFFEE, then backs away . . .]

Driver lift him stick
Was about to give Cuffee one lick
That would put him to sleep till morning
When another actor enter on the scene
And write a different script.[76]

The play develops to a climax as Driver is killed by Cuffee as he also strangles the young man. It is Miss Gatha who, as executioner, provided the weapon. Miss Gatha is the one who closes out the play as it were and reinstates some level of order and justice:

BRAINSY:
So is you, Miss Gatha . . .
I should have known.[77]

In "One Love—Rhetoric or Reality? Aspects of Afro-Jamaicanism," Wynter is very definite in identifying a "cultural matrix," which, she explains, "sprung out of a people's response to that dehumanization which would convert them into merchandise."[78] It is interesting as well that Afro-Brazilians have also recently defined an "African matrix"[79] as describing, as Wynter puts it, that "secret underground current of people's lives outside the time continuum of dates and surface deeds; the current of pervasive continuities."[80] It is this secret underground that she would operationalize in the play *Maskarade*, which had Jonkonnu, an African-derived Caribbean masquerade tradition at its center; but throughout the creative narrative, she allows commentary on a range of issues: poverty, creativity, survival, gender relations, age and youth, lust and love. These issues, together, inform a diasporic claim to place that is not linked to conquest but is instead evidence of everyday interactions that are tied to a people struggling to newly reinvent themselves. *Maskarade*, then, might be read as a textual invitation to think about how questions of displacement and encounter produce the conditions for living the world differently. Further clarifying her thoughts on indigenization, Wynter suggests that

> roots are never natural; roots are created in a new relation to the land.
> This is what indigenizes you. Amerindians had put down roots and created cultural matrices earlier, and in the post–Middle Passage matrix,
> African people had been the ones putting down roots in a nonexploitative relation to the land in the same way that Europeans had done this in
> Europe. When they became settlers in the New World, though, it was not
> so much putting down roots but extracting or exploiting its resources.
> It was the African-descended populations in the New World who were
> going to create something new out of what was received.[81]

This indigenization is also a continuous process, part of that underground cultural matrix out of which something new emerges each time.

Revindication of Blackness, the Native, the Human

While she is informed by a range of theoretical principles and positions from Marxism to African cultural critiques, Sylvia Wynter is always clear (pace

Aimé Césaire's declaration and in a kind of "left of Karl Marx" way) that "the black struggle goes beyond the usual Marxist definition, since the black is at once a member of the proletariat, and a member of the only race whose humanity has been questioned."[82] She also cites and agrees with Wilfred Cartey that the urgent concern of their generation was/is with the "literary and cultural revindication of the humanity of the black, [which] lies at the core of, and is essential to the solution of an urgent and fundamental problem with which all modern literature and art grapples—the reconstruction of man's humanity in a world of increasing and rapid dehumanization."[83]

In her "One Love" essay, Wynter is critical of empty forms of appropriation of creole language, creolization, and other opportunistic practices, which are linked to the plantation versions of European systems. She sees utility even here in Fanonian conclusions, suggesting that we work toward that "new clearing in the forest of liberated black and human experience of Being."[84] Indeed, she writes that it was only Fanon who had, at the time of her writing "One Love," grappled with the "complexity of our problem," that "we the New-World blacks, the first total colonials of capitalism, have internalized the 'standards and needs' of the external audience."[85] Here, too, she draws attention to the ways in which education—again following Fanon—was the "chief agent of indoctrination by which the colonized black internalizes the standards of the colonizer other."[86]

All of these early strands of analysis come together, then, in Wynter's theory of the human. Five recent essays/interviews will illustrate briefly. The essay "Unsettling the Coloniality of Being/Power/Truth/Freedom: Towards the Human, after Man, Its Overrepresentation—An Argument" begins boldly by asserting and proving that "the struggle of our new millennium will be one between the ongoing imperative of securing the well-being of our present ethnoclass (i.e. Western bourgeois) conception of the human, Man, which overrepresents itself as if it were the human itself, and that of securing the well-being and therefore the full cognitive and behavioral autonomy of the human species itself/ourselves."[87] She continues that all our present and local struggles are different facets of this larger struggle for humanity. The remainder of the essay marshals a wide array of evidence from a range of fields in order to consolidate this argument, but it ends, nevertheless with Césaire's call for a "new science of the Word."[88]

A number of Wynter's positions are clarified in two landmark interviews. In his interview with Wynter in *Small Axe*, "The Re-enchantment of Humanism," David Scott was able to do the kind of research on the early periods, which got Wynter to talk expansively on how she came to her current theoretical assertions. Wynter's interview with Greg Thomas, originally located in *ProudFlesh* as "ProudFlesh Inter/Views Sylvia Wynter" and reproduced in *The Caribbean Woman Writer as Scholar* as "Yours in the Intellectual Struggle," is where she summarizes some of her current preoccupations and provides her own assessment of her work over the years: "I came to the conclusion that the question of 'consciousness' cannot be solved within the terms of the Western system of knowledge, which is the system of knowledge in which the modern world is brought into existence. . . . And so I suddenly realized then that's what Black Studies in its origin had arisen to."[89] In a more specific essay on the critique of black studies as it now exists, "On How We Mistook the Map for the Territory," she offers a critical reading of what black studies has become. For her, then, it was not just "anthropology but also all the disciplinary discourses of our present order of knowledge, as put in place from the nineteenth century onward, that had to be elaborated on the a priori basis of this biocentric, *homo oeconomicus* descriptive statement and its over-representation as if it were that of the human."[90] Black studies was incorporated into the mainstream, then, in her view, "only at the cost of the pacification of its original thrust, by means of its redefinition in Man's normative terminology, no longer as a Black utopian alternative mode of thought but rather, as Ethnic sub-text of the Ideologies of Man's Word—that is, as African-American Studies."[91]

Wynter sees festival culture, what we might call "Behind Maskarade" ideas, as mechanisms of each human order and thus the stories and human practices holding together social and cultural materials and knowledges. These ideas induce and invent different kinship systems and uncover clues to thinking about the ways in which stateless societies—such as enslaved and postslave diasporic communities—were able to enact mechanisms and invent themselves as a people. In this way, Jonkonnu connects to the premonotheistic world out of which festivals come.[92] Like the Bakhtinian reading of carnival, there is that sense in which the carnival or festival overturns hierarchies and/or creates new ones. Jonkonnu, as understood and put forth by Wynter, is part of the foundational matrix that connects or "goes back to Africa" aesthetically as it also indigenizes in the Caribbean landscape. In a sense, then, *Maskarade* (and, related, Jonkonnu) offers a glimpse of a knowledge system beyond the workings of epistemological normalcy (and

Man): it creatively conveys the ways in which economies of transatlantic slavery and its colonizing twin—processes meant to comprehensively dispossess and thrive on land exploitation—produced the conditions through which black subjects developed alternative ways of human being and a sense of belonging based not on territorialization but through acts of localized/grounded (translocal) cultural production. Wynter identified this in a talk given at Wesleyan University in April 2009 that was titled "Human Being as Noun or Being Human as Praxis: On Laws, Modes of Institution and the Ultimate Crisis of the Global Warming and Climate Change."[93] From its titling alone, one gets a sense that Wynter wanted to offer an overarching discussion about the theoretical principles with which her work has been preoccupied; in her words, "like Césaire, she has been writing the same poem but advancing it technically each time."[94] For Wynter, it is not just "performing gender," as Judith Butler would have it, for she sees a danger in separating gender from genre, but performing being human that is the new challenge.[95] Being human as praxis can create a new order again, as evident in the British Petroleum environmental disaster in the Gulf of Mexico in 2010, in which the technical systems of capitalizing on nature by extracting mass wealth from the land and sea for corporate greed failed. The result is an epic-like spread of crude oil into the Gulf of Mexico and outward, to destroy land and sea, and people and animal life. The failure is poignant and demands new ways of living our world.

Maskarade, then, represents one early thread in the beginning of an analysis toward "ontological sovereignty," as Wynter terms it throughout many of her essays, which moves through the example of the Caribbean process as she identified: to "offer a thesis with regards to, and attempt an interpretation of, the Jonkonnu folkdance as *agent* and *product* of a cultural process which we shall identify and explore as a process of *indigenization*."[96] This initial process offers the building blocks for the much larger project as identified here but not without the politics of revindication of the black subject that is identified early as part of the black radical intellectual project, and not without as well the valorization of indigenization—which includes the reintegration with the land of the other debased and dehumanized "dysselected others." For Wynter, then, Jonkonnu and *Maskarade* become revelatory.

In *Maskarade* there is a conscious presentation of the Jonkonnu first as "shades" and then in full view as described in the stage directions: "The Jonkonnu band surges on stage for the second part, no gauze traverse, lights coming up slowly until they are full on by the time LOVEY rounds off his introduction:

Jonkonnu music noise up the air."[97]

Notes

1. Scott, "The Re-enchantment of Humanism," 133.
2. Scott, "The Re-enchantment of Humanism," 133.
3. Sylvia Wynter, personal letter to Carole Boyce Davies, May 26, 2010. Wynter indicates that her presentation was titled "Behind Maskarade" and that she presented it at Northwestern before the performance of the play. I have not seen a copy of the paper "Behind Maskarade" but have communicated with Wynter on some of the sequencing of events in relation to its public presentation.
4. A typescript copy was made available by the director of the production, Sandra Richards, of Northwestern University and is in the author's possession.
5. Wynter, *The Hills of Hebron*. Sylvia Wynter is identified in biographical entries as also a dramatist. In 1958, Wynter met Jan Carew, with whom she wrote pieces for the BBC and completed *Under the Sun*, a full-length stage play, which was bought by the Royal Court Theatre in London. She also is identified as the author of *Shh . . . It's a Wedding* (1961), with music by Carlos Malcolm, who had written all the music for the James Bond film *Dr. No*; this play is notably the first production of a folk theater company she founded in Jamaica. Wynter also wrote *Miracle in Lime Lane* (1962), *1865 — Ballad for a Revolution* (1965), the pantomime *Rockstone Anancy* (1970), and *Maskarade* (1973). Most of Wynter's creative texts, with the exception of the play *Maskarade* and *The Hills of Hebron*, are no longer in circulation.
6. Among these are works such as Wynter, "One Love," 64–97; Wynter, "Jonkonnu in Jamaica," 34–48. A range of subsequent works, however, consistently engage the Caribbean as a base but go on to analyze the pathways of the development of European modernity and its conceptions of the human through the destruction of native peoples and the enslavement of Africans, but also the dislodging of these now oppressed peoples from subsequent definitions of humanity. Wynter's "We Must Learn to Sit Down Together and Talk about a Little Culture," a two-part piece in *Jamaica Journal*, is identified by her in the David Scott interview as being critical but also without leaving out her own subject position, asking for a more "engaged criticism" while breaking through herself to a new way of thinking. See Scott, "The Re-enchantment of Humanism," 152.
7. Boyce Davies, "Preface," ix.
8. Lee, Wynter, and Chevannes, *West Indian Plays for Schools*, 26–55. For this essay, a copy was provided by Sylvia Wynter. All citations for *Maskarade* are from this version of the play.
9. Wilson, "Production Notes," 26.

10. Wynter, "One Love," 78. Here, as opposed to her Man1/Man2 project, Wynter's use of "black man" and her referencing of the masculine pronoun as generic is specific to its time and has already been addressed and revised by subsequent feminist scholarship. On Man1/Man2, see McKittrick's introduction to this volume.

11. Wynter, letter, May 26, 2010; Scott, "The Re-enchantment of Humanism," 145.

12. Wynter, "Jonkonnu in Jamaica," 34–48. As part of assigning appropriate credit, Wynter wants it known that the origin of *Maskarade* arose as well from the suggestion of a then young television producer, Jim Nelson, who, after having read the Jonkonnu essay, had called her up and asked her to "write it as a television play for me," with this resulting in the first version published for schools. Sylvia Wynter, personal letter to Carole Boyce Davies, May 26, 2010.

13. Wilson, "Production Notes," 26.

14. Price-Mars, *So Spoke the Uncle/Ainsi parla l'oncle*.

15. Sylvia Wynter, personal letter to Carole Boyce Davies, May 26, 2010.

16. Wynter, "Jonkonnu in Jamaica," 34.

17. Cf. Mohanty, "Under Western Eyes," 61–88.

18. For Wynter today, "creolization" operates on the same plane as does "multiculturalism." Wynter, telephone conversation with the author, April 29, 2010.

19. Wynter, "Jonkonnu in Jamaica," 35.

20. As Nandita Sharma comprehensively outlines in this collection, this argument is now very controversial as some indigenous peoples who had been destroyed by invading and colonizing powers see Africans, at times, as "settlers" (although not always voluntary settlers). This point was also made strongly at a conference in Toronto where an Indigenous scholar, Bonita Lawrence, reprised comments made by Pamela Kingfisher (Cherokee) at the UN Conference against Racism in 2000: "You can keep the mule but the 40 acres is still mine." Bonita Lawrence, "Land, Identity and Indigenous Survival." Andrea Smith, Cherokee, would challenge this by saying the logic of fighting over the land did not comport with the approach to the land that indigenous peoples had preconquest and that the question of landownership and the role of enslaved Africans should be read against or with native claims to prior residence rights as opposed to the *terra nullis* assertions that drive European conquest. See Smith, "Indigenous Feminist Perspectives on Reparations." The Kingfisher comment can be found in Andrea Smith, *Conquest*, 47.

21. Wynter, "Jonkonnu in Jamaica," 35.

22. Turner, "Junkanoo," 599–600.

23. The use of Amy Ashwood Garvey is politically interesting here as Amy Ashwood, who with Marcus Garvey cofounded and helped launch the Universal Negro Improvement Association, would be discarded after three months of marriage in favor of a lighter and younger woman, Amy Jacques Garvey, whom Garvey would marry later on. In effect the same thing takes place in the play as Driver finds a younger queen to play the lead.

24. Wynter, *Maskarade*, 49.

25. Abraham, "Introduction," xxi.

26. Wynter, telephone interview with author, May 1, 2010. On gender/genre, and thus *kinds* of human being, see Wynter's contribution to this collection.

27. Wynter, *Maskarade*, 39.

28. Wynter, "Jonkonnu in Jamaica," 42.

29. Wynter, *Maskarade*, 48.

30. Wynter, *Maskarade*, 50–51.

31. Richards, "Horned Ancestral Masks, Shakespearean Actor Boys, and Scotch-Inspired Set Girls," 254–271. This essay does not explore the meaning of jonkonnu but focuses on the horned ancestral mask and its multiple representations.

32. "Horned Ancestral Masks," 257–258.

33. "Horned Ancestral Masks," 258.

34. Hill, *The Trinidad Carnival*.

35. National Carnival Commission, "Canboulay Re-enactment 2010."

36. Wynter, *Maskarade*, 51.

37. Scott, "The Re-enchantment of Humanism," 135.

38. Wynter, "Jonkonnu in Jamaica," 36.

39. Edwards, *The Practice of Diaspora Literature*. See also Herskovits, *The Myth of the Negro Past*.

40. Neal, "Some Reflections on the Black Aesthetic," 13–16.

41. Wynter, telephone interview with author, May 1, 2010.

42. Kelley, "But a Local Phase of a World Problem," 1047.

43. Locke, "The Legacy of Ancestral Arts," 254–267.

44. Perry, *Hubert Harrison*; Wynter, "One Love," 64.

45. Wynter, "Jonkunnu in Jamaica," 35.

46. Wynter, telephone interview with author, May 1, 2010.

47. Wynter, "Jonkonnu in Jamaica," 35; Leopold Senghor, "Essay on the Problem of Culture," cited in Wynter, "Jonkonnu in Jamaica," 35.

48. Wynter, "Jonkonnu in Jamaica," 35.

49. Scott, "The Re-enchantment of Humanism," 142.

50. Williams, *Capitalism and Slavery*.

51. Wynter, "Jonkonnu in Jamaica," 36 (emphasis in the original).

52. Wynter, "Jonkonnu in Jamaica," 36.

53. Wynter, "Jonkonnu in Jamaica," 37.

54. Wynter, "Jonkonnu in Jamaica," 39.

55. Braithwaite, *The Development of Creole Society in Jamaica*; Glissant, *Poetics of Relation*.

56. Wynter, "Jonkonnu in Jamaica," 39.

57. For a recent critique of the theoretical uses of "creolization," see Palmié, "Creolization and Its Discontents," 433–456. For a discussion of creolization as a difficult and painful exchange that might anticipate the indigenization of hu-

manness (rather than lead *from* in-betweenness *to* integration), see Rinaldo Walcott's essay in this collection. Walcott is at pains here not to leave out the "brutality of the fusing and mixing of diasporic cultures into hybrid forms" but also sees it as possibility.

58. Wynter, "Jonkonnu in Jamaica," 43.
59. Trouillot, "Culture on the Edges," 8–28.
60. Trouillot, "Culture on the Edges," 17.
61. Trouillot, "Culture on the Edges," 23.
62. Wynter, *Maskarade*, 50, 51.
63. Baker, "The Necessity of Madness," 181.
64. DeLoughrey, "Provision Grounds and Cultural Roots," 205–224.
65. DeLoughrey, "Provision Grounds and Cultural Roots," 205.
66. Wynter, "Jonkonnu in Jamaica," 37.
67. Scott, "The Re-enchantment of Humanism," 142.
68. See, for example, Althusser, *Philosophy of the Encounter*, which examines some of the reaches of Marxism. It is my contention that a range of Caribbean leftists from Hubert Harrison to Aimé Césaire and Claudia Jones were doing this kind of work, not so much revisioning Marxism but recognizing how far this analysis could go and not seeing it therefore as the end point. For Sylvia Wynter, "indigenization" has to do with finding a way to make a landscape and a new socioeconomic reality habitable and therefore rehumanize a space and a set of conditions that had the intent to dehumanize.
69. The David Scott interview in *Small Axe* includes a full section on "Creole Criticism" highlighting the series of quarrels that Wynter would engage with regarding the nature of Caribbean literary and cultural criticism. Scott, "The Re-enchantment of Humanism," 151–173. See also Wynter, "Creole Criticism," 12–36; and Wynter, "A Different Kind of Creature," 153–172. She discusses this point in her David Scott interview, 146.
70. Wynter, "Rethinking 'Aesthetics'" 236–279.
71. Wynter, "Novel and History, Plot and Plantation," 95.
72. Scott, "The Re-enchantment of Humanism," 120–207.
73. Baker, "The Necessity of Madness," 180.
74. Wynter, "Novel and History," 99–100.
75. Wynter, telephone interview with author, April 29, 2010.
76. Wynter, *Maskarade*, 47.
77. Wynter, *Maskarade*, 49.
78. Wynter, "One Love," 65.
79. Sanabria, "African Matrix," 53.
80. Wynter, "One Love," 65.
81. Wynter, telephone interview with author, May 1, 2010.
82. Wynter, "One Love," 69; Boyce Davies, *Left of Karl Marx*.
83. Carty, "Three Antillian Poets."
84. Wynter, "One Love," 93.

85. Wynter, "One Love," 74.

86. Wynter, "One Love," 75.

87. Wynter, "Unsettling the Coloniality of Being," 260.

88. Wynter, "Unsettling the Coloniality of Being," 331.

89. Wynter and Thomas, "Yours in the Intellectual Struggle," 34–35.

90. Wynter, "On How We Mistook the Map for the Territory," 129.

91. Wynter, "On How We Mistook the Map for the Territory," 158.

92. Wynter, telephone interview with author, May 1, 2010.

93. A version of the Wesleyan talk has been made available to the editor as: Wynter, "Human Being as Noun."

94. Wynter, telephone interview with author, May 1, 2010.

95. Cf. Butler, *Gender Trouble*.

96. Wynter, "Jonkonnu in Jamaica," 34.

97. Wynter, *Maskarade*, 38.

10 **"COME ON KID, LET'S GO GET THE *THING*"**

The Sociogenic Principle and the *Being* of Being Black/Human

> We have no philosophers who have dealt with these and other problems
> from the standpoint of the Negro's unique experience in this world. . . .
> They have failed to study the problems of Negro life in America in a
> manner which would place the fate of the Negro in the broad framework
> of man's experience in this world.
>
> **E. FRANKLIN FRAZIER, "THE FAILURE OF THE NEGRO INTELLECTUAL"**

In its March 1928 edition, the *Crisis* published a letter written by Roland A.
Barton, a very enterprising high school sophomore from South Bend, Indiana. Barton felt compelled to write because he disagreed with the journal's
use of the term "Negro." He questioned why the official organ of the NAACP
would "designate, and segregate us as 'Negroes,' and not as 'Americans.'"
He was also opposed to the use of such a term for "the natives of Africa,"
whom he felt should be called Africans or "natives." According to Barton,
"The word, 'Negro,' or 'nigger,' is a white man's word to make us feel inferior." Therefore, as a young "worker for the race," he hoped that in the future
this term would no longer be used to refer to those of African hereditary
descent.[1]

Barton's inquisitive letter emerged at a critical moment in the trajectory
of the ongoing question posed by those of African hereditary descent, the
population that owed its group presence in the Americas to the massive
transshipment of the Middle Passage. Written in the context of the post–
Civil War and Jim Crow United States, his comments followed upon a specific intellectual tradition that had been wrestling with this issue of naming
for at least more than a century. Beginning in the early nineteenth century,

many blacks abandoned the designation "African" in order to distance themselves from the negative connotations associated with those who resided on the continent of Africa, as well as those who participated in the colonization movement. Given this development, the need for dual identification arose, one that could acknowledge both the African origins and the U.S./American status of blacks. In the 1840s, Martin Delany employed the term "Africo-Americans" to describe what he insisted was a unique people. Moreover, the titles of black journals and newspapers, such as the *Weekly Anglo-African*, the *Disenfranchised American*, the *Aliened American*, the *Colored Citizen*, and the *True American*, all reflected this tension, the two-ness of being both American and Negro that would later be paradigmatically defined as "double consciousness."[2]

Whether or not Barton was aware of such debates is not at issue, but his intervention does refer to a recurrent question that has remained central to black intellectual discourse. In response to Barton's letter, the editor, W. E. B. DuBois, did not in the least dismiss the young man's concern but rather took it quite seriously, attempting to fully engage him as to the wider implications of his inquiry. DuBois argued that the matter was less one of names than of what names represented, and thus, "if men despise Negroes, they will not despise them less if Negroes are called 'colored' or 'Afro-Americans.'" Based on an analysis of the U.S. and global racial hierarchy, DuBois noted that "you cannot change the name of a thing at will" as names "are not merely matters of thought and reason" but more profoundly "are growths and habits."[3] Thus, before the emergence of contemporary discourses that question the "unitary subject" and the naturalness of *Being*, DuBois had already insightfully noted that historically no name, "neither 'English,' 'French,' 'German,' 'White,' 'Jew,' 'Nordic,' nor 'Anglo-Saxon'" was ever completely accurate in describing the peoples to whom it referred; initially, all of these were "nicknames, misnomers, and accidents" that were rendered accurate through wide use.[4] A similar argument, he proposed, could thus be made for the use of the word "Negro" to describe peoples of African hereditary descent: "In this sense 'Negro' is quite as accurate, quite as old and quite as definite as any name of any great group of people."[5]

DuBois further asserted that even if the name "Negro" *could* be changed, such an alteration does not mean that the issues would necessarily be solved: "Would the Negro problem be suddenly and eternally settled? Would you be any less ashamed of being descended from a black man, or would your schoolmates feel any less superior to you?"[6] Strategically seeking to involve

Barton in the process of social change, DuBois declared: "Your real work, my dear young man, does not lie with names. It is not a matter of changing them, losing them, or forgetting them."[7] In the most unequivocal language, DuBois emphatically stated what he saw as the fundamental question: "Get this then, Roland, and get it straight even if it pierces your soul: a Negro by any other name would be just as black and just as white; just as ashamed of himself and just as shamed by others, as today."[8] Earlier in his response, Du-Bois had made this point in an equally compelling manner when he noted: "The feeling of inferiority is in you, not in any name. The name merely evokes what is already there. Exorcise the hateful complex and no name can ever make you hang your head." For this reason, he came to the inescapable conclusion: "It is not the name—it's the *Thing* that counts. Come on Kid, let's go get the *Thing!*"[9]

Toni Morrison also depicts the *Thing*, poignantly, in her novel *The Bluest Eye*. Morrison writes:

> If she was cute—and if anything could be believed, she *was*—then we were not. And what did that mean? We were lesser. Nicer, brighter, but still lesser. Dolls we could destroy, but we could not destroy the honey voices of parents and aunts, the obedience in the eyes of our peers, the slippery light in the eyes of our teachers when they encountered the Maureen Peals of the world. What was the secret? What did we lack? Why was it important? . . . And all the time we knew that Maureen Peal was not the Enemy and not worthy of such intense hatred. The *Thing* to fear was the *Thing* that made her beautiful, and not us.[10]

What *Thing* made Maureen Peal so desirable in contrast to Claudia and, most extremely, Pecola, whose only possibility of redemption is to pray for blue eyes? What is this *Thing* to which DuBois referred? In this respect, DuBois raised the central issue when he argued that a Negro would be "just as ashamed of himself and just as shamed by others," as he was describing the fundamental issue that coloreds, Negroes, blacks, and in contemporary terms, African Americans, would have to (and continue to) confront: the *representation* of those of African hereditary descent, as the ontological lack within the terms, as Sylvia Wynter has asserted, of the secularized auto-poietic field of meaning of the Judeo-Christian West. However, this representation has not gone unchallenged. Indeed, spanning from the earliest recorded writings of "black" thinkers in the late eighteenth century, it can be argued that confronting and undoing this *Thing* has formed the overarching thematic that has come to characterize the black intellectual tradition, whose efforts have enabled a reconceptualization of the *Being* of *Being Black*.

In this context, this essay will illustrate the wider implications of the nature of this counterintellectual tradition. In this respect, the challenge mounted by thinkers such as Olaudah Equiano, Frederick Douglass, Anna Julia Cooper, Carter G. Woodson, and Aimé Césaire not only constituted significant interventions within black intellectual discourse but also have consequences with respect to questions related to the instituting of human consciousness itself, and therefore, in the terms of Frazier, within "the broad framework of man's experience in the world."[11] Frantz Fanon's concept of sociogeny, together with Sylvia Wynter's amplification of this idea as the sociogenic principle, this as the analogue of the genomic principle that orients the behaviors of purely organic species, makes clear that the abject negation of those of African hereditary descent, the *Thing* of *Being Black*, can enable an understanding of the rule-governed nature of the system of representations by means of which we as "humans" come to know our social realities and to experience them in the *genre-specific* terms of a particular mode of what it means to *Be Human*.[12]

With its revelation of the kind of change that many underwent after being forcibly taken from their homes and transported to a new land where they would be subordinated in the terms of a new system of meaning, the transformation of Olaudah Equiano, as chronicled in *The Interesting Narrative*, can become quite instructive. Whereas early in his life Equiano was the son of an elder of the highest distinction, later he would be drawn into a new autopoietic field, within whose imperially expanding and secularizing monotheistic Judeo-Christian worldview he would become a member of a group represented as the embodiment of the lack of normal Being. In his former life, Equiano did not experience himself as an African. He could not have.[13] Yet, his transformation from a person of high status to one of low status, from Conceptual Self to Conceptual Other, was emblematic of how those who had formerly existed within their own auto-instituting self-conceptions would now come to realize their Being in the terms of a quite different ontology. Indeed, nowhere is the transformation effected by Western expansion better revealed than with the appellations whereby those of African hereditary descent would come to be identified as "colored," "Negro," and "African," all of which with some negative connotations that troubled the young Roland Barton.

Equiano was initially persuaded that he had somehow "gotten into a world of bad spirits," and such led to his being captured by Whites, whom he thought were cannibals: "I asked them if we were not to be eaten by those white men with horrible looks, red faces, and long hair?"[14] Yet, his self-conception would undergo a tremendous change in the wake of his interactions with Europeans as evidenced by the psychoaffective conversion in which he began to perceive himself in the terms of lack. After befriending the daughter of one of the mates of his then owner, Equiano acknowledged that he began to harbor a sense of shame about himself: "I had often observed, that when her mother washed her face it looked rosy; but when she washed mine it did not look so; I therefore tried oftentimes myself if I could not by washing make my face of the same colour as my little playmate (Mary), but it was all in vain; and I now began to be mortified at the difference in our complexions."[15] The citation from *The Bluest Eye* can be most illuminating in this context: What was the secret of this *Thing* that compelled Equiano to respond as such, giving rise to what Frantz Fanon would later identify as a "corporeal malediction"?[16]

Recently, in *Equiano, the African: Biography of a Self Made Man*, Vincent Carretta argued that Equiano's story is apocryphal, being authored by a "skillful rhetorician" who "could speak or write in many voices and in many styles appropriate to different occasions and audiences."[17] Based on evidence, including baptismal and naval records indicating that Equiano was born in South Carolina, Carretta was led to conclude that with careful construction, Equiano "probably invented an African identity," which suggests that his narrative should be classified as historical fiction rather than as autobiography.[18] Yet, even if invented and fictionalized, *The Interesting Narrative* would constitute a poignant example of what Richard Waswo has identified as "the history that literature makes," where "fictional imaginings, themselves a response to past events, can themselves become a cause of future ones."[19] Such an understanding of the power of literature would imply that Equiano's narrative could also be analyzed in terms of the powerful effects that it would have on the interpretation of a new experience and reality; this, reflecting a new model of identity, of Being Human, one that had been at the time only recently brought into existence.

As Sylvia Wynter has argued, "all literature, indeed all human narrative, functions to encode the dynamics of desire at the deep structural level of the order's symbolic template." In other words, literature can provide a unique and specific kind of insight—that is, knowledge of the "system-specific modes of mind" on whose basis social orders are instituted and reproduced.[20] From this perspective, the "truth" produced by Equiano's narrative can be seen to reside not primarily in the realm of objective facts (where he was actually born, lived, and traveled), "facts" that, according to Carretta, can be disputed. Rather, the "truth" that emerged from Equiano's narrative constitutes a *fact of consciousness*—the revelation of a completely new existential reality in which peoples of African hereditary descent would no longer be defined in terms of their pre-Encounter models of identity, but now in relation to, and as the lack of, the Western European, Judeo-Christian idea of the Self in its then increasingly secular modality.

In the vein of Equiano, throughout the nineteenth century, the intellectual productions of black thinkers made inescapably clear the fundamental nature of this *Thing* that confronted the population group, and thus the need to dismantle it. As an eloquent example, in his *Appeal to the Coloured Citizens of the World* (1829), David Walker repudiated the assertions of Thomas Jefferson's *Notes on the State of Virginia* (1787). In effect, Walker set out to deconstruct the hegemonic pre-Darwinian and proto-evolutionary explanatory model—a model which was founding to the Enlightenment schema of natural law and legitimated the subordination of blacks based on the representation of their differences being fixed in nature. For this reason, Walker insisted that he be shown a "page of history, either sacred or profane . . . which maintains, that the Egyptians heaped the insupportable insult upon the children of Israel, by telling them they were not of the human family."[21]

This American distinction of slaves being not only physically subordinated but also conceptually imagined out of the human species would be equally countered with the unique literature, what Arna Bontemps identified as "an American genre," in which former slaves authored narratives that challenged the plantocratic order of domination and the ontology that subtended it.[22] Given that slavery was a juridical institution, one that subtended the formal structure of national government (such as with the three-fifths ratio in the Article 1, Section 2, of the U.S. Constitution, which apportioned direct taxation and representation in the U.S. House of Representatives based on slaveholding), the individual personality of the slave was simultaneously a public personality. For this reason, even nonslaveholders felt allegiance to a system where they may not have necessarily benefited economically, but from which they certainly derived psychic and political benefits. Thus, rather than autobiography, slave narratives should be seen, in the vein of Equiano's *Interesting Narrative*, as a form of sociography, indeed, as one of the first iterations of American sociology, or countersociology since at this moment the field was taking shape with works such as George Fitzhugh's *Sociology for the South* and Henry Hughes's *Treatise on Sociology* that "looked to the early socialists or to Auguste Comte for the model of a science of society that would project a wholly different historical course."[23]

Frederick Douglass and Harriet Jacobs remained the archetypes of this genre, as both revealed not only the rigorous process by means of which those of African hereditary descent would be made into slaves, but also how such a process enabled the realization of others as fully human. In his classic duel with Edward Covey, Douglass made the evocative statement concerning the producedness of Being when he declared: "You have seen how a man was made a slave; you shall see how a slave was made a man."[24] And, while "man" in this context referred to a conception of Being Human to which the black population group remained its negated Other, there would also be a correlated allocation of gender roles in which the slave/Black Woman became the incarnation of the *Untrue Woman* to the represented *True Woman*, optimally white whether in its Southern slaveholding variant or its Northern middle-class/industrializing model. Jacobs documented this process when she described the divergent pathways of two young girls on the plantation, who biologically were sisters, though due to the governing symbolic code did not experience themselves as such. Whereas the "fair child grew up to be a still fairer woman" with a life "blooming with flowers," her equally beautiful slave sister had no "flowers and sunshine of love," but rather was forced to drink from "the cup of sin, and shame, and misery, whereof her persecuted race are compelled to drink."[25]

This impulse to challenge the U.S. racial hierarchy as it expressed itself in the allocation of gender roles was brilliantly undertaken by Anna Julia Cooper, whose scholarship and life's work represented a significant development in understanding the *Thing* confronting the black population group. Her intervention came in the wake of the contradictions and unresolved questions in what Eric Foner has identified as the "unfinished revolution" of Reconstruction.[26] Cooper formed a part of "women's era" club movement in which many middle-class black women took it upon themselves to address the systemic problems confronting the population group, doing so by creating social service and community organizations that filled in a gap left by the state and the society in general.[27] Moreover, her work would be one of the earliest enactments of Frazier's charge to place the study of the black experience in the wider context of that of the human.

In the essay "Woman vs. the Indian," Cooper made a compelling argument for the symbiotic relation between the question of the allocation of gender roles and the general conditions under which the total black population group suffered. This connection was articulated at a moment when Cooper described her experience traveling on Jim Crow trains, when conductors forced her, because she was not traveling in the capacity of a nurse or a maid, to leave the compartment designated for whites. Looking out of the window from the segregated compartment, Cooper noticed "convicts from the state penitentiary, among them boys from fourteen to eighteen years of age in a chain-gang, their feet chained together and heavy blocks attached," further remarking that such was occurring "not in 1850, but in 1890, '91 and '92."[28] This moment compelled Cooper to exclaim: "What a field for the missionary woman!" Moreover, rather than viewing herself in the dominant terms as an inferior subject, she proclaimed from her ostensibly marginalized position in the Jim Crow car to transform the general society: "The women in this section should organize a Society for the Prevention of Cruelty to Human Beings, and disseminate civilizing tracts, and send throughout the region apostles of anti-barbarism for the propagation of humane and enlightened ideas."[29]

This impetus was related to Cooper's overall belief that the particular disregard and mistreatment that she faced remained inseparable from the systemic hierarchies and injustices of the instituting society. For this reason, she asserted that women activists like the Reverend Anna Shaw should never "seem to disparage what is weak" for "the woman's cause is the cause of the weak."[30] According to her, when such a stance is taken, that is, "when all the weak shall have received their due consideration," it will follow that "woman will have her 'rights,' and the Indian will have his rights, and the Negro will have his rights."[31] In a brilliant synthesis of poetry and politics, Cooper insisted: "Hers is every interest that has lacked an interpreter and a defender. Her cause is linked with that of every agony that has been dumb—every wrong that needs a voice," and thus "the cause of every man and woman who has writhed silently under a mighty wrong."[32] Embodying Frazier's injunction, the question of women's rights opened onto the issue of the ordering of the society, which in effect illustrated, as Cooper insisted, the extent to which it was "broader, and deeper, and grander, than a blue stocking debate or an aristocratic tea," for it was "based on a principle as broad as the human race and as old as human society."[33]

This intellectual thrust that addressed the particularity of the *Thing* confronting blacks with its universal implications can also be identified in negritude and especially with the writing of Aimé Césaire. Césaire's *Cahier d'un retour au pays natal* (1938) was the first work to use the term "negritude," which could mean both the study (*étude*) of the Negro (*nègre*) and the new attitude of the Negro. While elaborating the specificity of the French colonial question, Césaire linked the liminality of the colonial subject to the general issue of alterity, as the protagonist of the *Cahier* noted: "I would be a jew-man/a Kaffir-man/a Hindu-man-from-Calcutta/a Harlem-man-who-doesn't-vote."[34] For Césaire, as he declared in his manifesto *Lettre à Maurice Thorez* (1956), authored upon his resignation from the French Communist Party, the uniqueness (*singularité*) of the situation of black people in the world could not be confused with any other issue, nor should it be reduced to be in the service of the Party's ideological fundamentalism of class.[35]

Yet this uniqueness, as was implied in Cooper's analysis, opened itself onto Frazier's issue of the broad experience of the human. For this reason, Césaire suggested in an interview conducted years after the publication of the *Cahier* that the concept of Négritude should not be interpreted in a programmatic manner, but rather should be understood in the context of a crucial human impulse: "You must not look for a political creed in it [*Cahier*]. But, perhaps you look for the essential man: a cry."[36] Moreover, for critics who viewed Négritude as a "vain and sentimental trap . . . based on an illusory racial community founded on a history of suffering," rendering it a "violent and paradoxical therapy . . . that replaced the illusion of Europe by an African illusion,"[37] Césaire provided a terse and insightful response: "As long you will have Negroes a little everywhere, Négritude will be there as a matter of course."[38] In other words, as long as there are humans who are intellectually and politically subordinated and therefore made to pay the price for the enactment of a social-symbolic system, there will be concomitant intellectual and political responses that will attempt to address their situation. Thus, one cannot simply do away with Négritude without dealing with the *Thing* that produces the negated category of Negroes that logically gives rise to it.

Writing during this same era, Carter G. Woodson offered a response to this question in *The Miseducation of the Negro* (1933), providing an insight that has become an indispensable component of Sylvia Wynter's thesis. Preempting the polemical IQ debates in the latter part of the twentieth century, Woodson explained the reason for black students consistently performing at a level lower than whites: "The same educational process which inspires and stimulates the oppressor with the thought that he is everything and has accomplished everything worthwhile, depresses and crushes at the same time the spark of genius in the Negro by making him feel that his race does not amount to much and never will measure up to the standards of other peoples."[39] Woodson generalized from this position that the conditions confronted by blacks had their origins in the system of knowledge, noting, "There would be no lynching if it did not start in the classroom. Why not exploit, enslave, or exterminate a class that *everybody* is taught to regard as inferior?"[40]

The more recent research of Claude Steele and his colleagues on "stereotype threat" has provided contemporary examples that verify Woodson's initial theses. In their work, the social scientists found that "the threat of being viewed through the lens of a negative stereotype, or the fear of doing something that would inadvertently confirm that stereotype" helped to determine black college students' performance on standardized tests and generally in college.[41] When told these tests were simply for diagnostic purposes in order to ascertain how certain problems are generally solved, black students performed in a manner similar to their white peers. However, when they were told that the tests were designed to measure intellectual ability, their scores decreased. In another example, a math test was given to white males, who were told that Asians generally performed better on it. With such a statement informing the context in which the test was administered, the performances of the white males was inferior to those who had taken the test without such a comment being made. This result led Steele and his colleagues to conclude that the power of "stereotype threat" was such that it "impaired intellectual functioning in a group unlikely to have any sense of group inferiority."[42] Here is an unequivocal example of how the *Thing* of *Being Black* can illuminate a mechanism functioning at the level of the *Thing* of *Being Human*. However, the nagging issue from this research remains as to what produces the "stereotype threat." That is, is it a natural phenomenon that can be found across time and space?

Following upon the breakthroughs of Fanon, from the ground of what she has defined as the perspective of black studies, the oeuvre of Sylvia Wynter has provided a most comprehensive response to this question. Wynter has linked the recognition of the systemic ontological—and, after Woodson and DuBois, it can be argued, epistemological—negation of blacks to a new scientific understanding of the instituting of human consciousness. She has therefore challenged the biocentric premise of our present conception of what it means to *be* human, as this "descriptive statement" continues to be elaborated in our contemporary disciplinary order of knowledge in the human sciences.[43] Adapting Fanon's thesis in *Black Skin, White Masks*, Wynter has argued that the subjective experiences of humans "cannot be explained in the terms of *only* the natural sciences, of only physical laws."[44] Rather being human is a hybridly auto-instituting process in which subjective experiences, which are "culturally and socio-situationally determined," have, at the same time, objective and "physicalist correlates."[45]

Fanon detected that many of his black and colonized patients, having assimilated the dominant's society conception of the Self, became autophobic to their own features, to their own physiognomy. Such a phenomenon led him to conclude that "antiblack" behavior was not aberrant, but rather constituted an attempt to embody the normative beliefs and behaviors that defined and structured the society.[46] Given that such internalization of negative representations could be understood logically, these behaviors could consequently be defined outside of the liberal humanist framework (based on the conception of an autonomous individual) as self-hatred. Indeed, as Pecola's unyielding desire for blue eyes so poetically suggests, such responses constituted attempts to realize one's being in terms of the rigorously elaborated status criterion and ideals that structure the social framework. It was this dynamic to which DuBois's concept of "double consciousness" referred, one that, as Alain Locke acknowledged during the New Negro / Harlem Renaissance era, implied that "we have been almost as much of a problem to ourselves as we still are to others."[47] For precisely this reason, the kind of change required would necessarily move beyond the economic realm as the psychic dimension of what Fanon identified as the lived experience of black (*l'expérience vécue du noir*) would at the same time need to be addressed. In this vein, the psychiatrist Alvin Poussaint noted in the wake of the civil rights movement that blacks "are not just seeking equality, full rights, and freedom. What's going on now is also a search and fight for an *inner* emancipation from the effects of white racism — to become somehow internally *purged*. So, it's not just a question of moving freely in white society."[48]

The question therefore remains: By what processes are such modes of consciousness instituted? How is it that, like Equiano, who came to view himself as the lack of having a rosy face, the Pecolas of the world (as a synecdoche for Conceptual Otherness) have come to see and experience themselves only as the lack of the norm rather than its embodiment? Certainly, in

Equiano's case, such was in opposition to the pre-Encounter understanding of himself, just as in much of Africa the Bantu physiognomy would be valorized and, as Georges Balandier has noted, it would be white skin, especially in the case of the albino, that was represented as being monstrous and, thus, the lack of the norm. Wynter has therefore proffered: "How do we account for the fact, that, . . . what was subjectively experienced as being aesthetically 'correct' and appropriate by the Congolese . . . was entirely the reverse of what is subjectively experienced by western and westernized subjects as being aesthetically correct and appropriate?"[49]

In other words, what has usually been identified as racism can be conceptualized in more comprehensive terms as the manner in which our particular genre of being human adaptively perceives, classifies, and categorizes our social world, this as the condition of instituting us as the specific mode of Being Human that we have come to live and embody. The sociogenic principle, as the analogue of the genomic principles that determines how organic forms of life adaptively perceive and classify their respective social worlds, implies that as humans, we cannot preexist our genres of Being Human or the representations of origins that give rise to them. The role played by the representation of blacks and other categories of lack and difference can therefore be understood in rule-governed terms, as being indispensable components of the instituting of our present biocentric model of Being Human, a representation whose premise remains that the human species exists within a line of pure continuity with organic forms of life; or, as Martin Heidegger phrased it with respect to Western metaphysics, the determination of the essence of being human in the "dimension of animality," as *homo animalis*, "one living creature among others in contrast to plants, beasts, and God." This understanding is maintained even when the elements of mind, spirit, and soul (*animus sive mens*) as also existing in humans is acknowledged.[50] As Heidegger further argued, the Enlightenment's transumptive rearticulation of the Aristotelian notion that "man is the animal who is endowed with *logos*," together with the concept from Roman humanism of *animal rationale*, precludes further questioning of the nature of the Being of Being Human, and as a result, metaphysics "does not ask about the truth of being itself."[51]

Our present hegemonic conception or genre of Being Human is of recent invention, that is, speaking in historical terms. As Michel Foucault has pointed out, "the figure of man" emerged toward the end of the eighteenth century as the result of a reconfiguration of the fundamental arrangements of knowledge. Wynter has identified this figure as fully secular *Man*, this in order to make a distinction from the partially secular variant that arose during the fourteenth and fifteenth centuries in the wake of lay humanism. Foucault has chronicled this transformative mutation from the pre-nineteenth-century classical episteme, or order of knowledge, to the contemporary one defined by the "quasi-transcendentals" of labor, life, and language. Within the terms of this trilogy, Being Human would now be conceptualized on the model of a natural organism, as one who labored and spoke, a reconceptualization of knowledge that made foundational the new disciplinary paradigms of biology, political economy/economics, and linguistics/philology (as opposed to the previous reigning frameworks of natural history, analysis of wealth, and general grammar).[52] Central to this reconfiguration would be a new historical chronology, one that now classified and evaluated societies on the basis of modes of subsistence and production, a process thought to have occurred primarily over the four sequential stages of hunting, pasturage, agriculture, and commerce.[53]

It is precisely from within this frame that the current dominant understanding of the world that insists it is the mode of economic production which determines human behaviors, whether in its normative liberal Smithian formulation or countervariant of Marxism, should be situated. Nowhere is the perspective, one that, in Wynter's terms, extrahumanizes agency, clearer than with statements such as "the market has spoken" or "the market has decided," assertions based on the ostensibly unerring laws of supply and demand.[54] Against this representation, Wynter has proposed that it is actually the mode of *auto-institution*, based on a specific narrative of origin and conception of Being Human, that determines human behaviors. As humans, we can therefore only fully realize ourselves in terms of a particular genre of Being Human, which is narratively instituted and then performatively enacted by its subjects. And we do not become human before or outside of this process. At the same time, this process remains inseparable from the implementing conditions of the biology of human by means of which we would become a narratively instituted species. From this conceptual frame, the specific mode of material provisioning to which the Western name of economics has been given becomes an indispensable, but nonetheless only a proximate, mechanism. In other words, Adam Smith's assertion that it is natural, if not the dominant imperative, for humans to barter, truck, and trade cannot be understood outside of the autopoietic field for whom the figure of *homo oeconomicus* (economic man) constitutes the referent subject.

It is therefore within this order of discourse, one premised on the rule of nature, that the black would serve as the ultimate Other to the representation of the normative Self now defined in the wake of the late nineteenth-century Darwinian revolution in bioevolutionary terms. Thus, just as in the Middle Ages, the presence of the Jews, Muslim, and pagan idolaters enabled the realization of the optimal status criterion of being Christian, people of African hereditary descent in a parallel manner enable nonblacks together with the non–middle class to experience themselves as being fully human in the terms of a conception premised on the nonhomogeneity of the human species, now enacted in biocentric terms. As the condition of the instituting of this conception, blacks necessarily experience themselves as the defect of whites, and indeed cannot experience themselves as white "in any way but as that fullness and genericity of being human, . . . a genericity that must be verified by the clear evidence of [blacks'] *lack* of this fullness, of this genericity."[55] Such a role implies that what Steele and his colleagues identified as "stereotype threat" can be positioned in a broader intellectual context as being neither an individual nor an arbitrary phenomenon, but rather can be understood as an organizing and integrating principle of the realization of what it means to Be Human in the present governing terms of biocentricism. Indeed, it is such a phenomenon determined by the representation of our specific *genre* of Being Human that allows for the instituting, stabilization, and reproduction of our social order and without which there can be no order.

As Wynter has pointed out, following upon Ernesto Grassi's thesis in *Rhetoric as Philosophy: The Humanist Tradition*, the coming of humans into existence was marked by a rupture with the "directive signs" of the genetic code that ordered the behaviors of purely organic species. With the emergence of language, a uniquely human code replaced the completely genetic one as the regulatory mechanism of behavior and would be initially embodied in the "sacred logos" of religious discourse. This Word "prescribed what *had* to be said, and what *had* to be done," and would compel the necessary behaviors of the specific modality of Being Human in an *equally* rigorous and powerful manner *as had been the case of the genetic code for purely organic forms of life.*[56]

Linked to the functioning of the human code, as the research on addiction conducted by the neurobiologist Avram Goldstein has revealed, are adaptive behaviors driven by a reward and punishment mechanism in the brain in which a natural opioid system is triggered with the performance of "good" and "bad" behaviors.[57] As a consequence, when a hungry animal finds food, when a dangerous situation is avoided, or when the promise and engagement of sexual activity arise, then an association is made with "good" behavior, and an opioid peptide (probably beta-endorphin) is released. However, with the occurrence of pain or harm, a "bad" signal triggers the release of dynorphin, and situations that should be avoided become clear. The negotiation of these opposing peptides constitutes the basis of the species-specific mode of understanding of its social world, its mode of mind. Thus, in order for organic species to reproduce themselves, their behaviors must be "adaptively suited to deal with the specific challenges of the environment in which the vehicle-organism (to use Dawkin's formulation) finds itself," and this ensemble of behaviors "can be ensured *only* through the mediation of the subjective experiencing by the organism of what is biochemically made to *feel* good and *feel* bad *to* it as it interacts with its ecosystem: only through the experience, therefore, of what it is like to *be* that organism."[58]

The difference for humans, however, occurs whereby nature has conditioned physiological responses to behaviors, yet what prompts the biochemical reaction to "good" and "bad" cannot be ascribed to nature. Rather, as Wynter has argued, being human is a hybridly auto-instituting process by means of which the narratively instituted *sense of self*, that is, *what we experience ourselves to be*, serves to induce appropriate behaviors indispensable to the realization and reproduction as a species of our genre-specific modes of mind/being.[59] In this context, metaphors of temptation and transgression found across human societies take on a far greater meaning. These schemas, including, as Wynter has noted, that of the secular Judeo-Christian discourse of race, can be understood as "artificial," or nongenetic, behavior-motivating mechanisms that "structure our culture-specific order of consciousness, modes of mind, and thereby of being."[60] Relating insights from the natural sciences, Wynter's thesis lays the groundwork for what she has defined as a new science of human systems: "It is these schemas and the coercive nature of their systems of meaning that make it possible for each mode of sociogeny and its artificially imprinted *sense of self* to be created as one able to override where necessary, the genetic-instinctual *sense of self*, at the same time as itself comes to be subjectively *experienced as if it were instinctual;* it is thereby not only to reoccupy the formerly hegemonic place, of the genetic self, but also to harness its drives to its now culturally defined sociogenetic own."[61] The implication remains that the discourse of race, "by mapping or totemizing negative/positive meanings (as part of a cultural series) on the non-humanly instituted difference (as a natural series)," activates by a process of semantic reprogramming the opioid system in genre-specific terms, thereby illustrating that the "*objectively* structured biochemical system . . . determines the way in which each organism will perceive, classify, and categorize the world in adaptive terms needed for its own survival and reproductive realization as such an organism."[62]

The compelling figure of Pecola in *The Bluest Eye* illuminates this process. Adapting Asmarom Legesse's elaboration of the role of liminal Others in stabilizing human order, Pecola can be seen to function, following Wynter's analysis, as the embodiment of the "liminally deviant category . . . through the mediation of whose negated mode of 'abnormal' difference the 'normal society' is enabled to experience itself both as 'normal' and as a socially cohesive community."[63] Moreover, the internalization of the dominant meaning of Self and Other, especially by those assimilated to the category of Otherness, has preoccupied much black thinking, producing Fanon's groundbreaking formulation of black skins having to wear white masks in order be human, which, according to Wynter, can be amplified as human skins always wearing autopoietic or auto-instituting masks. Morrison has most powerfully depicted this dynamic in the constellation of relationships defining the vortex in which Pecola remained ensnared:

> All of our waste which we dumped on her and which she absorbed. And all our beauty, which was hers first and which she gave to us. All of us—all who knew her—felt so wholesome after we cleaned ourselves on her. We were so beautiful when we stood astride her ugliness. Her simplicity decorated us, her guilt sanctified us, her pain made us glow with health, her awkwardness made us think we had a sense of humor. Her inarticulateness made us believe we were eloquent. Her poverty kept us generous. Even her waking dreams we used—to silence our own nightmares. And she left us, and thereby deserved our contempt. We honed our egos on her, padded our characters with her frailty, and yawned in the fantasy of our strength.[64]

The representations heaped onto Pecola can be seen to activate the neurological opiate reward mechanism, enabling those around Pecola, however marginalized and subordinated they might be, to realize themselves none-theless as human vis-à-vis this little girl.

In this context, literary knowledge reveals the dynamic structure of mimetic desire as it functions to encode the order of consciousness by means of which the Maureen Peals and the Pecolas of the world are instituted as human in *genre*-specific terms, thereby signaling the activation of the neu-rochemical reward and punishment mechanism according to the auto-instituting rules of representation. Pecola's metaphysical negation as well as her own desire for blue eyes can no longer be seen as arbitrary or in terms of self-hatred, as these psychoaffective responses remain indispensable elements to the "vernacular languages of belief and desire" of enacting biocentrism. As the preceding passage from Morrison reveals, this mechanism is the *Thing* that produces "the honey voices of parents and aunts, the obedience in the eyes of our peers, the slippery light in the eyes of our teachers when they encountered the Maureen Peals of the world."[65]

At the same time that *The Bluest Eye* illustrates the brutality implicit in the governing symbolic code that structured the order of consciousness of the postslavery United States, it also perceptively challenges the ruling terms of the order. By compressing the contradictions of our present order's biocosmogony in the suppressed voice of a young girl, who remained subordinated in terms of race, class, gender, age, and most profoundly, aesthetics, the novel lays the groundwork for detaching the opiate reward signifiers from the possession of blues eyes, and therefore from the dominant understanding of what it means to *be* black, to *be* Human: "And fantasy it was, for we were never strong, only aggressive; we were not free, merely licensed; we were not compassionate, we were polite; not good, but well behaved, and hid like thieves from life. We substituted good grammar for intellect; we switched habits to simulate maturity; we rearranged lies and called it truth, seeing in the new pattern of an old idea the Revelation and the Word."[66] The novel therefore proffers a critique of the ostensible freedom of the subjects, who, like all of us, remain *merely licensed* in the terms of the machinery of desire, that is, until they are transformed.

From this perspective racial hierarchy, together with other related issues of alterity and subordination that structure our present order, can be understood in both the *genre-specific* terms of biocentrism as well as in the general, *transgenre* terms of the enactment of the process of what it means for us as humans to realize our humanness. Wynter's intervention suggests that for neurobiologists the persistence of the "puzzle of consciousness" lies in the inability to grasp that consciousness or subjective experience, while inseparable from the physical processes of neurobiology, at the same time cannot be reduced to these biological/neurobiological processes alone: "If the mind is what the brain *does*, *what* the brain does, is itself culturally determined through the mediation of the socialized *sense of self*, as well as of the 'social' situation in which this *self* is placed."[67] In this context, the implication remains that in order to address the contradictions, if not the horrors, produced by the belief system of race, its function as a behavior regulatory and order-instituting mechanism must equally be addressed.

Following upon this idea, our contemporary global crises can be interpreted as epistemological ones that are generated from the premises that underlie our present secular disciplinary system of knowledge and the prototype of being to which it necessarily gives rise. On the one hand, as Wynter has always insisted, it remains important to acknowledge the epochal shifts that led to our modern world system, most centrally that of lay humanism, coming out of the transformations of the late Middle Ages, as well as that of the rise of the bourgeoisie, enabled by the Scottish and French Enlightenment, together with the Industrial Revolution and the abolition of slavery. Both of these moments of "great transformation" represented a mutation at the level of the human species.[68] At the same time, on the other hand, these emancipatory breakthroughs were to be accompanied by equally defining acts of subjugation, including in the Americas the expropriation of the lands inhabited by the Indigenous peoples as well as the juridical enslavement over centuries of those of African hereditary descent.

Each of these moments of tremendous change were effected by a calling into question of the then reigning *genres* of being human, in the case of former that of the theocentricism of Latin Christianity, and in the case of latter that of the ratiocentricism of the political order of the imperial state based on the empire of reason. In other words, these transformative shifts, even with their contradictions, make clear that humans do not always remain enclosed in a single mode of subjective understanding. In fact, it is precisely when such models are called into question that social change is made possible. Transformation of a social order can therefore occur when a society attempts to deal with the contradictions produced by its specific order of consciousness and, thus, what signals good behavior and what signals bad behavior, codes that are activated by the agency of narratives by means of which we are able to realize our humanness.

Another moment of "great transformation" occurred during the general social upheaval of the 1950s and 1960s, spearheaded by the global anticolonial movements as well as the demand of blacks for civil rights in the United States. These movements, both of which called for political enfranchisement in their respective contexts, can also be understood in terms of their epistemological challenges. Wynter has for some time now insisted that the black movement constituted a reenactment of the lay humanist movement, which detached ideal being from the theocentric representation that the feudal clergy embodied the redeemed spirit as opposed to the fallen flesh of the laity, a breakthrough of desupernaturalization (i.e., secularization) that also made possible the rise of the natural sciences. In a parallel manner, by detaching ideal being from the biocentric representation of the human defined purely in the bioevolutionary terms of natural selection (blacks as dysselected, if not "fallen," genes), the New Studies of the 1960s opened onto a new scientific frontier of the instituting of human consciousness.[69]

Wynter has therefore put forth a challenge defined as "the third emancipatory breaching of the law of cognitive closure."[70] Beginning in the sixteenth century, the first breaching was effected at the level of physical reality, with the rise of the natural sciences resulting from the breakthroughs of Copernicus, Galileo, Kepler, and their contemporaries, and the second on the basis of the nineteenth-century Darwinian revolution that provided scientific knowledge of the biological levels of reality. Her meta-Darwinian hypothesis argues that with Fanon another break has occurred—one with respect to the rules governing human consciousness. She asserts that the human is a hybridly, auto-instituting species, and therefore a third level of existence, from the event of our origin on the continent of Africa until today. The process of instituting us as humans derives from the sociogenic principle, that is, "the information-encoding organizational principle of each culture's criterion of being/non-being, that functions to *artificially* activate the neurochemistry of the reward and punishment pathway, doing so in the terms needed to institute human subjects as a culture-specific and thereby verbally defined, if physiologically implemented mode of being and *sense of self.*"[71]

However, the functioning of such laws, she has proposed, has hitherto remained beyond our conscious awareness, but from the liminal perspective of Fanon's "lived experience of the Black" (and related to other categories of liminality), this issue can be further developed. Fanon stated, "Each generation must out of relative obscurity discover its mission, fulfill it, or betray it."[72] In Wynter's terms, the mission would necessarily involve the reconceptualization of our present monohumanist sociogenic replicator code based on the representation of the human as a natural organism and optimally as *homo oeconomicus*. For it is within this specific system of meaning and being that peoples of African hereditary descent would always find themselves marked and treated as the lack of what it means to be fully human. Such a process would necessarily entail the restoration of our collective agency as humans, which, after the secularization with the rise of the natural sciences, has been in the sociohuman renaturalized by being reprojected onto the bioevolutionary laws of natural selection. Unless we attempt to carry out the challenge set forth by Fanon and Wynter, we shall otherwise remain, like those around Pecola, not free, but *merely licensed*—licensed in the prototype or *genre* of the biocentric definition of Being Human. Such an undertaking would also follow upon DuBois's charge to Barton, to "go get the *Thing*."

Notes

1. Barton, "The Name 'Negro,'" 96.
2. Sweet, *Black Images of America*, 50–52, 89; DuBois, *The Souls of Black Folk*, 5.
3. Barton, "The Name 'Negro,'" 96.
4. Barton, "The Name 'Negro,'" 96.
5. Barton, "The Name 'Negro,'" 96.
6. Barton, "The Name 'Negro,'" 96.
7. Barton, "The Name 'Negro,'" 96.
8. Barton, "The Name 'Negro,'" 96.
9. Barton, "The Name 'Negro,'" 96–97 (emphasis in the original).
10. Morrison, *The Bluest Eye*, 74.
11. Frazier, "The Failure of the Negro Intellectual," 60.
12. In an unpublished essay, "Meditations on History," Wynter first made the distinction between "gender" and "genre" in which the allocation of roles between men and women in all human societies remains an indispensable function of the overall enactment of the governing symbolic code of life and death. The question of gender therefore opens onto all of the role allocations in human orders, i.e., the *genre-specific* mode of Being Human.
13. Indeed, for this reason, the contention that "Africans sold Africans into slavery" only makes sense within an already racialized order of discourse in which all the inhabitants of the continent of Africa are represented as sharing a common (i.e., racial) model of identity. Such clearly was not the case as all who became slaves in Africa did so for reasons that had not been articulated in racial terms. Ottobah Quobna Cugoano, a contemporary of Equiano and one of the "sons of Africa," made this point most eloquently when he stated: "As to the

Africans selling their own wives and children, nothing can be more opposite to every thing they hold dear and valuable, and nothing can distress them more, than to part with any of their relations and friends." This phenomenon he saw as not being restricted to Africa, noting that "very few nations make slaves of any of those under their government; but such as are taken prisoners of war from their neighbors." See his *Thoughts and Sentiments on the Evil and Wicked Traffic of the Slavery*, 25–27.

14. Equiano, *The Interesting Narrative and Other Writings*, 55.
15. Equiano, *The Interesting Narrative and Other Writings*, 69.
16. Fanon, *Black Skin, White Masks*, 111.
17. Carretta, *Equiano, the African*, xv.
18. Carretta, *Equiano, the African*, xiv–xv.
19. Waswo, "The History That Literature Makes," 541.
20. Wynter, "On Disenchanting Discourse," 219.
21. See Walker, *Appeal in Four Articles*, 10. See also Jefferson, *Notes on the State of Virginia*, 124–143; and Cohen, *Science and the Founding Fathers*, 74–79.
22. Bontemps, "The Slave Narrative," vi–xix.
23. See Ross, *The Origins of American Social Science*, 32.
24. Douglass, *Narrative of the Life of Frederick Douglass*, 107.
25. Jacobs, *Incidents in the Life of a Slave Girl*, 28.
26. Foner, *Reconstruction*.
27. Lerner, "Early Community Work of Black Club Women," 161–162.
28. Cooper, "Woman vs. the Indian," 95–96.
29. Cooper, "Woman vs. the Indian," 96.
30. Cooper, "Woman vs. the Indian," 117.
31. Cooper, "Woman vs. the Indian," 117.
32. Cooper, "Woman vs. the Indian," 122, 125.
33. Cooper, "Woman vs. the Indian," 123, 125.
34. Césaire, *Notebook*, 43.
35. Césaire, *Lettre à Maurice Thorez*, 8, 12.
36. Rowell, "It Is through Poetry That One Copes with Solitude," 51.
37. Condé, "Négritude Césairienne, Négritude Senghorienne," 418; and Bernabé, Chamoiseau, and Confiant, *Éloge de la Créolité / In Praise of Creoleness*, 82.
38. Rowell, "It Is through Poetry That One Copes with Solitude," 55, 57.
39. Woodson, *The Miseducation of the Negro*, xiii.
40. Woodson, *The Miseducation of the Negro*, 3 (emphasis in the original).
41. Steele, "Thin Ice," 46.
42. Steele, "Thin Ice," 50.
43. The term "descriptive statement" comes from Gregory Bateson, who argues that cybernetic, self-corrective systems "are always conservative of something." See his "Conscious Purpose vs. Nature," 34–49.
44. Wynter, "Towards the Sociogenic Principle," 36 (emphasis in the original).
45. Wynter, "Towards the Sociogenic Principle," 36–37.

46. Fanon, "Racism and Culture," 37–40, where he stated: "We say once again that racism is not an accidental discovery. It is not a hidden, dissimulated element. . . . The habit of considering racism as a mental quirk, as a psychological flaw, must be abandoned. . . . The racist in a culture with racism is therefore normal."

47. Locke, "The New Negro," 3 (emphasis in the original).

48. Poussaint, "The Role of Education in Providing a Basis for Honest Self-Identification," 197 (emphasis in the original).

49. Wynter, "Towards the Sociogenic Principle," 51. See also Balandier, *Daily Life in the Kingdom of the Kongo*, 217–219, where he describes the role of the albino (*ndundu*) and how the *ma ndundu* was "an extraordinary and dreaded personage" who could preside over certain initiation ceremonies. In his research, Wyatt MacGaffey found as late as the 1960s traces of the idea that blacks constituted the norm and whites, the other. He saw this in the contemporary cosmology whereby blacks constituted "the realm of the living" and Whites the otherworld of the dead. See his "Kongo and the King of the Americans," 171–181.

50. Heidegger, "Letter on Humanism," 246.

51. Heidegger, "Letter on Humanism," 245–246. Aristotle's statement, from Heidegger's *Being and Time*, is cited in Spanos, *The End of Education*, 6.

52. See Foucault, "Labour, Life and Language," 250–302.

53. For an illuminating analysis of the shift in historiography, one in which the representation of Indigenous forms of life in the Americas enabled a new theory of society, see Meek, *Social Science and the Ignoble Savage*.

54. Wynter has argued that before the rise of monotheisms all human societies had mapped and therefore absolutized their criterion of being onto the heavens in a process that enabled them to experience their social realities "as if they had been supernaturally (and, as such, extrahumanly) determined." See Wynter, "Unsettling the Coloniality of Being," 271. Such a process, she insisted, projected agency outside of the collective agency by means of which through narrative we as humans bring into being our social order. This phenomenon is no less so with our contemporary discourse of biocentrism, which, after having desupernaturalized agency in terms of a discourse of nature, would reproject it onto the bioevolutionary laws of natural selection.

55. Wynter, "Towards the Sociogenic Principle," 40.

56. Wynter, "Towards the Sociogenic Principle," 46 (emphasis in the original); Grassi, *Rhetoric as Philosophy*, 106.

57. Goldstein, *Addiction*.

58. Wynter, "Towards the Sociogenic Principle," 50 (emphasis in the original).

59. Wynter, "Towards the Sociogenic Principle," 53–54 (emphasis in the original).

60. Wynter, "Towards the Sociogenic Principle," 47. It is important to note that Wynter prefers the terms "autopoietic" and "auto-instituting" to "culture," which, as Richard Waswo has noted, remains a Western conception based on

agriculture, that is, the representation of humans coming out of nature. See Waswo, "The History That Literature Makes," 548.

61. Wynter, "Towards the Sociogenic Principle," 47–48 (emphasis in the original).
62. Wynter, "Towards the Sociogenic Principle," 50, 53 (emphasis in the original).
63. Wynter, "Towards the Sociogenic Principle," 57–58l; Legesse, *Gada*, 114–115.
64. Morrison, *The Bluest Eye*, 204–205.
65. Morrison, *The Bluest Eye*, 74.
66. Morrison, *The Bluest Eye*, 205–206.
67. Wynter, "Towards the Sociogenic Principle," 37.
68. The phrasing here borrows from Karl Polanyi's classic examination of the rise of the industrial worldview. See Polanyi, *The Great Transformation*.
69. Wynter, "The Ceremony Must Be Found," 19–70.
70. Wynter, "The Ceremony Found."
71. Wynter, "Towards the Sociogenic Principle," 54 (emphasis in the original).
72. Fanon, *The Wretched of the Earth* (trans. Farrington), 206.

BIBLIOGRAPHY

Abraham, Keshia. "Introduction: Speaking Us into Being: Creating/Imagining/Theorizing." In *The Caribbean Woman Writer as Scholar: Creating, Imagining, Theorizing*, edited by Keshia N. Abraham, xvii–xxvi. Coconut Creek, FL: Caribbean Studies Press, 2009.

Adesanmi, Pius. "Disappearing Me Softly: An Open Letter to Sandra M. Gilbert and Susan Gubar." Accessed December 2007. http://zeleza.com/blogging/u-s-affairs/disappearing-me-softly-open-letter-sandra-m-gilbert-and-susan.

Adorno, Theodor W. *Prisms*. Translated by Shierry Weber Nicholsen and Samuel Weber. Cambridge, MA: MIT Press, [1967] 1981.

Agamben, Giorgio. *Homo Sacer: Sovereign Power and Bare Life*. Translated by Daniel Heller-Roazen. Stanford, CA: Stanford University Press, 1998.

Alcoff, Linda Martin, and Eduardo Mendieta, eds. *Thinking from the Underside of History: Enrique Dussel's Philosophy of Liberation*. Lanham, MD: Rowan and Littlefield, 2000.

Aledort, Andy, and Joff Jones. *Hendrix—Axis: Bold as Love: The Complete, Authoritative, Transcriptions for Guitar, Bass, and Drums as Performed by the Jimi Hendrix Experience*. Milwaukee, WI: HLP Publishing, 1989.

Alexander, Michelle. *The New Jim Crow: Mass Incarceration in the Age of Colorblindness*. New York: New Press, 2010.

Althusser, Louis. "Ideology and Ideological State Apparatuses: Notes towards an Investigation." In *Lenin and Philosophy and Other Essays*, 85–126. Translated by Ben Brewster. New York: Monthly Review Press, 2001.

Althusser, Louis. *Philosophy of the Encounter: Later Writings, 1978–1987*. London: Verso, 2006.

Anderson, Benedict. *Imagined Communities: Reflections on the Origin and Spread of Nationalism*. New York: Verso, 1991.

Appiah, Anthony. *Cosmopolitanism: Ethics in a World of Strangers*. New York: Norton, 2006.

Appiah, Anthony. *The Ethics of Identity*. Princeton, NJ: Princeton University Press, 2005.

Arendt, Hannah. "Social Science Techniques and the Study of Concentration Camps." In *Essays in Understanding, 1930–1954*, edited by Jerome Kohn, 232–247. New York: Harcourt Brace, 1994.

Arsuaga, Juan Luis. *The Neanderthal's Necklace: In Search of the First Thinkers*. Translated by Andy Klatt. New York: Basic Books, 2004.

Aslan, Reza. *No God but God: The Origins, Evolution and Future of Islam*. New York: Random House, 2005.

Associated Press. "Science Looks at Brain on Jazz." *Metro*, March 18, 2008.

Atkinson, Quentin. "Phonemic Diversity Supports a Serial Founder Effect Model of Language Expansion from Africa." *Science* 332, no. 6067 (2011): 346–349.

Augustine of Hippo. *The City of God*. Translated by Henry Bettenson. Harmondsworth: Penguin, 1972.

Axelson, Sigbert. *Culture Confrontation in the Lower Congo*. Falköping, Sweden: Gummessons Boktryckeri AB, 1970.

Bacon, Francis. *Novum Organum*. Edited by Joseph Devy. New York: Collier, [1620] 1901.

Badiou, Alain. "The Communist Hypothesis." *New Left Review* 49 (January–February 2008): 29–42.

Badiou, Alain. "The Emblem of Democracy." In *Democracy in What State?* by Giorgio Agamben, Alain Badiou, Daniel Bensaïd, Wendy Brown, Jean-Luc Nancy, Jacques Ranciére, Kristin Ross, and Slavoj Žižek, 6–15. Translated by William McCuaig. New York: Columbia University Press, 2011.

Baker, Houston A., Jr. *Blues Ideology and Afro-American Literature: A Vernacular Theory*. Chicago: University of Chicago Press, 1984.

Baker, Kelly. "The Necessity of Madness: Negotiating Nation in Sylvia Wynter's *The Hills of Hebron*." In *The Caribbean Woman Writer as Scholar*, edited by Keshia Abraham, 179–204. Coconut Creek, FL: Caribbean Studies Press, 2009.

Balandier, Georges. *Daily Life in the Kingdom of the Kongo: From the Sixteenth Century to the Eighteenth Century*. New York: Pantheon/Random House, [1965] 1968.

Balutansky, Kathleen, M., and Marie-Agnes Sourieau, eds. *Caribbean Creolization: Reflections on the Cultural Dynamics of Language, Literature, and Identity*. Gainesville: University Press of Florida, 2002.

Bannerji, Himani. *The Dark Side of the Nation: Essays on Multiculturalism, Nationalism and Gender*. Toronto: Canadian Scholars Press, 2000.

Barney, Gerald. *Global 2000 Revisited*. Arlington, VA: Millennum Institute, 1993.

Barton, Roland A. "The Name 'Negro.'" *The Crisis: A Record of the Darker Races* 35, no. 3 (1928): 96–97.

Bateson, Gregory. "Conscious Purpose versus Nature." In *Steps to an Ecology of Mind: Collected Essays in Anthropology, Psychiatry, Evolution, and Epistemology*, edited by Gregory Bateson, 432–445. Chicago: University of Chicago Press, [1972] 2000.

Bateson, Gregory. "Conscious Purpose vs. Nature." In *The Dialectics of Liberation*, edited by David Cooper, 34–49. Middlesex, England: Penguin, 1969.

Bateson, Gregory. "The Logical Categories of Learning and Communication." In *Steps to an Ecology of Mind: Collected Essays in Anthropology, Psychiatry, Evolution, and Epistemology*, edited by Gregory Bateson, 279–309. Chicago: University of Chicago Press, [1972] 2000.

Baudrillard, Jean. *The Mirror of Production*. Translated by Mark Poster. New York: Telos Press, 1975.

Bauman, Zygmunt. *Legislators and Interpreters: On Modernity, Post-Modernity and Intellectuals*. Ithaca, NY: Cornell University Press, 1987.

Bauman, Zygmunt. *Wasted Lives: Modernity and Its Outcasts*. Cambridge: Polity Press, 2004.

Benhabib, Seyla. *Another Cosmopolitanism: The Berkeley Tanner Lectures*, edited by Robert Post, 13–44. Oxford: Oxford University Press, 2006.

Bernabé, Jean, Patrick Chamoiseau, and Raphaël Confiant. *Éloge de la Créolité/In Praise of Creoleness*. Paris: Gallimard, 1993.

Berry, Ellen E., Kent Johnson, and Anesa Miller-Pogcagar. "An Interview with Mikhail Epstein." *Common Knowledge* 2, no. 3 (1993): 103–118.

Biko, Steven Batnu. *I Write What I Like: A Selection of Writings*. Chicago: University of Chicago Press, 1978.

Blumenberg, Hans. *The Legitimacy of the Modern Age*. Translated by Robert M. Wallace. Cambridge, MA: MIT Press, 1985.

Bogues, Anthony, ed. *After Man, towards the Human: Critical Essays on Sylvia Wynter*. Kingston, Jamaica: Ian Randle, 2005.

Bontemps, Arna. "The Slave Narrative: An American Genre." In *Great Slave Narratives*, edited by Arna Bontemps, vii–xix. Boston: Beacon Press, 1969.

Bourdieu, Pierre. *Distinction: A Social Critique of the Judgment of Taste*. Translated by Richard Nice. Cambridge, MA: MIT Press, 1984.

Boyarin, Jonathan. *The Unconverted Self: Jews, Indians, and the Identity of Christian Europe*. Chicago: Chicago University Press, 2009.

Boyce Davies, Carole. *Left of Karl Marx: The Political Life of Black Communist Claudia Jones*. Durham, NC: Duke University Press, 2008.

Boyce Davies, Carole. "Preface: The Caribbean Creative/Theoretical." In *The Caribbean Woman Writer as Scholar: Creating, Imagining, Theorizing*, edited by Keshia N. Abraham, xi–xvi. Coconut Creek, FL.: Caribbean Studies Press, 2009.

Boyce Davies, Carole, and Elaine Savory Fido. "Introduction: Women and Literature in the Caribbean." In *Out of the Kumbla: Caribbean Women and Literature*, edited by Carole Boyce Davies and Elaine Savory Fido, 1–24. Trenton, NJ: Africa World Press, 1990.

Boyce Davies, Carole, and Elaine Savory Fido. "Preface: Taking It Over: Women, Writing and Feminism." In *Out of the Kumbla: Caribbean Women and Literature*, edited by Carole Boyce Davies and Elaine Savory Fido, ix–xx. Trenton, NJ: Africa World Press, 1990.

Brand, Dionne. *Land to Light On*. Toronto: McClelland and Stewart, 1997.

Brathwaite, Kamau. *The Development of Creole Society in Jamaica, 1770–1820.* Oxford: Clarendon Press, 1972.

Briggs, John, and F. David Peat. "Interview: David Bohm." *Omni* 9 (1987): 69–74.

Brown, Wendy. *Regulating Aversion: Tolerance in the Age of Identity and Empire.* Princeton, NJ: Princeton University Press, 2008.

Browne, Simone. "Digital Epidermalization: Race, Identity and Biometrics." *Critical Sociology* 36, no. 1 (2009): 1–20.

Bullard, Robert D. "Let Them Eat Dirt: Will the Mother of All Toxic Cleanups Be Fair to All NOLA Neighborhoods, Even When Some Contamination Predates Katrina?" Environmental Justice Resource Center, April 14, 2006. Accessed April 4, 2008. http://www.ejrc.cau.edu/LetThemIntro.htm.

Butler, Judith. *Gender Trouble: Feminism and the Subversion of Identity.* New York: Routledge, [1990] 1999.

Campbell, Mark. "Remixing Relationality: Other/ed Sonic Modernities of Our Present." PhD diss., University of Toronto, 2010.

Carretta, Vincent. *Equiano, the African: Biography of a Self-Made Man.* New York: Penguin, 2005.

Carty, Wilfred. "Three Antillian Poets: Emilio Ballagas, Luis Palés Matos, and Nicolás Guillén." PhD diss., Columbia University, 1965.

Castro-Gómez, Santiago. *La Hybris del Punto Cero: Ciencia, raza e lustración en la Nueva Granada (1750–1816).* Bogotá: Pontificia Universidad Javeriana, 2005.

Césaire, Aimé. *Discourse on Colonialism.* Translated by Joan Pinkham. New York: Monthly Review Press, [1972] 2000.

Césaire, Aimé. *La Tragédie du Roi Christophe.* Paris: Présence Africaine, 1970.

Césaire, Aimé. *Lettre à Maurice Thorez.* Paris: Présence Africaine, 1956.

Césaire, Aimé. *Lyric and Dramatic Poetry, 1946–1982.* Translated by Clayton Eshleman and Annette Smith. Charlottesville: University Press of Virginia, 1990.

Césaire, Aimé. *Notebook of a Return to the Native Land.* In *Aime Cesaire: The Collected Poetry.* Translated by Clayton Eshleman and Annette Smith, 32–85. Berkeley: University of California Press, 1983.

Césaire, Aimé. "Poésie et connaissance." *Tropiques* 12 (1945): 158–170.

Césaire, Aimé. "Poetry and Knowledge." In *Refusal of the Shadow: Surrealism and the Caribbean,* edited by Michael Richardson, 134–146. Translated by Michael Richardson and Krzysztof Fijalkowski. New York: Verso, [1946] 1996.

Chorover, Stephen, L. *From Genesis to Genocide: The Meaning of Human Nature and the Power of Behavioral Control.* Cambridge, MA: MIT Press, 1980.

Christian, David. *Maps of Time: An Introduction to Big History.* Berkeley: University of California Press, 2005.

Cleaver, Eldridge. *Soul on Ice.* New York: Dell, [1968] 1991.

Cohen, Bernard. *Science and the Founding Fathers: Science in the Political Thought of Thomas Jefferson, Benjamin Franklin, John Adams and James Madison.* New York: Norton, 1995.

Comaroff, Jean, and John L. Comaroff. "Naturing the Nation: Aliens, Apocalypse, and the Postcolonial State." In *Sovereign Bodies: Citizens, Migrants, and States in the Postcolonial World*, edited by Thomas Blom Hansen and Finn Stepputat, 120–147. Princeton, NJ: Princeton University Press, 2005.

Condé, Maryse. "Négritude Césairienne, Négritude Senghorienne." *Revue de Literature Comparée* 48, nos. 3/4 (1974): 409–420.

Cooper, Anna Julia. "Woman vs. the Indian." In Anna Julia Cooper, *A Voice from the South*, 80–127. New York: Oxford University Press, [1892] 1988.

Cooper, Frederick. *Colonialism in Question: Theory, Knowledge, History.* Berkeley: University of California Press, 2005.

Cosby, Bill, and Alvin F. Poussain. *Come On People: On the Path from Victims to Victors.* Nashville, TN: Thomas Nelson, 2007.

Crichlow, Michaeline. *Globalization and the Post-Creole Imagination: Notes on Fleeing the Plantation.* Durham, NC: Duke University Press, 2009.

Cross, Charles R. *Room Full of Mirrors: A Biography of Jimi Hendrix.* New York: Hyperion, 2005.

Cross, Malcolm, and Michael Keith, eds. *Racism, the City and the State.* New York: Routledge, 1993.

Cugoano, Ottobah Quobna. *Thoughts and Sentiments on the Evil and Wicked Traffic of the Slavery and Commerce of the Human Species, Humbly Submitted to the Inhabitants of Great Britain.* New York: Penguin, [1787] 1999.

Danielli, James, F. "Altruism and the Internal Reward System, or the Opium of the People." *Journal of Social and Biological Systems* 3, no. 2 (1980): 87–94.

Darwin, Charles. *The Descent of Man.* New York: D. Appleton and Company, 1871.

Darwin, Charles. *The Descent of Man, and Selection in Relation to Sex.* Princeton, NJ: Princeton University Press, [1871] 1981.

Davidson, Basil. *Black Man's Burden: Africa and the Curse of the Nation State.* New York: Times Books, 1992.

Davis, John. *Exchange: Concepts in Social Thought.* Minneapolis: University of Minnesota Press, 1992.

Davis, Mike. *Planet of Slums.* New York: Verso, 2006.

Dear, Michael J., and Jennifer R. Wolch. *Landscapes of Despair: From Deinstitutionalization to Homelessness.* Princeton, NJ: Princeton University Press, 1987.

Debray, Regis. *God: An Itinerary.* London: Verso, 2004.

DeLoughrey, Elizabeth. "Provision Grounds and Cultural Roots: Towards Ontological Sovereignty." In *The Caribbean Woman Writer as Scholar: Creating, Imagining, Theorizing*, edited by Keisha Abraham, 205–224. Coconut Creek, FL: Caribbean Studies Press, 2009.

Derrida, Jacques. "The Ends of Man." *Philosophy and Phenomenological Research* 30, no. 1 (1969): 31–57.

Derrida, Jacques. *On Cosmopolitanism and Forgiveness.* Translated by Mark Dooley and Michael Hughes. London: Routledge, 2001.

Derrida, Jacques. *Spectres of Marx.* Translated by Peggy Kamuf. New York: Routledge, 1994.

Destro-Bisol, Giovanni. "Interview with Sarah Tishkoff: Perspectives for Genetic Research in African Populations." *Human Biology* 83, no. 5 (2011): 637–644.

Dodson, Michael, and Robert Williamson. "Indigenous Peoples and the Morality of the Human Genome Project." *Journal of Medical Ethics* 25 (1999): 204–208.

Douglas, Mary, and Steven Ney. *Missing Persons: A Critique of the Social Sciences.* Berkeley: University of California Press, 1998.

Douglass, Frederick. *Narrative of the Life of Frederick Douglass, an American Slave.* New York: Penguin [1845] 1986.

DuBois, W. E. B. "Does the Negro Need Separate Schools?" *Journal of Negro Education* 4, no. 3 (1935): 328–335.

DuBois, W. E. B. *The Souls of Black Folk: Essays and Sketches.* New York: Modern Library, [1903] 1965.

Dussel, Enrique. *The Invention of the Americas: Eclipse of "the Other" and the Myth of Modernity.* New York: Continuum, [1992] 1995.

Dussel, Enrique. *The Underside of Modernity: Apel, Ricoeur, Rorty, Taylor and the Philosophy of Liberation.* Atlantic Highlands, NJ: Humanities Press, 1996.

Dyer, Richard. *White.* New York: Routledge, 1997.

Edleman, Gerald. *Neural Darwinism: The Theory of Neuronal Group Selection.* New York: Basic Books, 1987.

Edwards, Brent Hayes. *The Practice of Diaspora Literature, Translation and the Rise of Black Internationalism.* Cambridge, MA: Harvard University Press, 2003.

Ehret, Christopher. *The Civilizations of Africa: A History to 1800.* Charlottesville: University Press of Virginia, 2002.

Ellison, Ralph. *Invisible Man.* New York: Random House, 1952.

Epstein, Mikhail. "Postcommunist Postmodernism: An Interview." *Common Knowledge* 2, no. 3 (1993): 103–150.

Equiano, Olaudah. *The Interesting Narrative and Other Writings.* New York: Penguin, 2003.

Erikson, Erik. *Life History and the Historical Moment.* New York: Norton, 1975.

Erikson, Erik. *Toys and Reason.* New York: Norton, 1977.

Eudell, Demetrius. "Afterword—Towards Aimé Césaire's 'Humanism Made to the Measure of the World': Reading *The Hills of Hebron* in the Context of Sylvia Wynter's Later Work." In *The Hills of Hebron,* by Sylvia Wynter, 311–340. Kingston, Jamaica: Ian Randle, [1962] 2010.

Eudell, Demetrius. "Modernity and the 'Work of History.'" In *After Man, towards the Human: Critical Essays on Sylvia Wynter,* edited by Anthony Bogues, 1–24. Kingston, Jamaica: Ian Randle, 2005.

Eudell, Demetrius, and Carolyn Allen, eds. "Sylvia Wynter." Special issue, *Journal of West Indian Literature* 10, nos. 1 and 2 (2001).

Eze, Emmanuel Chukwudi. *Race and the Enlightenment: A Reader.* Oxford: Blackwell, 1997.

Fanon, Frantz. *Black Skin, White Masks*. Translated by Charles Lamm Markman. New York: Grove Press, [1952] 1967.

Fanon, Frantz. *A Dying Colonialism*. Translated by Haakon Chevalier. New York: Monthly Review Press, [1959] 1965.

Fanon, Frantz. "Racism and Culture." In *Toward the African Revolution: Political Essays*, 29–44. Translated by Haakon Chevalier. New York: Grove Press/Evergreen, [1964] 1988.

Fanon, Frantz. *Toward the African Revolution*. Translated by Haakon Chevalier. New York: Grove Press, [1964] 1988.

Fanon, Frantz. *The Wretched of the Earth*. Translated by Richard Philcox. New York: Grove Press, [1961] 2004.

Fanon, Frantz. *The Wretched of the Earth*. Translated by Constance Farrington. New York: Grove Press, [1961] 1963.

Federici, Silvia. *Caliban and the Witch: Women, the Body and Primitive Accumulation*. Brooklyn, NY: Autonomedia, 2004.

Fitzpatrick, Peter. *The Mythology of Modern Law*. New York: Routledge, 1992.

Fodor, Jerry, and Massimo Piatelli-Palmarini. *What Darwin Got Wrong*. New York: Farrar, Straus and Giroux, 2010.

Foner, Eric. *Reconstruction: America's Unfinished Revolution, 1863–1877*. New York: Harper and Row, 1988.

Foucault, Michel. *The Archaeology of Knowledge*. Translated by A. M. Sheridan Smith. London: Routledge, 2002.

Foucault, Michel. "Body/Power." In *Power/Knowledge: Selected Interviews and Other Writings, 1972–1977*, edited by Colin Gordon, 55–62. Translated by Colin Gordon, Leo Marshall, John Mepham, and Kate Soper. New York: Pantheon/Vintage, 1980.

Foucault, Michel. *The History of Sexuality, Volume I: An Introduction*. Translated by Robert Hurley. New York: Vintage, [1976] 1978.

Foucault, Michel. "Intellectuals and Power." In *Language, Counter Memory, Practice: Selected Essays and Interview*, edited by Donald F. Bouchard, 205–217. Ithaca, NY: Cornell University Press, 1981.

Foucault, Michel. "Labour, Life and Language." In *The Order of Things: An Archaeology of the Human Sciences*, 250–302. Translated by Alan Sheridan. New York: Vintage/Random House, [1966] 1973.

Foucault, Michel. *The Order of Things: An Archaeology of the Human Sciences*. Translated by Alan Sheridan. New York: Vintage, [1966] 1994.

Foucault, Michel. *Society Must Be Defended: Lectures at the Collège de France, 1975–76*. Edited by Mauro Bertani and Alessandro Fontana. Translated by David Macey. New York: Picador, 2003.

Foucault, Michel. "Two Lectures." In *Power/Knowledge: Selected Interviews and Other Writings, 1972–1977*, edited by Colin Gordon, 78–108. Translated by Colin Gordon, Leo Marshall, John Mepham, and Kate Soper. New York: Pantheon/Vintage, 1980.

Franklin, Cynthia, and Laura Lyons. "Remixing Hybridity: Globalization, Native Resistance, and Cultural Production in Hawai'i." *American Studies* 45, no. 3 (2004): 49–80.

Frazier, E. Franklin. "The Failure of the Negro Intellectual." In *The Death of White Sociology: Essays on Race and Culture*, edited by Joyce Ladner, 52–66. Baltimore: Black Classic Press, [1973] 1998.

Fujikane, Candace. "Foregrounding Native Nationalisms: A Critique of Antinationalist Sentiment in Asian American Studies." In *Asian American Studies after Critical Mass*, edited by Kent A. Ona, 73–97. Oxford: Blackwell, 2005.

Fujikane, Candace, and Jonathan Y. Okamura, eds. *Asian Settler Colonialism: From Local Governance to the Habits of Everyday Life in Hawaii*. Honolulu: University of Hawai'i Press, 2008.

Fujikane, Candace, and Jon Okamura, eds. Introduction to "Whose Vision? Asian Settler Colonialism in Hawai'i." Special issue, *Amerasia Journal* 26, no. 2 (2000): xv–xxii.

Fukuyama, Francis. *The End of History and the Last Man*. New York: Perennial, 1993.

Fuss, Diana. *Essentially Speaking: Feminism, Nature and Difference*. New York: Routledge, 1989.

Gallop, Jane. *Reading Lacan*. Ithaca, NY: Cornell University Press, 1985.

Gauchet, Marcel. *The Disenchantment of the World: A Political History of Religion*. Princeton, NJ: Princeton University Press, 1997.

Gilmore, Ruth Wilson. *Golden Gulag: Prisons, Surplus, Crisis and Opposition in Globalizing California*. Berkeley: University of California Press, 2007.

Gilroy, Paul. *Against Race: Imagining Political Culture beyond the Color Line*. Cambridge, MA: Harvard University Press, 2002.

Gilroy, Paul. *The Black Atlantic: Modernity and Double Consciousness*. Cambridge, MA: Harvard University Press, 1993.

Gilroy, Paul. "Bold as Love? Jimi's Afrocyberdelia and the Challenge of the Not-Yet." *Critical Quarterly* 46, no. 4 (2004): 112–125.

Gilroy, Paul. "Multiculture, Double Consciousness and the 'War on Terror.'" *Patterns in Prejudice* 39, no. 4 (2005): 431–443.

Gilroy, Paul. *Postcolonial Melancholia*. New York: Columbia University Press, 2005.

Girard, Rene. *Deceit, Desire and the Novel: Self and Other in Literary Structure*. Baltimore: John Hopkins University Press, 1965.

Girardot, Norman, J. *Myth and Meaning in Early Taoism*. Berkeley: University of California Press, 1988.

Glass, Ruth. *London: Aspects of Change*. London: MacGibbon and Kee, 1964.

Glissant, Edouard. *Caribbean Discourse: Selected Essays*. Translated by Michael Dash. Charlottesville: University Press of Virginia, 1989.

Glissant, Edouard. *Poetics of Relation*. Translated by Betsy Wing. Ann Arbor: University of Michigan Press, 1997.

Godelier, Maurice. *Enigma of the Gift*. Translated by Norah Scott. Chicago: University of Chicago Press, 1999.

Goggin, Jacquelin. *Carter G. Woodson: A Life in Black History*. Baton Rouge: Louisiana State University Press, 1993.

Goldstein, Avram. *Addiction: From Biology to Drug Policy*. Oxford: Oxford University Press, 1994.

Gordon, Colin, ed. *Michel Foucault, Power/Knowledge: Selected Interviews and Other Writings, 1972–1977*. Translated by Colin Gordon, Leo Marshall, John Mepham, and Kate Soper. New York: Pantheon, 1990.

Gordon, Lewis. *Fanon and the Crisis of European Man: An Essay on Philosophy and the Human Sciences*. New York: Routledge, 1995.

Goveia, Elsa. "The Social Framework." *Savacou: A Journal of the Caribbean Artists Movement* 2 (September 1970): 7–15.

Grahn, Judy. *Blood, Bread, and Roses: How Menstruation Created the World*. Boston: Beacon Press, 1994.

Grassi, Ernesto. *Heidegger and the Question of Renaissance Humanism: Four Studies*. Binghamton, NY: Center for Medieval and Early Renaissance Studies, 1983.

Grassi, Ernesto. *Humanismo y Marxismo: Crítica de la Independización de la Ciencia*. Madrid: Gredos, 1977.

Grassi, Ernesto. *Rhetoric as Philosophy: The Humanist Tradition*. Translated by Michael J. Kroi and Azizeh Azodi. Carbondale: Southern Illinois University Press, 2001.

Green, Peter. *The Hellenistic Age: A History*. New York: Modern Library, 2007.

Grey, Stephanie Houston. "(Re)Imagining Ethnicity in the City of New Orleans: Katrina's Geographical Allegory." In *Seeking Higher Ground*, edited by Manning Marable and Kristen Clarke, 129–141. New York: Palgrave Macmillan, 2008.

Gugliotta, Guy. "The Great Human Migration: Why Humans Left Their African Homeland 80,000 Years Ago to Colonize the World." *Smithsonian Magazine*, July 2008. Accessed November 19, 2013. http://www.smithsonian.com/history/archaeology/humanmigration.

Haar, Michel. *Heidegger and the Essence of Man*. Translated by W. McNeill. Albany: State University of New York Press, 1993.

Haddour, Azzedine. "Sartre and Fanon: On Negritude and Political Participation." *Sartre Studies International* 11, nos. 1–2 (2005): 286–301.

Hall, Stuart. "Conclusion: The Multi-Cultural Question." In *Un/settled Multiculturalisms: Diasporas, Entanglements, Transruptions*, edited by Barnor Hess, 209–241. London: Zed Books, 2001.

Hall, Stuart. "Creolization, Diaspora and Hybridity." In *Creolite and Creolization*, edited by Okwui Enwezor, Carlos Basualdo, Ute Meta Bauer, Susanne Ghez, Sarat Maharaj, Mark Nash, and Octavio Zaya, 185–198. Berlin: Hatje Cantz, 2003.

Hall, Stuart. "New Ethnicities." In *Stuart Hall: Critical Dialogues in Cultural Studies*, edited by D. Morley and K. Chen, 441–449. London: Routledge, 1996.

Hallyn, Ferdinand. *The Poetic Structure of the World: Copernicus and Kepler*. Translated by Donald M. Leslie. New York: Zone Books, 1990.

Haraway, Donna. *When Species Meet*. Minneapolis: University of Minnesota Press, 2008.

Harding, Sandra, ed. *The "Racial" Economy of Science: Toward a Democratic Future*. Bloomington: Indiana University Press, 1993.

Hardt, Michael, and Antonio Negri. *Empire*. Cambridge, MA: Harvard University Press, 2000.

Hatton, Timothy J., and Jeffrey G. Williamson. *The Age of Mass Migration: Causes and Economic Impact*. New York: Oxford University Press, 1998.

Hawthorne, Susan. *Wild Politics*. North Melbourne: Spinifex Press, 2004.

Headrick, Daniel R. *Power over Peoples: Technology, Environments and Western Imperialism, 1400 to the Present*. Princeton, NJ: Princeton University Press, 2010.

Hearne, John. *Voices under the Window*. London: Faber and Faber, 1973.

Hegel, Georg H. W. *Philosophy of Right*. Translated by S. W. Dyde. New York: Cosimo, [1821] 2008.

Heidegger, Martin. *Basic Concepts*. Translated by Gary E. Aylesworth. Bloomington: Indiana University Press, 1998.

Heidegger, Martin. *Being and Time*. Translated by Joan Stambaugh. Albany: State University of New York Press, 1996.

Heidegger, Martin. "Letter on Humanism." In *Pathmarks*, edited by William McNeil, 239–276. Cambridge: Cambridge University Press, [1946] 1998.

Heidegger, Martin. *Ontology: The Hermeneutics of Facticity*. Translated by John van Buren. Bloomington: Indiana University Press, 1999.

Heilbroner, Robert. L. *Behind the Veil of Economics*. New York: Norton, 1988.

Henshilwood, Christopher S., Francesco d'Errico, and Ian Watts. "Engraved Ochres from the Middle Stone Age Levels at Blombos Cave, South Africa." *Journal of Human Evolution* 57 (2009): 27–47.

Henshilwood, Christopher, S., Francesco d'Errico, Royden Yates, Zenobia Jacobs, Chantal Tribolo, Geoff A. T. Duller, Norbert Mercier, Judith C. Sealy, Helene Valladas, Ian Watts, and Ann G. Wintle. "Emergence of Modern Human Behavior: Middle Stone Age Engravings from South Africa." *Science* 295, no. 5558 (2002): 1278–1280.

Herrnstein, Richard, and Charles Murray. *The Bell Curve: Intelligence and Class Structure in American Life*. New York: Free Press, 1994.

Herskovits, Melville Jean. *The Myth of the Negro Past*. Boston: Beacon Press, [1941] 1990.

Hill, Errol. *The Trinidad Carnival: Mandate for a National Theatre*. London: New Beacon Books, 1997.

Hill, Robert A., ed. *Marcus Garvey, Life and Lessons: A Centennial Companion to the Marcus Garvey and Universal Negro Improvement Association Papers*. Berkeley, CA: University of California Press, 1987.

Hocart, A. M. *Kings and Councillors: An Essay in the Comparative Anatomy of Human Society*. Edited by Rodney Needham. Chicago: University of Chicago Press, [1936] 1970.

Hochschild, Adam. *King Leopold's Ghost: A Story of Greed, Terror and Heroism in Colonial Africa*. London: Pan Macmillan, 2006.

Holloway, Jonathan Scott. *Confronting the Veil: Abram Harris Jr., E. Franklin Frazier, and Ralph Bunche, 1919–1941*. Chapel Hill: University of North Carolina Press, 2002.

hooks, bell. "Homeplace: A Site in Resistance." In *Yearning: Race, Gender, and Cultural Politics*, 41–49. Boston: South End Press, 1990.

Humphrey, Nicholas. *A History of the Mind: Evolution, and the Birth of Consciousness*. London: Springer, 1992.

Hunt, Edward E., Jr., et al. *The Micronesians of Yap and Their Depopulation*. Report of the Peabody Museum Expedition to Yap Island, Micronesia, 1947–78. Coordinated Investigation of Micronesia, 1947–1949, no. 24. Washington, DC: Pacific Science Board, National Research Council, 1949.

Hyers, Conrad. *The Meaning of Creation: Genesis and Modern Science*. Atlanta, GA: John Knox Press, 1984.

Ichikawa, Mitsou. "The Japanese Tradition in Central African Hunter-Gatherer Studies." In *Hunter-Gatherers in History, Archaeology, and Anthropology*, edited by Alan Barnard, 103–114. Oxford: Berg, 2004.

Isaac, Barbara, ed. *The Archaeology of Human Origins: Essays by Glynn Isaac*. Cambridge: Cambridge University Press, 1989.

Isaac, Glyn. "Aspects of Human Evolution." In *Evolution from Molecules to Men*, edited by D. S. Bendall, 509–543. Cambridge: Cambridge University Press, 1983.

Jackson, Fatimah. "African-American Responses to the Human Genome Project." *Public Understanding of Science* 8 (1999): 181–191.

Jacobs, Harriet. *Incidents in the Life of a Slave Girl*. Mineola, NY: Dover, [1861] 2001.

Jacques-Garvey, Amy, ed. *Philosophy and Opinions of Marcus Garvey*. New York: Atheneum, 1991.

James, C. L. R. *C. L. R. James and Revolutionary Marxism: Selected Writings of C. L. R. James 1939–1949*. Edited by Scott McLemee. London: Humanity Book Publishers, 1994.

James, C. L. R. "C. L. R. James on the Origins." *Radical America* 2, no. 4 (1968): 20–29.

James, C. L. R. *Notes on Dialectics: Hegel, Marx, Lenin*. London: Allison and Busby, [1948] 1980.

James, C. L. R. *State Capitalism and World Revolution*. Written in collaboration with Raya Dunayevskaya and Grace Lee. Chicago: Charles H. Kerr, [1950] 1996.

James, Joy. "Afterword: Political Literacy and Voice." In *What Lies Beneath: Katrina, Race, and the State of the Nation*, edited by South End Press. Cambridge, MA: South End Press, 2007.

Jefferson, Thomas. *Notes on the State of Virginia*. Edited by William Peden. Chapel Hill: University of North Carolina Press, [1787] 1955.

Jones, Gwyneth. *Bold as Love*. London: Gollancz, 2001.

Jones, Jessica. "Cherokee by Blood and the Freedman Debate: The Conflict of Minority Rights in a Liberal State." *National Black Law Journal* 22, no. 1 (2009): 1–55.

Jordan, June. "Poem about My Rights." In *Directed by Desire: The Collected Poems of June Jordan*, 309–311. Port Townsend, WA: Copper Canyon Press, 2005.

Julian, Isaac, director. *Young Soul Rebels*. London: British Film Institute, 1991. Film, 105 minutes.

Kauanui, Kehaulani J. "Colonial in Equality: Hawaiian Sovereignty and the Question of U.S. Civil Rights." *South Atlantic Quarterly* 107, no. 4 (2008): 635–650.

Kauanui, Kehaulani J. *Hawaiian Blood: Colonialism and the Politics of Sovereignty and Indigeneity*. Durham, NC: Duke University Press, 2008.

Kelley, Robin, D. G. "But a Local Phase of a World Problem: Black History's Global Vision, 1883–1950." *Journal of American History* 86, no. 3 (1999): 1045–1077.

Kevles, Daniel. *In the Name of Eugenics: Genetics and the Uses of Human Heredity*. Cambridge, MA: Harvard University Press, 1995.

Khan, Aisha. "Journey to the Center of the Earth: The Caribbean as Master Symbol." *Cultural Anthropology* 16, no. 3 (2001): 271–302.

Kincaid, Jamaica. "The Flowers of Empire." *Harper's*, April 1996.

King, Joyce E. "Race and Our Biocentric Belief System: An Interview with Sylvia Wynter." In *Black Education: A Transformative Research and Action Agenda for the New Century*, edited by Joyce E. King, 361–366. London: Erlbaum, 2005.

Krieger, Nancy. "Refiguring 'Race': Epidemiology, Racialized Biology, and Biological Expressions of Race Relations." *International Journal of Health Services* 30, no. 1 (2000): 211–216.

Kristeva, Julia. *The Powers of Horror: An Essay on Abjection*. Translated by Leon S. Roudiez. New York: Columbia University Press, 1982.

Kristeva, Julia. "Women's Time." Translated by Alice Jardine and Harry Blake. *Signs* 7, no. 1 (1981): 13–35.

Lamming, George. *In the Castle of My Skin*. Ann Arbor: University of Michigan Press, [1970] 1991.

Latour, Bruno. *We Have Never Been Modern*. Translated by Catherine Porter. Cambridge, MA: Harvard University Press, 1991.

Lawrence, Bonita. "Land, Identity and Indigenous Survival." Paper presented at the conference "Diasporic Hegemonies: Race, Gender, Sexuality and the Politics of Feminist Transnationalism," University of Toronto, Toronto, October 20, 2006.

Lawrence, Bonita, and Enakshi Dua. "Decolonizing Antiracism." *Social Justice* 32, no. 4 (2005): 120–143.

Lawrence, Sharon. *Jimi Hendrix: The Intimate Story of a Betrayed Musical Legend*. New York: HarperCollins, 2005.

Lee, Easton, Sylvia Wynter, and Enid Chevannes. *West Indian Plays for Schools*. Vol. 2. Kingston, Jamaica: Jamaica Publishing House, 1979.

Leeming, David. *Myth: A Biography of Belief*. New York: Oxford University Press, 2002.

Legesse, Asmarom. *Gada: Three Approaches to the Study of an African Society*. New York: Free Press, 1973.

Le Goff, Jacques. *The Medieval Imagination*. Translated by Arthur Goldhammer. Chicago: University of Chicago Press, 1992.

Leong, Russell. "Whose Vision? Asian Settler Colonialism in Hawai'i." *Amerasia Journal* 26, no. 2 (2000): xii–xiv.

Lerner, Gerda. "Early Community Work of Black Club Women." *Journal of Negro History* 59, no. 2 (1974): 158–167.

Lévi-Strauss, Claude. *Mythologiques*. Vol. 1, *The Raw and the Cooked*. Chicago: University of Chicago Press, 1964.

Lévi-Strauss, Claude. *Tristes Tropiques*. Translated by John Weightman and Doreen Weightman. New York: Atheneum, 1955.

Lewis, Rupert. *Marcus Garvey: Anti-Colonial Champion*. Trenton, NJ: Africa World Press, 1988.

Lewontin, Richard, C. "Not So Natural Selection." Review of *What Darwin Got Wrong*, by Jerry Fodor and Massimo Piattelli-Palmarini. *New York Review of Books*, May 27, 2010.

Lieberman, Phillip. *Uniquely Human: The Evolution of Speech, Thought and Selfless Behavior*. Cambridge, MA: Harvard University Press, 1991.

Limb, Charles J., and Allen R. Braun. "Neural Substrates of Spontaneous Musical Performance: An fMRI Study of Jazz Improvisation." PLOS ONE 3, no. 2 (2008): 1–9.

Linebaugh Peter, and Marcus Rediker. *The Many-Headed Hydra: Sailors, Slaves, Commoners, and the Hidden History of the Revolutionary Atlantic*. Boston: Beacon Press, 2000.

Locke, Alain. "The Legacy of Ancestral Arts." In *The New Negro*, edited by Alain Locke, 254–267. New York: Atheneum, [1925] 1992.

Locke, Alain. "The New Negro." In *The New Negro*, edited by Alain Locke, 3–16. New York: Atheneum, [1925] 1970.

Long, Alecia P. *The Great Southern Babylon: Sex, Race, and Respectability in New Orleans, 1865–1920*. Baton Rouge: University of Louisiana Press, 2004.

Lorde, Audre. *Sister Outsider*. Freedom, CA: Crossing Press, 1984.

Lyotard, Jean-François. *Heidegger and "The Jews."* Minneapolis: University of Minnesota Press, 1990.

MacGaffey, Wyatt. "Kongo and the King of the Americans." *Journal of Modern African Studies* 6, no. 2 (1968): 171–181.

Maldonado-Torres, Nelson. "The Topology of Being and the Geopolitics of Knowledge, Modernity, Empire, Coloniality." *City* 8, no. 1 (2004): 29–56.

Malthus, Thomas Robert. *An Essay on the Principle of Population*. New York: Penguin, [1798] 1982.

Mamdani, Mahmood. "Understanding the Crisis in Kivu: Report of the Council for the Development of Social Research in Africa (CODESRIA) Mission to the

Democratic Republic of Congo September 1997." Centre for African Studies, University of Cape Town, 1998.

Marcus, Griel. *Mystery Train: Images of America in Rock 'n' Roll.* 4th ed. New York: Plume, [1975] 1997.

Martin, James. "Interview with James Martin." In *Born in Slavery: Slave Narratives from the Federal Writers Project, 1936–1938*, Vol. 16, No. 3. Washington, DC: Library of Congress, 1937

Marx, Karl. *Capital: A Critique of Political Economy, Vol. 1, Pt. 2, The Process of Capitalist Production.* New York: Cosimo, [1867] 2007.

Maté, Gabor. "Capitalism Makes Us Crazy: On Illness and Addiction." *Making Contact, KPFA.* Accessed October 25, 2013. http://www.kpfa.org/archive/id/92075.

Maté, Gabor. *In the Realm of Hungry Ghosts: Close Encounters with Addiction.* Berkeley: North Atlantic Books, 2008.

Maturana, Humberto R., and Bernhard Poerksen. *From Being to Doing: The Origins of the Biology of Cognition.* Heidelberg: Carl Auer International, 2004.

Maturana, Humberto R., and Francisco J. Varela. *Autopoiesis and Cognition: The Realization of the Living.* London: Reidel, [1972] 1980.

Maturana, Humberto R., and Francisco Varela. *The Tree of Knowledge: The Biological Roots of Human Understanding.* New York: Shambala, 1992.

May, Vivian M. *Anna Julia Cooper, Visionary Black Feminist: A Critical Introduction.* New York: Routledge, 2007.

McClintock, Anne. *Imperial Leather: Race, Gender and Sexuality in the Colonial Contest.* New York: Routledge, 1995.

McKibben, Bill. *The End of Nature.* New York: Random House, 1989.

McKibben, Bill. *Enough: Staying Human in an Engineered Age.* New York: St. Martin's Griffin, 2004.

McKittrick, Katherine. *Demonic Grounds: Black Women and the Cartographies of Struggle.* Minneapolis: University of Minnesota Press, 2006.

McKittrick, Katherine. "On Plantations, Prisons, and a Black Sense of Place." *Social and Cultural Geography* 12, no. 8 (2011): 947–963.

McKittrick, Katherine. "The Science of the Word." Music-text mashup. Toronto-Oakland, 2008.

McKittrick, Katherine, and Linda Peake. "What Difference Does 'Difference' Mean to Geography?" In *Questioning Geography,* edited by Noel Castree, Ali Rogers, and Douglas Sherman, 39–54. Oxford: Blackwell, 2005.

Meek, Ronald. *Social Science and the Ignoble Savage.* Cambridge: Cambridge University Press, 1976.

Mercer, Kobena. "Introduction." In *Cosmopolitan Modernisms,* edited by K. Mercer, 6–23. Cambridge, MA: MIT Press, 2005.

Mignolo, Walter D. *The Idea of Latin America.* London: Blackwell, 2005.

Mignolo, Walter D. "Racism as We Sense It Today." *PMLA* 123, no. 5 (2008): 1737–1742.

Mignolo, Walter D. "Thinking Possible Futures: The Network Society and the Coloniality of Being." The Joan Carslile Irving Lectures, 1999–2000. Department of Fine Arts, Art History and Theory, University of British Columbia, March 30, 2000.

Mignolo, Walter D., and Arturo Escobar, eds. *Globalization and the Decolonial Option*. London: Routledge, 2009.

Mohanty, Chandra. *Feminism without Borders*. Durham, NC: Duke University Press, 2003.

Mohanty, Chandra. "Under Western Eyes: Feminist Scholarship and Colonial Discourses." *Feminist Review* 30 (autumn 1988): 61–88.

Morales, Rosalie. "We're All in the Same Boat." In *This Bridge Called My Back: Writings by Radical Women of Color*, edited by Cherrie Moraga and Gloria Anzaldua, 91–93. Watertown, MA: Persephone Press, 1983.

Morrison, Toni. *The Bluest Eye*. New York: Penguin, [1970] 2000.

Mudimbe, Valentin. *The Invention of Africa: Philosophy, Gnosis, and the Order of Knowledge*. Bloomington: University of Indiana Press, 1988.

Mudimbe, Valentin Y. "Romanus Pontifex (1454) and the Expansion of Europe." In *Race, Discourse, and the Origin of the Americas: A New World View*, edited by Vera Lawrence and Rex Nettleford, 58–65. Washington, DC: Smithsonian Institution Press, 1995.

Murena, Alberto. *El pecado original de América*. Buenos Aires: Editorial Sur, 1954.

Nabokov, Vladimir. *Pale Fire*. New York: Vintage, [1962] 1989.

Nagel, Thomas. *The View from Nowhere*. New York: Oxford University Press, 1986.

Nagel, Thomas. "What Is It Like to Be a Bat?" *Philosophical Review* 83, no. 4 (1974): 435–450.

Nas. "Life's a B****." From *Illmatic*. Sony CD, 1994.

National Carnival Commission. "Canboulay Re-enactment 2010." Accessed February 10, 2010. http://www.ncctt.org/home.

Neal, Larry. "The Black Arts Movement." *Drama Review* 12, no. 4 (1968): 29–39.

Neal, Larry. "Some Reflections on the Black Aesthetic." In *The Black Aesthetic*, edited by Addison Gayle Jr., 13–16. New York: Doubleday, 1972.

Nelson, R. H. *Economics as Religion: From Samuelson to Chicago and Beyond*. Foreword by Max Stackpole. University Park: Pennsylvania State University Press, 2001.

Nevins, Joseph. *Operation Gatekeeper and Beyond: The War on "Illegals" and the Remaking of the US-Mexico Boundary*. New York: Routledge, 2010.

Newberg, Andrew, Eugene D'Aquili, and Vince Rause. *Why God Won't Go Away: Brain Science and the Biology of Belief*. New York: Ballantine Books, 2001.

Niezen, Ronald. *The Origins of Indigenism: Human Rights and the Politics of Identity*. Berkeley: University of California Press, 2003.

O'Connor, Erin. *Raw Material: Producing Pathology in Victorian Culture*. Durham, NC: Duke University Press, 2000.

Ortiz, Fernando. *Cuban Counterpoint: Tobacco and Sugar*. Translated by Harriet de Onís. Durham, NC: Duke University Press, [1947] 1995.

Ottley, Roi. *"New World A-Coming": Inside Black America.* Boston: Houghton Mifflin, 1943.

Pagden, Anthony. "Human Rights, Natural Rights, and Europe's Imperial Legacy." *Political Theory* 31, no. 2 (2003): 171–199.

Palmié, Stephan. "Creolization and Its Discontents." *Annual Review of Anthropology* 35 (2006): 433–456.

Pandian, Jacob. *Anthropology and the Western Tradition: Towards an Authentic Anthropology.* Long Grove, IL: Waveland Press, 1985.

Pandian, Jacob. *Culture, Religion, and the Sacred Self: A Critical Introduction to the Anthropological Study of Religion.* Englewood Hills, NJ: Prentice-Hall, 1991.

Perry, Jeffrey B. *Hubert Harrison: The Voice of Harlem Radicalism 1883–1918.* New York: Columbia University Press, 2009.

Pfaff, Françoise. *Conversations with Maryse Condé.* Lincoln: University of Nebraska Press, 1996.

Philip, Marlene NourbeSe. *A Genealogy of Resistance.* Toronto: The Mercury Press, 1992.

Pocock, J. G. A. "Civic Humanism and Its Role in Anglo-American Thought." In *Politics, Language, and Time: Essays on Political Thought and History,* 80–103. Chicago: University of Chicago Press, 1960 [1989].

Pocock, J. G. A. *The Machiavellian Moment: Florentine Political Thought and the Atlantic Political Tradition.* Princeton, NJ: Princeton University Press, 1975.

Polanyi, Karl. *The Great Transformation: The Political and Economic Origins of Our Time.* Boston: Beacon Press, [1944] 2001.

Poovey, Mary. *Making a Social Body: British Cultural Formation, 1830–1864.* Chicago: University of Chicago Press, 1995.

Poussaint, Alvin. "The Role of Education in Providing a Basis for Honest Self-Identification." In *Black Studies in the University: A Symposium,* edited by Armstead L. Robinson, Craig C. Foster, and Donald H. Ogilvie, 194–201. New Haven, CT: Yale University Press, 1969.

Prashad, Vijay. *The Darker Nations: A People's History of the Third World.* New York: New Press, 2007.

Price-Mars, Jean. *So Spoke the Uncle/Ainsi parla l'oncle.* Translated by Magdaline W. Shannon. Colorado Springs, CO: Three Continents Press, [1928] 1983.

Prigogine, Ilya. Foreword to *The Arrow of Time: A Voyage through Science to Solve Time's Greatest Mystery,* by Peter Coveney and Roger Highfield, 15–18. New York. Fawcett, Columbia, 1990.

Quijano, Anibal. "Coloniality of Power, Eurocentrism, and Latin America." *Nepantla: Views from the South* 1, no. 3 (2000): 533–580.

Quijano, Anibal, and Immanuel Wallerstein. "Americanity as a Concept, or the Americas in the Modern World-System." *International Social Science Journal* 134 (1992): 549–557.

Redding, Noel, and Carol Appleby. *Are You Experienced? The Inside Story of the Jimi Hendrix Experience.* New York: Da Capo, 1996.

Rediker, Marcus. "The Red Atlantic; Or, 'A Terrible Blast Swept over the Heaving Sea.'" In *Sea Changes: Historicizing the Ocean*, edited by Bernhard Klein and Gesa Mackenthun, 111–130. New York: Routledge, 2003.

Reed, T. V. "Toward an Environmental Justice Ecocriticism." In *The Environmental Justice Reader*, edited by Joni Adamson, Mei Mei Evans, and Rachel Stein, 145–162. Tucson: University of Arizona Press, 2002.

Richards, Sandra. "Horned Ancestral Masks, Shakespearean Actor Boys, and Scotch-Inspired Set Girls: Social Relations in Nineteenth Century Jamaican Jonkonnu." In *The African Diaspora: African Origins and New World Identities*, edited by Isidore Okpewho, Carole Boyce Davies, and Ali Mazrui, 254–271. Bloomington: Indiana University Press, 1999.

Roberts, Martin. "Spanish Parliament to Extend Rights to Apes." Reuters, June 25, 2008. Accessed July 10, 2009. http://www.reuters.com/article/scienceNews/idUSL256586320080625.

Rodríguez, Dylan. "The Meaning of 'Disaster' under the Dominant of White Life." In *What Lies Beneath: Katrina, Race, and the State of the Nation*, edited by the South End Press, 133–156. Cambridge: South End Press, 2007.

Rolston, Holmes, III. *Three Big Bangs: Matter-Energy, Life, Mind*. New York: Columbia University Press, 2010.

Rorty, Richard. *Objectivity, Relativism and Truth: Philosophical Papers I*. Cambridge: Cambridge University Press, 1991.

Rorty, Richard. "Solidarity or Objectivity." In *Objectivity, Relativism and Truth: Philosophical Papers I*, 21–34. Cambridge: Cambridge University Press, 1991.

Rose, Hilary, and Steven Rose. "Darwin and After." *New Left Review* 63 (May–June 2010): 91–113.

Rosenblum, Bruce, and Fred Kuttner. *Quantum Enigma: Physics Encounters Consciousness*. Oxford: Oxford University Press, 2006.

Ross, Dorothy. *The Origins of American Social Science*. Cambridge: Cambridge University Press, 1991.

Rowell, Charles H. "It Is through Poetry That One Copes with Solitude: An Interview with Aimé Césaire." *Callaloo* 38 (winter 1989): 49–67.

Rue, Loyal. *Everybody's Story: Wising Up to the Epic of Evolution*. Albany: State University of New York Press, 2000.

Sahlins, Marshall. *Apologies to Thucydides: Understanding History as Culture and Vice Versa*. Chicago: University of Chicago Press, 2004.

Sahlins, Marshall. *How "Natives" Think: About Captain Cook, for Example*. Chicago: University of Chicago Press, 1995.

Sala-Molins, Louis. *Dark Side of Light: Slavery and the French Enlightenment*. Translated by John Conteh-Morgan. Minneapolis: University of Minnesota Press, [1992] 2006.

Sanabria, Alicia. "African Matrix." In *The Encyclopedia of the African Diaspora: Origins, Experiences and Culture*, edited by Carole Boyce Davies, 531. Santa Barbara, CA: ABC-CLIO, 2008.

Sartre, Jean-Paul. "Orphée Noir." Preface to Léopold Sédar Senghor, *Anthologie de la nouvelle poésie nègre et malgache de langue française*, ix–xliv. Paris: Presses Universitaires de France, [1948] 1969.

Sartre, Jean-Paul. Preface to *The Wretched of the Earth*, by Frantz Fanon, 7–31. Translated by Constance Farrington. New York: Grove Press, [1961] 1963.

Schmitt, Carl. *The Nomos of the Earth in the International Law of the Ius Publicum Europaeum*. New York: Tellos, 2003.

Scott, David. *Conscripts of Modernity: The Tragedy of Colonial Enlightenment*. Durham, NC: Duke University Press, 2004.

Scott, David. "The Re-enchantment of Humanism: An Interview with Sylvia Wynter." *Small Axe* 8 (September 2000): 119–207.

Scott, David. *Refashioning Futures: Criticism after Postcoloniality*. Princeton, NJ: Princeton University Press, 1999.

Segal, Ronald. *The Other Black Diaspora: Islam's Black Slaves*. New York: Farrar, Straus and Giroux, 2001.

Sephocle, Marie-Line. "Interview with Aimé Césaire." In *Ex-Iles: Essays on Caribbean Cinema*, edited by Mybye Chain, 359–369. Trenton, NJ: Africa World Press, 1992.

Sexton, Jared. "The Obscurity of Black Suffering." In *What Lies Beneath: Katrina, Race, and the State of the Nation*, edited by South End Press, 120–132. Cambridge: South End Press, 2007.

Shari'ati, Ali. "Modern Man and His Prisons." In *Man and Islam*, translated by Dr. Fatollah Marjani, 46–62. North Haledon, NJ: Islamic Publications International, 1981.

Sharma, Nandita. *Home Economics: Nationalism and the Making of "Migrant Workers" in Canada*. Toronto: University of Toronto Press, 2006.

Sharma, Nandita, and Cynthia Wright. "Decolonizing Resistance, Challenging Colonial States." *Social Justice* 35, no. 3 (2009): 120–138.

Sharpley-Whiting, T. Denean. *Frantz Fanon: Conflicts and Feminisms*. New York: Roman and Littlefield, 1998.

Sibley, David. *Geographies of Exclusion: Society and Difference in the West*. New York: Routledge, 1995.

Sibley, David. "Purification of Space." *Environment and Planning D: Society and Space* 6 (1988): 409–421.

Silva, Denise Ferreira da. "'Bahia Pêlo Negro': Can the Subaltern (Subject of Raciality) Speak?" *Ethnicities* 5, no. 3 (2005): 321–342.

Silva, Denise Ferreira da. "Mapping Territories of Legality: An Exploratory Cartography of an Emerging Female Global Subject." In *Critical Beings: Law, Nation and the Global Subject*, edited by Peter Fitzpatrick and Patricia Tuitt, 203–222. London: Ashgate, 2004.

Silva, Denise Ferreira da. "No-Bodies: Law, Raciality and Violence." *Griffith Law Review* 18, no. 2 (2009): 212–236.

Silva, Denise Ferreira da. *Toward a Global Idea of Race*. Minneapolis: University of Minnesota Press, 2007.

Simon, John, K. "A Conversation with Michel Foucault." *Partisan Review* 38 (1971): 192–201.

"Skin Bleach Ban Fails: Vendors Still Making Big Bucks Despite Ministry Clampdown." *Jamaican Star*, February 9, 2007. Accessed May 28, 2009. http://www .jamaica-star.com/thestar/20070209/news/news1.html.

Slabodsky, Santiago E. "De-Colonial Jewish Thought and the Americas." In *Postcolonial Philosophy of Religion*, edited by Purushottama Bilimoria and Andrew B. Irvine, 269–290. New York: Springer, 2009.

Smith, Andrea. *Conquest: Sexual Violence and American Indian Genocide*. Cambridge, MA: South End Press, 2005.

Smith, Andrea. "Indigenous Feminist Perspectives on Reparations: Beyond Capitalism and the Nation State." Keynote paper presented at the conference "Diasporic Hegemonies: Race, Gender, Sexuality and the Politics of Feminist Transnationalism," University of Toronto, Toronto, October 20, 2006.

Snow, C. P. *The Two Cultures*. London: Cambridge University Press, [1959] 2001.

Solomon, Anne. "Rock Art in Southern Africa." *Scientific American* 15 (January 2005): 42–51.

Spanos, William V. *The End of Education: Toward Posthumanism*. Minneapolis: University of Minnesota Press, 1993.

Spillers, Hortense. "Mama's Baby, Papa's Maybe: An American Grammar Book." In *Within the Circle: An Anthology of African American Criticism from the Harlem Renaissance to the Present*, edited by Angelyn Mitchell, 454–481. Durham, NC: Duke University Press, 1994.

Spivak, Gayatri Chakravorty. "Can the Subaltern Speak?" In *Marxism and the Interpretation of Culture*, edited by Cary Nelson and Lawrence Grossberg, 271–313. London: MacMillan, 1988.

Spivak, Gayatri Chakravorty. *A Critique of Postcolonial Reason: Toward a History of the Vanishing Present*. Cambridge, MA: Harvard University Press, 1999.

Stackhouse, Max Lynn. Foreword to *Economics as Religion: From Samuelson to Chicago and Beyond*, by R. H. Nelson, x–xiv. University Park: Pennsylvania State University Press, 2001.

Steele, Claude M. "Thin Ice: 'Stereotype Threat' and Black College Students." *Atlantic Monthly* 284, no. 2 (1999): 44–54.

Stein, Kathleen. *The Genius Engine: Where Memory, Reason, Passion, Violence, and Creativity Intersect in the Human Brain*. New York: Wiley, 2007.

Subramaniam, Banu. "Moored Metamorphoses: A Retrospective Essay on Feminist Science Studies." *Signs* 34, no. 4 (2009): 951–980.

Sutcliffe, Bob. "Migration and Citizenship: Why Can Birds, Whales, Butterflies and Ants Cross International Frontiers More Easily Than Cows, Dogs and Human Beings?" In *Migration and Mobility: The European Context*, edited by Subrata Ghatak and Anne Showstack Sassoon, 66–82. New York: Palgrave, 2002.

Sweet, James H. "The Iberian Roots of American Racist Thought." *William and Mary Quarterly* 54, no. 7 (1997): 143–166.

Sweet, Leonard I. *Black Images of America, 1784–1870*. New York: Norton, 1970.

Teruel, De Antonion. "Narrative Description of the Kingdom of the Congo." Unpublished manuscript. Madrid: National Library of Madrid. MS 3533:3574, 1663–1664.

Thomas, Greg. "ProudFlesh Inter/Views Sylvia Wynter," *ProudFlesh: New Afrikan Journal of Culture, Politics and Consciousness* 4 (2006). Accessed August 5, 2010. http://www.proudfleshjournal.com/issue4/wynter.html.

Tishkoff, Sarah, and Kenneth Kidd. "Implications of Biogeography of Human Populations for 'Race' and Medicine." *Nature Genetics* 36 no. 11 (2004): 21–27.

Trask, Haunani Kay. "Settlers of Color and 'Immigrant' Hegemony: 'Locals' in Hawai'i." In "Whose Vision? Asian Settler Colonialism in Hawai'i." Special issue, *Amerasia Journal* 26, no. 2 (2000): 1–26.

Trouillot, Michel-Rolph. "Culture on the Edges: Creolization in the Plantation Context." *Plantation Society in the Americas* 5 (spring 1998): 8–28.

Turnbull, Colin. *The Forest People*. New York: Touchstone, 1968.

Turner, Grace. "Junkanoo." In *The Encyclopedia of the African Diaspora: Origins, Experiences and Culture*, edited by Carole Boyce Davies, 599–600. Santa Barbara, CA: ABC-CLIO, 2008.

UNESCO. "Fossil Hominid Sites of South Africa." Accessed November 26, 2013. http://whc.unesco.org/pg.cfm?cid=31&id_site=915.

Unified New Orleans Plan. "City Wide Plan: Section 1—Introduction." Accessed April 4, 2008. http://www.unifiedneworleansplan.com/home3/section/136/city-wide-plan.

United Nations. "Evidence Is Now 'Unequivocal' That Humans Are Causing Global Warming: UN Report." Accessed July 2011. http://www.un.org/apps/news/story.asp?Cr1=change&Cr=climate&NewsID=21429#.

United Nations. *Statistical Yearbook for Asia and the Pacific*. http://www.unescap.org/stat/data/syb2008/3-International-migration.pdf. Accessed January 5, 2011.

Valaskakis, Gail Guthrie. *Indian Country: Essays on Contemporary Native Culture*. Waterloo, ON: Wilfred Laurier University Press, 2005.

Varela, Francisco. *Principles of Biological Autonomy*. New York: Elsevier Sciences, 1979.

Wade, Nicholas. "Eden Maybe: But Where's the Apple Tree?" *New York Times*, May 1, 2009, A6.

Waksman, Steve. "Black Sound, Black Body: Jimi Hendrix, the Electric Guitar, and the Meanings of Blackness." *Popular Music and Society* 23 (1999): 75–113.

Walcott, Rinaldo. "Caribbean Pop Culture in Canada: Or, the Impossibility of Belonging to the Nation." *Small Axe* 5, no. 1 (2001): 123–139.

Walcott, Rinaldo. "Pedagogy and Trauma: The Middle Passage and the Problem of Creolization." In *Between Hope and Despair: Pedagogy and the Remembrance of Historical Trauma*, edited by Roger I. Simon, Sharon Rosenberg, and Claudia Eppert, 135–151. New York: Rowman and Littlefield, 2000.

Walcott, Rinaldo. "Reconstructing Manhood; or, The Drag of Black Masculinity." *Small Axe* 13, no. 1 (2009): 75–89.

Walker, David. *Appeal in Four Articles; Together with a Preamble to the Coloured Citizens of the World*. New York: Hill and Wang, [1829] 1965.

Wallace, David Foster. *Infinite Jest*. New York: Little, Brown, 1996.

Wallerstein, Immanuel. *The Modern World-System*. Vol. 1, *Capitalist Agriculture and the Origins of the European World-Economy in the Sixteenth Century*. New York/London: Academic Press, 1974.

Wallerstein, Immanuel. *The Modern World-System*. Vol. 2, *Mercantilism and the Consolidation of the European World-Economy, 1600–1750*. New York: Academic Press, 1980.

Ward, Keith. *The Big Questions in Science and Religion*. West Constitution, PA: Templeton Foundation Press, 2008.

Ward, R. Gerard. "Earth's Empty Quarter? The Pacific Islands in a Pacific Century." *Geographical Journal* 155, no. 2 (1989): 235–246.

"A Warming Report: Scientists to Show New Evidence." *Time*, January 25, 2007. Accessed January 2, 2010. http://www.time.com/time/magazine/article/0,9171,1582333,00.html.

Waswo, Richard. *The Founding Legend of Western Civilization: From Virgil to Vietnam*. Hanover, NH: Wesleyan University Press, 1997.

Waswo, Richard. "The History That Literature Makes." *New Literary History* 19, no. 3 (1988): 541–564.

Wayman, Erin. "Evolution World Tour: The Cradle of Humankind, South Africa." *Smithsonian Magazine*, January 2012. Accessed November 26, 2013. http://www.smithsonianmag.com/travel/evotourism/Evotourism-World-Tour-The-Cradle-of-Humankind-South-Africa.html.

Weheliye, Alexander. *Phonographies: Grooves in Sonic Afro-Modernity*. Durham, NC: Duke University Press, 2005.

Wilfred, John Noble. "In African Cave, Ancient Paint Factory Pushes Human Symbolic Thought 'Far Back.'" *New York Times*, October 14, 2011.

Williams, David Lewis. *The Mind in the Cave: Consciousness and the Origin of Art*. London: Thames and Hudson, 2002.

Williams, Eric. *Capitalism and Slavery*. Chapel Hill: University of North Carolina Press, [1944] 1994.

Williams, Randall. *The Divided World: Human Rights and Its Violence*. Minneapolis: University of Minnesota Press, 2010.

Williams, Sherley Anne. *Dessa Rose: A Novel*. New York: Berkeley Books, 1986.

Williamson, Michael, and Robert Williamson. "Indigenous Peoples and the Morality of the Human Genome Project." *Journal of Medical Ethics* 25 (1999): 204–208.

Wills, Garry. *Inventing America: Jefferson's Declaration of Independence*. New York: Vintage, 1978.

Wilson, E. O. *Consilience: The Unity of Knowledge*. New York: Knopf, 1998.

Wilson, E. O. *Sociobiology: The New Synthesis*. Cambridge, MA: Harvard University Press, [1975] 2000.

Wilson, Jeanne. "Production Notes." In *West Indian Plays for Schools*, by Easton Lee, Sylvia Wynter, and Enid Chevannes, vol. 2, 7–25. Kingston, Jamaica: Jamaica Publishing House, 1979.

Wilson, William Julius. *The Truly Disadvantaged: The Inner City, the Underclass, and Public Policy*. Chicago: University of Chicago Press, 1987.

Woods, Clyde. "Life after Death." *Professional Geographer* 54, no. 1 (2002): 62–66.

Woodson, Carter G. *The Miseducation of the Negro*. New York: AMS Press, [1933] 1977.

Wynter, Sylvia. "Africa, the West and the Analogy of Culture: The Cinematic Text after Man." In *Symbolic Narratives/African Cinemas: Audience, Theory and Moving Image*, edited by June Givanni, 25–76. London: British Film Institute, 2000.

Wynter, Sylvia. "After the New Class: James, *Les Damnés*, and the Autonomy of Human Cognition." Paper presented at the conference "C. L. R. James: His Intellectual Legacies," Wellesley College, Wellesley, MA, April 19–21, 1991.

Wynter, Sylvia. "Afterword: Beyond Miranda's Meanings: Un/silencing the 'Demonic Ground' of Caliban's 'Woman.'" In *Out of the Kumbla: Caribbean Women and Literature*, edited by Carole Boyce Davies and Elaine Savory Fido, 355–372. Trenton, NJ: Africa World Press, 1990.

Wynter, Sylvia. *Beyond Liberal and Marxist Leninist Feminisms: Towards an Autonomous Frame of Reference*. San Francisco: Institute for Research on Women and Gender, 1982.

Wynter, Sylvia "Beyond the Categories of the Master Conception: The Counter-doctrine of the Jamesian Poiesis." In *C. L. R. James's Caribbean*, edited by Paget Henry and Paul Buhle, 63–91. Durham, NC: Duke University Press, 1992.

Wynter, Sylvia. "Beyond the Word of Man: Glissant and the New Discourse of the Antilles." *World Literature Today* 63 (autumn 1989): 637–647.

Wynter, Sylvia. "The Ceremony Found: Black Knowledges/Struggles, the Color Line, and the Third Emancipatory Breaching of the Law of Cognitive Closure." Keynote paper presented at the Collegium for African American Research: Black Knowledges, Black Struggles, Civil Rights — Transnational Perspectives, University of Bremen, Germany, March 26, 2009.

Wynter, Sylvia. "The Ceremony Must Be Found: After Humanism." *Boundary II* 12, no. 3 and 13, no. 1 (1984): 19–70.

Wynter, Sylvia. "Columbus and the Poetics of the *Propter Nos*." *Annals of Scholarship* 8, no. 2 (1991): 251–286.

Wynter, Sylvia. "Columbus, the Ocean Blue and 'Fables That Stir the Mind': To Reinvent the Study of Letters." In *Poetics of the Americas: Race, Founding and Textuality*, edited by Bainard Cohen and Jefferson Humphries, 141–164. Baton Rouge: Louisiana State University Press, 1992.

Wynter, Sylvia. "Conversation [with Daryl Cumber Dance]." In *New World Adams:*

Conversations with Contemporary West Indian Writers, edited by Daryl Cumber Dance, 276–282. Leeds: Peepal Tree Press, 1992.

Wynter, Sylvia. "Creole Criticism: A Critique." *New World Quarterly* 4 (1973): 12–36.

Wynter, Sylvia. "A Different Kind of Creature: Caribbean Literature, the Cyclops Factor and the Second Poetics of the Propter Nos." *Annals of Scholarship* 12, nos. 1/2 (1997): 153–172.

Wynter, Sylvia. *Do Not Call Us Negroes: How Multicultural Textbooks Perpetuate Racism*. San Jose, CA: Aspire Books, 1992.

Wynter, Sylvia. "Ethno or Socio Poetics." *Alcheringa/Ethnopoetics* 2 (1976): 78–94.

Wynter, Sylvia. "1492: A New World View." In *Race, Discourse, and the Origin of the Americas: A New World View*, edited by Vera Lawrence Hyatt and Rex Nettleford, 5–57. Washington, DC: Smithsonian Institution Press, 1995.

Wynter, Sylvia. "Gender or the Genre of the Human? History, the Hard Task of Dessa Rose, and the Issue for the New Millennium." Paper presented at symposium "Black Women Writers and the 'High Art' of Afro-American Letters," University of California, San Diego, CA, May 15–17, 1998.

Wynter, Sylvia. "'Genital Mutilation' or 'Symbolic Birth'? Female Circumcision, Lost Origins and the Aculturalism of Feminist/Western Thought." *Case Western Law Review, Colloquium: Bridging Society, Culture and Law: The Issue of Female Circumcision* 47, no. 2 (1997): 501–552.

Wynter, Sylvia. *The Hills of Hebron: A Jamaican Novel*. New York: Simon and Schuster, 1962.

Wynter, Sylvia. "Human Being as Noun, or Being Human as Praxis? On the Laws/Modes of Auto-institution and Our Ultimate Crisis of Global Warming and Climate Change." Paper presented in the Distinguished Lecture and Residency Series at the Center for African American Studies, Wesleyan University, Middletown, CT, April 23, 2008.

Wynter, Sylvia. "Human Being as Noun? Or Being Human as Praxis? Towards the Autopoetic Turn/Overturn: A Manifesto." Unpublished essay.

Wynter, Sylvia. "Is 'Development' a Purely Empirical Concept or Also Teleological? A Perspective from We the Underdeveloped." In *Prospects for Recovery and Sustainable Development in Africa*, edited by Aguibou Yansané, 299–316. Westport, CT: Greenwood Press, 1996.

Wynter, Sylvia. "Jonkonnu in Jamaica: Towards the Interpretation of Folk Dance as a Cultural Process." *Jamaica Journal* 4, no. 2 (1970): 34–48.

Wynter, Sylvia. *Maskarade*. In *West Indian Plays for Schools*, by Easton Lee, Sylvia Wynter, and Enid Chevannes, vol. 2, 26–55. Kingston, Jamaica: Jamaica Publishing House, 1979.

Wynter, Sylvia. "Meditations on History: *Dessa Rose* and Slavery Revisited." Paper presented at symposium "Black Women Writers and the 'High Art' of Afro-American Letters," University of California, San Diego, CA, May 15–17, 1998.

Wynter, Sylvia. "New Seville and the Conversion Experience of Bartolomé de Las Casas: Part One." *Jamaica Journal* 17, no. 2 (1984): 25–32.

Wynter, Sylvia. "New Seville and the Conversion Experience of Bartolomé de Las Casas: Part Two." *Jamaica Journal* 17, no. 3 (1984): 46–55.

Wynter, Sylvia. "Novel and History, Plot and Plantation." *Savacou* 5 (1971): 95–102.

Wynter, Sylvia. "On Disenchanting Discourse: 'Minority' Literary Criticism and Beyond." *Cultural Critique* 7 (fall 1987): 207–244.

Wynter, Sylvia. "One Love—Rhetoric or Reality? Aspects of Afro-Jamaicanism." *Caribbean Studies* 12, no. 3 (1972): 64–97.

Wynter, Sylvia. "On How We Mistook the Map for the Territory and Reimprisoned Ourselves in Our Unbearable Wrongness of Being, of *Désêtre*: Black Studies toward the Human Project." In *Not Only the Master's Tools: African American Studies in Theory and Practice*, edited by Lewis Gordon and Jane Anna Gordon, 107–169. New York: Paradigm Press, 2006.

Wynter, Sylvia. "The Pope Must Have Been Drunk, the King of Castile a Madman: Culture as Actuality and the Caribbean Rethinking of Modernity." In *Reordering of Culture: Latin America, the Caribbean and Canada in the 'Hood*, edited by Alvina Ruprecht and Cecilia Taiana, 17–41. Ottawa: Carleton University Press, 1995.

Wynter, Sylvia. "ProudFlesh Inter/Views: Sylvia Wynter." *ProudFlesh: New Afrikan Journal of Culture, Politics and Consciousness* 4 (2006): 1–35.

Wynter, Sylvia. "Rethinking 'Aesthetics': Notes towards a Deciphering Practice." In *Ex-Iles: Essays on Caribbean Cinema*, edited by Mbye Cham, 237–279. Trenton, NJ: Africa World Press, 1992.

Wynter, Sylvia. "Towards the Sociogenic Principle: Fanon, Identity, the Puzzle of Conscious Experience." In *National Identities and Socio-political Changes in Latin America*, edited by Mercedes F. Durán-Cogan and Antonio Gómez-Moriana, 30–66. New York: Routledge, 2001.

Wynter, Sylvia. "Tras el 'Hombre,' su última Palabra: Sobre el posmodernismo, les demnés y el principio sociogénico." In *La teoría política en la encrucijada descolonial*, edited by Alejandro De Oto, 51–124. Compiled by Walter Mignolo. Buenos Aires: Ediciones del Signo y Globalization and the Humanities Project, Duke University Press, 2009.

Wynter, Sylvia. "Unsettling the Coloniality of Being/Power/Truth/Freedom: Towards the Human, after Man, Its Overrepresentation—An Argument." *CR: The New Centennial Review* 3, no. 3 (2003): 257–337.

Wynter, Sylvia. "We Must Learn to Sit Down Together and Talk about a Little Culture: Reflections on West Indian Writing and Criticism." *Jamaica Journal* 2, no. 4 (1968): 23–32.

Wynter, Sylvia. "We Must Learn to Sit Down Together and Talk about a Little Culture: Reflections on West Indian Writing and Criticism." *Jamaica Journal* 3, no. 1 (1969): 27–42.

Wynter, Sylvia, and Greg Thomas. "Yours in the Intellectual Struggle." In *The Caribbean Woman Writer as Scholar: Creating, Imagining, Theorizing*, edited by Keshia N. Abraham, 31–70. Coconut Creek, FL: Caribbean Studies Press, 2009.

Yanagisako, Sylvia, and Carol Delaney. "Naturalizing Power." In *Naturalizing Power: Essays in Feminist Cultural Analysis,* edited by Sylvia Yanagisako and Carol Delaney, 1–22. New York: Routledge, 1995.

Zinn, Howard. *A People's History of the United States: 1492–Present.* New York: Harper and Row, 1980.

CONTRIBUTORS

Bench Ansfield is a doctoral student in American studies at Yale University. His research revolves around the interplay between gentrification, imprisonment, and feminist and queer antiviolence organizing.

Carole Boyce Davies is an African diaspora studies scholar who is professor of Africana studies and English at Cornell University. She is the author of *Left of Karl Marx: The Political Life of Black Communist Claudia Jones* (2008) and *Black Women, Writing and Identity: Migrations of the Subject* (1994) and has edited the following: *Ngambika: Studies of Women in African Literature* (1986); *Out of the Kumbla: Caribbean Women and Literature* (1990); and the two-volume *Moving beyond Boundaries* (1995): *International Dimensions of Black Women's Writing* (vol. 1) and *Black Women's Diasporas* (vol. 2). She is the coeditor with Ali Mazrui and Isidore Okpewho of *The African Diaspora: African Origins and New World Identities* (1999) and *Decolonizing the Academy: African Diaspora Studies* (2003) and general editor of the three-volume *Encyclopedia of the African Diaspora* (2008).

Demetrius L. Eudell is professor of history at Wesleyan University in Middletown, Connecticut. He has worked closely and extensively with Sylvia Wynter for the past two decades, including having published essays on her work.

Denise Ferreira da Silva authored *Toward a Global Idea of Race* (2007) and is professor of ethics at Queen Mary, University of London.

Katherine McKittrick is associate professor of gender studies at Queen's University in Ontario, Canada. She is the author of *Demonic Grounds: Black Women and the Cartographies of Struggle* (2006) and the coeditor, with Clyde Woods, of *Black Geographies and the Politics of Place* (2007). Her research explores black intellectual history as it co-relates to geography, science studies, and the arts.

Walter D. Mignolo is William H. Wannamaker Professor of Literature and Romance Studies at Duke University. He authored *The Idea of Latin America* (2005), *Local Histories/Global Designs* (2000), and *The Darker Side of the Renaissance* (2003).

Nandita Sharma is associate professor of sociology at the University of Hawai'i at Manoa. Her research interests address themes of human migration, migrant labor, national state power, ideologies of racism and nationalism, processes of identification and self-understanding, and social movements for justice. Sharma is an activist scholar whose research is shaped by the social movements she is active in, including No Borders movements and those struggling for the commons. She is the author of *Home Economics: Nationalism and the Making of "Migrant Workers" in Canada* (2006).

Rinaldo Walcott is director of the Women and Gender Studies Institute and associate professor at OISE University of Toronto. His research is in the area of black diaspora cultural studies, with an interest in queer, multicultural, and postcolonial concerns.

Sylvia Wynter is professor emerita in black (i.e., African and Afro-American) studies and Spanish and Portuguese at Stanford University. She had, however, initiated her first career as a Jamaican/West Indian anticolonial writer in London, where, as a then British colonial subject, she attended King's College, London, as well as Madrid University, Spain. After returning to a newly politically independent Jamaica in 1962, she joined the Mona faculty of the newly established University of the West Indies, teaching there for roughly a decade and writing for the newly established periodical *Jamaica Journal*.

With the eruption in the United States, in the wake of the civil rights movement, together with the struggle against several other *isms*—of major issues resonant with those that she had pursued in an anticolonial context, Wynter was invited to join the Department of Literature at the University of California, San Diego. Her task at UCSD was to aid in the development of the new Program in Third World Studies, which had been fought for by a range of nonwhite student activists. As the Third World umbrella category came to prove more and more unworkable, however, she moved to Stanford in 1974, where, resulting in a major part from student struggle in the wake of Martin Luther King's assassination, the Program of African and Afro-American (i.e., Black) Studies had also been established.

During the course of this historico-specific itinerary, Wynter has written more than sixty essays, all of which attend to questions of race and its ostensibly extra-humanly mandated hierarchical locations of "labor" and of "being human," this correlatedly thereby with the thematics of (mono)humanism, knowledge, and modernity. A first collection of these essays, titled *We Must Learn to Sit Down Together and Talk about a Little Culture: Decolonizing Essays, 1967–1984*, is forthcoming from Peepal Tree Press. She is the author of several plays and the novel *The Hills of Hebron* (1962), recently republished in 2010 by Ian Randle Press—introduced by Anthony Bogues and with an afterword, "Towards Aimé Césaire's 'Humanism Made to the Measure of the World': Reading *The Hills of Hebron* in the Context of Sylvia Wynter's Later Work," by Demetrius Eudell.

Note: Italicized numbers indicate a figure; n indicates an endnote behavior (*continued*)

human, 24, 63, 65, 196, 218, 240–41; institutionalized suprahuman influences on, 28, 69, 72–73; mimetic desire and, 19–20, 34–35, 49, 53, 60–61, 241–42; neurochemical elements underlying human, 11–12, 57–58, 72, 239–40; as product of mankind's *bios-mythoi* character, 28–29, 32; religion as a regulator of, 25–26, 37, 75n14; Wynter on human, 20, 33, 238, 239–41. *See also* reward-and-punishment

Bellarmine, Cardinal Robert, 14, 18, 35, 75n14

belonging: as context for racism and sexism, 90, 106, 148, 165–67, 171–77, 197; as product of cultural production, 219–20

biocentrism: as hindrance to the development of knowledge, 142, 145–47, 150–52, 156; alternatives to, 156–57, 160, 192; as assumption of secular, liberal thought, 14, 16, 18, 20, 34, 75n19; as influence on colonialism, 122n1, 145; challenges to, 23, 48, 59, 63, 69, 77–78n33, 152–53; challenges to by Césaire, 65, 66, 70, 73, 154; challenges to by Fanon, 57, 58, 59, 63; challenges to by Wynter, 33–35, 42, 44, 57, 94–95, 99, 235–36; consciousness and, 242–43, 244; cosmogony-based, 65; gender and, 162n23; global reach of, 18–20, 29, 103, 219; Heidegger's definition of, 30; humanness as conceived through, 16–17, 23, 29, 161n4, 247n54; and macro-origin stories, 11, 70, 107–8; race and, 6, 57–58, 102, 146–47, 237, 239, 242

bios-mythoi: as challenge to Darwinian concept of humanness, 29–30, 39, 155, 157–58, 199; alignment of with Fanon's concepts of skins and masks, 23, 25, 33, 54, 57; *bios* as agency of the human brain, 26–27, 44, 65, 156; and Césaire's hybrid human, 32, 66, 70, 75n13, 148; human initiation as evidence of our

hybrid nature, 35, 68, 80–81n69, 82n92; and Third Event origin of mankind, 28–29, 31, 32; Wynter's call for humanness based on concepts of, 5, 11, 16–18, 31, 35, 144–45, 152–54, 190. *See also* hybrid human beings

blacks: crossing of historico-cultural traditions from Africa to the Americas, 82n80, 208–9, 211, 219–20; diaspora, 61, 143–44, 155, 156, 158; double consciousness of educated, 47–54, 56; the DuBois-Barton exchange on names and naming, 226–28, 229, 245; DuBois on black mankind, 51–54; as dysselected or symbolically dead human beings, 47, 58–61; intellectuals, 205, 210–11, 226, 228–29, 231–34, 236; Jim Crow practices against, 226, 233; Locke on internal emancipation, 236; Marcus Garvey's UNIA-ACL, 41, 210–11, 222–23n23; Maroon, 213, 214; Middle Passage, 61, 62, 82n80, 171, 178, 217, 226; negritude, 60, 63, 88n144, 206, 210, 233–34; "nigger" as bourgeois malediction, 46–47, 54, 56, 60, 77–78n33, 146, 190; "nigger" in Wynter's Cartesian axis, 152–53, 155; plight of the *evolué* Frenchman, 48, 49, 52, 55–56, 58–60, 85n111; Poussaint on internal emancipation, 236; and Western hierarchical model of humanness, 95, 115–16, 119–21, 190; women's social service organizations, 232–33; Woodson on effects of stereotyping, 234–35. *See also* slavery

Black Skin, White Masks (1952), 13, 48, 52–53, 60, 77–78n33, 86n126, 88n144

Blombos Cave, 62–63, 66–69, 73

Bluest Eye, The (1970), 60, 228, 230, 236–37, 241–42, 245

body: the black, 126, 132; and concept of *pieza*, 113–15; and concepts of taint and filth, 126–27, 131, 134; in the context of space, 127, 128, 131–38, 139n3, 139–40n7, 140n9; portrayal of non–

Western corporeal aesthetics as not normal, 125, 230; portrayal of Western corporeal aesthetics as normal, 18–19, 60; the post-1492 realignment of human corporeal spectrum, 124, 125, 130, 180n9; and social construction of race, 149

brain: Césaire's theory of the human, 66, 70–72; and co-evolution of human language, 25–26, 69, 70–73, 80–81n69; and consciousness, 80n63, 88n147, 100, 145, 155–56, 159, 243; human *bios* as the, 32, 65, 66; and human creativity, 142, 154, 156–57, 159; implementing agency of the human, 26–27, 65; opioid system of the human, 10–11, 58, 65, 72, 80n63, 239–40, 241

Brathwaite, Kamau, 187, 200–201n8

brutality, 137, 143, 188, 193–94, 197–98, 242

capitalism: as outgrowth of colonialism, racism, and slavery, 6, 114–15, 122n6, 177, 212, 218; and market economy, 22, 113

Caribbean islands: as site for modernist experimentation in humanness, 186–88, 191–94, 197–98; black struggle and rebellion in the, 41, 46–47, 214, 216; colonization in the, 168, 177–78; ex-slave archipelago of the, 2, 39, 42, 46–47, 48, 50; as first site of the modern world system, 42, 92–94, 111, 164, 191, 221n6; indigenization of blacks by the environment of the, 203, 206–7, 209–10, 211–15, 219–20; intellectual heritage of the, 204–6, 210, 212, 215–16, 224nn68–69

Carnival, 209, 219

Carretta, Vincent, 230–31

Cartesian axis, 105n32, 124, 139n3, 152, 160

Césaire, Aimé: arguments by for a new science, 18, 30, 73, 75n13, 218; science of the word, 26–27, 32, 62–63, 65–66, 69–71, 154

cholera, 126, 139–40n7

civic humanism, 21, 35, 91, 94, 182n42

civil rights: struggles of the 1950s and 1960s, 137, 144, 184, 191, 211, 236, 243–44; Wynter on the struggles, 22, 23, 39, 41, 151–52

cleanliness, 131–32

code: DNA, 19, 29, 35, 70, 77n27, 87n130, 149; genetic, 33, 239; sociogenic of symbolic life or death, 56, 80–81n69, 83n92, 245n12; Wynter on the sociogenic code of symbolic life or death, 29–37, 42, 45, 47, 58, 65, 72; Wynter's concept of the biocentric master, 95, 96, 99, 103

cognition: autopoietic qualities of, 27–28, 107, 121, 136; shifts of human in response to change, 4, 32, 144–45; and shift toward ecumenical humanness, 44, 45, 66, 144, 148, 154–55; Wynter on shift toward a new human, 164, 166, 179, 218, 244. *See also* consciousness

colonialism: as incentive to reinvent humanness, 143, 147–48, 167, 234; antiracism as product of, 151, 175; autochthonous discourses, 172–78; basis of in human inequality, 5, 145, 148, 153, 171–72, 174, 176–77; and creation of Creole society in the Caribbean, 187, 191, 193, 194, 198, 204; Fanon on, 90; influence of on definition of humanness, 95–99, 104n9, 110–11, 113–18; migration as by-product of, 173, 176, 185–86; race-based exploitation as product of, 90–94, 106, 113, 120; racial violence as by-product of, 171, 173–74; Scott on, 189; the status of evolué Frenchmen, 48–49, 55, 59; victims construed as agents of, 174–75; Wynter on, 2, 21, 113, 120, 204, 206, 209–10. *See also* anticolonialism; coloniality; decolonialism

coloniality: decolonial reaction to, 107, 114, 115, 192; systematic character of, 108, 111, 192, 247n54; Wynter on concepts of, 1, 4, 90–92, 101, 111–13, 190. *See also* colonialism color line: as divider between native and non-native, 172–73; breaching of the, 52, 57, 60, 139n6; DuBois's concept of the, 51, 52, 95; Fanon's perception of a, 52, 59–60; Wynter's ideas concerning the, 87n130, 130–31, 146

Columbus: influence of his arrival in the Americas on the concept of habitability, 129–30, 167–68, 180n9; influence of his arrival in the Americas on the concept of humanness, 109, 130, 166–68; initial Columbian exchange, 170–71, 177–78; religious millenarian ideas of, 168; worldviews prior to the voyages of, 121; Wynter on the voyages of, 124, 164–68, 179, 182n39, 190

consciousness: challenges to the biocentric concept of, 59–60, 64, 154, 229, 231, 235–36, 243–44; Cleaver on, 83n98; collective sociocultural, 68–71, 109, 112, 116, 157, 240, 242–43; double, 45–46, 83n98, 84–85n106, 116, 118, 227; DuBois on double, 46, 47–48, 50–52, 227, 236; Fanon on, 46, 49–50, 56; Foucault on, 90; Freudian unconscious, 115; improvisation and, 159; as location of the *bios-mythoi* element of mankind, 31, 33, 35, 45; and perception of causality, 88n147; response of to extrahuman sociocultural mandates, 24, 28; Wynter on, 50–52, 56, 100, 118–19, 145–47, 201n22, 219. *See also* cognition

contamination, 125–26, 134–35, 137, 139–40n7. *See also* purification

Cooper, Anna Julia, 229, 232–33, 234

Copernicus, Nicolaus: tassertions of regarding Earth's movement, 14–15; contributions of to a self-correcting approach to cognition, 13–14; Copernican leap, 1, 13, 24, 46, 143, 144; influence of on ideas of man's place in the universe, 14–16, 73, 75, 121; influence of on science and astronomy, 13–14, 62, 121, 129, 244

cosmogony: Darwinian biocosmogony, 35, 38, 42, 47, 55, 58, 95; extrahumanly mandated elements underlying, 28, 36–38, 45, 80–81n69, 100, 238, 247n54; as necessarily preexistent to individual organisms, 21, 35, 36, 72, 83n92, 237; theo- regarding the origins of humanity, 16, 58, 80–81n69; trans- as cognitively empowering, 46, 49–50, 54, 56, 57–59; Wynter's hypothesis of auto-speciation and origin myths, 25, 30, 37, 57, 83n92, 93. *See also* origin myths; storytelling

cosmopolitanism: Appiah on, 194–97; based on multicultural values, 193, 194–95, 196–99; based on Western values, 192, 193–94, 196; and creolization, 193; Derrida on forgiveness and, 183, 192, 193; and multiculturalism, 186; vernacular, 193, 194, 198

cosmo-political ethics, 186, 193, 194, 197

creative work: as medium for ecumenical social change, 44–45, 61; creativity, 142, 144, 146, 155, 156, 209, 217; as product of all hybrid humans, 142, 144, 149–50, 154–60; Wynter's, 1–2, 203–5, 207, 210–11, 215–16

Creole: populace in Great Britain, 185, 200n4; society in the Caribbean, 186–88, 214

creolization: brutal context underlying, 187–88, 214, 223–24n57; and cosmopolitanism, 193, 196, 198; and indigenization, 206, 213; Wynter on, 200–201n8, 203, 213–14, 214–15, 218, 222n18

culture. *See* auto-instituting processes; autopoietic social systems; kin-recognizing behavior

damnés, les (the damned), 39, 87–88n139, 108, 124, 209

dance: as element of Carnival celebrations, 209; Jonkonnu folkdance, 204–6, 210–11, 213, 215, 220; Pygmy, 87n130

Darwin, Charles: revisions of theories of, 87n131; studies of natural selection by, 81n70, 84–85n106, 94; studies of phenotype-based ideas of beauty by, 76n23

Darwinism: as basis for biocentrism, 16, 29, 42, 75n19, 91, 95, 102, 161n4; as basis for Western origin stories, 10, 35–36, 58, 65, 80n67, 146, 239; as complement to the concept of economic man, 14; challenges to biogenetic theories based on, 66–67, 69, 72–73, 101, 147–48, 231, 244; influence of on ideas of man's place in the universe, 4, 121, 130; Malthusian, 10, 35, 37, 45, 80n65, 148–49, 151; Wynter on humanity's meta-Darwinian hybridism, 11, 16, 30–31, 36, 44, 67, 72–73

Dasein, 101–2, 104, 105n32

decolonialism: and claims of "natives," 172, 175, 176; and institution of a new form of humanness, 81–82n79, 115, 120, 179–80, 206–8; Wynter's *decolonial scientia* approach, 5, 116–18; Wynter's work in support of, 106–9, 112, 115–17, 169. *See also* anticolonialism; colonialism

decolonial scientia, 5, 116–18

deconcentration paradigm, 124, 127–28, 133–35, 137, 140n11

dehumanization, 105n24, 212, 217, 218, 220, 224n68

Derrida, Jacques, 5–6, 23, 63, 183, 192–94

difference: and concepts of cosmopolitanism and multiculturalism, 102, 193–94, 195, 197; importance of to establishing social hierarchy, 108–11, 130, 145, 148–49, 151, 155, 180n9; Wynter on racial as tool of Western colonialism, 91–92, 94, 97–98, 116, 165–66. *See also* lack

displacement: of indigenous peoples, 5, 21–22; of nonwhites from their communities, 61, 125, 128, 134, 137, 200n4,

217; transatlantic slavery as violent, 6, 112

DNA Code, 19, 29, 35, 70, 77n27, 87n130, 149

double consciousness, 83n98, 84–85n106, 116, 118; DuBois's concept of, 46, 47, 50, 227, 236

Douglass, Frederick, 229, 232

DuBois, W. E. B.: the concept of double consciousness of, 46–52, 56, 59, 83n95, 116, 227–28, 235–36; the concept of the color line of, 52–53, 95, 130–31; exchange with Roland Barton, 226–28, 228, 245

dysgenic status: as Western sociocultural construct, 57, 77n28, 126, 130, 134, 137; as symbolic death, 17, 18, 37, 42, 47, 59, 133. *See also* eugenic status

dysselection: as natural human category, 7–8, 10, 37, 47, 95, 107, 145–46; as sociocultural condemnation against outsiders, 7, 95, 99, 146, 155; blackness as natural, 46, 47; the Darwinian concept of, 81n70, 84–85n106, 91, 95; rejection of the concept of, 44, 64–65, 146–47, 220, 244

Earth: as theocentrically degraded location, 14–15, 93; discovery of the movement of, 14, 17, 18, 75n14; navigable, habitable nature of, 166, 167–68; temperate versus torrid regions of, 93, 129–30; Wynter on land as, 212, 213, 215

Enlightenment: concepts of freedom, 103; concepts of humanness, 124, 130–31, 133, 186, 192, 231, 237; ideas regarding cities, 131–32, 186, 195; Wynter's criticisms of post- thought, 91–92, 98–99

episteme. *See* knowledge

epistemological resignation, 124, 128, 133

Equiano, Olaudah, 229–32, 236–37, 245–46n13

Erikson, Erik, 25, 38

ethics, 36, 68–69, 91, 197–98, 207, 216

eugenic status: as an implication of symbolic life, 37, 42; as a Western socio-cultural construct, 17–18, 47, 57, 77n28, 130–31, 133. *See also* dysgenic status
eusocial systems: the autopoietic character of human, 29, 32–38, 43, 84n101; beehives as, 28, 34; the interaltruistic character of human, 27, 28–29, 38, 71

Fanon, Frantz: *Black Skin, White Masks*, 13, 48, 52–53, 60, 77–78n33, 86n126, 88n144; concept of corporeal malediction of, 13, 78n36, 230, 236, 241, 247n46; and concept of double consciousness, 45–46, 51–54, 56; concept of sociogeny of, 2, 11, 53–54, 74n6, 115–16, 147; influence of on Wynter's thought, 5, 10–11, 25, 218, 229, 235–36, 244–45; plight of as an *evolué* Frenchman, 48–49, 52, 55–60, 85nn111–12, 86n126, 116, 161–62n20; skins-masks model of humanness of, 16, 22–23, 31, 33, 63, 69, 77–78n33, 81–82n79; work of on auto-centered societies, 50, 54–60, 86n123, 87n129, 90, 108, 206–7
feminism: consciousness and, 48; feminist thought, 40, 151–52, 207–8; and humanness, 60, 162n23, 191; and racism, 49
filth, 131–32
First Event, 31. *See also* Second Event; Third Event
1492: as turning point in history, 5, 85–86n118, 109–11, 122n6, 127–29, 164–68, 182n39; geo-racial restructuring following voyages of, 42, 127, 128, 133, 136, 171, 177; Wynter on significance of, 45–46, 124, 168, 170, 179, 180n9, 182n42, 190
Foucault, Michel: on consciousness, 50, 81n71, 84n103, 84–85n106, 90, 103–4; philosophical concepts of, 112–13, 132, 237–38; Wynter on philosophical thought of, 91–92, 94–100

Frazier, E. Franklin, 226, 232, 233, 234
freedom: struggles for, 61, 197–99, 209; universal human, 60, 62–63, 236; Western concepts of, 11, 62, 103, 196–97, 242; Wynter on, 61–63, 94, 97, 100, 152–53

Galileo, 14, 75n14, 116, 148, 244
Garvey, Amy Ashwood, 207, 211, 222–23n23
Garvey, Marcus, 41, 210, 211, 222–23n23
gaze from below, 11, 21, 22, 42, 50, 51–52, 76n24
gender: Cooper on defense of socially weak, 233; Morrison on blackness and, 60; as role performance, 33, 74n7, 220, 232–33, 245n12; Wynter on, 7, 33, 78–79n39, 79n58, 204, 207–8, 216
genetic codes, 25, 26–27, 28, 35, 71
genre-specific models: as basis for defining kin and communal relationships, 27, 31, 33–34, 37–38, 67–69, 83n92, 245n12; the autopoietic character of, 28, 71; as being embedded in human consciousness, 50, 52, 55, 57–58, 72, 241; as formulations designed to define humanity, 25, 28–30, 38–39, 229; homogenizing influence of, 19, 20–21, 76n23, 77n23, 242; need to replace, 44–45, 66, 71, 240; presentation of as based in extrahuman mandates, 28, 32–33, 35, 38, 58–59, 71–72; as tools for explaining economic dynamics, 17–19, 22, 40, 42–43; and the Westernized approach to human interactions, 17–20, 47
geo-racial thinking, 124, 127, 132, 135–36, 137, 139n3
ghetto-specific behaviors, 127, 128, 133, 140–41n26
Glissant, Edouard, 2, 5, 187, 188, 205, 206
global concerns: ethics of knowledge transmission, 18, 29, 59, 64, 70, 83n91, 104, 116–19; global linear thinking (of 1492), 110–11, 113, 165, 177–78; global warming and climate instability, 20–22, 24, 65, 77n29; human rights,

39, 102, 118, 193, 195; interconnected
nature of, 44, 169–70; internationalism as means of addressing problems,
196; market-oriented economics, 19,
26, 37, 43, 66; migrations, 181n25; 187;
nuclear politics, 43; poverty, 24, 37,
43, 66, 139n5; protection of vulnerable
populations, 39, 102, 103, 110; racism, 7,
10–11, 102, 130–31, 227; recovery from
colonialism, 39–40, 42, 44, 51, 170–71,
178–79, 180n9; thinking globally,
43–44, 187, 189, 192–93, 195–97; Western biocentric attitudes, 19, 21, 22, 24,
29–30, 69, 76nn23–24; Wynter's work
on, 92, 95, 97–101, 113, 120–21, 143–44,
243–44

God: and concept of *propter nos*, 15–16,
168; religious conceptualizations of,
21, 80–1n69, 87n130, 109, 129; Renaissance reconceptualization of, 15–16

guide quotes: locations of, 12–13; regarding, 11–12, 62, 63, 78n36

habitability: degrees of, 136, 139n3; and
humanness, 125, 128–30, 138, 166, 168,
224n68; versus uninhabitability, 124,
129, 130, 135–36

Haiti, 17, 20, 46, 64, 194

Hall, Stuart, 175, 185, 187, 189, 193, 194

Harlem Renaissance, 210–11, 236

Hawai'i, 174–75, 176

Heaven/Earth divide, 15

Hegel, Georg Wilhelm Friedrich, 96, 98,
101, 110

Heidegger, Martin: on being human,
13, 23, 30, 62, 93, 237; on being in the
world, 101–2, 105n32

Hendrix, Jimi: the music of, 156, 157,
159–60, 163nn44–45; the social commentaries of, 157–58, 160

hierarchical system: extension of to
colonial societies, 166, 171, 177, 208;
globalization of the Western, 109;
Marxist assumptions concerning the
Western, 41, 42; of medieval Western

society, 15, 244; of modern Western
society, 7, 29, 192, 242; overlay of racial
difference in the Western, 46, 53, 116,
130, 153, 208, 227; as something to be
overthrown by global society, 166, 170,
211, 219, 232–33

Hills of Hebron, The (1962), 203–4, 207,
209, 214, 215–16

homeplace, 126–28, 133, 134, 136, 140n9,
140–41n26

homo narrans, 25, 30, 44, 63, 67, 69, 72

homo oeconomicus: as basis for Man2, 10,
12, 14, 35, 69; as creator of a globalized
origin narrative, 24, 26, 29, 35, 38,
42–43; displacement of, 42, 44, 66,
70, 77–78n33, 244–45; as normal and
virtuous man, 19, 20, 21, 22, 24, 26,
238–39; overrepresentation of as a natural being, 21, 38, 47, 65–66, 82n84, 219

homo sapiens, 67, 69

human: as a natural organism, 16, 18, 21,
23, 29–30, 37, 47, 63; neurological
aspects of being, 144–46, 149–50,
154–57, 241–42

human body. *See* body

humanity: and concept of the *referent-we*,
24, 36, 38–39, 45, 63; Western mo-
nopolization of concept of, 76n23,
77–78n33, 102–4, 161–62n20, 196–97,
221n6; Wynter's desire for a more ecumenical concept of, 66, 72–73, 91–92,
106–10, 118–22, 166–70

humanness: colonial encounters as an
incentive for redefining, 143–44, 150,
153, 180n9; and conceptualization
of Human Being as a verb, 3, 23, 122,
155–56, 160–61, 179; and consciousness,
242–43; hybrid nature of, 29, 156–57;
the interaction of with habitability, 125,
128, 130–31, 133, 135–36, 138, 139n3; non-
European ideas of, 5, 73, 88n144, 137,
160, 194; Western hierarchical model
of, 7, 16, 18, 46, 94–95, 107, 109; Wynter's reconceptualization of the term,
8–9, 11–12, 93, 108, 111, 151–52, 190–91

hybrid human beings: as challenge to bio-centric Man, 93, 144, 145, 149, 157, 169; as nullification of concept of natural *selection/dysselection*, 17, 44–45; the autopoietic quality of, 27–28, 68–69; and Césaire's science of the Word, 17–18, 32–33, 66, 69–71, 73; as embodiment of genetic and nongenetic codes, 17–18, 26–29, 34–35, 57–58, 75n11, 236; Third Event origins of, 63, 68–73, 83, 84n101, 240, 244; Wynter's concept of, 11, 16–18, 23, 25, 31–37, 50–54, 72–73. See also *bios-mythoi*

identity: categories of, 78–79n39; and cosmopolitanism, 195–97; intellectual movements to address, 151; place as an element of individual, 133–38; politics of, 19, 184–85, 198

imperialism, 44, 46, 51, 62, 85n111, 88n144, 198

indigenization: and creolization, 185, 213, 223–24n57; indigenism, 181n22, 200–201n8; and Jonkonnu dance, 208, 211; Wynter on, 203, 206, 213–15, 217, 219–20, 224n68

indigenous peoples: autochthonous discourses, 172–78; black slaves as to their settled locations, 6, 181n22, 200–201n8; blood quantum rules, 173; concept of indigeneity, 170–71, 173; concepts of the Native and Native-ness, 173–74, 175; conflicts of with imperialist settlers, 51, 85n111, 243; connectivity to the land as a challenge to, 171–72, 173; construed as lacking humanness by early Western thinkers, 81–82n79, 94–95, 119; co-victims construed as agents of colonialism, 167, 174–77, 222n20; and decolonization, 172, 175, 176; migratory or stateless, 22–23; nonnative status as a denial of connectivity and rights, 171–75, 176, 177; settler colonists cast as non-, 5, 6, 171–75, 181n25, 229; as symbols of

nationalism, 174–76; as victims of Western racial discrimination, 130, 143–44, 146, 172

initiation: as social rebirth, 33, 34–35, 67–69, 78n35; as sociocultural auto-instituting tool, 25, 32, 49, 55, 83n91, 84n101, 85n124; the Blombos Cave site, 66–69

instructions: first set of (genetic codes), 25, 26–27, 28, 35, 71; second set of (nongenetic codes), 25, 26–27, 33–35, 38, 58, 71, 83n92

international. See global problems

Isaac, Glyn, 36

Jacobs, Harriet, 232

Jamaica, 41, 187, 205–6, 210, 213

James, C. L. R., 81n79, 111–14, 121, 199, 205, 212

Jews: conceptualization of as Other in some societies, 119, 239; forced immigration of Spanish, 110–11; and traditions of initiation, 84n101

Jonkonnu: as cultural manifestation, 203, 208–9, 211, 219–20; banning of, 208–9; as portrayed in *Maskarade*, 207, 208, 217, 220–21; Wynter's work on, 203, 205–6, 211, 213, 216, 217

Judeo-Christian worldview, 93, 120, 143, 228, 229, 231, 240

Julien, Isaac, 184–86, 198

juridical power: as tool to subjugate colonized peoples, 91–94, 96, 97–99, 231, 243; global dominance of Western-based, 102, 103–4

Kant, Immanuel, 96, 97, 101, 102, 195

Katrina, Hurricane, 5, 125–26, 134–36, 137–38

kin-recognizing behavior: initiation as tool for ensuring, 34, 68; within human groupings, 25, 27, 32, 33, 38, 45, 57

knowledge: assumptions underlying modern Western, 26, 43–44, 65, 81n71,

96, 136, 238; challenges to modern Western, 23, 66, 91–92; dominance of the Church over medieval, 10, 14, 16, 20, 24, 93–94, 178; failure of modern academia to facilitate new, 22, 44–45, 119, 150–53, 162n23; modern hegemony of economics over, 26; and modern system of learning, 32–33, 43–44, 47, 65, 66, 71, 83n91; pre–Renaissance hegemony of theology over human, 26; Scholastic, 15, 16, 20, 91, 129; Wynter's challenges to modern Western, 95–96, 199; Wynter's criticisms of modern academic, 146–47

lack: as a necessary attribute to validate the social status of not lacking, 136, 235, 237, 241–42; as applied to homosexuality, 84–85n106; attributed to blacks by Western social thinking, 3, 138, 174, 245; and concept of inferiority, 47, 54, 85–86n118, 110–11, 146, 226–28, 235; role of corporeal aesthetics in construing a sense of, 18–19, 60, 77n28, 236; sense of among some blacks, 228–31, 236–37, 239; and social concepts of being normal or abnormal, 47–48, 55–56, 59; and social concepts of being rational or irrational, 10, 85–86n118, 93–94, 97–99; tolerance and, 183–84. See also difference
land: as a means of controlling or empowering people, 167, 174–75; as basis for distinguishing native from nonnative, 170–71, 173, 222n20; as basis for sense of self and belonging, 167, 181n22, 200–201n8, 206–7, 217, 219–20; and concept of property, 136, 167, 174, 177, 215; connectivity and, 171; geo-racial thinking, 111, 127, 140n9, 173–74, 177; imperialist claims to, 113, 219–20; medieval ideas of habitable and uninhabitable, 129–30, 135–36; slave provision grounds, 211–13; sovereignty

and, 189, 199; the territorialization of, 167, 170–71
language: as characteristic of the Third Event of humanness, 25–26, 69; as constraint on creativity, 27–28; as tool of colonialism, 5, 117–18; as tool of power, 12–13, 115–17, 119, 131, 135, 137; the co-evolution of with human brain, 72, 154–55; as embodiment of cultural conceptions, 108, 112–13, 115–17, 126, 127–28; and human genetics, 70, 89n163, 239; Wynter on, 205–6, 218. See also storytelling
Latin-Christian Europe, 10, 14, 15, 20, 24
Locke, Alain, 211, 236
logos. See bios-mythoi

Malthusian scarcity, 24, 35, 37, 45, 65, 80n65, 131
man: as an organism, 13; cultural concepts regarding the good, 83n92; Douglass on, 232; Fallen, 14, 15, 36; Fanon on, 63, 81–82n79, 85n112; Foucault on, 91, 237–38; the Shari'ati explanation of man, 119; Smith's concept of economic, 238–39; Western concepts of, 24, 30, 49, 81n71, 91, 93–94, 211–12; Wynter on, 78n36, 92. See also overrepresentation of Western Man as human
Man1: as invention of Renaissance thought, 10, 35, 39, 46–47; Wynter on the epistemological transformation of, 9–10, 83n93, 93, 107, 143; Wynter's model of humanness, 39, 46
Man2: challenges to dominance of, 39, 42, 77–78n33, 94–95; as one representation of humanity, 46, 47, 69, 77–78n33, 83nn92–93, 107; Wynter's conceptualization of as economic man, 10, 35, 69; Wynter's conceptualization of as monohumanist man, 22, 24, 37, 44–45, 143
markets: free, 19, 22, 41, 43; global, 113, 196, 212

Marxism: acceptance of Smith's economic behaviorism by, 40–41, 238; concept of "opium of the people" of, 89n165; Fanon on colonialism and, 81–82n79, 90; the influences of on modern thinkers, 196, 224n68; the of C. L. R. James, 5, 112–13, 122n8; Wynter on the limitations of, 39–41, 42, 96, 114–15, 212, 215, 217–18

Masai people, 21, 22, 78n35

Maskarade (1973): as critique of the Western social order, 200–201n8, 203–5, 207; as analysis of Caribbean plantation society, 216; character of Miss Gatha in, 207–8, 216–17; performance of, 203–4, 220–21, 222n12; place of in Wynter's formulation of her theories, 215–16, 217, 219–21; significance of Jonkonnu as portrayed in, 207–9, 211, 217

Maturana, Humberto R.: "realization of the living" concept of, 3–4, 7, 145; work on autopoiesis, 25, 27–28, 106–8, 110, 111, 121

Middle Ages: concepts of purity and taint and Other during the, 94–95, 99, 131, 239; dominance of the Church over human knowledge during the, 10, 14–16, 20, 24, 93–94, 178; Latin-Christian Europe during the, 10, 14, 15, 20, 24; medieval concepts of the world, 124, 125, 128–29; social hierarchies and tensions during the, 182n42, 244; Wynter's study of social transitions during the, 95, 97–98, 113, 118, 190, 243

Middle Passage, the, 61, 62, 82n80, 171, 178, 217, 226

migration: borders and, 117, 176–77, 181n25; forced and the concept of *decolonia scientia*, 117, 125–26, 128, 137, 139–40n7; immigrants, 5, 171–72, 173, 200n4; influence of on modern globalization, 187–88, 189, 194; native hostility toward mobility, 167, 171–72, 176, 181n25; relationship of people to land, 173–74; seasonal as a lifestyle, 78n35; settlers forced into, 167, 171–72, 174–76, 181n25

mobility, 167, 171–72, 176, 181n25

modernity: as an outgrowth of violence and colonialism, 143, 145, 178, 181n22, 182n42, 187, 221n6; Enlightenment modernity, 184, 186, 192, 198; European modernity, 189, 197, 204, 212; forgiveness as a factor in facilitating, 193–94; and promises of the future, 2, 157, 186, 188–89, 194, 197

monohumanism: as a product of extrahuman or divine mandate, 37, 58; autopoietic character of, 44–45; creation of the concept of biocentric man by, 23, 37; creation of the concept of economic man by, 10, 14, 21, 35, 42, 77–78n33; globalization of by the West, 21–23, 31–32, 47, 57, 60, 82n84, 245; Man2 as a creation of, 22, 23, 24, 35, 42, 45, 77–78n33; need for the global replacement of, 11, 24, 62, 65, 76n24, 77–78n33; premises of liberal, 10, 11, 14, 21–23, 31–32, 35

Morrison, Toni, 60, 228, 241, 242; *The Bluest Eye*, 60, 228, 230, 236–37, 241–42, 245

multiculturalism: Appiah on, 194–96; in the Caribbean, 186, 194, 199; and cosmopolitanism, 186, 193, 195–96; and creolization, 185; popular, 185

mythoi. See *bios-mythoi*

myths. *See* origin myths

names and naming, 197, 226–28

nationalism, 174–76

natives. *See* indigenous peoples

naturalization: academic theory as a tool of, 124–25, 127; of concept of race, 10, 151, 154; concept of natural man, 92, 94–95, 145, 161n4, 238; desupernaturalization, 13–14, 35, 244, 247n54; of idea that economic man represents all men, 65, 238, 245;

of opinion as knowledge, 86n124,
107, 108, 139n5, 245; of racially biased
colonial interactions, 91, 94, 115, 175; of
the selected-dysselection dichotomy,
7–8, 10, 133–34, 146–47, 244; of social
injustices, 11, 127–28, 156; of Western
ideas concerning humanness as being
universal, 13, 18, 35, 48, 59, 91
natural rights, 49
natural scarcity: modern acceptance of
the idea of Malthusian, 19, 24, 26;
Wynter on Malthusian, 11, 37, 65, 70
natural sciences: Césaire's criticisms of
the, 17–18, 30, 64, 71–72; and ethics,
20; the influence of Darwinian theory
on the, 21, 35, 87nn130–31; popular
acceptance of the models and theories
of the as facts and givens, 15, 23, 24,
29, 35; and the revolution in thinking
initiated by Copernicus, 16; Wynter
on the, 2–3, 100, 103, 145–50, 236, 240,
244–45
natural selection, 76n23, 81n70, 87n131, 91,
94, 244–45, 247n54
negritude, 60, 63, 88n144, 206, 210, 233–34
Negro. See black
New Orleans: antidemolition struggles
in, 5, 138; as site of deconcentration, 134, 135, 140n11; as symbol of
contamination, 125, 126, 134, 139n6;
controversy over public housing in,
138, 140n11; gradations of habitability
exhibited in, 136; post–Katrina, 5, 125,
135, 137–38
Newton, Sir Isaac, 116, 148
nocebo, 34, 50, 58, 65, 72, 80n63, 80–81n69
nongenetic codes, 25, 26–27, 33–35, 38, 58,
71, 83n92
nonnegotiable imperatives, 57–59, 72–73
normal and abnormal. See lack

opiate-blocking behavior, 58, 72, 80n63
opiate-rewarding behavior: as neurochemical response, 34, 58, 72, 80n63;
and societal sanctions or censure on

the individual, 25, 48, 50, 58–59, 68, 72,
80–81n69
origin myths: as basis for eusocialization,
25, 27, 34, 58; connection of mankind
to the divine in, 36, 38, 57–58, 72–73,
80–81n69; Darwinian science as,
72n23, 80n67; French, 49, 52; and
human faculty of language, 72; Pygmy,
54; Western post–Renaissance, 77n28,
84nn101–2. See also cosmogony;
storytelling
Other: as basis for denying connection,
171; as epitomizing symbolic death, 47,
48, 116, 130–31, 191, 229; as necessary
for confirming humanness, 143–44,
150, 152, 190, 232, 236–37, 239–41;
spaces occupied by, 133, 193n3; Western attributions to those regarded as,
46–47, 54, 99, 117–19
overrepresentation of Western Man
as human, 6, 38–39, 92, 118, 151, 157;
Wynter on the, 9–10, 31, 186, 191, 218.
See also man

Pecola. See *Bluest Eye*
phenotype, 76n23, 77n28, 87n131, 98, 127,
146, 148
placebo, 34, 50, 58, 59, 65, 72, 80n63,
80–81n69
plantations: and colonization, 145, 181n22,
188; and creolization, 213–15; folklore
and folk cultures as outgrowths against,
212–13; Hawaiian, 175; provision
grounds, 211, 213–14, 215, 216; and race-
based social hierarchy, 153, 209–21; and
slavery, 6, 187–88, 194, 200–201n8, 205
post–Enlightenment thought, 91–92, 98,
99, 103, 124, 133
poverty: archipelagos of, 3, 39, 186, 191;
and blackness, 5, 125; concentrated,
126–27, 128, 132, 134, 140–41n26;
deconcentration of, 124, 127–28; as
one of many interconnected human
problems, 43–44, 81n76, 124, 139n5,
148; as social illness and death, 37, 43

praxis: gender as, 33–34; humanness as a praxis of being by humans, 3–4, 5, 7–8, 23; mind as, 44, 70–71; ritual initiation as transformative, 68–69; Wynter on the need for a new intellectual, 62–63, 67–68, 144, 154, 160–61

Price-Mars, Jean, 20, 181n22, 200–201n8, 205–6

property, 136, 167, 174, 177, 215

propter nos ("for us"): need to reject a particularistic understanding of, 167, 169–70, 174;

propter nos homines ("for us men" or "for mankind"), 16, 73; Renaissance reconceptualization of, 15–16, 73, 75, 168; Wynter's ideas concerning the concept of, 3, 5, 15–16, 116, 167–70, 220

pseudospeciation, 25, 37, 38, 42, 69, 70–71

purification, 125, 127–28, 134, 137, 140n11. *See also* contamination: contagion as a the link between toxic bodies and places, 131, 134–35, 136, 137; purity and humanness, 131; racial and ethnic purity, 139–40n7, 175; removal of urban blight as geo-racial, 126, 134–35, 137; Victorian concepts of purity and cleanliness, 126, 131, 139–40n7

Pygmy people, 22, 50, 54–59, 86n123, 87n130

Quijano, Anibal: work of on race, 92, 114; work of on the concept of coloniality, 90–91

race: as category of identity, 78–79n39, 192; as unsolved global problem, 7, 76n24, 77n28, 154–55, 175, 183–85, 242–43; as product of economics, 40, 179, 208; in context of colonialism, 51, 90, 109, 111, 116, 167; Darwinian-Malthusian naturalization of the idea of, 10; DuBois on, 52–53; Foucault on, 91–93, 97–99; and ideas of superiority and inferiority of peoples, 47, 88n144, 125, 140n9, 218,

232–35, 242; minority discourse, 199; "the idea of," 91–93; Wynter on, 91–93, 120, 130–31, 151–53, 164–65, 240–41

racism: antiracism, 175; as sociocultural hatred, 77n28, 77–78n33, 105n24, 122n6, 174, 247n46; dependency of early capitalism on, 114; and early voyages to America, 109–11, 122n6; and European concept of Man, 118, 154, 237; influence of on science, 87n130, 142, 148, 149, 150, 155; land-based as tool of autochthonous discourse, 173–76

rational and irrational. *See* lack

reason: as primary characteristic of the Renaissance *homo politicus*, 15–16, 94; as a quality of Western man, 3; lack of as quality of inferior beings, 3, 56; transcendental, 91–92, 96, 98, 101–2; Wynter on, 92, 94, 97–98, 118

rebellion: Canboulay Riots (Trinidad), 209; grand and petit marronage as forms of slave, 214; Guyana Riots (1961), 212; world-changing in medieval Europe, 178–79, 182n42

referent-we: as defining quality of community, 27, 33–34, 38, 57–58, 67–68, 70–72; as goal in achieving humanness, 7, 25, 44–45; and concept of us-not us, 58; the of Man, 24, 38–39, 56, 57, 73

Renaissance: conceptualizations of mankind, 10, 91, 108, 118, 119, 121; the Copernican leap as iconic of the transformation, 13, 15, 24, 116; and the decline of theological hegemony, 73; humanism, 15, 16, 73; sociopolitical change during the, 113

representations: autochthonic of native versus nonnative, 172–74, 176, 177; auto-instituting quality of societal, 238–42; in context of colonialism, 169–71, 181n22; Darwinian of human origins, 69, 76n23; of difference, 91; of European man as symbolizing all of humanity, 191, 218–19, 245; of options and opinions as being natural, 86n124, 91, 95, 97, 99–101, 103; societal of human origins, 34, 36, 37–38, 58–59, 72, 80n67; stereotyping and negative of blacks, 226–28, 228–29, 231–32, 236–37; symbolic of people and places, 127, 130, 132, 134, 169, 244; Wynter on modes of, 165

resistance. *See* violence

reward-and-punishment: as neurochemical system of the human brain, 10, 25, 34, 65, 239–40, 244; as social tool for controlling behavior, 45, 48, 50, 58–60, 68, 71–72, 146; and Marxian concept of "opiate of the people," 89n165; mimetic desire, 19–20, 34–35, 49, 53, 60–61, 241–42; placebo and nocebo, 34, 50, 58, 59, 65, 72, 80n63, 80–81n69. *See also* behavior

Rorty, Richard, 22, 30, 65, 71

San people, 22, 78n35, 84n101

Scholasticism, 15, 16, 20, 91, 129

science of the word. *See* Word

scientia: decolonial, 5, 116–18; Hendrix's music as an embodiment of, 159–60; Wynter's vision of, 100, 115–16, 142, 148–50, 154, 156, 158

Scott, David, 189, 196, 219, 224n69

Second Event, 25, 31, 72. *See also* First Event; Third Event

segregation, 41, 48, 135, 227, 233

sense of self, 25, 167, 200n4, 240, 243, 244

settler: the antisettler bias of autochthonous discourse, 172–78; land as the basis for distinguishing native from, 170–71, 173–76, 222n20; settler colonialism, 5, 6, 171, 174–75, 181n25, 229; settler imperialism, 85n111, 217

slavery: as a basis for Western modernization and expansion, 42, 62, 114, 171–72, 178; African slave trade, 112–14, 245–46n13; in ancient world, 85–86n118; and concept of freedom, 152; concept

of slaves as separate species, 49, 231–32; grand and petit marronage, 214; influence of ex-slave archipelago of the Caribbean, 2, 39, 41–42, 45–50, 55, 181n22, 200–201n8; man-to-earth relationship within, 213, 215; race and, 114, 149, 231–32; the slave rebellion in Haiti, 46–47; symbolisms of slave ships, 61–62, 82n80; Western abolition of as a paradox, 46–47; Wynter on, 61, 83n93, 143, 212, 219–20. *See also* blacks

Smith, Adam, 39–40, 238–39

soap, 131

social change: black women's clubs that addressed broad, systemic, 232–33; importance of challenging established thinking to achieve, 138; and matter of true forgiveness, 193–94; state intervention to promote healthy, 195, 196, 198

sociogeny: as element of humanness, 16, 23, 69; *decolonia scientia* in context of, 116–17; Fanon's concept of, 2, 5, 11, 23, 53–54, 74n6, 115–16; Wynter's ideas concerning, 6, 11, 54, 115, 147, 229, 240

Steele, Claude, 235, 239

stereotype threat, 235, 239

storytelling: as tool of human auto-speciation, 28–29, 31, 44–45, 50, 63, 71; as tool of Western sociopolitical influence, 29–30, 32, 65; connection of mankind to the divine in, 36, 38, 57–58, 72–73, 80–81n69; use of by man to represent himself, 11, 25, 33–34, 55, 58, 69, 71–73. *See also* cosmogony; language; origin myths

studia humanitatis, 9–10, 13–14, 15

symbolic death, 19, 32, 33–34, 37, 47, 58–60, 80n69

symbolic life: auto-instituting quality of, 30, 32–35, 45, 57–59, 80–81n69, 83n92, 96; as Western sociocultural construct, 18, 29–30, 37–38, 42, 47, 65, 83n91; kin-recognizing quality of, 25, 27, 45, 67–68, 71–72

temperate zone, 93, 124, 129, 130

territorialization: as act of imperialism, 44, 51, 76n23, 104n9, 167, 177–79; as act to deny rights to long-term residents, 170–71, 173–76; globalized humanness as replacement for, 70, 151, 167–70

theocentrism, 14, 18, 73, 89n165, 120, 243, 244

theology: Christian as basis for knowledge in pre–Renaissance Europe, 10, 14–15, 16, 18, 24; influence of on human behavior, 37, 80–81n69, 88n147, 108, 116–17, 143, 182n42

Third Event: and inception of supra-individual consciousness, 35, 44, 63, 67, 84n101; as origin of the *bios-mythoi* human being, 25, 28–29, 30–31, 58, 69, 70–71, 73

Third Event. *See also* First Event; Second Event

tolerance, 183–84

Trobriand Islanders, 83n92

Trouillot, Michel-Rolph, 214

truth of solidarity, 20, 22, 29–30, 32, 45, 67

uninhabitable spaces: areas of concentrated poverty as, 127, 128, 132; association of with the bodies that inhabit them, 133, 134; European concepts of torrid zones as, 124, 129, 180n9; Wynter on humanist merging of habitable with, 129–30, 135–36

urban homeplace. *See* homeplace

urban renewal: gentrification, 128; in post–Katrina New Orleans, 124, 128, 140n14

Varela, Francisco J., 3–4, 7, 25, 27–28, 106, 107, 145

violence: as incentive for resistance and change, 61, 171, 178–79, 181n22, 193, 234; brutality, 143, 188, 193–94, 197–98, 242; concentration and extermination camps, 105, 184; continuing influence of colonial on society, 3–4, 113, 143, 160, 162n23, 167; fears of within a dominant group, 208, 209; forgiveness following, 193–94; indigenization as cultural resistance to, 206–7, 213, 214; mass displacement, 21–22, 78n35, 137, 140n9, 167, 176; racial, 3, 125, 185, 212; rebellions, 178–79, 209, 212; Rediker on "four violences," 178; and terror, 61, 165, 178, 184, 200; transatlantic slavery as, 6, 214

Vitruvian Man, 108–11, 120

Woodson, Carter G., 229, 234–35

Word: Césaire's concept of science of the, 62, 65–66, 69, 74n1, 218; theological, 81n79, 88n147, 239, 242; Wynter on science of the, 14, 17–18, 26–27, 29–30, 32, 70–73, 100

wretched of the earth (*les damnés de la terre*), 39, 87–88n139, 108, 124, 139n3, 209

Wynter, Sylvia: on black studies, 219; on creolization, 214–15, 218; the dramatic works of, 203–4, 221n5; on indigenization, 214–15; on Marxism, 40, 212, 215; *Maskarade*, 200–201n8, 203–5, 207–9, 211, 216–17, 220–21, 222n12; on the novel as medium of communication, 215–16; *The Hills of Hebron*, 203–4, 207, 209, 214, 215–16

Young Soul Rebels (1991), 184–86